FOREVER, SIDE BY SIDE

FOREVER, SIDE BY SIDE

JOHN J CUFFE

This novel is a fictionalized portrayal of the lives of Elisha Benton, Jemima Barrows, and their families, at the outset of the American Revolution. Content drawn from the limited source documents available, such as state archives detailing the military service of the Benton brothers, was adhered to faithfully. Other real people from neighboring towns and colonies also appear. Their actions and words are likewise fictionalized, but every attempt was made to accurately portray any historical actions credited to them. The guiding principle was to honestly convey any known fact, and to create plausible actions and dialogues that would support the facts, while telling the story of Elisha and Jemima.

ISBN: 1515308022
ISBN 13: 9781515308027

$19.95 U.S.
www.Foreversbsjjc.gmail.com

DEDICATION

To Elisha and Jemima, who I hope rest in peace, and who within these pages live Forever, Side by Side

CAST OF MAIN CHARACTERS

Historical Person:	As Appears in Novel:
Daniel Benton I	'Grandsire'
Sarah Benton	'Mother Sarah' – Grandsire's 2nd wife & grandmother to 'Elisha'
Daniel Benton II	'Father' - to 'Elisha' - son of 'Grandsire'
Mary Benton	'Mother' – to 'Elisha' – wife of 'Father'
Elisha Benton	'Elisha' - first born son of 'Father & Mother'; 'My Boy' – name used by 'Grandsire' for Elisha
Daniel Benton III	'Daniel' - brother to 'Elisha'
Azariah Benton	'Azariah'- brother to 'Elisha'
Jacob Benton	'Jacob' - brother to 'Elisha'
Hannah Benton	'Hannah' - sister to 'Elisha'
Sarah Benton	'Aunt Sara' - widow of 'Grandsire's son William & aunt to 'Elisha'

Jemima Barrows	'Jemima' – daughter of 'Jon Barrows' & 'Elisha's betrothed'
Heman Baker	'Heman' – friend of 'Elisha'
Elijah Chapman	'Eli' – friend of 'Elisha' & nephew of 'Col. Chapman'
Capt. Solomon Willes	'Captain Willes' – commander of 'Elisha's' militia unit

LIST OF DRAWINGS

(Follows Historical Notes at end of book)

BOOK I

Tolland, Connecticut - 1774

Chapter 1

How many harvest times had I stood thus on Tolland's town green, surveying those who scurried towards me? Not so few that I dreaded, as once I used to, hiring one of whom Father disapproved. So easy a thing it was to incur his wrath. No, nor not so many seasons that the excitement of such a role should have waned. Yet it had. Standing there, with Daniel all silence and obedience beside me, I could fathom neither why nor when.

Most of the men of the town came 'round by the packed dirt lane. More than one plowed straight across this singularly level stretch of common land, heedless of the soaking to hose and shoe. Hats whipped from heads when these men, adults all, were still many rods distant. A tingle started at the base of my neck and spilled down, like twin rivulets, raising the hair along my arms. Shame soon vanquished this tiny pleasure. I knew it would. Never had I reconciled the warring emotions this power of the purse, and so men's fortunes, conferred in me. Never would there come enough autumns that I might.

"Elisha," Daniel said. "Brother, did Father instruct you as to how many laborers..."

"I have a number in mind."

"If I may, Brother. Does it match Father's?"

I held up my hand for I had heard a sound- a voice or voices rather. The movement stopped Daniel's lips, and the feet of the landless men. I dropped my hand at once. Too late, for they adorned the ground before me like statues. Embarrassed though I was, and bathed in prickly heat, a frown spread upon my face – for I knew those distant voices well.

"Is that Brother Azariah?" Daniel asked.

The laughter pealed from within the open, double doors of the Meeting House. "None other. Nor is he alone."

Even Daniel and I and the promise of wages for labor was forgotten by the semicircle of men upon the Meeting House Green. Heads turned as one to discover who it was that flaunted the community's place of gathering and prayer.

Through this wide space burst our younger brother Azariah, and hard upon his heels - Jemima, Jemima Barrows. He seemed to glide over the ground like a creature of the wood, sure of every footfall at any speed. She was all motion: a blur of flying auburn hair, wide eyes and mouth, and billowing dress revealing white ankles and bare feet. So close they ran that one could swear their hands were entwined, but they were not.

I knew what I thought of her in days past. A free-spirited child who never seemed to grasp the time or her place. Yet for all that, intriguing in some way - like an object in the store window that one has never seen before; that alighted as if from some exotic land; that draws one within and yet prompts thoughts of flight at the same instant. Thinking back, perhaps I never have understood this girl. But if that was so, I've no yardstick by which to measure her in this new season; in this her fifteenth year.

Catching sight of us, Azariah raised an arm. Instantly he changed direction. Now she saw us. Saw me, too, I think. Just as quickly her steps slowed.

Shifting my weight, I returned my brother's greeting. How he loped along. He was the farm's dog, cavorting playfully amongst the beasts of burden. Daniel, he was one of those beasts, though of course a prized one all stolid and willing; and if he was so then what was I, why a beast as well, but only partly so, for I've equal parts a plowman, and I drive myself and every living thing up one furrow, and down the next, till day gives way to night. Ever have I been thus, to my lasting pride; and pain.

"Your cap, child," Jon Barrows called out as they approached. "How many times is it yer mother must remind you." He kneaded the worn brim of his hat in those sturdy fists of his. At my glance he lowered his eyes.

Jemima cast long fingers at her head and felt about as if discovering it bare. "Oh Father! I forgot."

"Greetings, brothers," Azariah said. "Can I steal you away, Elisha? We bring news."

Her darting gaze seemed to grasp our purpose at once. What she saw displeased her. I drew Azariah aside, lest her displeasure extend to me. "Will it keep?" I replied. "Pray join us, Brother. Our business will be brief."

He surveyed the assemblage. "Ah, I see there's no mystery as to what you're about."

"There is much you can learn," I offered, though I sensed he was lost to me.

He laughed. Just a single note but with his head tossed back and his loose-clubbed hair spilling upon his broad shoulders, the sound carried in the thin, crisp air. "No, not I, Elisha. This is not an office for which I'm suited."

"Not suited?" Daniel challenged. I touched his arm to encourage his patience. "Please, Elisha, you heard him. His impertinence. Just what is he suited for I'd like to..."

"Enough," I said, "from both of you."

Daniel stood down. Azariah flashed that grin of his and shrugged. "As you wish."

"What I wish is to accomplish what we had in mind when we set out this morn. To contract three hands. The apple crop awaits," I added for the benefit of the half circle of expectant faces.

"The hiring it is!" Azariah said, mocking my announcement with a bow. "So, they'll be no disturbing you this day."

"You've had your warning, little brother," I whispered.

"Come, Jemima, let's make what we can of your news from Boston. The great man is otherwise engaged."

He stepped away as he tossed out this last remark, which was well enough for him that he had. His mouth had run quite enough...

"Elisha," Daniel confided at my sleeve. "Three? Are you certain Father desires so many."

"The number is my own, Brother," I replied, grateful for his interruption. "I have my reasons and I'll take pains to make them clear to Father. I'll not involve you if that is your wish."

"No, I will stand by the count. If you believe it true."

His calloused palms worked together as he spoke. I patted his shoulder and smiled. "All will be well," I said, though his fears had stirred my doubts. Father's image shaped in my mind till a movement close at hand dissolved it. Jemima drifted through the clump of men. On she went despite Azariah calling her name from beneath the massive oak that edged the hilltop green. One by one the men parted before her. She smiled for each then glanced at me. Glance after glance she aimed. Each struck hard as a blow. How her eyes blazed. I had to mind myself that I didn't flinch before them. What had I done to deserve such heat? Such impudence in that look. What had I said? Reaching her father she wrapped his thick forearm in both her hands, and stared fixedly at me.

Clearing my throat I addressed the assembled men. "Neighbors. Thank you. For coming. As I've no need to explain, the time of harvest is at hand. Two men..." I felt Daniel's eyes upon me, if only for a moment. "Two will be needed. Benton fruit must be picked, and Benton soil must be turned..."

"He claims the earth itself for the Bentons."

It had been she who had spoken. The group of men huddled close as cattle might when threatened by a wolf. They stared up at me. My mind had drained like a mill pond gone to mud.

Her father whispered, low yet harsh. She was not done. "But Father, must it be so? With you and every man of the town cringing like curs; begging one and all for his scraps?"

Jon Barrows silenced her then but I cared not. Words gushed back into my head, my mouth. "You, Silas Avery, I will have. And you, Ben Wright. My brother Daniel will explain the terms. We have need of no others." Daniel's slack jaw prompted me to add, "Thank you. My family, as always, thanks you."

Dazed, it took a moment for the small crowd to begin drifting apart. Many wandered directly across Meeting House Green, despite its calf high, damp grasses. Here and there a man wore a bitter look. It pleasured me that these few were reserved for her, not me.

"Elisha?" Daniel began.

"Make the arrangements clear to them," I snapped. "Let there be no confusion as to terms, as they are to be contracted." I turned away and whistled for my mare. Far too shrilly it turned out, for April snatched her head from the prime grazing as though shot. Even Azariah roused himself at the unfolding scene.

I stood at the center of it all. The townsmen scattering amongst the one- and two-story structures that lined both sides of the common land. Daniel spoke hurriedly behind me to the hired help. Jon Barrows and his daughter gestured and traded words in the corner of my vision. I had not meant for this to happen. Did not comprehend in fact what had. Doubtless I'd brought no honor to the family name this day. Father would hear of it soon enough, and fashion his judgment just as quick. Whatever that was to be, I had no other to blame, for I'd brought his disfavor onto my own head.

April sidled alongside me as I trailed the departing crowd. She wedged her long brown muzzle with its single white spot beneath my palm. "No," I assured her, "I am not angry with you. Good girl. There, there."

Azariah came up on her opposite side. "I'd lay odds Father learns of this before ever we arrive home."

"Thank you for that, Brother."

"What happened, Elisha? Though little did I hear, someone must have provoked you something fierce." I turned towards Jemima. "Not her, surely?" he continued. "What is it with the pair of you? The one is always vexing the other."

"I vex her? Why I hardly ever converse with her. What could I have possibly done...?" Her father's rapid approach, with Jemima in tow, clapped a stopper to my mouth. "Azariah," I muttered without turning. "Walk April, would you."

"Mister Benton, sir, if I may be so bold?"

Jon Barrows, shorter than me by half a head, but unlike most, even more thickly built, released his daughter's hand. With both meaty paws raised and close together, he fiddled with his worn straw hat. It put me in mind of a tame bear I'd seen once in Hartford. Chained he'd been, and made to dance for fools. Jon Barrows. As big a man as that; made small. And some of the blame fell to me. "Of course, Jon. What would you ask of me?"

"Ask, why nothing, sir. It's my daughter. Jemima. There's something she would say."

"Of course." Though my anger had not drained full away, I'd avoided her gaze. I knew not why. Now I had no choice. I caught sight of her as she rose from a curtsy- her first in my recollection, though young ladies curtsied often enough. The top of her head reached halfway up my chest. Unrestrained by cap or ribbon her hair cascaded in all directions. A toss of her head and the brush of her hand set it to rights. Near at hand the color defied description. Red, auburn and black it was, and seemingly all at once. My anger quite gone, I sucked at the cool air.

Her face met mine. Never had we stood so close. Her words flowed quick and soft. They contained all manner of apology. She had not meant to speak out of turn. No right had she to interrupt the dealings of men. Yet her eyes seemed to credit little of that. Beams, they were.

Beams that bore deep into me. Such a blue and so ablaze. I would have stepped back if I held mastery of my legs.

In the long silence that followed, I sensed some word was due of me. "No harm is done," I feebly offered. Jon Barrows nodded, with a smile that came and went. Jemima waited as if more was warranted. Daniel stood waiting too. And Azariah beside him, though I had asked him not to tarry. "Our business is concluded," I ventured. "Successfully I might add. So..." I nearly repeated that no harm had been done but managed not.

"Good," Jon said. "Good, good."

"Is it truly?" she asked.

"Is what?" I asked blankly.

"You've hired merely two men whereas earlier you cited three."

"Now, Jemima..." Jon Barrows said, his brim twisting once more.

"I may have mentioned something of the sort. To my brothers."

"Three you did say. Even over your father's objections."

"Daughter," Jon protested. "You try this gentleman's patience. And mine."

"Elisha," Daniel interrupted. "Did not Father tell us, well you, that two..."

"I have not forgotten, Brother. Thank you." Must everyone remind me of my father's wishes, and publicly too. Daniel at least was family. Jemima could claim no such right to weigh in on Benton business. Why, she...

"Elisha," she said, in such a way that for a moment I believed we stood in the road alone. "Azariah tells me that the harvest is so plentiful it bends your trees' branches to the ground. 'Tis you told him so. You do need a third."

Her eyes still blazed but not with heat. Gold flecks floated in twin seas of blue. I could not fathom their intent nor could I look away. "I did. I do."

"Then as you intend hiring another, why not my father?"

"Daughter!"

"He has the strength of any two other men whom you might name. And none work harder, or give such satisfaction. Your grandfather knows this to be true."

"Elisha..." Daniel urged at my side.

She could have made no stronger plea than to invoke Grandsire. With my own ears I had heard him praise Jon Barrows - over Father's objections. There before me the big man's hand restrained his daughter, but his mouth hung open with hope. "I can contract you for a week, Jon Barrows. Not a day more. If it is hard work from sunup to sundown you seek."

Without word or warning he stepped forward and snatched up my right hand. A bear he was and his grip near forced the air from my throat.

"Bless you, Mister Benton, sir! Ya'll not regret it. I promise you that!"

Behind him, I caught sight of Jemima's retreating form. Already she'd nearly reached the small house rented by her family. No outward indication did she give that she'd heard our exchange. The door opened; it closed. In the blur of movement she might have glanced back. Of this I could not be certain.

Chapter 2

With arrangements finalized with Jon Barrows and the other laborers, I dispatched Daniel to the blacksmith's shop, and leaving Azariah in charge of the horses, kept my appointment with Eli Chapman. My abrupt commands and hasty departure had delayed my brothers' inevitable questions. The set, business-like expression on Mister Chapman's face, seated there within the tavern, caused me to set aside my own.

Not half an hour on, I re-emerged. Both April and the gelding wandered the opposite end of the common lands. Of Azariah there was no sign. Striding forward I whistled once. The mare pricked her ears at the sound. She hopped once in my direction and began bounding across. Not to be either outdone or abandoned, the gelding pursued her. April's head tossed repeatedly as she neared.

I laughed out loud, the morning's events and my mood quite forgotten. "What has come over you?" I demanded. "1774 it is, and you, dear girl, are fully five years of age." I stroked her muzzle. "Not some senseless filly. And what of you, a gelding, and smitten. What good will such behavior do one such as you?" I gathered up his reins. In truth, I was grateful for his infatuation for otherwise it would be I pursuing him all about the green. Circling round him I re-positioned the saddle and tightened the cinch strap. She waited patiently for her turn.

Daniel appeared outside the smithy a moment later. By his hurried walk it was clear he had tidings of some import. Azariah's absence would normally have caught his attention straightway, but he came on as if wholly unaware. "Elisha!"

"It must be urgent news you bear, Brother." He slowed as if I'd snatched away some momentous secret. "Come, Daniel. Your haste gives you away. Tell me. Has someone taken ill?"

"It is Boston, Elisha. The port has been closed. People are said to starve in the streets..."

"Take a breath, Brother. By whose authority could such a thing happen? This cannot be."

"But it has! The letter tells us so."

"Letter?" I said. "Ah. Azariah. He spoke of correspondence. And Boston, too." Wrong I had been to send him away. Her too, for as Jemima served the Captain, she would be privy to…

"Where is our little brother? Shirking once more? Why, Elisha, he left the care of the horses to you!"

"He did, yes. The letter, Daniel. Have you seen it? Read it?"

"No, but there is much talk. They say it arrived by express rider from the Committee of Correspondence in Boston. Perhaps by the hand of Dr. Joseph Warren himself."

"Yes, I am certain rumors have spread far and fast, which is why we must see it with our own eyes." I surveyed the buildings both near and opposite. "And our missing brother intended to show it to us I'm willing to wager. If I'd but listened."

Daniel stretched out his arm. "There! There he is!"

Our vanished brother stepped from out Jemima's parents' house. And she it was who followed. "I see him. Come Daniel, mount up."

We had scarce begun when the mare's nostrils flared. "Yes, that is young Azariah yonder," I whispered at her ear, checking the reins ever so slightly. We proceeded at a walk whilst Daniel kept up a steady stream unaided by me.

"It is he and they who should come to you," he said. "Not us to them. We are his elders after all. He owes it to you at least, Elisha, as the first born son!"

I watched the two of them, thick as thieves, or children up to mischief. "Calm yourself, Brother. What signifies is that we learn the way of it."

"You're right, of course, Elisha. And quite certain I am that you will get to the bottom of this Boston business. I only mean..." I doffed my cocked hat at the appearance of two town selectmen at the Meeting House entry. Both men were well known to us Bentons, but as the distance was too great for a hail, I merely returned their wave. Daniel followed suit. "This is precisely what concerns me," he whispered. "Father will be upset enough with what transpired this morn. Think what he'd say should he learn we ventured here as though summoned." The sweep of his arm encompassed Azariah and Jemima standing outside the small home tucked farthest back from the road. "Oh, and he will surely hear of it," he added, casting a glance back towards the pair astride The Meeting House steps.

I stopped April. The gelding eased in beside us.

"Must we, Elisha?" Daniel exclaimed. "Must our entire family be thus held captive, and twice in one day?" In a fierce whisper he added, "She is daughter to a mere tenant!"

I snatched Daniel's arm so swift and hard he jerked in the saddle. I released him at once but confusion and hurt filled his eyes. "Hear me now," I whispered. "This house before us. Empty it sat for many years. Season after season it stood thus, Mister Ellis and his wife praying all the while that their first-born son would find his way back to them, and to the home purpose built for him. Yet never would William return. He had fallen as had so many other men of Tolland, in the King's expedition to Cuba. Back in 1762 that was, when you were still a boy. Trust me when I tell you, Brother that the elder Ellis is most grateful to now receive the rents that Jon Barrows pays. It helps sustain him and his mistress in their lonely old age."

"I am sorry, Elisha. I did not grasp the way of it."

"Perhaps then you should listen more to your conscience, and less to the prattling of loose-tongued men." I knew my words would singe him and they did. But he had vexed me exceedingly with his gossip and petty fears. Besides, such talk did not suit him, for Daniel ached to do right in all he did. I let my breath out long and slow. Reaching out I patted his knee. I straightened only to discover that Azariah and Jemima had approached. I had to fight the urge to ask what it was she sought from me, for a question lingered there, suspended in those eyes so blue.

"Are you quite finished, Elisha?" Azariah asked.

He had used his most serious, most grown-up voice - one rarely heard from him. "We are at your disposal, Brother," I replied. I glanced from him to her. "I trust that some of what you have to say concerns the goings on in Boston."

They exchanged looks. "Aye, Brother," he replied. "Yet I would speak to you alone. If I may."

Though Daniel stiffened at this request, he said nothing. "On the way home, then," I said. "Though you will speak with your brothers together."

"Very well." He flashed a smile for Jemima. Instantly he moved alongside the gelding. Daniel stared at his outstretched arm for a long moment. Seeming to reject the impulse to knock it away, he hauled our younger brother up behind him.

My hand had found my hat again. "Miss Barrows," I said, though Jemima had been upon my lips.

She smiled so with her eyes and mouth that I nearly replaced my tricorne upon April's head rather than my own. "Thank you, Elisha Benton," she said.

"For what?" Daniel whispered when he might as well have shouted.

"Your brother knows full well," she said, and smiling still, whirled about by way of parting.

I backed the mare a bit so that I might watch her take her leave. Jemima turned at the entry and so I yanked April's head left, and spurred her on. Our pace over the next mile barely kept up with my racing thoughts. Only out of pity for our mounts did I check our speed. The gelding immediately closed the gap and sidled close.

"Why, Elisha, do we race?" Daniel asked, his breathing near as heavy as his mount's. "Should we rather, take the time to ponder what to say to Father?"

Father? How could I have forgotten? "We've time aplenty," I replied, for two miles of road lay before us.

"Of course, but has word reached him, do you think? What would you have me say?"

Azariah laughed and relaxed his grip 'round Daniel's waist. "If our elder brother is thinking at this moment," he said, "it is not of Father."

Daniel made as if to shake him off. "You! Just you keep your laughter and your comments to yourself. First you fail to keep the horses near at hand, and then, well that whole business at the Barrows."

"Business? What business is that? If this is to be another lecture about keeping up appearances, save it, Brother. Such talk is all well an' good for those who wish to curry Father's favor..."

Daniel twisted halfway 'round. "You fathom nothing of my rationale!"

"I know enough to grasp that both of you stand to inherit, whilst Father has made no provision for me."

"Elisha! Hear how he insults us both. Not a day's work does he without being pressed to his duty, yet he mocks our reasons for laboring."

Only inches apart, their red faces bobbed and hissed like stirred up snakes. My God how I had grown weary of separating them. More and more often of late, it seemed. It was of little consequence that both were right in their way...

"Elisha?" Daniel insisted. "Is it not wrong that he took refuge in the Barrows' residence? The ink was barely dry on the contract for this man's labor yet he..."

I stopped April, which stopped us all. "Have you wondered at it, Brothers," I asked, "as do I, why Jon Barrows declined a shilling and a half in coin for each day worked? And chose instead the equivalent in cordwood?"

"I did find it strange," Daniel said at once. "The others leapt at the silver. Seldom does any man refuse ready cash. Yet Jon Barrows did, though he has rents to pay."

"What of it?" Azariah demanded.

"Leave it be, Azariah," I said. "Think now. As you know the family best, why would he make such a choice?"

"I don't know. Maybe the one is harder to get than the other. And without firewood, he would freeze come winter." After a pause he added, "As would Jemima, and Mistress Barrows too."

"That's it," Daniel agreed. "As a townsman he has no access to a wood lot of his own..."

"Men of the town versus landowning men!" Azariah exclaimed. "Must it always be a matter of social standing with you? If a man lacks our 500 acres or whatever ungodly sum it is, he simply..."

"Never do you listen! How many times has Elisha explained that barely 100 can be relied upon to yield good hardwood?"

"Forgive me! One hundred acres. I stand corrected!"

They'd come to blows more than once. For all their spitting and sputtering back and forth, this did not seem to be one of those times. Though prepared I was to intervene, as I watched them seated front to back; twisting and glaring. After a time, the odds of a battle lessened. They turned to me.

"Tell him how wrong he is," Daniel said.

"It's you who's wrong-headed," came Azariah's instant retort.

"I marvel at it, but I believe you are both right. A man makes his choices based on need. Jon Barrows needs food for his family. Yet since he tends the Ellis' kitchen garden, Mister Ellis grants him access to that plot's ample bounty."

"How do you know these details of his arrangements?" Azariah asked.

Daniel scoffed. "Elisha's business dealings involve him in all manner..."

"As I was saying. For shelter Jon must pay rents. His cabinet business surely clears enough for this, for his craft is respected near and far. Though here I merely speculate."

"Oh, so you are not all-knowing, Brother."

"Sssh," Daniel hissed.

"This leaves the need for warmth. And for this he must hire himself out. Our family's habit of providing well-seasoned wood, and willingness to deliver it to a man's door, makes this option difficult to ignore - no matter the allure of the King's coin."

"What, Brother? Will you allow Mister Barrows nothing for a new hat, or cloth for his mistress to fashion clothes?"

Though Daniel chided Azariah's flippant tongue, it pleased me to glimpse the mirth restored to our younger brother's eyes.

Azariah at once caught sight of my smile. "So, wise elder, what lesson have we learned in all this?" His playful tone caused Daniel to also turn towards me.

"What you have learned, Brother, I will not hazard a guess. As for myself, though, in considering Jon Barrows, I see us Bentons more clearly." As they both waited, I continued. "One poor harvest, or one crop left to languish on the branch, will risk not the roof above Father's head, nor the fire in his hearth, but would see a forfeit of the luxuries Mother above all cherishes."

"Is this why," Daniel began, "why you chose three men, not the two that..."

"He is not finished," Azariah interrupted. "And besides, there is more than this logic behind that decision."

I ignored his wink, and even the image that sprang to mind. "Two such failures, one following the other, and it would be the Benton clan found huddled around cold, dark grates."

"Us?" Daniel exclaimed. "Why would Bentons face such a fate, what with 100 acres of prime forest?"

"And how would the cutting, the hauling, be accomplished?" I asked him, though in truth I wondered what a man might suffer who possessed but a fraction of that total. What might befall a farmer just starting out?

"The Chapmans' oxen. Would we not have coin enough to hire them out, as in other years?"

"Not with two bad harvests, it appears," Azariah said. "So, class is a less fixed thing than it would appear. Even for a Benton."

Daniel looked from one of us to the other. "Surely Father would have sufficient credit to fetch fresh seed for one last planting."

"'Tis certain the Chapmans would never rent their precious beasts on such terms," Azariah speculated.

How easy it would be for a single man to fail, I thought. How easy for him to starve. "One could rent oneself out," I murmured. "As does Jon Barrows."

"To the Chapmans!" Daniel exclaimed.

"Or their like," I replied, trying to imagine such a conversation with the heir to the better part of the Chapman fortune, and Eli of an age with me. "We would be forced to seek the favor of men who hire out beasts and slaves, and whose fates are not tied so tight as ours to fickle nature."

"Well, my brothers," Azariah said. "It appears that even your assured wealth is no guarantee of prosperity. Perhaps you will bond with me now, in my poverty and despair."

What I said next I immediately regretted. Azariah's rediscovered mirth vanished, and Daniel's face assumed the despair that his brother had merely feigned. How heavy the thoughts must have weighed, somewhere deep in my mind, for them to have sprung so unconsidered to my lips. “No wealth is assured me,” is what I said. “Nothing is or ever was promised me.”

“Nothing?” Daniel murmured at last. “Not ever? But all those talks with Father. In the parlor; just you and he...”

Cursing my selfishness, I could do naught but shake my head. “Chores. Always was it about the next season and its endless chores.”

“The selfish bastard,” Azariah said quietly.

I would have struck him if closer. If only out of instinct. Daniel would normally have scaled a tree to do so. He moved not a whit. “You should not speak so,” I managed at last. “He is our father.”

“But Elisha,” Daniel said as though he’d heard none of this exchange. “This fall marks your twenty-sixth year. Father was younger by three years when Grandsire gifted him his own parcel. The house we live in, too. And this despite Father’s ailments having kept him from doing the half for Grandsire, what you have rendered him. Surely, surely Father has...”

“Father and Grandsire are different men.”

“Do you not see what Daniel is saying,” Azariah added. “This is not just about you. If Father can break his word to his first born, he can certainly break it to Daniel. To me, to everyone.”

“I understand you, Azariah, but he broke no promise for he made none.”

Azariah slipped from the horse’s bare back as most men might rise from their table. “You’re wrong! What he owes to you is a promise sure as any writ in blood. You must hold him to it. Only you can. How can you fail to see this? Most lack your forbearance.” He waved at Daniel whose face had drained clear of blood. “Will you let Father steal our future as he’s stolen yours?”

“I’m going now,” Daniel said to the open road.

“Where?” I asked. “Where to? Stay a moment more.”

“I’m going.” He repeated. “I must leave.”

“Daniel,” I said. “If you return alone it will be alone you face him.” My words only served to deepen his shock.

Azariah touched our brother's knee. "I will stay on," he explained. "There is more I must speak to Elisha about."

This broke the spell that had anchored Daniel at our side. Without speaking he drove his heels into the gelding and they barreled down the road into a roiling cloud of their own construction.

"I cannot tarry, Azariah. There will be hell to pay and I'll not have Daniel face it by himself. Not when it's of my making."

"And he in this state."

"Precisely." I reached down to him. "Then take my hand."

"I must speak to you even so."

"Of Boston?"

"Yes, and I've a favor to ask of you. One greater than I have ever asked before."

He had never been in such earnest. My heart hammered in my chest as I conjured possibilities. I struggled to keep the mare's head still for my mood had infected her. "Then be quick, Brother."

"I would go to Boston."

"You? To Boston." Little did he care of events in Hartford and it a mere day's ride from Tolland. The port city was easily four times farther off. "Do you jest at a time like this?"

"Never would I. I wish to go in your stead."

I reclaimed my offered hand, not aware whether anger, or perhaps fear, bade me to do it. "You'll need to tell me more. Much more."

"Then it must be tonight, and I have so much to tell."

"Come then, your hand. We must be off."

He smiled as though I'd acquiesced to all that he had asked. "I wager I'll reach home before you!" With that he glided across the road, leapt the broad ditch, and disappeared amongst a copse of yellow-leaved birch trees on a crow's path to the Benton Homestead.

Abandoned there, I set off in the less direct path which Daniel had taken.

Chapter 3

The mare pressed on with all of the eagerness I felt. To check myself I tugged at her reins. She slowed to an impatient walk as we turned off the road that ran southwest out of town. The trees lining the lane that bordered Benton lands now engulfed us in a deeper chill. Armies of maple leaves swayed above us in the breeze, shimmering in their bold new coats of crimson.

So much had happened in this single morn. So much had not yet taken place. April tossed her head and strained forward when I bid her wheel at the opening in the stone wall. "Not to Grandsire's, though I long to follow where you would lead." I patted her neck. "No, Daniel must be our emphasis, for surely Father has hold of him by now."

Father's house and the barn too had an abandoned look. How strangely at odds it was with the bright sun that blazed in the crystal blue sky. The front door yanked inward and Sister Hannah flew forth. Curls of her long, brown hair poked from beneath her cap. Her hands and forearms practically wind-milled as she rushed to my side.

I chuckled despite all that was crammed in my head. "One would almost think you spied upon me," I teased. "To fly at me so upon my arrival."

"But I was, Brother. I mean, that is, Mother bade me keep watch for you."

"Did she now?" I dismounted.

"Yes, Brother. Daniel arrived afore you. Never have I seen him look so, so..."

"Upset?"

"Yes, Brother, that's what he was. But stunned, too, I think." I glanced at the parlor windows yet the ripples and swirls of the crown glass revealed nothing. When Father entered that room it became his study, and he occupied it now, of that I was certain. "Did I speak out of turn, Brother? Was it not my place?"

"No. Far from it. Your choice of words was apt, I'd say."

"Azariah returned, too. Just before you this was. He pledged my silence about his coming. Strange, too, whereas Daniel was all fret and silence, Azariah smiled." Her thin arm flung towards the far corner of the house. "Then he slipped round to the side entry with his finger to his lips. Can you tell me what has happened, Brother?"

"If he asked you to keep his confidence, Sister, why ever did you tell me?"

"I am sorry, Elisha. I thought I ought."

"One's elders need not know each solitary thing you come upon."

"Not even you, Elisha? I only thought, if anyone can make right what's amiss, you can."

Smiling, I handed her the reins. "Well, let us hope then, that I can justify your faith in me. But do think on it, Sister, before giving your word so lightly. Now, before you take the mare to the barn, tell me this. Has anyone called upon Mother and Father? Any visitors from town?"

"Not one soul, but Father spoke to the Grants." My puzzled expression led her to continue. "Father came outside. When the clock chimed noon it was, and you had not returned. To and fro he paced, and at each turn stared down the lane. Finally he walked the entire way to where it meets the road..."

"Father did? He had his cane of course."

"Oh yes, Brother. And when he came back again, he said he'd met the Grants, the elder and his son Noah, and had they a tale to tell."

"He told you this, girl?"

"No, not me! Mother. And before you say it, Brother, I am sorry that I eavesdropped, but Brother Jacob and I were frightened by how Father returned, all red-faced and stomping about. Practically shouting, and to Mother at that." Covering her mouth she whirled towards the parlor and its lifeless panes of glass. "Forgive my speaking so..."

"Noah Grant?" I muttered aloud. "I would not think him a likely source of gossip."

"Oh, Father complained most bitterly. Like squeezing water from a beet to get anything from that man. Well," she added, fiddling with the reins in one hand, and her hem in the other, "that is what he told Mother."

"And I thank you for telling me. Now it's best I get indoors. And rescue Brother Daniel."

"Rescue him?"

"A manner of speech, Hannah, that is all. Best remind Brother Jacob to rub the mare down good. And ask him to cover her with a blanket. I rode her harder than I ought."

While Azariah's route inside appealed, what sufficed for one would not for another. Instead I grasped the front door latch, squeezed, and pushed it wide. The warmth of unseen fires enveloped me at once. Young Jacob had been busy in our absence. Breathing out, I let the latch drop softly into place. So quiet was it that the crackling of those same fires could be heard. The clang of iron striking iron proved Mother moved about within the kitchen. I longed to discover her read of Father's mood, but to pass through the hall meant to avoid him, and purposely so. That simply would not do.

I took hold of the knob to the parlor door. It yielded with its too-familiar creak. Daniel came into view, standing in the room's center with his hat clenched in one hand. He turned towards me now - relief flooding his drained features.

Opposite him sat Father. We made eye contact. Father leaned hard against his straight-backed chair. "Well, at long last. The prodigal son."

We shared the same block-like head; the thick mass of hair. Nothing of myself, though, had I ever discerned in his eyes. They bored into me now, dark and cold despite the fire's glow upon his cheek. "Greetings, Father." To my brother I nodded. He must have confided little to be kept in such a miserable state.

"Late you are, Elisha," Father said. "Though you at least had courage enough to not steal through the hall." He cast a contemptuous look at Daniel. "Leave us!"

Daniel glanced my way then stepped 'round Father and disappeared through the entry to the kitchen.

Father's walking stick lay across his lap and beneath his withered right hand. He freed it with his powerful left, and pointed to the chair before me. "Sit there. I hear troubling and conflicting reports and I would have the truth of it from you."

The chair lay within the reach of the gnarled head of that stout branch of hickory. I sat.

"I will be blunt, Elisha. Rumor has it that the hiring was at best an awkward affair. Setting that aside, I've learned you contracted three men, when it was two we agreed upon. Your brother offers nothing to explain the way of it. Have you so stretched your authority that you would spend my money without so much as a 'by your leave'?"

He had not always spoken so. Not to me, at least, and not so often as in recent years. I glanced down that I might see where the head of that stick slumbered. A pang of fear burned through me at the sight of it. But when that had passed, some other emotion crept forward, and I disliked how it whitened the knuckles of my fist.

"Speak up, boy! Have I charged you at last with a role too big for your britches?"

"You spoke at length, Father, of who you favored, and how many townsmen we might need. Never did I voice agreement. My mind was unsettled in this until this very morn. I rose before any had awakened. 'Round the orchards I rode once more. Your trees, Father, and Grandsire's too, droop to the ground with their fruit. Two men would never do. I did hire those of whom you spoke. I chose the third. My brothers had no hand in it. The man is to work for firewood, which we both know that Daniel and I will split and haul. It costs you nothing but our time, and us our sweat."

He stared at me for a moment prolonged by the tick-tock of his prized mantel clock. Flames danced- reflected in his unblinking eyes. In his broad hand the hickory twitched. "You dare mock me?"

"I intend not."

"Years," he said at last, "yes, years may have passed since I applied a switch to you. But I remind you now of another thing we both of us know. I've other ways I can punish you boy. And if need be, I'll use these ways. To remind you of your obligations, as a Benton, and to me as my eldest."

Whatever regret I'd felt, transformed to hatred. "We should both of us be grateful, Father," I said, in a voice I scarce recognized as my own, "that never have I forgotten what is owed between a father and a first-born son."

The dense mass of his stick rose straight up and slow, then drove down against the wide, pine floorboard. The blow echoed in the silent room. His knuckles trembled on the knob. "Leave me! Do not come before me once more; not till you've restored a civil tongue to your head."

He turned then to the fire, quite as though I had already left. So I stood. Had I really spoken thus to him? A moment I needed to collect myself but I was not to find one. The crash must have startled Mother and Daniel for they both stared with wide eyes as I entered the kitchen.

"My son," Mother whispered. Still with a dripping spoon in hand she abandoned the hearth and came to me.

"All will be well, Mother."

"But that horrid sound." She glanced beyond me towards the parlor. "And the state of your brother..."

From the table fashioned of pine Daniel murmured, "I said nothing I ought naught. Made no mention of Jemima."

My pulse quickened at her name. I had suppressed thought of her, and her part in this affair. I must continue to.

"Jemima?" Mother asked. "Daughter to Jon Barrows?"

"Please Mother," I replied. "Have we not complication enough."

She patted my arm as once she had my head. Her eyes searched mine. Her words came soft and low. "I will see to your father. You may wish a private word with your brothers, for Azariah has come home to us as well." At this last, her gaze shifted to the unseen loft above.

"I do, yes." With that I kissed her head and took my leave. Despite the commotion, or perhaps because of it, Daniel had chosen his familiar seat midway along the trestle table's length. I squeezed his shoulder. "Father knows the decision to be mine alone."

"Thank you, Elisha. I had in my head what to say to him, then he herded me in there with that club. My mind went blank as a lamb's..."

I drew his head into my shoulder. "Do not trouble yourself, Brother. All will be well. Warm yourself by the fire. I'll be down directly."

My shoulders practically brushed both walls as I climbed the steep set of stairs tucked off the rear of the kitchen. Though sundown was still an hour hence, there was need of the candle set safely in the center of the loft.

Azariah paused long enough to cast a smile my way. "You survived the interview with Father."

"No thanks to you. As always you kept a safe distance from the day's events." Insult him I must or he would guess the way of it. He had looked to me to hold Father to his obligations, and I in my weakness could not even hold my temper.

"I merely maintain the distance you set for me, Brother."

"Do you mock me, beardless one?"

He laughed. “Never you, oh exalted one. No, a simple reminder that you exclude me from weighty decisions. Like how many to hire.”

“You do mock me!” Ducking beneath the rafters I made a playful grab for his sleeve. He easily backed over his straw-filled mattress despite the clutch of clothes spilling from his embrace. Even in such a confined space he proved elusive to a lumbering opponent such as me. I settled on his bed. He moved to Daniel’s. “At least I am capable of making difficult decisions,” I said.

With an eye on me he continued his industry. “You! Your decision. So, you credit Jemima not one whit?”

Again, her name. My cheeks warmed as I recalled her reminding me that the number three had been mine. The smirking little man had got the better of me once more. Worse still, now it appeared two such people existed in this world who could best me at will. “What is it you’re about?” I challenged him. “Rarely do I see you work as hard, and never unbidden.”

“I pack for Boston. Is it not obvious?”

I sprang forward in an instant. A twin miracle was that I managed both to snare his arm and avoid knocking myself senseless on the slanting beams. He appeared shocked that I had even attempted such an act, and this must have led to his capture. But once in my grip there would be no escape. He knew this, and settled himself as though he had become captive by choice. “You will relate all to me,” I demanded, “without exception.”

“You do remember I tried once before.” I released him despite his smugness. He rubbed at his arm. “Now, where to begin...”

“Try explaining why it is you have cause to journey to Boston.”

“Because the harvest finds you far too busy, and the selectmen will expect a Benton to be among the party.”

“As God is my witness, Azariah, I will give you a thrashing if you make sport of me.”

“I speak the truth, Brother.”

"Then no more riddles!" The smile fled his mouth. If the light had allowed a proper look at those eyes of his, one gray and one green, I'd wager a look of hurt surfaced there. "Please, Azariah. Speak plain is all I ask."

"As you wish, Brother." He faced me. "You know now about the port. General Thomas Gage, named Military Governor by the King himself - it was he ordered the closure. No ship enters or leaves unless on business of George III. The harbor is near empty. Only soldiers are aplenty, 'tis said. More than barracks alone can quarter. Wait. I should back up."

While he settled himself more comfortably, I conjured images of Boston's Long Wharf, crammed with people and topped with shops; jutting far into the bay. Either side bristled with docked ships, Indiamen even, whose masts stood taller than the Meeting House steeple. Only I among we Bentons had seen these sights. Never would I forget them. How could wharves such as these be empty, and worse by far, as empty as the bellies of those thousands I had walked among?

"You may not know," Azariah was saying, "that Captain Willes has asked Jemima to take down his official dictation. You'll recall how the schoolmaster boasted of her pretty hand."

My own surprise at her appointment had been overshadowed by the vocal opposition of certain elders to having a woman in such a delicate role. "I remember dragging you to the school house," I admitted. "That I remember."

"Only when the sky was prime for game..."

"Go on," I insisted. "Boston. The Captain." I mentioned not, Jemima.

"Yes. Let's see. In this role she learns firsthand of correspondence. And this very day the letter arrived of which we spoke."

"And what of the selectmen? Grandsire has not been consulted. Or has he?"

"By this evening so we're told. Word will come that Boston starves. That an urgent appeal for aid spreads from colony to colony. And that the selectmen thus far made aware wish to answer this plea."

"As they have in the past, I imagine. With generosity and dispatch."

"Exactly so, Elisha. So certain is the Captain of what men like Grandsire will say, that he employs Jemima in taking down a draft reply to the Committee. It promises just that."

I leaned against the nearest rafter. Thoughts careened in my skull. The harvest at hand; citizens starving in Boston's cobbled streets; Grandsire's near certain endorsement of providing succor; Father's equally certain opposition. "And you," I asked, prying my head from its support, "you propose joining the party, should one be sent?"

"I am not a fool, Brother. I can guess you will second the notion. You and Grandsire have always chosen charity on such occasions."

"But I will conveniently be too consumed by the harvest. Thus leaving an opening for you to travel in my stead. You, little brother, who never cared a fig for putting food in our own cellar or on our table unless a gun must be fired to accomplish it. Yet it's you who will set forth to nourish strangers."

"Now you mock me, my Christianity and my ability to hunt of all things."

"No, truly I mean no insult."

"Elisha," he whispered. "Allow that I know this as fact. You are far kinder than you will ever admit. And no sacrifice of yours is too great if it satisfies the needs of others. You will argue with Father that Benton beasts be included in the herd to be driven to distant Boston. You will likely argue too that as Benton beasts go, so too must you see them there and safe. For once let me be the one chosen."

His wish was real. The need great. "Why, Brother? Why is it you would do this?"

"Why not? None here will miss me." I would, I knew. "Allow me to go, Elisha. Let me see the city with my own eyes. You of all people understand that this, this here, is not the life for me. I am not a farmer nor never will be. Whatever you may attempt at Father's behest."

The candle wavered as we sat silent and close. At last I touched his arm. "I will not speak against you."

"You must plead for me, Brother, or never will he grant me leave!"

I rose. "I go now. To Father and Grandsire both. They must learn of this, and before a rider reaches them from town."

"But Elisha..."

"Enough, Brother. I will not forget what you have asked of me." He released me and I made my way down.

Chapter 4

Within the hall, Father had taken a seat at the family dining table. He'd chosen his accustomed place at the head. Though he disregarded Daniel, he scowled a bit less than was typical. I hovered between this room and the kitchen, where Mother stood before the large, iron pot suspended on its hook. She shared a sly smile with me. So, she had worked her magic upon him once more. And here came I to squander whatever goodwill she had won.

Hannah darted 'round me with an armload of the broad, wooden plates put out when no guests were expected. Jacob, willowy yet sprouting taller each year, called up the stairs to the loft, asking Azariah to come down for dinner. He then hurried across the kitchen to me.

"Elisha, I placed two wool blankets over April." I squeezed his shoulder. Smiling, he took his place.

Bathed already in luscious scents, the room now began filling with kin. These and the roaring fire, the brick-lined hearth and laden serving vessels, spread a delicious warmth that promised to cast its spell over all of us, over me, as it so often had. Azariah appeared. Quietly he took his place - watched by Father. No longer could I delay.

"Father..." I said.

Daniel's head came up. Azariah had not taken his eyes from me. Mother's gaze I felt upon my back. And the children stared back and forth, then down.

"You will sit, boy."

"But Elisha," Mother said, speaking as though Father had not. "The meal; it's ready."

"Forgive me, Mother, but I must go out."

"Now!" Father demanded. "Where to?"

"I must speak to Grandsire, and at once."

Father's face darkened through shades of red to plum. "And just what have you to say to my father?"

"My son..." Mother began.

"What I must say is for the ears of both our family's patriarchs."

"Both? You would have me rise from my table, though grace is on my lips?"

Despite his blustery tone I sensed his interest in learning whatever I had to say to Grandsire. "I go this instant," I said, "for there's not a minute to be lost. Will you join me?" I extended my hand.

All manner of emotion warred on his face. Finally and with a growl, he plucked his stick from his chair back and hauled himself upright. My hand he ignored. Ignored my gaze, too, as ever he had since I surpassed him in height- leastways when standing so close.

My stomach growled, reminding me I had fasted since break of day. Instinctively I scanned the table. Not quickly enough for Mother caught me at it. "Hannah, break off a chunk of that bread," she instructed. "Wrap it and some cheese for your brother." Hannah had hold of the loaf in an instant but Father stepped twixt her and where I stood.

"If his time's so precious, we've no time for that," he declared. To me he added, "Well, go on if we're going!"

I stepped around Mother. Daniel then did the most amazing thing. He stood directly before Father and me.

"Should I, I was wondering?" he managed to blurt out. "Should I accompany you?"

"You?" Father replied. "Why would we need you with us?"

Daniel had so surprised me my mind went blank. He shrank down. Father snatched the coat held in Mother's hand and left. My brother's head hung too low for me to glean his expression as I followed Father outside.

Father's stump echoed some steps ahead. So well did we both know this well-trod path, no wider than a cart, that neither required a lamp. Even so, the uneven ground posed a danger to him. I should have caught him up. In a stride or two I could have. Yet it was wrong of him to disrespect Daniel. How much courage it must have taken my brother to ask what he did. By rights, he was of an age that he should join with us elders - for a talk such as this one was wont to be.

"Well keep up, boy! Near twice your age, and what with my condition... Such a damnable hurry. And for what I ask?" He talked as much to himself as to others at times. Not sensing which was addressed to me I let it all pass. He fell into a deep silence as we closed on the distant light, winking through the branches.

Many were the times he and I had come this way. His arm on mine, our entwined voices planning what we had come to share with my Grandsire; or what we would ask of him.

A poor plant of father's stick and he nearly went down. I had hold of his weakened right arm in a heartbeat.

"Let me be!" So loud was his shout I released him and fell back a step. "I need no man's help. And certain I am, not yours!" Motionless, I stood, like a tree whipped by a gale. Shocked again I was, this time by tears. They blurred my vision though I blinked them furiously away. He fussed at his coat, oblivious to my state. If anything he deserved my wrath. Not this. Not weakness. I thanked The Lord for the dark, and the selfishness that prevented him paying any heed.

He set off again. Soon we had entered the clearing. Grandsire's barn stood like a chiseled black boulder far to our left. In contrast, the home that had brought me so much joy emitted a glow that guided us in as might a lighthouse. I caught sight of Mother Sarah as she crossed from one room to the next. A moment more and Father's hickory shaft barred my way.

"You will not speak of what passed between us in my parlor," he commanded. "I'll have your word on it."

I swallowed hard. I fought to keep my heart and hands still, for the lumpish shape of his stick's knob pressed like a stone against my chest. "Father. I treat that conversation as any between us- as one destined for you and me alone."

The silence weighed heavy, on both of us I thought, though scarce any time had passed. The walking stick slipped away. His withered hand appeared in the home's soft light and brushed my sleeve. "Son. Perhaps I have been..."

A rush of sound and movement from within stopped what I would have, for all the world, wanted to hear. Inward went the door.

"Elisha!" Mother Sarah hollered. "Husband, your grandson Elisha!" She enveloped me at once with words, fussing, and a hug that jammed her face, still rosy and warm from the fire, full against my cheek. When Grandsire had at last recovered from Grandmother's loss, and re-married, I had thought to withhold affection from his second wife. That first year was not yet out when Mother Sarah had brushed my feeble defenses away. She had done so with embraces just like the last.

"And also your father," she said. "Welcome, Daniel. To what do we owe the pleasure of your visit?" Before he could answer she pulled me indoors and steered me towards Grandsire's parlor. "We expected you so much earlier, Elisha. Did you find men enough in town?"

"Let him breathe," Grandsire called from the parlor. I turned just in time to see Father enter and close the door.

Grandsire beamed up at me from his rocker, drawn almost within the wide hearth. His block-like head, still covered in a thick mass of hair, now white, nodded up and down. "There he is. Come, My Boy."

Mother Sarah pushed me on, though she knew I needed no encouragement. "You must be famished," she said as she hurried to her kitchen. "I'll warm some of that delicious stew. Azariah brought a brace of rabbits by, though you know that sure!"

I went to Grandsire's side. I bent low so he could cradle my face in those platter-sized hands of his, and kiss my forehead. Always had he welcomed me thus. He did so now and the tears nearly began again. What was happening to me?

"Are you unwell, My Boy?"

"No, I am fine, Grandsire." He would have got to the bottom of it in but a moment more; if Father had not entered the room.

"My son. What brings you out so late, and on such a chill night?"

Father bowed his head. "Elisha would speak with us."

"I see. Then sit. Here, we have chairs enough. Sarah, dear. Some tea is all for now I think."

"Tea, of course, Daniel," her deep yet womanly voice responded. "I'll warm the stew regardless. Young Elisha looks fit to devour a cow."

Father took the straight-backed chair opposite his own father. I positioned a rush-seated one between them. As I relayed what I knew, I realized how little I understood of events unfolding in Boston. Any number of questions could prove upending to what I planned to recommend, and Father, by habit and by the deepening furrow of his brow, would throw all manner of obstacle in my path. When I had shared my news, but not yet my recommendations, I paused to catch my breath. Grandsire's patience showed in the deliberate way he refilled the bowl of his pipe, tamped the tobacco, and then held a lit taper close whilst he sucked at it.

Father had observed all this in a tight-lipped silence that produced at last a bead of sweat there at his temple. "Surely our past help to these self-same unfortunates relieves us of more sacrifice." He had leaned so near Grandsire it appeared he might nudge that venerable knee with his own pale limb.

"You are correct to remind us, Daniel that always we Bentons have looked to charity as a means of guiding us." Father's chair creaked as he leaned back against it.

"We were blessed in lambs this spring," I reminded them. "And the many are now grown plump on the meadow's grasses."

"Would you have us part with this rare bounty, boy?" Father demanded. "And with the starving time so near at hand."

Grandsire released a great cloud of smoke that billowed against the wood-paneled walls. "Precisely the time, when Christian men ought to extend a helping hand to those in greater need than they."

The words of these two men, the men I had heeded my entire life, hung longer in the air than Grandsire's smoke. How could Father's utterances, so devoid of charity, usher from his lips. The import of the former and the twist of the latter did him no credit. Had his health, never good, begun to shrink his soul as well as his body?

Grandsire had been observing me before he spoke. "Elisha, how many, do you think, could we afford to part with?"

"Sheep?" I asked, while my mind re-counted the herd at shearing time, and the lambs born since. "Five, I reckon, Grandsire. Six if you prefer."

"Five? Six?" Father exclaimed. His stick thrust up above the mantel. "Go higher still, boy. Why not a dozen full? What matter our family's empty bellies as long as those of strangers are full up."

Grandsire turned his pipe upside down and tapped the bowl against the rocker's burnished arm. Ash sprinkled down, drawn into the flames. "Six. That will suffice."

The moment was wrong, but it must be now. "There is more," I said. Father thrust himself back but Grandsire's upraised pipe gave me the chance to continue. "A Benton should join the party of drovers. And whilst I agree, it was Azariah who first recommended doing so."

"Azariah?" Father said. "How is he connected to a matter such as this?"

My mind raced. Jemima, my brother, Captain Willes; how could I address all these and still...

"I agree with your recommendation, Elisha," Grandsire said. "Such clear thinking is what we have come to expect from you. Yet it is a pleasant surprise to hear the same from Azariah. Is it not, Daniel?"

"What? Yes, Father. Of course, but..."

"Azariah has volunteered," I blurted. "And I think it right."

Father came straight out of his chair. Heedless of the pain it surely cost him, he squared his shoulders and thumped the floor with his stick. "Azariah! What does that boy know of driving beasts? We'll be made laughing stocks. Slandered our name will be and by the wagging tongues of townsmen no less!"

Mother Sarah waited with burdened tray till Father caught sight of her. His stick lowered the moment he had. She smiled for her husband, set down, then poured out a steaming cup of tea for each, and winked at me before finally bustling away.

"What say you, Elisha?" Grandsire asked. "Of your father's concern? Your brother does want in experience."

"He is right to worry that Azariah has little practiced the art, but he learns fast when a thing interests him, and this does."

"Bah!" Father interrupted. "Your brother interested in sheep? Why never has he shown a whit of care for cows, chickens, nor any beasts that need a farmer's hand. He has fooled you in some way, boy. What is he up to, is what I want to know."

Grandsire left this flurry to me, which proved he shared an interest in the answer. "I agree, Father," I said, ever so carefully. "That of all creatures, only game interests him. I believe that, the drive itself, the destination, is what..."

"Oh that is too plain to see. Do you not?" Father asked of us both. "Not only will the young ne'er do well embarrass on the road, he will sully us with his whoring in that festering great port. Do you not recollect that girl of the town we're forever hearing it said he sniffs after? Daughter to your cabinet maker, Father. Barrows! Aye, that's the one."

Somewhere in all that I had come to stand, though what had made me do so I could not say. Before ever I opened my mouth, however, Grandsire bid me sit. That I couldn't do but at least his gesture stayed my hand. Never in life had I thought to strike Father, but now the impulse had rattled through my being, setting my limbs aquiver.

Grandsire's right hand settled on Father's powerful left - blanketing it entirely. It must have clamped down with its vaunted strength, for Father caught his breath. "Not another such word shall you speak, Daniel. Not under my roof and about my grandchild. Is this understood?" Father's head jerked up and down as though yanked by a string. The hand lifted away revealing mottled white and red fingers, quivering in its wake.

If my mind had not quite been made up, it was now. "And I also aim to join those setting off for Boston." Before Father could draw sufficient air into his gaping mouth, I plowed on. "My experience from past drives will surely benefit the party chosen, as will my presence likely please the selectmen. As for our Azariah, I can look to what he might lack along the way."

Father's mouth opened and closed twice more. I prepared myself for whatever may come out of him by way of reply. Unprepared I was for Grandsire's prolonged silence, and the way that he probed at me- almost how Father so often did.

"Your offer, Elisha," he intoned at last, "has much to commend it." My offer? He had not agreed. "Your presence among Tolland's men would satisfy my son's legitimate worries. It does mine. However, and I beg your indulgence My Boy in the asking - but what of the crops ripening in the fields? We Bentons have, one and all, turned to you to bring home the harvest, and so safeguard our futures, lo these many years. Without you..."

The sound of his voice trailing off, nearly breaking, near to broke my heart. "Daniel is ready, Grandsire. It is his time."

"Daniel?" Father exclaimed with a newly discovered pitch. "You cannot mean my son, my second son. Why he holds not a candle to you."

"I have taught my brother all that I can teach. All that I learned from the two of you. He is ready. He just needs the doing of it. Alone."

Father shook a finger at me. "Ah! Ah ha! Now I see it. This is why you hired that third man! So that the pair of you may run along to Boston. You think I haven't sensed how you tire of your duties. Teach Azariah, heh! It is to be he teaching you; in the ways of corrupted flesh!" Father was babbling now, despite Grandsire's grip upon his sleeve, and Mother Sarah's stern expression there in the entry. "Or will it now?" he persisted. "Perhaps you and that great whoremaster, Heman Baker, and he that unfortunate man's first-born son, scheme to reenact your first visit to that den of sin." Grandsire had a good hold now and Father had just about said his last. "I bear witness to how you've turned from us," he croaked. "Don't you think I haven't?" Then he was still.

I sat at last, brought low by Father's fury. Nor could denial be sought in remembrance of my inaugural trip to the Colony of Massachusetts, and its great city by the sea. Heman, my closest friend then and now, and both of us but seventeen years of age, had accompanied the Tolland party. Little we knew of driving beasts, and less did we know of city living. The drive a success, we'd been allowed to wander by the town elders. Soon we found ourselves down by the docks where we fell in with a knot of sailors whose tales snared us at once and completely. We strode the narrow streets with them, our chests puffed out like cocks of the walk. Already taller than some of our companions we were, but our hearts hammered at what we longed yet feared to do. A brothel we sought and a brothel we found, tawdry on the outside it was, and stinking of dank sweat within. We learned the mysteries there, and had not known the shame of it till the minister hauled us from the place. Father, Heman's too, learned of our trespass before ever we reached home. I drove no beasts to market for two years after.

"Sarah," Grandsire said flatly. "Lead my grandson from the room." He had hold of father's ear and into it he poured words low yet fierce. I could not make them out if I had wished it, and I did not. Whatever I had hoped to achieve this night, I had failed, and miserably.

Mother Sarah's loving yet firm embrace guided me forth. In the kitchen, she plied me with soft words which I failed to hear, and hot stew that I could not taste.

Chapter 5

Time passed while I sat staring into the fire. Now and again Mother Sarah poked it to sustain life. I levered the spoon into the clay bowl till it scraped against the bottom. She came to my elbow; stew reappeared. And I saw to its disappearance once more. My mind, which had buzzed with thoughts like hornets in a shaken nest, drained quite as empty as the bowl.

Such was my state when she led me back to the parlor. Neither Father nor Grandsire sat within, though both men's subdued voices from the entry kept a band tight about my chest. I sat where I had earlier. Only after Mother Sarah drifted away did I realize how strangely quiet had been her manner.

Grandsire's tobacco lingered in the room. I breathed easier at the scent. His rocker faced the front door as though waiting for his return. I recalled that Jon Barrows had fashioned the piece for him. The name sent a quiver through me, for the man and his daughter had set this day in motion. But from that moment it had been of my doing. I sought comfort in the memories this room held. So well did I know each item and its placement that I could have walked from one end to the other blindfolded. Always had I been given the run of Grandsire's abode yet never had I run through it.

"My Boy," Grandsire said. "There you are." He walked slow and steady forward and settled himself with a sigh. "Your father has left us," he said, answering a question I'd yet to ask.

"Without a word of parting?"

"Perhaps it is for the best." When I did not respond, he added, "Sarah and I hope that you will stay the night."

"Has he forbid me his roof, then?"

Grandsire's hand found my knee. "Come now, My Boy. It is not as bad as that. I make a suggestion is all. The morn will see us restored to our former selves." Anger began seeping into the vacuum of my chest. Bile bubbled up which I struggled to swallow. "Elisha. Do not let what has passed make of you a bitter man."

"Like my Father?" His hand and its comfort withdrew. "Forgive me, Grandsire. It is not right for me to speak so."

"Tell me true. Had other words passed between you and my son this night? The look you wore when first you arrived..."

"They were between he and I. And on another matter entirely."

"The hiring was it? My son mentioned that you acted counter to his wishes."

"We need the third man, Grandsire. Besides, his hiring had nothing to do with me going to Boston. Or Azariah either. I only made up my mind to accompany him while I sat right here. You must believe me."

"Never have you given me cause to disbelieve you, My Boy." He plucked his pipe from the mantel and produced his pouch from his waistcoat. "Something, however, is amiss. All this talk about you turning from your duties."

"I have not! Father lies!"

Grandsire's raised hand and arched eyebrow shut my mouth. I could scarce believe the words that had escaped my lips. Could barely control the waves roiling in my chest. A man possessed I was. He drew on the pipe till minute flecks of red sprouted in the bowl. All the while he watched me. Despite the scrutiny his deliberate manner calmed me. "Avoid your duties you would not," he said. "My son is in the wrong there, that's certain. Yet a change has come; at long last." Before I could inquire as to his meaning, he continued. "Daniel has glimpsed it as have I, though he has misdiagnosed it."

"What? What change?"

"It's not for me to say, but for you alone to name. Though, you may not as yet understand what's come over you. Fear not My Boy. In time we may see that it is for the best. Meanwhile, there is something I must ask, and it is this. Has my son threatened your inheritance over this? Time passes and still neither of you come to me with his proposal. You are no longer a mere lad, apprenticed as it were, to your father and me. You have a birthright as the first-born. Of this my son is well aware. I have made some modest arrangements for you as well, yet I hold my tongue till one or both of you say matters are settled between you."

So much he seemed to comprehend. Always I tried to act the man with him; to still my tongue though my heart might cry out. Yet he uncovered my hopes and fears as though I had bared my soul. Already this day I had burdened my brothers on this very point - wailing to them as might a child for its mother's milk. And instantly had I lived to regret it. Would I now drag Grandsire into my misery and shame? Especially after my behavior under his very roof. I would not. I would reveal no more this night. No, not even to him; and not even to acknowledge what he had guessed.

"I see," he said, "that I will need to take this up with my son. Perhaps that is best regardless. Come, what say we convince your Mother Sarah that we need a cup before we turn in."

My body melted into the chair in its relief. "Forgive me, Grandsire, but I must disappoint you once more. I am to ride into town, and without delay."

"At night? And risk a fall?"

"The promised rider has not come. What if enough selectmen were in town this day? A pair I saw with my own eyes. They may have had a quorum and even now be selecting the party. A Benton must be among them. On that point at least we three agree."

"Surely they would hold a spot open till they spoke with me."

"Eli Chapman was among those at the inn."

"Was he?"

"I spoke to him myself; about the rent of a pair of his oxen. That man will make no provision for a Benton. Not unless doing so turns a profit for the Chapman clan."

The white-haired head nodded at last. "Your words are devoid of fellowship, My Boy, but 'tis certain he is an enterprising fellow. If only his grandfather were still alive. Nothing came between the Captain and I. Ah well, that's long ago now. Perhaps you should make the journey at that."

Just then a horse whinnied in the clearing. I sprang to the window. Even by moonlight there could be no mistake. "It's Heman!" I said with as much surprise as I felt. Heman, not of my Father's conjuring but my friend himself, and in the flesh. "May I let him in?"

"Go, My Boy. Sarah, we have company! Young Heman Baker."

"I've more water on the boil, husband," she called – her proper carrying voice recovered. "Have Elisha show him in."

By that point I'd reached the door. "Heman, my friend! What brings you to this part of Tolland? And after nightfall no less."

"Elisha Benton as I live and breathe!" Winding his mount's reins about the hitch post, he came on with that loping stride of his. We clapped each other's backs.

"Shall we lead your mare to the barn?" I asked. "You'll come in of course."

"No time for that, my friend. Great doings in the town this day! I ride back directly. And hope you'll ride beside me," he whispered as Grandsire and Mother Sarah appeared in the entry.

"Welcome!" they said in unison as Heman stepped right up and wrapped each in turn.

"What was that I oft said of you two?" Grandsire asked. "When you were mere lads."

"If Elisha is fashioned of sturdy oak..." Heman began with a grin.

"Then Heman is wound from rope," I finished.

"Well, indeed, and so you have become. Just look at the pair of them, will you Sarah. Strapping young men indeed."

"None more handsome in the whole of the town," she agreed.

Their words and obvious joy quite extinguished the image Father had painted earlier. Returning their smiles I draped an arm round my friend's shoulders. "This is why I keep turning up," Heman insisted. "Flattery and open arms. But tonight I'm not to have my fill. I bring word for you, Grandfather Benton, and would deliver it here if you'll forgive me."

Grandsire looked to me, then nodded to my friend. Mother Sarah had already hustled inside.

I released Heman. "I, too, was in town this day. Early, when the letter arrived. I've told Grandsire of Boston's plight."

"And the relief, too?" Heman asked. "Good, good. Then, Elisha, will you return with me?" He glanced at Grandsire. "So that, well, other men of our acquaintance may know your wishes."

Mother Sarah returned. Despite Grandsire's blushing, she wrapped a shawl snug round his shoulders. "My grandson will join you," he said over the top of her head. "It is he who will tell them how the Bentons will act in this."

I went to him and bent so that he may kiss my head. Never had his touch so reassured me. "Grandsire," I began. "About this evening..."

"Ssssh, now. All will be well. Go, and speak for us."

I hugged Mother Sarah and fell in beside my friend, for I did not trust myself to peer into my Grandsire's warm and forgiving eyes.

"Is something amiss?" Heman asked as we led his mare away. I did not answer straightway and he said, "A family matter, then." Always had I treasured that part of his nature. His sense of when talk would do no good. Father's house was pitch dark. He may not have forbade me his roof, but neither was I welcome. By the moon's pale light Heman glanced from the black outline of the house to me. "You'll want to fetch your horse, I trust."

"I won't be a moment."

So often had I saddled her before break of day, both the mare and I arranged the tack without candle or commotion. The other beasts shuffled about a bit, but April satisfied herself with a nudge or two of her head against my chest. From the yard we led our mounts away. I wondered if a candle still burned in the loft, with Daniel and Azariah huddled close, fret in their features and their voices. "I must see this right," I muttered.

"What's that?" Heman asked.

Before us stretched the road heading northeast into town. "It's safe to ride," I answered. We mounted and rode abreast at a walk. The moon shined cool upon the hard-packed earth.

Heman confirmed my fears regarding the maneuverings of Mister Eli Chapman. First had the man been to donate sheep. Then, when other men, townsmen who had nothing to offer but themselves, volunteered to drive his beasts, Eli countered that his slaves could handle this task. Heman had ridden out alone in hopes that I might argue for his inclusion as well as my own – so that we could journey together as on past market days to Hartford and Boston. The urgent tone in which he relayed this news caused me to flick my heels into April's flanks. And so we risked a faster pace. Contemplation of the day's events, and what lay ahead, drew me into a silence that may have held till we reached town. Heman's voice broke through.

"Would you welcome good news?" he asked.

"Of course," I replied, though in my mind's eye I saw only Eli Chapman's lean jaw and pale blue eye. With Chapman sheep and Chapman slaves, the glory of Tolland's succor would be his family's to claim.

"Well then," Heman said. "As I've often bored you with the telling, my friend, long have I wished to hear what my father had in store for me this day." I braced myself for it was now clear what he meant to share.

"My father," he began, "has gifted me the parcel I coveted so long. You know the one. The corner of his land where the stream cuts through."

I could see the shallow, sparkling water as clear as if we stood upon its bank at midday. So often had he and I skipped stones across it. Swallowing hard, I reached out. "Congratulations, Heman!" I grasped his left hand with my right, and pumped it up and down.

"Thank you, Elisha! So my news is not unwelcome. I wondered, you know," and he jerked his head in the direction we had come, "whether I should let it age for a time. Not talk of fathers this night."

"Perish the thought! This has been your dream. Land to call your own! I am truly happy for you."

"I knew you would be. And guess what? There's more. Father also granted me the timber I'll need for a house. My own house!" I cursed my heart that wanted to seize up at my best friend's good fortune. So this was how badly I wanted what he now had. "Would you, Elisha, as once you said you might; help me select the trees? We could fell them together, and haul them out. Once the ground hardens, of course."

Despite the light that rendered us and our mounts but ghosts, I swore I could see the freckles that had always dotted his cheeks. "You know I will. You've but to name the day, and I am yours." Now it was my turn to have my hand and arm worked like a pump. That at least produced a trickle of warmth into my numb chest.

"You make me so happy, Elisha! I knew you'd keep your promise, as I will to you when your turn comes. So happy," he repeated. His hat he pulled from his head and waved to and fro. The moon turned his red hair white.

"Just there," I said. "The lights of the town." Gratefully I spurred the mare towards what promised to be true unpleasantness ahead.

The Meeting House glowed at every window. So many horses had been hitched outside we had to dismount before the tavern. Our long strides brought us quickly along the green and up the wide steps.

Inside men crowded the pulpit area down front despite the lateness of the hour. Not one among them sat.

Captain Solomon Willes' sharp eye caught sight of us almost the moment we entered. I returned his wave. "Heman Baker," he called. "Welcome back. I see you found Mister Benton. Elisha. Join us, will you."

Heman followed me down the center aisle. Men parted as we came on. They had arranged themselves as they might on a Sunday. Landless men stood nearest the door. Jon Barrows was among them, and for some reason his presence surprised me. Heman prodded me on. Those who owned small farms or claimed a trade came next. Finally, I led us up to the knot of selectmen standing before the pulpit. Greetings and handshakes were exchanged. Eli Chapman, near tall as me and wiry as Heman, met my grip with iron of his own. His eyes remained locked on me even after he released my hand.

"Close we are to our mark," the Captain related. "We agreed upon a number at sundown and now are nearly there."

"May I repeat that we Chapmans are happy to make up the shortfall," Eli stated flatly.

"You have already pledged a dozen sheep, Mister Chapman," Captain Willes replied. "Your generosity does your family name great credit. Yet we seek a town-wide response to our neighbors' dire need." Gray-haired heads nodded on either side. "And so it is our humble wish that every family be given the opportunity to offer aid." At this last he turned to me.

"How many do you need, Captain?"

"Seven would bring us to an even four dozen. But," he hastened to add, "Any contribution by the Bentons would be gratefully accepted."

"Seven it is," I said. "Tolland has met its mark."

Even as the selectmen stepped 'round Eli to slap my back, I sensed I had spoken too loud; too quickly. That's when I saw her. She was seated just beside the pulpit at a small desk. A quill was poised in her right hand. Jemima Barrows, whose blue eyes had dropped away at the sound of my bragging.

Chapter 6

With the donation secured, and citing the lateness of the hour, the Captain made a motion to close the proceedings. The selectmen voiced agreement. Only Eli Chapman protested that other business begged our attention. He was especially insistent that with the size of the herd established, the makeup of the party itself could be settled.

The Captain's next statement surprised me, and upset Eli Chapman, judging by his set jaw. "Come sunup," Captain Willes announced, "this item, together with ensuring an adequate supply of gunpowder, will be our first priorities. Now, gentlemen, I bid you goodnight."

The crowd needed no further urging. With a self-satisfied air, the men of Tolland noisily filed out. All the while, Eli shot looks my way. No attempt did he make to hide his disdain. His pale gaze had taken on the glare of a circling hawk. I ignored him, best I could, and tried to locate Jemima's slender figure amongst the newly covered heads of my chatting neighbors.

"You set yonder Chapman down a notch or two," Heman whispered at my side.

"Nor will he let me forget it." For a moment I thought I saw her thick, auburn hair.

"Don't let him trouble you, Elisha. Those Chapmans are wealthy sure, but they don't own the whole town."

"They do own the oxen you'll need to rent if we're to clear your land," I reminded him.

"Oh damn. You're right."

There she was. I stepped forward, blocking her way, before ever realizing her father stood at her side. Whatever I had thought to say to her, fled.

Mister Barrows doffed the hat I saw more often in his hands than upon his head. "Mister Benton, sir. That was right generous of you just now."

"It was nothing," I replied lamely. Had I truly offered up seven plump lambs? Suddenly Aunt Sara's face came to mind. "I, my family, we are happy to oblige."

"You know my daughter, of course. Jemima. Wasn't it kind of Mister Benton…"

She met my gaze. "Most kind, Father. Why, I wonder whether a single soul would even know of Tolland, if not for the generosity of the Bentons. And the Chapmans of course."

"Exactly so," her father agreed. "Well said, Daughter. Now we must be getting along." He waved his crushed hat by way of apology to the people backed up behind them.

I stepped aside and watched them walk down the steps. "Quite a compliment, that," Heman said. "And from the prettiest girl in town."

"That was not her intent," I replied. I watched her go until the night swallowed her and her father both. It made no sense to me. She made none. Had she not come up to me this very morn, to thank me especially for hiring her father. The man's gratitude lingered, yet all she had for me was what, ridicule?

"What is it, Elisha? If she irks you, then forget her. She may be pretty but she's only a girl."

"I know her to be practically sixteen even if you don't." His silly freckles stood out in the lamps set out above the Meeting House steps.

"Next you'll be reminding me of her father's trade. Telling me he owns no land..."

Heman wrapped one of his cable-length arms about my shoulders and guided me down to the nearly empty road. "It appears I missed some goings on in town this morn." He laughed at my half-hearted gesture to throw him off. "None of that now," he counseled. "Come along real quiet like. I'll hear the tale if it takes till sun-up." By this point we'd reached our tethered mounts. He looked one way, then the other. "Where are we to take our ease this night?"

The chill had crept inside my open coat after the warmth of the crowded building. Our breath spilled out in vapors. "I've no idea," I replied. I laughed and Heman joined in.

"One thing's certain," he said. "We won't be riding. Not with all those clouds." Sure enough the moon rarely peaked between layers that hung like lengths of cotton stretched across the heavens. This inky night would pose risks to mounted men. And should we choose to walk our mounts, the Baker homestead was as far west of the town green as the Benton homes were southwest. At least his father would welcome us.

"I know a place where there's room for the three of us," said a voice from the shadowed porch of the tavern.

"Azariah?" I asked.

He stepped into what little light there was. "Aye, Brother."

"What are you doing here? You're supposed to be home. In bed."

"What, and miss your fine oratory Brother? I must say you parted with the makings of a herd of Father's sheep. And quickly too. Though you have yet to see me included in the party. Not a fair trade he might judge."

"The little man has a point there," Heman said.

"Don't encourage him," I replied, though indeed I had been generous - with beasts that belonged not to me, and quite indifferent to the need of others, such as our aunt. "Were you in earnest concerning sleeping quarters?" I challenged.

"Completely, Brother. Oh, and Heman, I can relate what passed between my brother here and my friend Jemima."

"Lead on, little man," Heman insisted. Laughing, he shoved at my back. I offered no resistance.

The quarters were none other than Doctor Cobb's barn. I held back at first but Azariah did locate the padlock's key as easily as he might retrieve his own. The escaping heat of the animals within proved sufficient to draw us in. Once we settled our mounts in their unfamiliar quarters we found a goodly supply of fresh hay for lying down.

"Are you sure the good doctor has no objections?" I repeated.

"Enough, Elisha," Heman urged. "The boy said he's got the use of the place in exchange for the rabbits he provides. Now let him get back to telling me what you won't. Go on, little man."

I had no choice but to let them rattle on. Not unless I wanted to tackle them both at once, and that would be no mean feat. Besides, as I wormed my way into the yielding bedding, I had to smile at their conspiratorial chuckles. Though their laughter came at my expense I would not begrudge it them. Of a sudden I realized Heman was like a fourth brother to me; and I loved him as I did the other three. Their voices floated above as I drifted off to a troubled sleep.

I woke to the name of he who had troubled my dreams. "Rise, Elisha, rise!" Heman insisted. "Azariah says that Eli Chapman campaigns to lead the Boston party."

The barn's rear door had been propped open. Through it I could see the sun had already cleared the distant horizon there beneath Tolland's hills. "What time is it? Why was I not wakened?"

"Not now, my friend. Your brother says you are needed. Urgently! Come!"

As I scattered the hay-stalks from my clothes I realized that Heman too was just now rising. How could we have slept so long, far from the comfort of our beds? I relieved myself behind the barn and caught up with Heman in the road. A minute more found us standing where we had stood mere hours ago. My vision strove to recover from a direct glance at the bright sun. At the threshold I nearly stumbled. All who had been in attendance had found their prior place. I had failed to note Jon Barrows in my haste and he nodded to me now. His daughter merely showed me the top of her head.

The Captain surveyed my state right quick. "Mister Benton. Good day to you." I nodded. "We are discussing a motion by Mister Chapman. He offers to lead our party to our neighbors to the north." Before I could speak, he added, "You should know that many of our brethren believe Eli's appointment to be a good one, as his family has contributed so much to Boston's bounty."

Ambition and persistence Eli possessed in abundance. If only he had experience to match. Precisely so. I smoothed my hair and took a step forward. Jemima's face turned upwards. Her appraisal added to the weight of Father's expectations, and Grandsire's too. "Gentlemen. Mister Chapman is a fine choice indeed. Not only for the reason you cite, Captain, but also because he is experienced with the long and difficult road that must be traveled." The gray-haired heads nodded. Eli's eyes brightened, though only for a moment and even then he seemed to sense I had not finished. "Why, it was on my second trip to Boston I believe," I continued, "that his family asked him to ride along with us who were driving the town's beasts to market in that distant city. Yes, his experience, as well as his family's generosity, commends him, and I would be happy to make the trip under his leadership. That is, if my own application for the role is deemed unsuitable by the selectmen." Eli's gaze abandoned me, but only to scour the faces of those gathered about the pulpit.

"Thank you for your words, Mister Benton," the Captain said. "And your offer. If we might confer a moment." With that, he gathered the elders in an even tighter knot. Their heads bent so far inward they nearly touched.

I risked a glance at Jemima. She had turned away, perhaps convinced more than ever of my arrogance.

"Smartly done," Heman whispered. "Though the girl of your fancy was little moved."

"Girl of my fancy?"

"You've won them over at any rate," Heman went on. "And they're the ones who matter. Mister Eli over there knows it full well. Look at the dour expression he wears will you."

Azariah leaned in close. "Do you forget your promise to me whilst campaigning for yourself?"

"I've forgotten nothing," I replied. Peevish I was and now with the pair of them. "Nor should you presume to advise me on town politics."

Azariah merely chuckled. "We both know I comprehend little and care even less about such matters. But Heman is right. Those old men are set to name you over Eli, which will make for a less than joyous journey."

"'Tis true," Heman interrupted. "For us all I dare say."

"I can handle Eli Chapman," I challenged them, though that gentleman blinked not as we traded hard stares across the narrow space.

"And what of when we arrive in Boston?" Azariah asked. "Are you prepared for that?"

"What would you know of it?"

"I? Nothing. Nor have I need of such knowledge. I merely pass on what Jemima tells me. Of the troubles there." She met my gaze, even as Azariah's words poured into my ear. No censure lurked in her eyes. Nor anger, either. Could it be concern that registered there? Or was it hope?

I broke contact with her; with Eli; with all the rest. What did I know of Boston really, and the events unfolding in that distant port? So caught up in the affairs of Tolland, and the Chapmans and Bentons was I. "Captain," I said. "If I may."

"We near a decision, Elisha..."

"Before you announce it then. A suggestion only I wish to make."

Captain Willes turned to the others. "But of course."

"Thank you. All of you. I have argued that Mister Chapman and I lend equal qualities to this enterprise. I do believe that either of us would prove able." Over their murmurs of assent I continued. "Yet we are not the most able persons to lead this party, or to represent Tolland in Boston – especially during its troubled times." Here I fought the urge to glance at Jemima.

The Captain took advantage of my hesitation to intercede. "Then whom do you have in mind?"

"You, sir. I move that you, Captain Willes, lead us. I, as well as my brother and friend here, long to join you in this mission of mercy."

A pause followed, during which the learned heads nodded as one. Their assent was quickly overtaken by a roar that quite drowned out the Captain's protests. Unanimous agreement unleashed the crowd towards the doors. A chorus of "Huzzah!" echoed in the beams above. Azariah pumped my hand then vanished. Heman clapped my back and managed to utter something about telling his father before he was spirited from my side. Only the most influential citizens remained behind to sort out particulars like where the herd would be penned, and by what date. In time, the Captain relinquished all of his protests but one. And passionate indeed did he speak about the need to secure additional gunpowder. The selectmen had authorized doing so, after all, and definitive steps were required.

He was silenced by an unlikely source. Eli Chapman it was who offered to convey the matter to his uncle, the Colonel. My surprise deepened when I found no trace of self-promotion in Eli's manner or words. "I will ride at once to my uncle's home," he promised. "Uncle speaks often in favor of the town's decree, and the urgency of augmenting our stockpile. I am certain he will appoint a capable man. As for our party, Captain, I do hope you will include me upon my return?"

"I aim to depart two days hence."

"And I shall be at your service by sunrise tomorrow."

A handshake sealed their understanding. With that, Mister Chapman passed me by. His glance may or may not have betrayed a grudging respect, but the disdain at least was gone. I turned full circle yet saw no sign of Jemima Barrows.

Chapter 7

I paid my respects to Doctor Cobb, being sure to thank him profusely for quartering guests he had not expected, and whom had already departed. Within his barn, autumn's air and mid-morning sun bathed the stall that April occupied alone. A layer of straw in the neighboring one still revealed the depressions from where my companions and I had passed the night. Absently, I brushed the mare's coat, responding to her whinnies with soft words. "It smells of October, does it not," I said to her, though the calendar insisted a goodly portion of September remained. Upon my return home, I would have much to explain to Father. Only then did my heart catch, like a horse at a gate. "Good Lord! The orchards. Daniel!"

April tossed her head and even stomped a front hoof as I slung the saddle onto her back and snugged the bridle over her muzzle at lightning speed. Moments more found us pounding from the town center like burglars fleeing the scene of a crime. I waved my cocked hat and cried pardon as people hurried towards the road's shoulders.

The mare, with me slipping against her neck, plunged down the steep roadway. Despite the slope I goaded her on. Her wild eye sought mine. I ignored it. How could I have forgotten that the hired hands were directed to our orchards this very morn.

The roadway leveled out and bent southwest. Here the marsh stretched away to my left. So high had the sun risen that it cleared the strand of pines on the far shore and fairly set the waters to shimmer. "Whoa girl, easy now." Her pace slackened at once. Loosening the reins I reached forward and patted her neck. "What's done is done," I murmured. "You should not pay the price of my folly." At a trot, now, we proceeded along the un-rutted crown.

The evening spent with Azariah had somehow convinced me all was well with my brothers. Yet Daniel, so anxious to please, had been left with no instruction whatsoever; not regarding the hirelings nor management of the harvest in my soon to commence absence. Not unless he had word of it from Father. At this thought I groaned aloud.

That's when I saw her. Jemima Barrows. She appeared some hundred meters off, as though floating directly out of the long grasses that hemmed the road. The mare and I stopped short, as if we had witnessed some mythical creature of the wood. Only then did it occur to me that Benton orchards lay in that direction.

Jemima spotted us. The twig that trailed from hand to earth now fell clear. Her feet walked a straighter path. They were bare. "Miss Barrows," I called. My hands were suddenly full of folded reins and my hat. "Good morrow."

The rays that set the marsh aglow blazed red in her long, wafting hair. "Mister Benton," she replied. High color flooded her cheeks. I felt the warmth of it rise in my own face. We were quite alone. Thankfully her gaze dropped and then her shoulders followed. She curtsied there in the road. For a moment her slender fingers clutched a fold of her dress. How ridiculous to be seated so high above her. I had resolved to dismount when she spoke again.

"I come from your family's orchards." She gave a wave of her arm for emphasis.

My eyes scanned the horizon though I knew full well a succession of knolls barred sight of them from here. A sudden relief flooded my being. "So, the men are set to work after all," I wondered aloud. "Well done, Daniel. Did you see him? How fares my brother?"

The sudden fierceness of her expression shocked me. "I saw him, yes, but my only care was for my Papa. You might recall him as one of your laborers."

"Forgive me," I stammered. "It's just that Daniel occupies my thoughts. I fear I have neglected him. As regards your father, are you not pleased that he has found work?" She seemed to come to a decision of sorts. I swallowed.

"I will answer truthfully," she said. "And fully. If you ask it of me."

"Of course I want the truth." I laughed, though hollowly, for her frankness had set my insides to quiver. The breeze toyed with her dress, her hair, yet despite all that her willowy form seemed rooted to the bare earth like the mightiest oak.

"Papa seemed happy at his tasks just now. I am glad of that. Yet, I wish he did not labor on Benton land."

"But you yourself played a part in his hiring!" I had spoken fast without thinking.

"And I regret it."

"But why? Do you resent that your father works for me?"

"Would you wish for your father to toil for a man half his age?"

I had no answer for that. Father had never worked for any other than himself, well, apart from Grandsire. Realizing too late that this was her precise point, I occupied myself with the lay of the reins in my palm. "So it is not me, specifically," I said, in a whisper.

"You I do not understand," she replied. "Yesterday morn, and again last night, you spoke with all the Benton conceit I have come to expect." At this impertinence my anger overspread my every limb. "But then this morn," she added, so calmly, so quiet, that the words soothed my very soul, "you paid compliments to Captain Willes, and put forward his name. So wise is the choice, and so caring your evident concern for those who might perish if our aid fails to reach them." Her overgenerous praise shamed me into a prolonged silence.

"Elisha," she said, and my name on her lips stopped my breath. "Azariah tells me that you possess many such fine feelings. This day, I saw the proof of it."

Never had I received a compliment so direct. The honesty of her words, and the spell of her unflinching gaze, quite rendered me speechless. I bent far forward and reached out. For a moment she simply stared at my outstretched limb. Then her hand rose up. I took it. The coolness of the air lingered on her soft skin. How delicate were her fingers. I meant to address her but could not. There were things I should say; wanted to. Bending lower still, I brushed the back of her hand with my lips. Releasing her I spurred the mare across the road and bade her jump the ditch. At the crest of the first knoll I saw that Jemima remained where I had parted from her; her hand still somewhat raised. An instant more and she was snatched from my sight.

From time to time I had joined Azariah when he hunted this portion of Father's land. I knew this tract of forest but not well. Certainly not enough to ride at speed through its many copses of trees and the occasional thickets that guarded the low-lying, damp places. I stopped beneath the leather brown canopy of an aged oak. From here, the stone wall bordering the orchard could be seen. The apple trees and duty beckoned but I dismounted regardless.

None had ever spoken to me as she had. Her criticisms stung less than Father's, yet delved deeper. Her praise gushed less than Mother's, yet wrought a fulfillment never tasted. I knew not whether to loll about in this newfound raiment, or shake myself so that I might reclaim my well-worn yet comfortable garb.

A man's shout reached me from such a distance that at first I could discern neither the location nor the source. Then I glimpsed Daniel amongst the laden trees.

Immediately, I set off in his direction. The mare matched my hurried pace. Knee-high grasses cast their ample wet upon my breeches with each stride. Daniel clearly had been laboring with the others for he had shed his coat and waistcoat despite the bite to the air. His waves revealed a mix of joy and anxiety. How to explain my delay? Harder still, I must find the way to tell him that Azariah and I would both soon be off. With a start I remembered practically promising him the next drive to market, whether it be Hartford or Boston.

"Elisha! At last! How glad I am to see you."

"Brother," I replied, squeezing his upper arm.

"The men are here, Elisha. Jon Barrows among them."

"I know of it." To ease his confusion I added, "I came upon his daughter on the road. Listen, Daniel, there is much that I would relate to you."

"Do you speak of Boston?"

"Why, yes. But how could you..."

"Azariah told me all."

"Azariah?" I flared with anger that our little brother had preempted me. Divulging such news was my responsibility, nay, my right to share.

"Aye. He returned early this morn. He meant to speak with me alone but Father overheard us. In the barn this was. Father seemed none too pleased, though unsurprised it appeared to me. Had you begged his permission?"

"He knew of my plans, yes. Is he at home?"

"Father went at once to Grandsire's."

I nodded. Grateful I should be that the news was out; to everyone it seemed. Grateful I supposed I was, though gratitude was difficult to enjoy what with the mixture of anger and shame that accompanied it. "What of you, Daniel? I fear I have let you down. My promise..."

"It is not for me to question you, Elisha. You had good reasons. I'm sure of that."

Reasons I had, certainly, but they failed to excuse a promise broken or the bind I had placed him in. "The men from town," I began. "I should at least have been here..."

"I am glad you speak of them." He gestured expansively towards the heart of the orchard. His relief bloomed anew, and thus we set off together. "So anxious was I for your advice," he said. "When I saw Azariah had returned alone, I went at once to where our lane intersects with the road. I hoped to spy you, of course, but Jon Barrows was the first face I saw. He and his daughter, I mean." He glanced sidelong at me but I let the mention pass. "The other two came up while we talked. I could think of nothing to do but lead them amongst the trees. Eventually I had to stop. They stared at me but my mind had gone blank."

"Daniel," I interrupted. "I do apologize..."

"Wait, wait!" His face lit with a secret smile. "That's when I suddenly remembered how you match the skill of each man to the tasks at hand. Ben you have hired before, and been pleased, so I asked him to assume the delicate role of twisting the low-hanging fruits from the branch. Silas, being not only an experienced picker but also slim and nimble, I set him to work upon the ladder, and with the use of the rake to coax the top-most apples from the trees. And when the rest of Jacob's chores are done, I will assign him the collection of drops."

If my actions had affronted Daniel, he showed it not. Quite the contrary, his present joy was barely contained. These truths raised a lump in my throat.

"Jon Barrows presented the greatest challenge," he continued, using both hands to illustrate its size. "In a moment I discovered he knew nothing of harvesting. Yet you had hired him, so clearly you had seen something there in him. I observed him more closely, and found him to be very strong and utterly willing."

Daniel had inherited his eyes from Mother; her lack of height too, though his broad shoulders could be claimed by Grandsire, or even Father. Just now, gazing into those eyes of his I wanted to throw my arms about his stout chest. With but a dash more confidence he could be the best of us.

"So I set him to the hefting of the bushel baskets. Yonder he stands. As he fills the cart faster than the other two can harvest, I demonstrated the use of the wooden rake for him. He shows a deftness of touch that surprises in one so powerful. I believe ere long he shall wield it as skillfully as he might one of his carpenter's tools."

Sure enough, Mister Barrows stood no more than a dozen rods off. At that moment his upstretched arms guided the long-handled implement betwixt the gnarled lower branches. He proceeded to tap the high, slender ones with the rake's teeth. We both flinched as a short length of last year's growth tumbled down with a trio of ripe fruit.

I chuckled. Daniel reddened. "His technique is still a bit raw," he admitted, "but Jon has the endurance to hold the tool high all day if need be. Perhaps I need to describe the necessary movements to him again..."

So eager was my brother to please. This fervent desire made him, on occasion, appear weak. The impression was false. "I think that he gets on rather well," I said. "And what's more, you have done me a great service this day. Whatever you decide in this is fine by me."

"Right then." He paused, and sized up yonder tree and he who labored there. "Then I will show Jon Barrows the way of it once more."

"Do not let me detain you, Brother," I stepped aside and encouraged him further with a smile. He strode off straight and true. Stronger he was than he knew. Stronger perhaps than I imagined, and I harbored the notion that my brother possessed a rare, inner strength. Father's hardness had not helped him discover it. And I, too, had played my part in its shyness. I would endeavor to change my ways.

April's affection, for I allowed myself to think it was that and not mere obedience, kept her at my side, allowing my thoughts to roam free whilst continuing on to Father's house. With luck he would still be with Grandsire, meaning I could postpone that conversation. So many things to put in place before this unexpected departure. As I began ticking them off one by one, so too did my doubts grow. "Why exactly?" I pondered aloud, had I put my name forward, and at such a time as this.

Before I could discover an answer I caught sight of Jacob outside Father's barn. He had progressed far in reducing what must have been a goodly pile of brush into kindling. "I see you honed a fine edge to the hatchet, little brother. And put it to good use."

"Oh, yes, Elisha. The axe, too. Would you care to see?"

"I would, by and by. Just now I must attend to matters most pressing. Have you seen Azariah?"

"Yes, Brother. He returned an hour ago."

"And he is now where?"

"Oh. Out behind the barn I think. He was melting lead. For hunting, most like."

He had turned up his face at this last, obviously proud that he had shared this nugget without being asked. Masking my frustration at Azariah's selfishness I tousled Jacob's hair till he giggled and ducked away. "Thank you, Jacob. And take care with that hatchet. Mind you get along to the orchard soon as you finish." I headed into the barn's cool, dark interior and relieved the mare of the saddle's weight. A few pitchforks full of hay saw to whatever hunger lingered after her recent browsing. My own stomach growled but I had no time to pay it heed.

The smokehouse stood between the barn and the house. The far side had been reserved for the covered woodpile while that nearest sported a brick encircled area for open fires. One smoldered there now. Azariah sat cross-legged before it, stuffing something into a pack.

"Nearly finished!" he proclaimed on seeing me. "No lead remains but we've balls enough to hunt the winter through. As to powder, though..."

"So that's what you've been up to. Always hunting it is with you. Have you forgotten the commitment just made to Boston?" I took advantage of his suddenly slack jaw to add, "I could have used your help in town."

"With what? You seemed to have matters well in hand when I left." My peevishness had got the best of me, for certainly he was right. But I glared regardless, for always he thought of no one and nothing but himself. Snatching up the bulging pack he stepped before me.

"What's this?" I asked when he held out what I now recognized as Uncle William's rucksack, handed down to me from Aunt Sara.

"I filled the cartridge box, though you'll want to carry it separate on the road. And Mother insisted on more shirts than you'll need, and every pair of socks you own."

My brain struggled for something to say by way of reply. I received its not inconsiderable weight into my hands. Hot blood rushed to my cheeks which would be fairly glowing red by now. "Where is yours?" is all I managed.

"I go now to start on it," he said, and left my side.

A fool I had been on many occasions, but never a more humbled one than on this day. I watched him go with the full knowledge that unless I changed my ways with all my brothers, Father's impression of my recent behavior would be proved too true.

Chapter 8

By this time of day the flock would normally have been led out to the pasture. Enclosed by stone walls it granted the sheep acres in which to roam. Yet when I first came through the barn the sheep hovered in the pen just beyond it. Someone, and I could only credit Daniel, must have kept them penned after hearing Azariah's news. Grateful, I returned there now. The selecting would be much easier in this confined space.

With a whistle I summoned the dog to my side. It proved the most reliable way to lure him from whatever sunny spot he had curled up in; His given name was Willie, yet Hannah, whose job it was to see him fed and who adored him, called him Woolly, on account of his thick, curly coat. The consequence of this was that he often refused to respond to either name, unless it was Hannah who sought him.

With my brindle-colored, shaggy companion at the ready, I edged the flock towards one corner. Willie held them at bay, and I waded in to find the seven destined for Boston. I had a dilemma. Do I select the plumpest, healthiest animals to squelch our neighbors' dire needs? Or should I choose weaker, lesser beasts, thus saving the prime animals for Benton needs – including that of Aunt Sara and my young cousins? Hannah's gay laughter reached me from the house. That sound, so near, so dear, could be no more real; whereas Boston's pain I could only guess at. I chose the seven, though perhaps none of them would be most pleasing to either Father or the selectmen.

Even as I set the fence rail dividing the smaller group from the rest, my sister skipped across the yard. "Brother! Mother wants to know how many days she should plan on."

"For what, Sister?"

"Why the food for your journey. With Azariah."

"Of course. I should have thought she would tend to that. Tell her I have made arrangements. Tell her, oh well tell her I will come in directly but that we have no need of foodstuffs."

"What? No need? Of food?"

The tone of incredulity matched Mother's exactly. I couldn't help but laugh. "Come here, Sister. Come." I held out my arms. Her puzzlement had not faded. Not one whit but she slipped within my arms anyway. Her head, her brown waves of hair smelled fresh from a washing. I found it hard to draw away.

"Are you well, Brother?" When I didn't answer straightway, she whispered to me. "Did you and Azariah argue?"

"We might have done. A little. It was all my fault too." I wrapped her in one arm and steered her towards the house. "Not to worry, Sister. I will make it up to him. All will yet be well."

At the doorway Hannah squirmed free. Taking me by the hand, she tugged me towards the kitchen. "Here he is, Mother!" she proclaimed. Hannah's face then fell as she took in the hall's food-blanketed table, and seemed to recall why she'd been sent for me. "Elisha says," she valiantly began, "that he, that..."

"Perhaps it's better I make explanations to Mother. Now then, Sister," I said to her in a confidential tone, "can I rely on you to release the sheep to pasture?"

"Me, alone! I need not ask Jacob?"

"Willie obeys you best. Besides, your brother is busy at the moment."

"Thank you, Brother! Woolly and I both thank you!" She curtsied and made for the door.

"Mind now. Leave the seven I placed in the inner pen. They'll need hand-feeding."

"Yes, Brother," she sang.

Mother had waited through all of this with arms folded across her chest. Her eyes swept the table and then snared me. "You have no need of this, I gather." It was not a question.

"It appears the root cellar has been moved upstairs," I said in my embarrassment.

"Nonsense. When you journeyed to Boston last autumn you were gone a fortnight. Besides, this time Azariah is to go with you." Suddenly she clasped a hand to her mouth. "You did not refuse him?"

I stepped forward. "No, no I did not. Would not. Though I have been most unkind to him." Her eyes searched mine. "A misunderstanding," I continued. "He had prepared a rucksack. For himself I thought. And so, well, I accused him of being selfish, even as he handed it to me."

"I know."

"He told you?" I glared at the dark corner that concealed the loft stairs.

"Fie, Elisha! You know he never would. I saw it in his face when he returned - without you and empty-handed."

I squeezed my forehead. "I have behaved so uncharitably towards both he and Daniel. What is wrong with me?"

She drew my arms down to my sides. "If you have, it is only because you are caught up in the arranging of charity for others, in greater need than we. What's more, I have never seen Azariah so inspired. Your brother Daniel, too."

Her choice of words lit a spark of hope. "Is Daniel also somewhat scared? I have not helped him prepare for this near as much as I should."

"There you are wrong, Elisha. He is ready, and for that he has you to thank. Always, my son, you are too hard on yourself."

"And you, Mother, are far too kind where I am concerned." We embraced for a moment. "I should go up to Azariah."

An occasional bang and the movements of hasty feet echoed from the rafters above. "Let him have a moment more," she counseled.

"You are right, of course. Then I should hurry along to Grandsire's. There are pressing matters that I must arrange with he and Father."

"It is not for me to interfere with men's affairs, but other matters there are that are of equal importance. Sustenance, for one. Tell me. When did you eat last?"

"Eat?"

"If you cannot remember it has been far too long. Sit!" She easily led me to a chair for there was no protesting. Besides, my stomach made great pains to remind me that it needed feeding. Hurriedly Mother cleared a space and in a flash had a steaming mutton pie, fresh from the warming oven, set before me. As I ate she rearranged the root cellar's bounty, shaking her head from time to time as though regretting that none of it would yet be used. "If I might, Mother," I managed to say between mouthfuls, "a jar of your raspberry jam for the journey?"

She kissed my head. "You shall have two. One for each of my boys."

I finished and sat back. Only the rustling of Mother's skirts and the occasional pop from the fire did I hear. From upstairs there came no sounds. I glanced at the stairs and stood. Mother laid a hand upon my arm.

"Azariah has calmed himself. You and he will have time enough on the road. Perhaps you should speak with your Father now."

I nodded. "Was he much angered with me?"

"My Daniel is a loving man. He loves you, my son. Very deeply." I pulled back, but she refused to release me. "I know he can be hard. On you, especially. Try not to doubt his love. Will you do this? For me."

I held her. "Aye. For you I will try." I stepped back and plucked my hat from the mantle. "When Azariah comes down..."

She smiled. "I will tell him."

The entire way to Grandsire's I thought of what she had said of Father.

Mother Sarah took hold of both my hands at the door. A stillness had taken root in her. She led me before Grandsire and Father before I could inquire as to the cause. Standing before them it occurred to me how much I had come to rely upon her loudly whispered confidences. Without her preamble, the reserved expressions on the faces of my elders doubly confused me. Mother Sarah left us without a word.

"My Boy," Grandsire said. His smile disappeared as fast as it had come. Father merely nodded.

As neither had invited me to sit, I plowed straight on whilst standing. Seven sheep had been promised I told them straight off. To this an eighth should be added to provide meat for my aunt. Father's eyes widened and his jaw quivered. He said nothing. "This generous commitment to Boston," I hastened to add, "enabled the town to make its self-imposed quota, and needless to say, pleased the selectmen to no end." Both nodded. "What's more, I argued that having also committed two men to the drive, it would be unfortunate if we Bentons should further be expected to furnish provisions for the journey. As a happy consequence, food will be provided for both me and Azariah. This lessens the toll on our smokehouse and root cellar," I added. The clarification had no impression on my silent audience. I shifted course. "As to the farms, much has been accomplished. Your planting fields, Grandsire, and yours too, Father, have been tilled. Daniel and I, we have likewise seen to the safe storage of choice seed for the spring planting. The smokehouse is now full. I may have told you this. Let me see. Ah! Come sunrise, I intend to visit the cider mill. I will let Mister

Stimson know the apple harvest is underway and we will soon have need of his services. He expects me. And, yes, I did mention previously that arrangements are made with Eli Chapman. The rental of his family's oxen to haul the felled trees? Of course, I expect to return to Tolland well before winter's advance…" Mother's stew had set me up proper, but I suddenly felt an urgent desire for the chair to my right.

"You have done well, My Boy," Grandsire said at last. "Done us Bentons proud, I'd say. Has he not, Daniel."

Father looked me in in the eye. The moment lasted longer, and his gaze appeared less angry, than I had seen in, well, further back than I could remember. I tried in vain to prolong the connection but he turned to the fire. "What is it?" I asked - of one, then the other. "What has happened?"

Grandsire patted Father's knee. "Nothing, My Boy. Reminiscing we were, is all, as men sometimes will. Allow me to lead you out. You've had quite a day by the sound of it, and should get your rest." He hauled himself upright. "The good Lord knows you will have need of it." Mother Sarah appeared with a tray laden with cups of tea, bread, and jam. "Say goodnight to our grandson, Sarah dear. Twill be a fortnight fore he sleeps in a bed again so he must be off."

She set down her burden and hurried forward. "God keep you, Elisha." The power of her embrace always surprised me.

Grandsire escorted me from the parlor. I hesitated at the front door. Before I could speak, he said, "Earlier your father happened upon Azariah. As he packed a rucksack for you."

"Uncle William's?"

"Yes, it belonged to your father's younger brother," he murmured. "William was to him as Daniel or Azariah are to you."

Long I had understood the order of their birth. Of my father and uncle as brothers I had seldom considered.

"Yet my Daniel never tutored William; as you do your brothers. That you never knew, I'd wager. His health was the cause, you see. Afflicted even as a boy he was."

I glanced at the parlor entry. Mother Sarah could be heard within as she served Father. Now I understood the emotion in his eyes just now. Loss. Her cheery words continued, speaking for herself and answering for him.

"When war came with the French," Grandsire continued, "it was young William who went, not your father, though he was the first born."

"And he died."

"War. It took one of my sons. And left another as you see him."

I could not fathom the impacts, not at once. "But what has this to do with this evening, Grandsire? Or with this journey?"

He laid his broad hand upon my shoulder. "There is an anger in the land," he replied. "And Boston is its beating heart."

I knew not what to say to this. Certainly Grandsire received numerous reports. And not all I imagined were shared with me, but there had been no violence. Not for years. Not since the massacre at that city's customs house. "But..."

"Be careful, My Boy," he said. "That is all I ask. What we ask. And keep young Azariah from that which might bring him harm." He opened the door then, and so I stepped out into the night. So fast did it fall at this time. Grandsire paused as if something remained unsaid. Only when he had pushed the door closed did I realize I had not bent for his kiss.

Chapter 9

A hint of dawn revealed lead-colored skies. None stirred in Father's house but I. In the loft's half-light I could just make out my brothers' outlines. They had lain prostrate since my return last night. Daniel was duly exhausted from the prior day's events. Azariah had, or so I guessed, merely feigned sleep. He could be pretending now for all I knew. As Mother had said, however, he and I would have ample time to set things right on the road. Quietly as a man my size could, I descended. Coals glimmered in the kitchen hearth. Jacob and Hannah were charged with keeping the fire lit but they slept on as only children could, stacked one above the other in the trundle beds placed in the far corner. Remembering how hard they had worked the day before, I smiled at their sleeping forms, and coaxed colors from the embers. Whilst I donned my outer garments, I fed first kindling, then split logs to the now awakened flames.

Rain threatened, so I plucked my greatcoat from the hook before heading to the barn. Should the temperature fall further still, an early snow could prove as likely.

The cows were unfazed by my presence, for often I came among them at hours early and late. No, it was the urge to be milked that caused them to shift noisily about within their stalls. Soon they would begin lowing and this would draw the young ones from their warm beds.

Having saddled April, and secured a bulging bag to the pommel, I led her out. She snorted at the cold and the hour, but stood still so that I might mount her. The house's chimney smoke rose in a column as we left at a walk.

Where the lane met the road we crossed straight over. In less than a mile I spotted a light just ahead. "We're in luck," I confided to the mare. "Mister Stimson is awake."

The candle's soft hue served to infuse the miller's cheeks with an even ruddier glow than he naturally possessed. The effect was that his face gleamed as shiny red as the ripe fruit overtopping the mill's hopper. "James. I hope I do not disturb you at this hour."

"Why, young Mister Benton. Come in, sir, come in."

Dismounting, I hefted the sack of carefully selected fruit, and joined him inside. Seeing that his cheese needed only one more layer, I offered my services. James' broad smile proved sufficient for me to shed my greatcoat. He tapped the Skungamaug's rushing waters to force the crusher round and round whilst I fed the hopper with the last of a neighbor's crop. Together we then employed short-handled shovels to scoop the surging mass of pumice out from the trough and onto the cheese. Satisfied, we put the top board in place and with his forearms rippling, he began the press. A slowly building stream of juice, as if escaping the relentless pressure, trickled, then poured down the channel; cascading at last into a barrel positioned just below the lip.

The sun's rays slanted inside even as we completed the press. Mister Stimson wiped his brow and sat on a barrel that had already been bunged. "Thankee, Elisha." I took a perch beside him. "Might those be some of yours you've brought me?" he asked with a thrust of his chin.

"Some from Father's trees. Grandsire's too." I plucked forth a pair and held them out.

"You do take such pains, Elisha. What's say we call the lot Benton fruit. For so it is."

I returned his smile. "If it suits, James, my brother Daniel can have the first cartload here before sundown."

The crunch of his bite brought a smile to both our faces. Bits of straw drifted lazily in the sunbathed air as he took his time eating till only the core remained. Within minutes we had settled on a timeline and his fee, which Mister Stimson was more than happy to accept as a percentage of hard cider that the crop would yield. He proved well aware of Tolland's commitment to Boston, and thus had no objection to my hurried departure.

Back home once more, I found the children up and about their morning chores. I surrendered the mare to them, but only after insisting that brother Jacob spoil her with an apple for each day I was away.

The kitchen and hall were near to overflowing with Bentons. Even Grandsire and Mother Sarah had come down to see us off. Pleased as I was to see them gathered together, the assemblage threatened any hopes I'd harbored of speaking in private to my brothers, especially Daniel. And in his flitting gaze I saw his gnawing fears betrayed. As the noisy mass of us edged closer to the front door, I began edging closer to him.

Father's figure at one of the hall windows distracted me. Leaning left, I caught a glimpse of what he saw- the seven sheep held at bay by Jacob, Hannah and Willie. Father frowned at the sight, at the loss they represented I imagined, whilst his back he offered to Azariah and me. My back I turned to him. Daniel had closed to an arm's length but the womenfolk came between us. Mother embraced me at the waist, while Mother Sarah, being somewhat taller, did her best to encircle my chest. Within a minute I had agreed to all that they asked of me and more than I could possibly remember. I promised to keep safe and look after my younger brother even as they extracted similar promises from him. And then out of doors we spilled.

"What of the hired hands?" Daniel demanded of my right ear. I had not seen him come round me but I certainly felt the clutch of his right hand upon my forearm. "Should I feed them?" His wide eyes verged on wild. "I reread the contract at first light. It fails to address..."

I coaxed him to the edge of our smiling, crying clan. "Be calm, Brother. We have seen to these harvests many times over, you and I."

"But you were always here with me, Elisha."

"You've but to recall how much I have ceded to you each season, Daniel. As to the men's feeding, let judgment be your guide. If they please you, see to their every need. If a man is found lacking, speak to him. Privately and at once. As you did with Jon Barrows yesterday."

"That did go well," he recalled with a shy grin. "I congratulated Jon. Then made a suggestion regarding the use of the pole. He altered his technique straightway."

I patted his back. Mother's gaze took us in. Her eyes glistened and she smiled. "A word on the cider mill, Daniel. Terms are laid with Mister Stimson. He will be ready for you. This noon if need be."

Daniel breathed out. "Thank you, Elisha. I had not thought to call on him."

"Trust your experience, Brother. And your instincts." I grasped both his arms. "For I do."

Grandsire appeared before me. "Allow me," he said, with a smile for us both. He grasped my right hand in his. His fine, old head nodded. I did not miss my chance to kiss it.

And then we were off. The sheep had made a break for it and Jacob set off in pursuit. At once Willie darted forward and turned the flank back towards our lane. Already laden with his pack, Azariah gave a joyful shout, hoisted his musket by way of a wave, and followed after them. Daniel likewise departed, but he towards the orchard.

No sooner had I settled the weight of Uncle William's rucksack on my shoulders, Hannah buried her head against my midsection. I kissed her and handed her over to Mother. "Jacob will return with your Woolly," I promised. "Until our return!" I called out to them. Only then did I realize Father alone had not emerged from the house.

Of the three of us, Jacob's skills at driving were the freshest. I had played at being a drover on many occasions but not of late. And Azariah, he immediately showed his inexperience by alternating quick forays with indifference. His mercurial behavior unsettled the placid beasts no end. Not wishing to humble him before our baby brother, nor start what promised to be a long journey on the wrong foot, I ignored these missteps.

"Azariah," I said. "Perhaps you might hurry forward and discover where in the town the herd is being assembled. I imagine the green will prove a hectic place just now, and knowing what's to be done..."

"Splendid idea!" His pace doubled on the instant. Jacob groaned as his older brother's advance divided the flock into two unequal portions.

"And Brother," I hollered. "Learn if you can whether we are to return this way this very day. After the counting is done."

"I shall! And if not I'll find quarters for us."

How gracefully he moved. Already he had put near on fifty yards between us. Even burdened as we both were, Azariah covered ground like the hunter he was. Pity the quarry caught in his sights. "Jacob, well done, lad. You've brought them all together again."

"It was mostly Willie did all the work, Brother. Sister will be so proud of him." It occurred to me that I had failed to inquire as to dogs for the journey. Willie would indeed be a fine choice but the family could ill afford his absence. More than mine most likely.

"Are you laughing at me, Elisha? Have I done something wrong?"

"Perish the thought. Why, on my return Daniel and I will arrange to have you take over all of the herding chores."

"Truly? Even into town? Hartford, too!"

"One thing at a time. For now, though, let's help Willie get that lamb away from those barberries."

"Oh. Oh no!" Jacob scampered off to the far side and I casually waved my musket to keep the other six moving down the road.

Soon enough we would arrive in town. There we would find Azariah. Heman, too, and Eli Chapman of course. There would be one other, and thoughts of her I had stored in the recesses of my mind. They spilled forward now that Jacob's diligence left me but a minor role. What might she say to me, after that bold, rash snatch of her hand? Might she have reported the act to her father? Class differences counted for little when a man of any station took such liberties with a maid. Would I tell him my intent should he question me? Jon Barrow's habitually friendly face appeared, scowling, in my mind's eye. What had been my intent after all?

Chapter 10

With little more than an occasional whistle and Willie's vigilance we drove the seven sheep up the main road that ascended to Meeting House Green. Jacob and I heard our neighbors before we saw them. Louder than a market day, the waves of sound washed downhill over us. The rap of hammers, the creak of wheels and the clop of horses' hooves all vied with a torrent of human voices. We topped the rise. The turnout rivaled a Sunday yet the commotion signaled anything but. Children had even been given liberty to frolic. Zigzag across the common they raced. Some darted between carts, startling a horse in one instance, and no adult took them by the ear.

"Elisha?" Jacob breathed; his mouth agape.

"Mind the animals now," I chided. Stripped of pack and musket, I caught sight of Azariah moving fast through the throng.

"This way, Brother," he called when still a few yards distant. "The selectmen await you. For the count."

"Jacob," I said. "Guide the flock by way of the green." The children were not so out of control that they needed to be told to give way. My height enabled me to easily track Azariah as he retraced his steps. We soon reached the stone enclosure used on market days.

"Fine specimens, Mister Benton," Selectman Lathrup intoned, as one by one the Benton beasts were coaxed inside the open gate. "You and your family are to be congratulated on your husbandry, as well as your charity."

Two other selectmen in attendance nodded to me. I returned the courtesy. Azariah had disappeared as he often did. Within the pen approximately two dozen sheep huddled. At least ours were not the last to arrive. The flock began moving in a nervous circle as newcomers fell in with them. Similar to our own, the occupants were a respectable mix of well-fed lambs and full-sized sheep born the prior year. If there were no prize specimens, neither were there any ill or underweight ones.

Only then did I make note of Eli Chapman. He had been leaning against the enclosure's far wall. Now he moved away. Had he been waiting for our arrival, I wondered? Clearly he had been observing our animals as they scampered inside. I couldn't suppress a grin, for just as surely I had been judging the Chapman beasts.

I glanced down to see Jacob smiling up at me. Willie stood beside him with his tail flapping like a flag. I messed the boy's hair. "You should be proud. The pair of you."

At that Jacob tousled the dog's fur. "Can I remain in town awhile, Brother?" he asked. "Promise we'll go straight home afterwards."

"You have earned it, surely." With a squeal, he launched himself towards his fellows on the common. "Not so fast!" I commanded. He returned at once. It was hard to determine whether my baby brother or the dog appeared more downcast. I bent low, gave his thin shoulders a squeeze, and kissed his head.

"Elisha! They'll see," he said, squirming about to discover if his mates had seen this horrid display.

I released him. "Obey Father and Mother whilst I'm away." He nodded most earnestly. "Good lad. And here. This is for you." I produced a copper half pence. "It's little enough, yet may fetch a candy for you and Hannah at the store."

His arms clutched at my shoulders. "Thank you Elisha!" Then he was gone. "Come home soon!" he hollered with the briefest of turns.

I swallowed as I watched Jacob fall in with his friends. How few had been the occasions that I had run carefree, when I was of an age. Now where had Azariah gone off to? Surely he'd learned whether we had sufficient provisions on hand, or, perish the thought, whether promises made could not be kept; leaving us with last minute procuring to do. I had begun to mentally recount the ready cash Grandsire and Father had entrusted me, when I spied Azariah and Heman both. They made as straight a course for me as the milling crowd allowed.

Azariah's grin assured me we would soon be off. "We're to leave the moment the flock is assembled!" he hollered.

"A word," Heman said, ignoring all pleasantries and taking me by the arm.

"What troubles, my friend?"

"Never was there a more ambitious man..."

"Do you speak of Eli Chapman?"

"The very one. Why just now I overheard him. Petitioning the Captain. Trying to volunteer, he was, to procure the powder."

"Jemima spoke of it," Azariah added.

"Well," I insisted. "What did she say? In the Meeting House, Eli seemed to care naught for the role."

"Calm thyself, Brother. I will tell what I know. She said Captain Willes convinced the Colonel of its importance. Another letter has come, from Boston. Their Committee of Correspondence I believe she said. They request every militia member in each town be supplied with two pounds of powder. Think on that, Elisha!"

"Two pounds per man?" Heman asked.

I tried to think, in spite of my brother's excitement and my friend's shock. "But Boston's Committee holds no sway beyond the colony of Massachusetts," I replied. "They might ask whatever they wish, yet they have no jurisdiction here in Connecticut. Good lord, think on the cost to the town." A special tax would be levied for such an outlay, I imagined, and how Father would rebel at that.

"A princely sum, to be sure," Heman agreed.

"Word comes from a higher power, I'm told," Azariah continued. "The Continental Congress I think she said."

"The one meeting in Philadelphia?" I asked.

"I imagine so. Don't look at me that way, Elisha. You know how little I care for politics. Even of the local variety," and he waved his arm dismissively.

"Can they decree such a thing?" Heman asked.

"If the Captain believes so," I replied, whilst I searched the crowd for him. "Then we should."

"What does it signify, do you think?" Heman asked. "That much gun powder."

"Nothing good," I replied, and set off in search of an answer. I trusted that they followed in my wake. The town residents, and the inhabitants too, had respected a space between themselves and the gathering of leaders. I strode across that now and joined my peers. The Captain was addressing them so I made my greetings with mere nods. Eli wore a frown so intense he saw me not. Noah Grant returned my salutation. With him in attendance, his family's sheep must now be among those that filled the enclosure near to bursting.

"And so I introduce to you," the Captain intoned, "Lieutenant Parker, of Coventry. Whilst I and the party are away, he will oversee the vitally important procurement of powder."

"Coventry?" Azariah whispered at my elbow. "Why should a man from a neighboring town..." I shushed him with a shake of my head.

"The Lieutenant," Captain Willes continued, "heads a detachment of militia that shall join us, should the need ever arise." After a pause he added, "Let us pray it never does."

In silence, then, men shook the Lieutenant's hand. I stepped forward as I wished to meet this man, and as it was expected of me. The Captain did the honors. Lieutenant Parker was a slim man, tidy almost, in proportions and dress. His eyes met mine dead on. When we shook hands I liked him straight off.

I stepped aside so that others might have an opportunity. And I saw her then. Jemima wore, to my amazement, a cap of linen beneath a straw hat. I tried to recall seeing her with two coverings at once. Gathering her hem, she ventured across the space dividing the townspeople from the elders. Shoes adorned her feet. I removed my hat before ever she arrived. She stopped in front of me, though she faced Azariah.

"Did you tell your elder brother?" she asked him.

"He's only just come." Azariah smiled and gestured towards me. "But here he is, as you plainly see."

She turned to me. The color of straw set off the blue of her eyes. "Mister Benton." My bow brought me nearer still. She blushed. "I asked your brother to convey some news to you."

"The allotment of powder, yes. He spoke of it as did the Captain just now." Suddenly martial stocks seemed irrelevant.

"There is more news than this," she said, her voice lower by far. "Captain Willes does not want this broadly known, but as he wished you to be made aware, I offered to share it with you." The blush deepened. "Seeing as I suspected our paths would cross..."

"Naturally," I replied. "It stands to reason..."

"He, the Captain, says to tell you that hundreds, perhaps thousands of militia turned out in Worcester."

"Massachusetts?" I said, as I struggled to comprehend the reason for such an event, and its relevance.

"Yes. An alarm had been raised. Word had come that powder was to be confiscated." Perhaps my expression betrayed my complete ignorance of the gist of this news, for she hurried on. "Our northern neighbors feared that soldiers would come. The King's men, and they from Boston."

My gaze broke from her now intense gaze. I sought and found Captain Willes, he a veteran of the war against the French and also the expedition to Cuba. Lieutenant Parker, too, I studied – he whose services the Colonel had thought necessary to secure. "The King's men," I murmured. "To Worcester from Boston…"

"Gentlemen," Captain Willes said in the voice he employed when drilling the company. "If those of my party can see to their final arrangements. We depart forthwith."

At once, men hurried in all directions. Parents recalled children from their play. People parted to reveal the center of the road. Eli Chapman stepped up and shouted for Newport, his Negro. With the flick of a slender switch, the fellow urged forward an ox that pulled a heavily laden cart.

"We're to place our packs aboard," Azariah confided. "Your musket, too, if you choose." He pressed his face against hers, and headed for the cart. "Wish us well, Jemima!"

"Godspeed," she called after him.

Heman paused when he noticed me rooted beside her, then drifted farther off. I cleared my throat.

She looked up at me. "You will watch over him, will you not?" she implored.

"I will. Yes, of course." We found ourselves isolated as everyone else had strung out along both sides of the road, anticipating the party's departure. How natural had it felt the last time we two had stood alone in the center of a road. And this, how awkward.

"Stay safe, will you?" she said.

I hesitated then, wondering whether I might be so bold as to experience the softness of her cheek. She extended her hand. I had no choice but to shake it. "Your servant, Miss."

"Release the sheep!" Captain Willes ordered. The gate swung open. Eli hurried inside, and out the animals raced. Down the gauntlet of people they ran, with we drovers hurrying after.

Chapter 11

Always had these drives to market been planned to a fare thee well. Not so this one. We began as a rabble that surged along our route. We headed southwest so that we might reach the main road and our true course to the north and east. The flock was small and men with dogs practically surrounded it. Our mere presence served to divide the sheep into frenzied groups of three here, five there. The more active our members, and of these Eli proved the most eager, the more did we stir the poor creatures into near panic.

"Captain!" I hailed, from the rear of the swarm of men and beasts. "Might I offer a suggestion to the men?"

"For Heaven's sake do!"

"Gentlemen!" I called out. "If we draw back from the front. And from the midst of the herd as well." I let my voice carry, yet kept it steady too. Eli surprised me by being the first to abandon the swirling, dusty center. Others mirrored his withdrawal, even Azariah, who must have resented following Eli's lead. "Take up positions along both flanks. Very good. And keep the dogs to the fringe. Best you're able."

The dogs still yapped at the sheep and each other, but for the most part they followed their owners. As if by magic, the heretofore harassed creatures drew together as a single, woolly host.

"Huzzah!" Heman cried. "Huzzah! Huzzah!" chorused the company. Joy at their collective relief kept any embarrassment at bay, even when the Captain clapped my back.

In orderly fashion, a sight of which the townspeople had been deprived, we skirted the marsh. Seven souls we numbered, including the Captain, Eli Chapman and his slave who went by the single name, Newport, Noah Grant, our nearest neighbor, and, of course, Heman, Azariah and me. We could have managed with half our number, in fact fewer would likely have added to our efficiency, but all present seemed willing.

Three dogs there were as well. Heman admitted to owning the mostly blond, noisy thing. It had followed him from home and he had failed to persuade it to leave his side. He, for the dog's incessant marking of anything growing more than three feet in height betrayed him as a male, knew absolutely nothing of sheep. A second dog of mottled colors and tipping the scales at four stones if an ounce, turned out to belong to Eli. Another male, he likewise paid heed to our flock only when it suited him. Eli did endeavor to convince the Captain of the animal's qualities as a sentinel. The final dog happily turned out to be a bitch owned by Noah, and she proved our salvation. Black with white smears, she moved quiet with her snout held low and always pointed in the direction of the cloven hoofed band.

Before I realized it, we had drawn abreast of the lane, which led off towards Benton lands. Azariah, alone on the right flank, caught my eye and smiled to me as we passed by.

The Captain fell into step beside me. Realizing he planned to let me speak first, I said, "It always seems odd to head opposite our intended destination."

"We follow where the roads take us," he replied in his affable yet practical manner. "None has completed more of these drives than you, I trust." I glanced at our companions, for I knew his words to be true. "Just so," he said. "I wonder, then, what shoes each of us might best fill."

His way, despite his perpetual friendliness, was straightforward. "My brother there," I said, starting with him I knew best, "is completely at ease alone in the wood." Captain Willes nodded. "Scouting ahead for open meadow or water will serve the persistent need for grazing lands and drink. And should we require fresh game, none is better suited than he." Such a role, I knew, would also sustain my brother throughout the monotonous days to come.

"Agreed. Go on, Elisha. Please."

Next, I mentioned that Noah, whose family possessed a goodly herd of sheep, was quite familiar with the keeping of them. I suggested Noah could be best employed out on the flanks, where he and his dog could keep the beasts from straying. To this, too, the Captain agreed.

"What of you and your friend, Heman?" he asked.

"'Tis true we comprehend a thing or two about being a drover. Perhaps the pair of us might secure the opposite flank. Assuming we can corral his unruly dog." My words must have carried for Heman caught hold of his dog's shaggy coat and shushed him proper.

"Sold!" Captain Willes proclaimed. "Capital notions one and all. Now then," he added, in a voice meant for me alone. "What of Mister Chapman yonder. And yours truly."

Since abandoning the center, Eli had tried his hand at one side then the other. On both occasions ewes had scampered beyond his reach and lambs had found thickets in which to entangle themselves. "Perhaps, sir, he might serve where we now stand. A steady pace and the occasional wave of an arm or switch will provide all the encouragement required."

The Captain tilted back his head and laughed. "A suitable situation indeed. For Mister Chapman, and allow me to spare you the embarrassment, Elisha, for myself too." With another clap on my back, he embarked at once, seeking out our companions for a private word, in the same order in which I had described a role for each. The Captain made no mention of Newport, and as the fellow led the ox, much as he had each time we Bentons had rented one from the Chapmans, I saw no occasion to comment on him.

By the time we climbed the short, steep hill leading to the Grant properties, our party had been sorted out. Generations of Grants stood along the west shoulder, hooting and hollering as we passed. The children ran along, clutching at Noah's sleeve until that farm too had turned vague in the small cloud of dust suspended in our wake.

Four miles or more of southing had brought us into the neighboring settlement of North Coventry. There we made our long anticipated turn to the east, and thus onto the Middle Post Road. This wider, more traveled way would see us clear to Boston within the week, should the weather hold. Seemingly unaware of the loan of their Lieutenant, the people of Coventry center paid our middling band little mind. We pushed on, eager to cover at least fifteen miles whilst daylight remained.

We re-crossed the Skungamaug. Here we paused so that the sheep might quench their thirst. Though I drank but little, I made sure to top off my canteen. The Captain ensured that the others did likewise. Eli shot me a hard look before complying.

"He seems a petty man," Heman offered, "despite his family's standing."

Heman had sprawled on the bank with his boots just clear of the surging current. I joined him. "He harbors no love for me, that's plain," I replied.

"Nor will he if the Captain keeps taking your advice."

Soon enough Captain Willes had us on the move once more.

Miles of unsettled country rendered driving all the easier. The thick forest on either side kept the flock confined and out of trouble. It offered little, however, in the way of grasses. Azariah proved capable in locating clearings. In these virgin meadows our pace slowed, so that grazing could commence. Lest the sheep wile away the day, we eventually guided them back to the highway.

The sun sank low at last, dragging the temperature down with it. By this time we had long crossed the wood bridge spanning the waters of the Willimantic. The people of Mansfield graciously allowed us use of their empty stone enclosure. Safe inside, our herd would have no risk from bear or coyote. Even so, our party chose to bed down just outside the gate. Everyone, that is, but Mister Eli Chapman. This gentleman alone chose to retrace his steps so that he might spend the night in the comfort of Brigham Tavern, situated along the river and thus the town line. Captain Willes let him depart with the promise of a return by break of day.

In darkness leavened only by occasional shafts of moonlight, I stood guard beside Heman and Azariah. The Captain, Noah and Newport lay two rods off, snugged close to a meager campfire.

"Are these really called for?" Heman whispered, hefting his musket.

"The Captain," Azariah replied, "he must fret that Mansfield folk will rise from their beds and make off with our herd."

"Stop snickering you two," I said. "You'll wake our companions. Besides, I imagine he merely prepares us for the nights to come. When we sleep in the wilds."

"That time can't come soon enough to suit me," Azariah said.

"Well, we shall soon see if you stand by that sentiment, Brother. When you're quaffing a pint before yonder tavern's hearth."

"Is our watch nearly up then?" Heman asked.

"The tavern keeper promised to come to his door promptly at midnight. Not a quarter hour more I reckon."

Heman settled his gun's stock on the ground and blew on his hands. "Kind of the chap to keep his fire stoked so late, and just for the likes of us."

When I spoke to the old man he had not had charity uppermost in his mind. Rather, he had confided that his sympathies lay with

Boston's Sons of Liberty; so much so that had he been two decades younger, or even one, he vowed he would have responded to their call for minutemen. Few such appeals had reached as far off the beaten track as Tolland. And given my younger brother's nature, it seemed better not to share the man's passion. Soon enough we would discover what was afoot in the streets of that distant city. So I kept my peace, though this newfound knowledge brought me none.

"Ah, there's the fellow now," Heman said. We roused the others and made for the tavern's warmth.

A few minutes on found us crowding a wide hearth that sported a lively fire. I gratefully accepted pewter mugs from the tavern keeper's tray, and passed them 'round. "Remember the Captain's admonition..."

"Aye, aye," Azariah mocked. "A pint per man, warm your bones, then off to bed with ya." We all laughed at his attempt to cock his eyebrow as Captain Willes was wont to do.

"Bed, indeed!" Heman said.

"For the life of me I cannot remember when last I slept beneath the stars," I replied.

"Nor I, my friend."

"Saddled with old men, I am," Azariah moaned. We shook him on either side, but not so much that his or our precious draughts would spill, no not a drop.

Talk soon turned to the day's events and our woeful beginning. It took but little time for Eli Chapman to bear the brunt of our self-mockery.

"I feared for him," Heman jested. "In truth, I did. Caught in the center of all those flailing beasts."

"Near trampled in his prime!" Azariah exclaimed with a swipe at his eye. "Beneath the hooves of lambs."

Both roared at this jibe, testament to the hour and our fatigue I reckoned. "If only the poor man possessed your skills as a drover," I said, and raised my mug in a mock toast.

His met mine with a clink. "Well put, Brother, but do I not possess skills of another sort? The Captain at least seems to think thus."

Sorely tempted was I to confess that I had convinced the Captain to make him a kind of scout. Instead, and with a solemn nod I said, "I withdraw."

"You are forgiven."

"Grand to see all is well among us three," Heman announced. He stood and drained the last of his drink. "Now, bear with me, for I go forth to liberate this fine brew."

No sooner had my friend stepped outside I seized the moment. "Azariah. I have meant to have a word. In private."

"I can guess at what you have to say. There is no need, Brother."

"There is. You did me a kindness, and I threw it in your face."

"Well, in that case, here's hoping that your rucksack is so heavy it carves dents upon your back."

This time I raised my glass to his. "To dents, it is," I said. "Deep as ruts in soft mud." We laughed. We drank down the last of it.

Azariah glanced about the room, empty now of even the tavern keeper. "Tell me, Brother. If this place had rooms to let, would you have taken one?"

"As Eli did, you mean?" I scanned the crude yet welcoming tables and the benches set beside them. "The cost would be more than our poor purse can bear."

"You cannot justify the expense to yourself? Or do you have Father in mind?"

Heman stepped into the doorway. A broad smile of relief spanned his face. I gave Azariah's upper arm a pat. "To answer that, we would need a good deal more time than we have, would we not." Smiling, he stood, and together we walked out into the night.

I fell into a deep sleep, and nearly at once. Only when staring into the Captain's lined and whiskered face did my bones feel the effect of the night spent upon the ground. Dew clung to everything. "I am awake," I promised him, rubbing the wet from my heavy eyes. Heman looked as I felt. We exchanged grins of commiseration. Of Azariah there was only the matted grass to show where he had slept. His absence surprised me not at all.

What did bring me full awake was the sight of Eli Chapman striding through the half-light towards where we roused ourselves. Moments more the surprise turned to shock when he presented a basket carefully packed with eggs plucked fresh this morning. His treat for the entire party, as he told the Captain.

"Is there nothin' he won't do to curry favor," Heman growled in as surly a tone as ever I heard from him. Oddly, Eli's manner in this instance seemed guileless. Without further conversation with the Captain, or as much as a look in our direction, he fell in with his Negro and began reloading the cart.

Even Heman glanced at me and shook his head. "Guilty conscience?" he asked. "After a night in his down bed?"

"I'm sure I know not."

Sitting in front of the tavern's fire we soon consumed all of Eli's eggs, along with a few pounds of pork carved from the loin now carefully re-wrapped and stored amongst Tolland's provisions. The Captain decreed that reaching Pomfret, a distance of some 20 miles, would be the day's objective. Given our early start and the firm state of the roads it seemed quite possible, if not a tad ambitious.

"Methinks our leader has confused us with soldiers," Noah said, with a grin that split apart his thick, dark beard. "It will be forced marches by midweek."

His remarks caused me to glance over at Captain Willes, for certainly the Grant family knew a thing or two about soldiering. Just then, the Captain waved his hat. The act set the flock in motion. Me too, for I hastened to take up my position alongside Heman. Everyone soon resumed his role from the day before. For his part, Azariah had already reported back with news of a likely watering stop. Just as quick he had vanished into the fog up ahead. Only then did it occur to me that the threat of a change in the weather might underscore our ambitious pace.

Whereas the day before we had raised a cloud of dust that trailed behind us, today tiny puffs appeared with every exertion of man and beast. Like smoke lightning our visible breaths flashed all about us. When we reached where Azariah had disappeared, evidence of our breathing was swallowed in the gray eddies of air.

"Captain!" I hollered.

"I see it, Elisha. Men, pack the beasts in close! Close as you can or we shall lose half their number."

"I can hardly make you out," Heman said, though he proceeded not ten paces distant.

"Should we stop?" a voice questioned. It may have been Eli, though sound took on an echoing quality in this murk.

"Captain?" I called out behind me, for I could see him not. "It may be just a pocket. Best we push on through if we can."

"Do you still hold the flank?" his voice asked.

"Aye. Heman is within my sight. The left edge of the flock too. If we all move close enough to see each other, we're unlikely to lose any of them."

"Do so, men, and at once. Keep calling out. Move towards each other's voices. By rights the sheep will be confined within our ring."

First Noah appeared off to our right. Moments later the Captain's stocky outline and a leaner one beside him took shape. A jumble of snouts and the occasional wild eye came and went in the middle space.

Not a hundred yards on, though it took an age, the mist simply vanished. So shockingly plain did we suddenly see one another that the entire party stopped. Once our laughter died away the Captain ordered a count. Not a solitary beast had we lost.

"Good girl," Noah cooed as he hugged his little dog.

"All right, men. We have time to make up." With another wave of his hat, the Captain propelled us north and east.

Chapter 12

Another crisp day gave way to dusk. Stopped we had, but we labored still. The Captain saw to that. My thoughts drifted even as my fatigued body worked, as though part of me slumbered while I stood, like cattle content in a pasture. Often had I wondered how many miles I logged in the Benton fields at harvest time? In my mind, I pictured the rumps of the oxen urged on by Daniel. I trailed behind, both hands clamped to the plough's handles, my steps awkward as I sought good footing on either side of the furrow carved deep by the blade. I swore I caught the earth's enthralling scent as this memory flooded over me. With a start I refocused on the here and now, for my task involved a heavy machete that I swung again and again. Yet with the repetitious motion my thoughts drifted, immune to the risk. Whatever tally those days wrought in miles, it surely fell short of the score and more we had covered this day. Pomfret we had left in our rear. For a time Massachusetts had seemed possible, yet man and beast succumbed to the allure of the French River that flowed south across our route. The persistent urgency of its rushing waters brought me back to where I stood close on the bank.

Here we were to bed down. The place was well chosen. A bend in the inky water provided a natural barrier that encircled the flock on three sides. They would not venture into its depths other than to drink along the bank, nor could predators cross at this point. To use the peninsula this way had been Eli's idea. For my part I was too fatigued to do more than numbly follow the Captain's orders. And so I cut and dragged thickets of barberry across the open end as a makeshift gate.

"Well done, Gentlemen," he said at long last. "Azariah, Heman, Noah and I shall stand first watch. Elisha, you, Eli and Newport turn in."

In Heman's face I saw that he, like me, questioned the change in the make-up of the watches. Also like me, he seemed far too fatigued to ask why. Nor did my brother seem inclined to raise a fuss. They simply hoisted their muskets from the cart whilst I spread my bed roll on the ground, and as close to the fledging fire as prudence allowed. Soon Eli and Newport had done the same. I have no recall of the plunge into sleep.

I awoke in the same posture in which I had lied down, on my left side and facing the flames. Judging by the depth of ash, I had slept some hours. Noah's dog licked my face before rejoining Azariah, Heman and the others who still stood watch. Back and forth they went in pairs before the piled thickets. Warmth was their sole purpose, I imagined, for what creatures of the night would approach a party of such strength.

My gaze drifted over my nearest companions. What a pair, they made. One of the most prominent men of our town, young Eli Chapman no doubt was; yet so near to him they almost touched, lied his slave. How could Eli own another man and share breakfast with him too. I recalled that despite the tavern keeper's many kindnesses towards us, he had balked at Newport coming under his roof. And so, Eli there had taken his meal out of doors and shared it with this fellow who was so black I could scarce discern his face from the blanket tucked about it. A man of contradictions this Eli was, I decided.

Newport shifted, but not before his stocking-covered foot stretched from beneath its covering. Just inches away from my head it rested. Never had I come this close to a Negro, or even looked directly at one. Always had I transacted business with Eli, while his man hitched the yoke to the oxen, or led them to where I wanted, and always without a word. I half-wondered if Newport spoke the King's English, though I had seen him and his master joined in conversation. Extending my arm towards him, I re-arranged his covering.

Soon I drifted off once more. This time I dreamt, though not of my companions. It was Jemima's face I saw. With eyes so blue she held my gaze, quite as though they'd wrapped my entire being in their embrace. Sun peeked in and out from behind me. One moment I could see her plain. The next, only the outline of flowing locks could I make out. She spoke. I strained to comprehend.

"Time to wake, Brother. The watch is yours."

"Azariah? I did not, did not recognize you."

"'Tis certain was not my name you called." My vision had cleared enough to recognize the broad grin he wore, and this despite it being the dead of night. I busied myself with my bedding for I had not recovered sufficient wit to fence with him.

Heman came up. I took hold of his proffered hand, and stood. "Anything of note?" I asked.

He shook his head no. Then his eyes shifted towards Newport there at the cart's open rear. "Strange, is it not?" he asked. "Consider, Elisha. Does it not strike you as odd to see a man who keeps slaves, also arms them?"

It did seem odd at that, but having already been embarrassed by my little brother, I was in no mood to seem guileless before my friend. "In the wilderness, the more guns the better. After all, you're the one about to lie down."

He grinned. "I suppose you're right."

"You know I am. Now sleep. For soon we'll be on the march again. A score plus 10 come sunup!" This last I whispered in such a fiendish way that Heman lay down laughing. I laughed too, for my brother and friend had restored my wits.

Difficult it was to tell when night ended and day began. Even so, the time had come to resume our journey. Low and near to bursting hung the clouds, like a herd of cows heavy with calves. Tiny pellets stung our faces, and melting, trickled along our cheeks. Far too early it was, for weather such as this. With hats snugged tight, we broke camp.

A few hours on, the Captain and I reckoned we had crossed over into Massachusetts. No sign marked one's arrival and the visibility offered no landmarks to confirm or deny the accomplishment. With Mother Nature having turned on us, he backed off of today's objective. For my part, I respected his decision to drive us hard the prior day. Long had I believed, as Grandsire and Father had taught me, make hay while the sun shines.

The temperature climbed a grudging few degrees as the morning wore on. Sleet gave way to rain. This small mercy towards our skin brought fresh torment to our bodies for by then the roads had turned slick.

The Stone Arch Bridge that spanned the Blackstone River gave evidence we had reached Uxbridge. There we halted so that the animals might drink and the men rest. Eli left Newport's side and approached the Captain. "Join us, would you," our leader bade us soon after. "Eli tells me that the cart's wheels are so caked in mud, and the road so soft, that the ox cannot manage. Not with this load."

"Captain," I said, "the sky has been lifting; for the last half hour. If the rain stops, this road will turn from the soup that it is, to a mud that will allow no wheel to pass. Mendon is but a few miles on. It happily lies upon a post road that runs from Worcester to Providence. Services are sufficient there that man and beast could take their ease, at least till the roads firm."

"Thirty-five miles from Mendon to Boston by my map," the Captain said. "That would put us two days out, should we stay the night."

"The night's cold will for certain firm the road, though we'll find it bumpy going come morning."

"Better that than this," the Captain replied. "What of the load itself?"

I glanced at Eli. He held his head up high under my gaze, though he did shift his weight. "Each could carry his own pack, and musket," I added, with a nod towards Azariah.

"Men? What say you?"

We turned to where Newport, covered from chest to foot in muck, stood beside the beast similarly encased. Heman shrugged. Noah tugged at his beard. Only Azariah seemed unperturbed. Both hands had he folded over the mouth of his musket barrel. Over them he merely watched me, waiting.

"Lessening the load thus might suffice to tip the scale," I said, facing him.

He grinned, shouldered his piece, and then made for the rear of the cart. As a body we followed. "Mista," Newport said with hat in hand as Azariah passed by. "Mista," he said to me, and I noticed gray hairs in the tight curls above his ear. "Newport," I replied, with a tug at the corner of my tricorne.

"Many thanks for this, my friend," Heman said as he wedged his sopped self within the snug straps of his pack. I aided the rest until only Eli remained.

Pulling my rucksack from beneath the oilskin, I turned to him. "Where is yours?" I asked.

Red blotches mushroomed on his pale skin. "I did not think to bring one. What with the cart and its provisions, I never..." His voice trailed off.

For a moment I wanted to swing at that gaunt, white jaw of his. All that complaining about a loaded cart and he no means to lighten the load. Then I considered that this man had probably never carried something on his back his entire life. Why, he might not even own a pack. I scanned what remained on the wide wood boards. "I could fashion a sling of sorts with one of these blankets and some rope," I told him. "You could tuck some of the foodstuffs into it. If you've a mind."

"I do. I do indeed."

At his urging I burdened him with the remains of the pig's quarter and a sack of potatoes. He may carry less in weight than some of us, but his would prove far more awkward.

"Elisha." He placed a hand on my arm. "I want to thank you. For this," and he gestured at the crude sling stuffed with goods. "And for helping Newport and I."

"You are quite welcome, Eli, but in truth, your suggestion was far too reasonable to let pass. We all of us require this conveyance."

I had not yet reached my place on the flank when he called out, "And Ben thanks you too!"

"Ben?"

"The ox, of course."

As our stopping point lay but a few miles on, the Captain had seen no need for scouting. Azariah had fallen back with Heman. I joined them as we began to move.

"What was that all about, back there?" Heman asked.

"Laughter, was it not?" Azariah replied for me.

"And from Eli Chapman, no less?" Heman went on.

I played along with these two merrymakers. "A great discovery this day. Our new friend possesses a sense of humor."

Heman glanced back. "Can it be?" he asked. "Then perhaps he'll be further amused at my attempt to negotiate the rental of his ox." With that, Heman drifted from us and nearer to Eli at the rear.

I wished to follow this development but Azariah cast a glance in my direction that I could only describe as calculating. So unusual was this that it completely distracted me. Ignoring Heman, Eli, as well as the bedraggled sheep, I ventured, ""Well, dear Brother, you alone appear unfazed by our labors. The role suits, it would appear."

"And I thank you for it."

"What on this earth for?"

"No need to play coy, Elisha. Your friend back there confessed it was you sung my praises to our good Captain. Heman's purpose, 'tis certain, was to convince me of your affection, and not expose the Captain's ignorance of whatever worth I possess." Azariah laughed as he spoke, and his eyes twinkled as only his could. For all that it had pained him that his attributes were not more obvious to another; and I resented that my good friend had passed on what he had overheard.

"I see it in your face, big brother. You are angry, and he your oldest friend."

My brother's eyes could, on rare occasions, convey a type of soulfulness. It might have been that one was green, and the other gray. Whatever the cause, they had that quality now. "It matters not," I assured him. "Never could I remain angry with him. Any more than I could with you." I seldom saw the little rascal reduced to speechlessness. This was one such time. It would not do. "Besides," I went on, "I am not at all convinced that I do love you."

Restored, he rapped my chest with the barrel of his musket. So many layers of cloth and leather binding crisscrossed me that I felt it little. It was the merely the state of the road that caused me to lurch from a misstep. I nearly went down as the weight shifted on my back.

He roared. "I do imagine the straps of your pack must cut plenty deep by now," he jested once he had breath enough. So infectious was his joy, even born as it was from sarcasm that I could not help but join in.

"Aye. You can claim your vengeance," I said. "Courtesy of Mother Nature."

"She can be a cruel mistress."

"Indeed." We slogged on, barely keeping upright along the matted grass of the shoulder. The rain at least had stopped.

"Speaking of the fairer sex," he said. "I am amazed you have yet to speak with me of Jemima."

"What of her?" So here at last was the subject he had planned upon.

He grinned. "Any would find it odd, Elisha that you call her name in your sleep, yet hold your tongue when awake." Before I could counter this he added, "She harbors no such reservation."

"How so?"

"She speaks freely of you, Brother. Well, of your time together." He frowned at my silence. "Come, come, I know you kissed her hand. She told me so."

"Did she now? And to whom else did she make such a claim?"

"Nonsense. She told no one. But surely you admit…"

"I admit nothing," I protested; all the more loudly as there was no denying the charge.

"What are your intentions, Brother?"

"You cannot be in earnest."

"Are you in love with her, Elisha? Is it that, or do you lust after my dearest friend?"

I would have preferred a minute alone with my thoughts; a moment even to sort out my reactions to her taking my brother into her confidence in this way. His expression prevented me doing so. It was precisely how I must look when some lad's gaze lingered overlong on Hannah. "Azariah…" I said.

"I have a right to know," he insisted. "I do!" My dawning smile fueled his temper. "What are you doing?_Are you laughing? At her or me?"

"Most assuredly at you, Brother," I replied. "Though I will answer you; and my answer is aye."

"But to which?"

"I will leave that for you to decide," I said, draping my arm over his shoulders.

"Can it be so? You? In love?" He hopped beyond my reach. "Can those paws of yours - that crush the handles of axes and ploughs; can they have cradled a thing as delicate and light as Jemima's palm?"

"Tell me her parents do not know of this..."

"Then you admit it! You, Sir Benton. You took her hand. And kissed it." Further away he leapt, though I'd made no real attempt. "Calm thyself, Brother," he said, laughing. "She told no other. Not even her mama and papa whom she holds so dear."

Heman had been watching us for a time. He chose this inopportune moment to approach. "What are you two carrying on about? What am I missing?"

"Jemima Barrows, of course," Azariah said. "Come! Join us." His words shocked me, for a tattletale was not one of his many faults. Before I could devise a means of stopping him he went on. "Your friend here was just remarking on, what was it Elisha, the softness of her hands?"

Heman winked at me. "I wondered when I would hear more in regards to that lass. Was it truly her hands, though, ya have in mind, my friend?"

Again I proved too slow for Azariah's wit and tongue. "Oh, indeed, my brother does. For I was just about to explain how wrong he surely is. No person's skin can remain soft when one labors for hours on end as does Jemima." Azariah now took my friend's arm in his. "Helps her mama she does, at every opportunity. Tends the kitchen garden all by herself. Cooks using that great iron pot. Sews. Makes candles too, and even us men know how bad a burn boiling tarrow can prove. Why, a marvelous wife she will one day make. But as I was saying, I find it hard to believe what Elisha insists – that despite all these trials, her skin remains soft as, well, as what, Brother?"

Heman stared over at me, then back at Azariah, then finally back at me. He grinned widely. "A baby chick?" he whispered, and chuckled.

"Or a rabbit?" Azariah snorted.

"Aye," my best friend agreed. "A wee bunny!"

Together they roared. On and on they went. So loud did their cackling grow that all of our companions eventually joined in, though they had no clue that I was the butt of this joke. Even Newport smiled. Only with difficulty, then relief, I heard the Captain announce that we had reached Mendon at long last.

On learning of our mission, the people of Mendon proved even more accommodating than had our Mansfield hosts. Their own market drives long passed, they not only offered us use of the common enclosure to pen our flock, they also insisted on standing watch. Their graciousness enabled every member of our party to scrub away the worst of the caked mud from our footgear and clothing. I privately chastised myself for having bemoaned the near ruin of my fine boots, when I discovered that what I took to be Newport's boots were in fact his stockings and shoes.

Presentable at last, we went together to the larger of the inns. The host and a nearly full house of animated, smoking inhabitants cleared a table so that we may claim the choice seats nearest the fire. There, we dried our clothes and warmed our aching limbs. A round of tankards brimming with hard cider reached us, courtesy of Captain Willes it turned out.

"What civilized folk," Eli, who had chosen a seat beside me, said. He raised his drink to those at the nearest table, touching off a chorus of "huzzahs!" In turn, we stood and drank to their health.

"Amazing reception," Heman said, beaming.

"Indeed," I agreed, though I kept an ear cocked towards the voices 'round us. A current was emerging, and more than gratitude nourished its force.

"What ails, Brother?" Azariah asked.

I smiled for him, and shook my head. Eli had caught my gesture, and he too now glanced about. Partly to lighten the mood that I had darkened, I asked of him, "Is Newport about?"

"He is seeing to Ben. The ox," he added with a smile that did sit well upon his features. "He expects to bed there at the stable. It is quite clean, and snug despite the recent rains."

Before I could inquire further, Captain Willes leaned between us. "Gentlemen. A word with the two of you."

We excused ourselves from our companions and followed our leader to a small table tucked in a corner.

"Pardon the secretive nature of our meeting," he began. "This place, as Elisha mentioned on our journey, sits upon a crossroads. One road leads to Boston; the other to Worcester. Both have provided useful information, as I had dared hope they might." He let the possibilities sink in. "In the latter case, the Powder Alarm proves true. Stay calm, gentlemen, for though there was a bit of trouble up Charlestown way, much rumor attended the news. In truth, not one of the King's soldiers marched on Worcester." I felt my shoulders relax upon hearing this. "But neighbors in towns all about that city believed they had. And they responded by coming together, armed, by the hundreds; intent on safeguarding their precious stores."

"Should we turn about?" Eli asked. "Is there a threat to Tolland?" Whatever I had once thought of Eli Chapman, I had no reason now to doubt either his courage or loyalties.

"A moment, Mister Chapman. There is more to tell. The new military governor, a certain General Gage, has recalled troops to Boston from the outlying boroughs. It is said the garrison there is also strengthened by troops conveyed by ship from New York."

"As far away as that?" I asked. "Whatever for, do you think? Does he fear...?"

"An uprising? Is that what you thought to suggest, Mister Benton? In answer I can say that the people of Worcester tossed out of office every official of the crown. And if you but listen a moment, what do you hear; at each table; from practically every throat?"

"If there is indeed an anger in the land," I said, "in this place it dwells."

Eli nodded as he scanned the room. Raised tankards punctured the wafting smoke. "The port closure has destroyed trade with the city, and livelihoods. And here I believed it was charity, or fellowship that inspired them to help us."

"It may have been those feelings too," the Captain agreed, "but there is raw emotion here, and anger plays its part. You might care to know that they have mustered four company of militia."

"Four!" Eli and I exclaimed together. Doubtless we both thought on Tolland's single force.

"Just this fall it was. And one entire company is of minutemen, charged with responding to an alarm within a mere thirty minutes." I gasped at the thought. Why it would require an hour at least for word to reach Benton lands from the town green, and give even a mounted man time to return.

"What would you have us do?" Eli asked.

"Well, I called you here much as would have happened at home. Both of you gentlemen would have been among those summoned..."

"We should tell our companions," I interrupted. "If, sir, you are asking our opinion."

"I agree that each one of us needs to be on our guard from this point on."

"Then you mean to press on," I said. "You do not believe, as Eli questioned, that our homes, our families..."

The Captain interrupted me. "If I thought that, I would order us back and at once. No, Tolland is safe. I am sure of it. But trust that I will muster our company, and count on you gentlemen to help us prepare for whatever may follow, the very day of our return."

I nodded. "And our companions?"

"I agree with Elisha," Eli said. "They should be told."

"Very well. I shall do so before we turn in. And soon, I think, for we will all of us need our rest."

"Forgive me, Captain," Eli said. "But I took the liberty of renting rooms."

"For all of us?"

"All, yes, but the innkeeper only had two rooms unspoken for. We might be a tad crammed..."

"These old bones of mine would cherish a night spent off the ground. Even wedged in a bunk with the likes of you two," Captain Willes replied. "Many thanks, Mister Chapman."

"Indeed," I said, clinking my mug against theirs. "Many thanks, my friend."

Chapter 13

The fourth day of our journey dawned cold and clear. We were grateful for each. The crystal blue sky spanned one horizon to the other. Beneath this dome we were afforded an unimpeded view of the surrounding landscape, for the leaves, like slain armies of yellow and brown, had fallen to the earth. Even the road fared well, for yesterday's ooze had filled the low spots, and few had been as foolish as we to brave travel, leaving little in the way of ruts. As a consequence we made record time in our transit.

At Medway we paused in search of rest, sustenance and news. We nearly found, or caused more like, a riot. It started innocently enough. The Captain had asked me to accompany him. We went off to arrange for word to be sent ahead that we expected to arrive in Boston, with our promised flock, one day hence. Meantime, around the town pump the balance of our party had gathered to refill canteens. A number of inhabitants milled about, the presence of strangers having drawn them from the blacksmith shop and the tavern across the street. Noah mentioned to one of their number that we hailed from Connecticut, intent on driving sheep into Boston. Either he never clarified that the beasts were a gift intended for the citizens, or the townspeople fashioned an intent of their own construction. Whatever the cause, Captain Willes and I hurried back into a swarm of shoving men. Womenfolk drew back, some clutching little ones to their breasts. Eli was doing his level best to restrain the most animated among the throng, but oaths had begun to fly. Fists would doubtless follow.

"Hold!" the Captain shouted. "Hold, you there!" Heads turned towards that martial voice of his. I trailed him, and seized one fellow's wrist. A chunk of firewood fell from his grasp. Keeping hold, I forced the pair of us forward until we reached my brother. "My name is Captain Willes," our leader declared. "I have responsibility for this party. We are men of Tolland, down Connecticut way. Long have we befriended the people of Massachusetts. What's all this then?"

His natural authority stilled the crowd for a moment, but as more angry faces packed the square, a chorus of epithets were hurled at us. "You give aid to our enemies!" one shouted. Enemy, I wondered? "Fer profit!" spat another through wretched teeth.

Captain Willes seized upon this charge. "Nothing of the sort! We come at the urging of Dr. Warren himself. He begs food for our Boston neighbors, and to them alone do we respond."

Raised fists fell. Had it been our Captain's air of command, or was it the name Warren that quieted our host?

"I am Captain Nathan Thayer," declared a voice among the later arrivals. The throng parted to let him pass. "We welcome you to Medway. You and your party, Captain." He surveyed his close-packed neighbors. "Forgive us this misunderstanding. The recent troubles are to blame. Come, Captain, tell us what we can do to speed your endeavor."

"Aye!" hollered he who Eli still restrained. Others took up the call. I let go of my captive and he immediately offered, "Count me in too. What needs have you?"

Soon our message had been hand delivered to the driver of the daily coach. Provisions, some necessary, others not, had been piled into our cart. The sendoff by men, women, and children nearly erased worries of how this visit could have ended.

For the next hour we skirted the Charles River. Its waters wound into our sight, and then away again, off to our left. It flowed eventually I knew, into the harbor at Boston. At my side Heman said, "For a time, back there..."

"Indeed," I finished the sentiment for him.

As dusk fell we made our final stop in East Medway. We could barely make out the inky, serpentine presence of the Charles River. Here we managed to remain nameless and unimportant, which following the exuberance of Mendon and the chaotic scene in Medway, suited us just fine. The next day should see us safe into Boston.

Towns came and went almost as steadily as the stone mile markers set along Boston Post Road - first Medfield, then Dedham. We cared naught for any of them, though only because we longed for the journey's end. Even so, my comrades wondered at what we would find, as did I.

Late in the afternoon, with a feeble sun lighting our party from the left, we veered nearly dead north. Recognizing the outskirts of Dorchester to my right, I knew we would soon climb up into Roxbury. From that town's center we should glimpse Boston.

Eli advanced along the perimeter of the herd, careful not to alarm them as he drew alongside Heman and I. "Elisha. Heman."

"Greetings," I replied. "What news?"

"Captain says that our destination lies just beyond the town up ahead." I nodded at this. He added, "You knew that I trust. He also says that we have done well. All this way in a mere five days, and with the loss of only a single ewe."

"It was a good transit," I replied. "This late in the season makes for a chancy affair."

"Aye, that muttonhead of a ewe," Heman burst out. "Straight off the bridge she walked. Have you ever seen the like?"

"Gone in a flash, she was," Eli agreed.

From my vantage point at that unfortunate moment, I thought the barking of a certain dog had startled the poor creature. But, what was done was done. "All in all," I offered, "we did well to lose just the one. I have heard tell of drives on which a quarter of the flock is lost — to predation, mishap or plain bad luck."

"Then we were fortunate," Eli replied. "Well, best I get back. The Captain will, wont as not, expect us to arrive in good order."

When Eli had gone, Heman said, "That fellow tries a bit too hard for my taste."

A week earlier I had never thought the particular fellow capable of caring, to say nothing of making too earnest an attempt. "Perhaps," I said. "But his effort is commendable."

My friend looked rearward and shrugged.

In Roxbury the town militia could be seen tromping across the green. Only the sight of a company of armed men alerted me to what I had not seen along this entire journey. Not one red coat had we spied.

"They're a serious-minded lot," Heman said.

"Aye. A hundred strong I dare say."

Our work as drovers was soon accomplished by a row of buildings that hemmed either side. The flock grouped together and we, enjoying the narrowed divide, chatted with each other over their craning heads. Townspeople watched us from doorways and shop fronts. One and all they wore guarded expressions.

"Soon, Elisha!" Noah called. "Soon we can bid farewell to the King's Highway. And good riddance to these woolly pests!"

"We call it the Boston Post Road, hereabouts!" I turned to see a gray-haired man shift his pipe so that he might spit in our wake.

"Go home, Tories!" came another shout from behind us.

Azariah alone had carried his musket into the town, as was his custom. He now swung the barrel so that it crossed his chest. When he glanced back my way I shook my head.

"Walk on!" Captain Willes commanded. Together we followed the fleeing flock down the long, winding road that fetched our destination at last.

The road straightened onto the causeway that would carry us into the heart of Boston. Orange Street people called it, though no houses fronted it hereabouts. Vast mud flats gleamed like dark glass to our left, for the tide was at its ebb. On the right The Atlantic lapped at the causeway's stones, and the city beyond. My comrades only had eyes for the fortification that spanned the width of Boston Neck. Through its open but heavily guarded gate we must pass.

"It appears higher than I remembered," Heman whispered, though none but we two could hear his words.

"Perhaps it is the number of troops," I replied, for along the wall ahead, here patrolled the red-coated soldiers who had proved noticeably absent from our route. Our little band fell silent as we stopped beneath the dominating mass of that bristling structure. A half dozen of the King's troops confronted us. Only the yapping of our dogs disturbed the peace.

"Silence those mongrels!" ordered the sergeant of the guard. The privates who flanked him took a step forward. Bayonets half the length of a sword had been affixed to their muskets. These they leveled.

"For the sake of God," Eli said. He clamped his dog's jaws with both hands. Meanwhile Captain Willes strode forward and presented his papers.

"The army could do with these sheep," the sergeant said. The hostility of his glance mirrored that which we had faced in Medway. The words, 'an anger in the land…' cycled in my head.

"...as the documents plainly state...," Captain Willes was explaining.

"'For the express purpose of satisfying the needs of the people of Boston...'," the sergeant mocked. "Aye, I can read same as you Mister Willes." If the Captain felt the slight he made no indication. I stared long at this unshaven soldier who would omit the title and rank of another who had served the same King, and in our Captain's case, throughout two horrific campaigns. I despised the fellow and at once. No. Something else, something far darker stirred in my guts as I glared at his grizzled jaw.

"What's that you're about?" he demanded, squaring up to face me. Captain Willes turned. I saw his eyes fly wide in warning.

I swallowed hard. "Only to discharge our duty, Sergeant. As Captain Willes informed you."

"Your duty is it? Well yer duty is to our King. And that's God's truth. All right." He stepped aside. "Be off with the lot of you." To his men he commanded, "These sheep herders may pass!"

Azariah's face reddened at the remark. I pushed through the flock and, taking him by the elbow, hurried us along Orange Street.

"The arrogant bastard!" Azariah cursed.

"Sssh now. Don't give him the satisfaction."

Chapter 14

"So many names there are," Noah said. "Newbury becomes Marlborough, which in turn begets Cornhill. Is there no end of this way, nor of the lanes leading off of it?"

The Captain laughed. "Our destination lies farther on," he said.

Even Eli's head cranked back as he strove to get a clear view of the buildings that pressed in upon both sides, thus seeming to narrow what was a broad avenue. Three-floored structures were common, whilst some edifices soared four stories above. Down this cavern we proceeded. Clad in deep shade, it sucked away whatever heat our fatigued bodies possessed.

Men and women hustled past our party, intent upon one errand or another. Chins were tucked within collars as each battled the pervasive chill. Some pinched faces stared out from blankets wrapped about their heads and shoulders. Here and there a fellow pushed a hand cart or led a horse-drawn conveyance. With whistle and gesture we steered our flock from the road's crown so that each in turn may pass.

Along the curb, children begged, their filthy, upturned palms and thin voices pled for coin. My heart went out to them.

With our precious sheep we scampered back to the high ground. The creatures' anxiety simplified matters; for the strange sights, sounds and smells caused them to move as one. All of us had been awed, I thought. For myself, like each prior visit, it felt as a first time. So vast a place this Boston was.

Even Azariah, seldom impressed or awed, pivoted his head from side to side. The stiff movements betrayed his discomfort. 'Tis likely sharpened by his empty hands I thought. Still, I harbored no regret at having convinced him to lay his musket within the cart, for everywhere could be seen the red coat. Soldiers milled about within and without every shop we passed. Flanking the entrance to each official building stood a pair of armed sentinels.

"Elisha!" Heman shouted. A detachment approached. The Captain reacted first. He directed us to the curb.

"Give way!" ordered a thin-shouldered but impeccably coated lieutenant. "You drivers! Yield the high ground!" He made no attempt to slow his pace so that we might comply. In fact, his excited state seemed to have just the opposite effect on his booted feet. He led three ranks of four abreast and they responded like a mount spurred by its rider's crop.

Our flock scattered. Terror filled their eyes. With bare hands I yanked two ewes clear. My companions sought to do likewise. Despite this, hobnailed boots kicked two or three of the bleating creatures aside. One was driven against the curb. Another rolled over a beggar-child and slammed against a storefront.

And then the soldiers swept on by. Their officer made no attempt to silence their guffaws or the oaths they flung at us.

Newport, trailing our party by rods, managed to guide the ox and our cart out of harm's way. Towards the rear of this my brother now strode. I hurried after. He rummaged beneath the oilskin as I feared he might. Even as he got hold of his musket's stock I managed to pin his arms. "Azariah, hear me! You must control yourself."

"Will you do nothing, Brother? If we let this pass..."

"What's done is done. Would you make matters worse?" Heman had rushed to our side. At the shake of my head his outstretched hands stopped short of my brother. "We are fine now. Are we not, Azariah?" His chest still heaved, but his breath came and went with less ferocity. I marveled at the change in his power since he and I had last come to serious grips. "Is it safe to release you?" I asked.

"Aye." I did so. He stood quite still, massaging his upper arms. My eyes he would not meet.

Worry still laced Heman's face. Farther along the street, the Captain was helping a beggar-child to a sitting position. He glanced back with similar concern. I raised my hand to signal all was well. Nothing could be more false. We remained more scattered than our sheep, whom strangers had helped Noah and his faithful dog to rally. Eli hovered part way between the Captain and where we three stood, as if unclear to whom he could best offer assistance. Newport busied himself with old Ben though his movements showed evident distraction.

"Why, Elisha?" Heman asked. "What had we done..."

"Nothing. Absolutely nothing."

Azariah was studying the corner around which the soldiers had wheeled. "What manner of men are these?" he asked.

Despite his tone and the helplessness that had overcome his passion, it calmed me to see my brother before me once more. "Angry," I replied. "And frightened, too, I think." And it afeared me to say as much, for that same dangerous look lurked in the eyes of those now venturing forth to render us aid.

Our physical losses had been light. One ewe limped along with the rest, whilst one lamb suffered a broken leg. This unfortunate we had placed within the high-walled cart. Memories of the encounter would linger far longer in my mind, and that of my companions.

Without further incident we made our way to the town house which anchored the intersection of King and Queen Streets. "Dock

Square lies just ahead, men," Captain Willes assured us. The calmness of his voice did assuage me to some degree.

We veered around the corner. Here the street widened considerably and split. The angular wedge of the town dock occupied the central space. Beyond lay the vast harbor. Both appeared near empty, and thus easy for the eye to ignore. The left and right-hand branches of the cobbled way drew our attention. Numerous stalls lined them with a vendor standing by each. At sight of our party, their voices rose, hawking all manner of wares and foodstuffs. On closer inspection I saw not one offering meat either fresh or smoked.

At the Captain's urging we drove the sheep onward. Before a majestic building fast against the water's edge, our journey finally came to an end. A small contingent of officials awaited us. Captain Willes stepped up, and introductions were made all around. Apologies were made for Dr. Warren who had been pulled away on urgent business. His surrogates then began a series of speeches, thankfully brief though flowery every one. I turned my attention elsewhere lest I begin to believe we men of Tolland were as saintly as these fine gentlemen intended painting us.

I sensed a gnawing disappointment and realized I had longed to meet Dr. Warren, he an orator of note and by all accounts a leader even among distinguished men. My eyes took in the hall whose upper floors were constructed of the same brick as the town house. The sun's slanting rays still blazed upon the countless red courses of the upper floors; blindingly so off the tall, narrow windows that stood in precise ranks, floor by floor.

Already, the square had begun to drain of vendors. Apparently they had decided our newly arrived party had come to sell, not buy. Prodded by our indifference and the lengthening shadows, they began packing up what had not sold. Here and there a goodwife hurried by, a covered basket in one hand with the other pinning a shawl close about her shoulders. Other citizens remained but the majority of these were men; men who simply stood about in small groups, talking low and pulling on their pipes. The caps that clung tight to many a head identified most as sailors, fishermen or other dock laborers. Winds funneling betwixt the buildings and out to sea whipped their wide-legged trousers. So many men, prime laborers at that, standing idly on a frigid, late afternoon. It bode ill.

"My memory fails," Heman whispered, "for I had this down as a lively spot; filled always with folk, and noisy ones at that. And what of the great ships? Where have they gone?"

"Your memory is not at issue here, my friend. The port's closure has…"

"Amazing!" Azariah said, stepping between us and sweeping wide both arms. "Never have I cared for town living, but heavens! If I had… what? What ails you two?"

Eli and Noah had also drifted over to us, relieved, finally, of tending the sheep. Like Azariah, they now stared at Heman and me. Before I could say something, a scuffle started not 10 paces off.

As the carts had been wheeled away, vendors had cast off bits of this or that. Two beggar boys had apparently laid claim to the same mound of rotted cabbage. They rolled this way then that across the cobbles, kicking and biting as chance offered. Other boys, some tall as men, leapt into the fray, drawn by the spoils or related perhaps in some way to the first combatants.

Our party advanced on them and began plucking one youth after another from the pile. The one in my left hand, filthy blond hair dangling over his eyes, clipped my mouth with a wild blow. It startled more than hurt me, but leaked blood into my mouth all the same. Snatching his wrist with my opposite hand I corkscrewed his arm.

"Ow!" he cried. "Blast you!" He flipped his hair back, saw me looming over him, and went completely limp. "Please, sir! I'll cause ye no trouble." I released him. He sank down, bawling and clutching his arm.

My companions had seen to the rest. Most of the lads scampered off to one of the alleys leading from the square. Not one of the sailors had seen fit to lift a finger. I glared at them. Only then did a spark light in the eyes of these men. Only then did I realize that they must have witnessed this scene playing out again and again. So oft, perhaps, that the squalidness and blood-letting seemed quite commonplace. I turned away.

"That offered some excitement at least," Azariah said. "I had two on my hands, Brother. Two to your one."

"Did you indeed," I replied, but my attention turned to Captain Willes. He had taken his leave of the city officials and was now headed our way.

"What was that commotion about?" he asked.

Since he faced me, I replied. "Nothing out of the ordinary it appears." I had been unable to dress up my remarks, even for him.

He took another glance at the stragglers, then me again, before addressing all of us. "Bored were you men, by the ceaseless speeches? Well, I don't blame you there. Do take heart, for you have done well. Exceeded expectations even; the city elders' as well as mine. You have done Tolland proud! Come! A feast of sorts has been laid on for us. We shall all of us dine, and sleep in real beds. But before we head back on the morrow, there is a spectacle I am told we must witness with our own eyes."

Chapter 15

Darkness fell like a drape dropped over the narrow street on which we found ourselves. By a passing watchman's torch I made out the sign. "Union Street, sir."

"That's the very one," the Captain said. Thankfully it was only a few streets over from where we had stabled the ox and cart. "Look for the sign of The Green Dragon," he instructed. "A large, rectangular building facing on the street."

With its beckoning candles in the front windows of the first floor, and a steady stream of men coming and going, the tavern proved easy to find. With only Newport absent, we six gently shoved our way through the animated throng. Eli and I procured tankards of beer at the bar while the Captain sought the man he had been told to meet.

"Our money proves no good here," I told my companions as we handed over the drinks.

"How generous," Azariah said. Up went his mug, leaving him with a frothy upper lip and a broad smile.

"Have you heard the talk, my friend?" Heman asked, as he took his swig in turn. His arched eyebrows convinced me he was even more shocked than I at the sentiments swirling about the room.

"George III would find no love hereabouts," Azariah said with a chuckle.

"'Tis hardly a laughing matter," Eli chastised him. "Some here talk treason."

"Would you defend him?" Azariah countered. "After his troops ran us down in the street!"

"You mistake my meaning, sir!"

I wedged between them. "You are both right. These men love him not but we would be wise to keep our voices low, and our heartfelt opinions to ourselves. We know none here; nor whose ears may be planted among them."

"Is it not enough, Brother, that they welcome us with open arms?" Our companions seemed to want to be convinced by Azariah's boundless enthusiasm, but for better or worse my warning had taken root. We all of us kept shoulder to shoulder after that, and sipped at our tankards' lips, watching and searching for the Captain. It nagged at me that among the faces surrounding us, I glimpsed more than one whose knowing glance seemed to say he knew all about us, or at least all that he needed to know; whereas I and we knew nothing of him. In time, a pleasing fatigue settled over me such that I barely felt the jostling we endured standing there; nor minded the dense smoke that filled our nostrils. A full score of miles we must have traveled on that final leg, and as to legs, mine reminded me that they had had enough.

At last Captain Willes reappeared from a door along the opposite wall. Two men accompanied him; one tall, the other middling sized though tending to a prosperous portliness. Both were dressed as gentlemen. Even across that opaque expanse the keenness of the stout one's glance could be felt.

"The Captain seems to be pointing you out to his companions, Brother."

"Elisha and Eli both," Heman agreed.

Whatever those three discussed had an end. The Captain waved to us. A trestle table had already been set in a choice spot before a wide hearth. To this we'd been summoned. The stout gentleman had taken his place at the head. His companion sat on his right side, and the Captain on his left. At their urging I sat beside our Captain, with Eli opposite. The rest of our number settled around the long table. Then a thing happened that I had never experienced in polite company: Our hosts asked our names without offering theirs in return. Whilst Eli and I fumbled about over how to respond to this breach of etiquette, my brother cheerfully said, "Azariah Benton, younger brother of Elisha, just here."

Our central host, who at this modest distance looked barely older than me, smiled. So comely were his features that with but a nudge he could have been said to be womanly. I had just hit upon the color that matched his cheeks, the hue of a pink rose, when he addressed me. "Ah, Mister Benton is it. Greetings, sir. Your Captain Willes lavishes you with praise. Praises all you fine men, in point of fact. You will forgive me, gentlemen, for not introducing myself. It is an absurd machination, to be sure, but I am not supposed to have appeared in this tavern tonight. Some in authority would be grievously upset should they learn otherwise. So, if asked, you can honestly deny having met me. Well, enough of that." He stood; his glass in hand. Chairs scraped as our party rose as one. "We will come to rely," he said, looking each of us in the eye, "upon the character and capabilities of many such gentlemen, as you most assuredly are. This I both trust and regret. Gentlemen of Tolland, Connecticut! Boston is, and forever will be, in your debt. To your health!"

Behind and along the entire side of us one hundred voices thundered out, "Huzzah! Huzzah! Huzzah!"

Plates followed in course after course. Great hunks of cod there was, which I had savored but only in chowder previously. There were corn cakes and puddings, coffee and pies. "Our apologies for the absence of teas," our host said in mock horror. "There seems to have been a problem bringing a shipment ashore." When those not at our table guffawed over this jest, I realized there was little he or we might say that would not become grist for the public mill; but also comprehended that this gathering of men was no ordinary assemblage. I tucked into my goblet of wine, which had replaced the tankard and which had no bottom that I could discover. As the evening wore on, I heard and comprehended less, yet smiled more and more.

When the candles had burned to stubs, and long after our host had been called away, the Captain led our vanquished band up a steep set of stairs. "Our room lies this way," he said.

"Did he say 'room'?" Azariah slurred. "A single room..." Convinced I was, that his breath stank of the vine; until I realized I had lost the sense of smell.

"How many are we?" Heman asked no one in particular. He glanced about and so then did I. We found ourselves in a long hall. Muted were the voices from below our feet.

Captain Willes unlocked the last door on the left. We followed him in. The furnishings were first-rate, though the pair of beds, complete with ornately carved posts, filled the room to near overflowing. "Whatever happened to Eli?" he asked.

"He went to retrieve Newport," I said. "Did you not order him to?"

"I did not. No, not I." The Captain glanced about him, scratching his jaw all the while. "As it turns out," he said, "we have but the one room. The finest mind you, yet only the one. It's all on account of The First Continental Congress. Sessions over. The Massachusetts men, they expect their delegates any day. Any hour even. Warren said as much. Anyway, rooms are reserved for the meetings you see."

"Meetings." Heman said. "What meetings?"

"Doctor Warren..." I muttered.

The Captain stared at us. Not angrily, though he was not used to being questioned so directly. No, his glance had more of a contemplative aspect. I studied him. He looked vacant. Perhaps our Captain had imbibed too much. No sooner had this thought dawned on me, then he nearly shocked me off the edge of the bed I had come to rest upon. "THE meetings!" he insisted so loud and so close to Heman's ear that an onlooker might have thought my friend to be deaf. "The ones to be held hard on the delegates return! Which meetings indeed," he murmured to the key still held upright in his hand. Then to me he said, "Will you sleep there, Elisha? In that bed?" By way of answer I pushed down upon its surface. He nodded. "Sleeping arrangements may be complicated," he counseled our companions. "More so with the addition of, well, with one more."

Never had I slept in such luxury. Mahogany and fine linens greeted the eye wherever I turned my head. Even so, with my wine-soaked mind I doubted that seven of us could find comfort in two beds, especially given my bulk and Heman's length. A knock, the door opened, and in came Eli. Newport followed. A quick glance 'round at us and his gaze fell to the thick woolen rug.

"Ah, there you are," the Captain said. "Eli. How good of you to come. We are just working on, working out the sleeping arrangements. The larger bed. Why it can accommodate three, certainly. Perhaps. While the smaller..." His voice trailed off as he noticed Newport standing there, looking positively black against the myriad splashes of white. "How on earth, Eli, did you manage to..." he stopped again, with his hand drifting towards Newport.

"Sir. I simply reminded the landlord I was a member of your party. Hosted by Doctor Warren. The landlord then showed us to this room, personally."

"Doctor Warren…" I said once more. Our host? The stout fellow?

"Of course," Captain Willes said. "Well. As to the arrangements. We have the two beds, as you can see."

Eli nodded. "And so a pair must sleep on the floor. Yes? Newport and I, then. Right here by the door will be fine."

"That is not right." I had spoken. I had stood up to do so. Everyone turned to me but what next to say was quite a mystery to me. I licked at my lips to aid their working. "Should not Eli claim a bed? After all, he paid for our room, back in, back there in..."

"Never mind where, Brother," Azariah said. "I'm not one for mattresses regardless." He squatted on the floor. Off came his boots.

"Brother, toss me that blanket would you. Thank you. Newport old chap. Here's a spot of room just here beside me."

That settled it for everyone. Eli joined me on the smaller bed, with his lean body taking up the slice unoccupied by my bulk. Heman and Noah flanked the Captain in the big, high-posted one. With the candle snuffed I could just make out my brother's outline beside another, darker form. I should have offered to lay where Azariah lay now. Even with the drink still sloshing about my insides I felt this to be so. But I had not. Something made me hesitate as I had stood there, swaying. Something that had not occurred to me out in the night around that campfire. A tiny voice whispered that it had been Newport's blackness set in amongst all that finery that snared my tongue. I told it no; that it must be some other reason why my brother had simply done what I ought to have. At some point in my confusion, I fell into a troubled sleep.

Daybreak found me awakened by a persistent hand. One far too rough to be the one I dreamt of. Begrudgingly my eyes opened to find Azariah inclining his head towards the door. It stood ajar. Heman leaned against the frame. From his posture his entire being suffered quite as badly from the night's excesses as did my banging skull.

"You promised to show me the town," my brother whispered.

"Did I?" With heroic effort, assisted by more tugs than one, I managed to locate the floor with my feet. He guided me carefully over our sprawled companions. Out in the hall Azariah knelt and jammed my feet into my boots. Heman and I allowed him to finish his ministrations, and we staggered off.

Even in our state it required no feat of navigation to wend our way along Union Street. Rays of the infant sun played upon the dock area just ahead. We turned left and faced the dawn. Instantly our hands shot up to shield our burning, unfocused eyes.

"Watch out below. You men there!" Barely did we give way when the contents of a piss pot splashed in the street where we'd stood.

"A bit of warning next time!" Heman growled.

"I did warn ye," the goodwife protested.

Grumbling, we made our way. "That was piss!" Azariah said. "A full pot at that!"

"Aye," I agreed, slowly coming around to the fact that my younger brother had like as not never seen one emptied from a second story window before. Through a haze far denser than the fog still clinging to shaded corners, I recollected promising my brother a look at the great ships. We had come so far on this journey, it would be unfair were he to not glimpse their grandeur. "Come along," I said, a bit of excitement stirring in me as well.

The Town Dock marked our destination the prior day. The angular wharves enclosed a wee bit of sea but again no vessels were tied up along its length. In the surrounding market place a few stalls were in the act of being set up. Here and there small gatherings of women waited upon the vendors. We circumnavigated the dock, aiming for a sight that would surely awe my brother.

Turning down Merchants Road we passed by a number of racks. Some fish lay drying but for the most part it stood as empty as the market area behind us. I felt my newborn elation deflate. Gulls circled above, kept from snatching morsels by the waves of a boy positioned there for just that purpose. Their calls mocked us as we passed below them. Nothing it seemed, was as it had once been. Sullen looks seemed to follow us wherever we set our feet. I tried shaking free of all of it. "Come!" I said to my companions. "Gaze, Brother, upon the wonders of Long Wharf!"

We turned left onto the broadest boulevard any of us had ever walked. Again we squinted from beneath raised arms. We then proceeded directly towards the sun - rising clear of the sea. "This expanse?" Azariah said aloud. "'Tis a wharf?" Never had I seen him so astonished.

"Wait," I promised. "Wait till you see!"

"Amazed ya'll be!" Heman promised too, as caught up now as any of us.

On either side of this great, broad way, I could now make out the towering masts of live oak that pierced the crystal sky. "Behold, Brother!" I proclaimed. "The majesty of the East Indiamen. The largest merchantmen the world has ever known." I had spread wide my arms in a vain attempt to imitate their scale, one massive deck rising from the one below, spars crossing those masts at unheard of heights, all draped with miles of rigging. Even then I had sensed something amiss, but I continued on. "From far across the vast oceans have they sailed to reach, to reach...."

"Elisha," Heman said. "I do not think..."

"You Yankees there! Yes, you, fool. Step away from His Majesty's ship." A pair of red-coated Marines it was who blocked our way. I saw now that they guarded either side of a gangplank that rose up and up till it entered the side of a ship - a ship of war. Massive, black, iron snouts protruded from her side which curved away as far as we could see. Cannon, and two decks of them at that she boasted.

"Mother of God!" Azariah said. "Will ya look at that!"

"No blaspheming," I scolded without thinking.

"You've been warned!" shouted the Marine on the left. He advanced with leveled musket. The probing steel of his bayonet gleamed along its deadly length. His comrade fell in beside him. He too made short thrusting motions that stopped just shy of our ribs. No choice had we but to back hurriedly away. They halted then and let their oaths pursue us. "That's it ya curs. Run, Yankees, run! Back to the whores that breached ya!"

"Never again!" Azariah spat out. "Not one more time will the likes of them cause me to turn tail." Heman and I had hold of either arm. Though we dragged my brother away, I felt inside that he had spoken for us three together.

Chapter 16

Back at The Green Dragon we spied our party gathered around the same table that had witnessed our debauch mere hours earlier. Once more a feast of sorts had been laid. This one I had no stomach for. While the outside air had cleared my head, the scene at Long Wharf had subdued any appetite the walk might have encouraged. Thinking of the journey to come, I did force down chunks of bread and cheese, fortified with a bowl of pottage. I washed it down with a small beer. Heman and Azariah sat sullen for a time, and then tumbled like items onto their wood plates. Every member of our party other than Eli had avoided the platter piled with meats. Only his head held high. He smiled and nodded. I did my best to smile back. "And Newport?" I asked, scanning our company.

"He offered to retrieve the ox and cart. We insisted he at least take some of this fine food with him."

"Ah, good." Even this exchange taxed me. Prepared I was to lapse back into silence, but Eli had apparently had quite enough of that for one meal.

"Did you take in the sights?" he inquired. "You and Heman, and your brother?"

It occurred to me then that he might have been awakened by our stumbling departure. His tone led me to wonder whether he might have wished to accompany us. I did my best to straighten in my chair before responding. "Much we saw, Eli, but not that which we sought. I had promised Azariah the wonders of Long Wharf. It was the gold-painted merchantmen I had in mind to show him. Towering three-masted ships we did see, but of East Indiamen not a one." The Captain's head lifted. His eyes might have been bloodshot but his jaw had ceased to chew. "A two-decker was tied up along one side of the wharf. A frigate just opposite. And lesser ships farther out."

"Never have I seen such cannons," Azariah murmured. "True behemoths!"

"Nor so many," Heman added, wiping his mouth with the back of his hand.

The tavern-keeper leaned across to refill my tankard. "Ya might not wish to mention His Majesty's warships so specific like," he whispered. "We are not alone this day, and a royalist might mark ya as a spy. Counting the strength of the King's arms and such." I glanced around his ample girth. Individual men were seated here and there, and nothing like the crowd of the night before. I nodded. "Can I fetch anything else for ye gentlemen?" he cheerfully inquired. We all of us thanked him for his kindness yet declined.

Captain Willes craned forward. Our heads leaned towards him. "There is still a thing I would have you see ere we return to Tolland," he whispered. "Perhaps now it is more important than ever."

The air had warmed considerably as we ventured forth once again. With a full stomach and my greatcoat fastened, I felt quite snug. Our contented band retraced our steps across Dock Square. There Newport awaited us with the ox named Ben harnessed before Eli's cart.

"This must be what passes for full nowadays," Heman said at my shoulder.

Many more peddlers lined the bordering buildings. Their shouted offerings and rival claims created a din that made one wince, but twice their number could have easily found a place. And no trouble had we to traverse the square in a body. Our only inconvenience was taking care not to plant an errant boot upon a beggar's outstretched hand. Thankfully my stomach lacked a conscience, for otherwise it would have relinquished the ample food I had lavished upon it this day. At faces much the age of Jacob and Hannah, I could not bear to look.

What I most sought was to march straight south and away from this city and her suffering, but the Captain's surprise remained. We swept right at Queen Street, our backs to the sea. As we turned left on Tremont, Azariah poked my ribs. "Brother, what do you make of it?" I followed his pointing arm yet saw only rooftops lining our route.

"The wood shipments," Captain Willes said. "They've been stopped."

"No wood?" I asked, seeing as did they, countless chimneys from which no smoke curled. "Not for the entire city?"

"Well, a cord here and there still manages to find its way. Some privileged folk there are who will always have their fire I suppose." Seeing my expression he added. "It's the way of it now, Elisha. The Doctor himself told me so. Come then, men. Cast your eyes right. Here lies what I meant for you to see."

The Common had always been one of my delights in journeying this far. Acres and acres of open green space, in the heart of this great city. The low, rolling mounds of Beacon Hill still traced the northern side, whilst the flats of the Charles River created a horizon in the background. Everything in between had, however, changed. Gone were the grazing cattle and sheep. In their place marched columns of red-coated soldiers. Four men abreast, in rank after rank, they maneuvered from left to right across our front. Further off files wider than I could quickly count swung about as if anchored to the ground at the far end. Sunlight shimmered off the fixed bayonets that stabbed the air like steel horns above this many-headed host. The clear, dispassionate voice of an officer carried to where we stood. Sergeants shouted his orders along the line. The red-coated, white-legged, gleaming mass, whirled as might a single, merciless, relentless beast. It turned on us.

We none of us said a word as we hastened along The Mall, which ran the length of The Common. Numbly I noted that much of the grazing fence, and even some of the trees that had shaded this popular path on summer days, had been chopped down, and crudely too. Likely the wood now fed the many campfires burning there amongst the taut, white tents - arranged row upon row.

Our silence held even as we waited on the King's guards along the causeway. My companions' jaws quivered as the regulars riffled through our carefully packed possessions. When a sack of provisions spilled at Azariah's feet his eyes flared. I leaned down at once and returned it to the cart.

"Sir?" asked a different sergeant than the first we had encountered. "Did the papers grant permission to take these forth?"

"Yes, Sergeant," Captain Willes replied. "Here it plainly states that we brought these muskets in with us."

"Seven, aye. Thank you, sir. You men are free to pass." The sergeant's unexpected civility calmed my heart. I searched my brother's face to see if it had a similar effect.

Beyond the fortification the northwest wind, unhindered by the expanse of the mudflats, smacked us full from our right-hand sides. We needed little reminder that an early winter's fury was near at hand.

On the journey to the coast we had spoken often of the reception we would receive, and Boston's civilian leaders had certainly not stinted in that regard. Also, though, we had joked about and much anticipated the carefree return trip. Indeed we had no sheep with which to concern ourselves. The dogs could roam where they willed, yapping at every squirrel and chipmunk that darted across our path. Only Newport had the unenviable task of keeping Ben moving. The rest of us merely needed to walk for hours and miles at a time; something we were quite used to; and make camp each dusk. Nevertheless, the expected levity eluded us. Exchanges lasted mere minutes before the speakers fell silent once again. Constantly my feet began forcing the pace. I had to consciously restrain them, before Newport and the cart fell too far behind. I was hardly alone in this.

"Anxious to be home?" Captain Willes asked, coming up from behind me.

I gave him a nod. "My apologies, sir. I am at that."

"So are all the men. As am I."

We moved along the hard-packed earth, our boots crushing the ice-crusted ridges of dirt. I marveled at our Captain, for here was a man who could accompany other men, saying not a word, yet causing no awkwardness by either his presence or his silence. Both behaviors served to increase the respect which men felt towards him. I stole a glance when he turned to survey our party with his ready smile. Men would follow such a man. I would. "Sir," I said, "a word if I may about Boston. I hardly recognized the place. It is become, a, a..."

"Aye, Elisha. It is an occupied city now, I fear. Not as one thinks of such things, of course. There is no age-old enemy there to fight, like the French. No, it is a nightmare of our own King's construction. English soldiers deployed by the thousands and why? Not to protect English subjects; rather to put them down. More's the pity, but 'tis so."

"What's to be done, Captain? Doctor Warren. Did he say?"

Captain Willes laid a hand on my forearm. "No man knows, Elisha, not even him. Or if he does, it is perhaps so terrible a prospect he will not give it words for fear of it coming to pass. No, a minute. What we must do is prepare ourselves. That is a thing we can do."

"Prepare? But for what?"

"For anything." He squeezed my elbow, smiled that smile of reassurance, and moved across to Eli. Despite that calm demeanor, his very words lent shape to the forebodings that had slithered in my guts since we first passed within the city gates. Perhaps this had been the Captain's intent after all - to prepare me, and Eli too, as I watched the worry deepen in those eyes now turned towards me.

"What was that about, then?" Heman asked as he and Azariah flanked me. "Ya look as though you've glimpsed a ghost." My brother just watched me.

It was not right to divulge the Captain's words, addressed as they'd been in private, yet there was also no point in denying what was on my mind. Azariah would pry it from me eventually. "The warships and the troops," I admitted; "the martial presence weighs upon my mind."

"Mighty fine language, my friend," Heman chuckled. "Call it what it is - an army, that's what. Why, when they wheeled to face us I nearly pissed myself. I know for a fact Azariah did." Laughing, he leaned across me to smack my brother's chest.

Banter and play of that sort were as common as air and breathing to my little brother, but he ignored that now. "I could have slain a pair of those bastards," he said to me. "You know the ones I mean, Elisha. Even now I could." When Azariah had been a boy, and Daniel and I had taken him out to hunt, I knew from the first he was born to it. So calm and confident had been his way, even when leveling a weapon longer than he was tall. But never from then till now, had I seen anger stirred in with killing. Always had he hunted as he'd been taught - to kill at such a time is a necessary thing. Now he wanted to. I disliked the look in his young face. Feared it too. Was he testing me, I wondered, or had a beast unknown to either of us been born out of this journey to Boston?

Heman had begun jesting about the soldiers' white leather cross-belts. Those bright, silver buckles in the center offered a proper aiming point he started to say. Hard to tell it was whether my glare or the fire in Azariah's eyes that caused my friend's voice to trail off.

I turned to my little brother. "You know what Grandsire would say about such talk. The taking of another's life. Why Father..."

"Is that all you have to say to me, Brother? After what we experienced; what we saw. You hide behind Father's tired preaching!" He turned on his heel. A moment more and he had retrieved his musket from the cart and came trotting back through our party - this time along the far shoulder.

I made to cut him off but Heman restrained me. "Let him go, my friend. For now at least. He's upset."

"Him? I'm upset. All of us are. That does not justify the urge to..."

"Sssh," Heman said, dragging me ahead of the others who did their best to look without staring. "I agree with you, but Azariah is younger than we. He needs more time to understand this."

"Damn," I muttered aloud. "How could I have invoked Father of all people..."

"Do not judge yourself harshly, my friend. What can anyone have said? The times are so confused."

They were, of course, but I had behaved like an idiot. How easy a thing it was to chastise rather than strive to understand. Such easy solutions, those that had worked once, or nearly so, were unlikely to in the future – whatever it held for us. "All right," I said. "You can unhand me now. You oaf."

He laughed and released me. "For my part, Elisha, I was wrong to make light of the redcoats."

"Damn right you were. It is all of it your fault." I clapped his shoulder. With a half turn I touched my cap so that the Captain and the rest could see all was well. At least among my friend and I. As to Azariah, I scanned the road ahead but he had already moved around the next bend.

Chapter 17

The barking of the dogs signaled Azariah's return before any of us had set eyes upon him. He would, of course, have scouted locations to bivouac. Though the sinking of the sun had drained color from the landscape, and despite the score of miles put behind us, I guessed I was not alone in wanting to press on.

Azariah mock wrestled with Eli's brute, both man and beast exchanging playful growls. Between my brother's frolicking, which pleased me no end, and the brace of rabbits strung about his neck, the three dogs soon ran delirious circles about him. When we came abreast, he broke free, leaving our furry companions to carry on their romp. "Medway lies just ahead," he reported. Captain Willes gave a nod. Stroking his chin, he studied Boston Post Road as though he could see the town from where we stood. "If you've a mind to press on, sir," Azariah offered. "I did find a high and dry place but a mile farther. Plenty of fresh water too."

"What say you, men?" our Captain asked. "Are we for going on?" He had correctly gauged our mood. Not a man wanted to sleep within a town this night, heedless of its creature comforts. "There you have your answer, Azariah."

We resumed our march with somewhat lighter steps, for each brought us nearer to home. The breeze had died throughout the day such that the air, though cold, felt almost pleasant. Through the town we went without pause. Few made note of our passage, given the lateness of the hour and the silence surrounding our small band.

As we gathered sticks for our fire I made a point of picking my way towards my brother. His more direct route made clear he sought me as well. "A good spot you found, Azariah," I said. "Kindling so plentiful a blind man could readily supply himself. That and the Charles right at our door."

Brushing aside these idle compliments, he eased the wood from my arms. "About our quarrel, Brother." I made to speak but he held up his hand. It was a gesture I recognized, for I used it too often, but never did I recall him quieting me this way. "Your mention of Grandsire, Elisha. Father too. It got me to thinking about our family." How rare a thing it was to hear him struggle so. "What I mean is," he resumed, "that what we saw back there; if that should happen in Tolland, at our parents' house..."

I now understood both my brother and myself. That armed men, clad in coats of red, might one day bar entry to our Meeting House with hostile glances and bayonets of steel; or worse, demand quarters within Grandsire's home. It was a prospect that had haunted me since our feet had first trod Boston's cobbled streets.

It was he who broke the silence; with a chuckle. "Well, Brother," he said. "What now?"

"We gather up this kindling, that's what. Come on. Get a move on. The sooner we're to bed, the earlier can we make a start." Laughing, we each snatched up an armful of sticks, keeping one hand free to fence awkwardly with stout branches.

The following morning a light drizzle greeted us. Drops formed on my greatcoat and rolled down as we broke camp. Though it caused mere discomfort, if it should persist the road would suffer, as would the cart's pace. Heman and I had just settled Noah within it. The ankle he had rolled the day before had swollen and stiffened in the night. Nothing was broken, but walking was out of the question.

"I can feel the ruts already," Noah complained, though smiled.

"Lay back and bear it," Heman replied, giving his chest a push. "Captain's orders."

With Noah stretched out in the rear, Newport moved along the cart's side to fetch hay for the ox. Given his stature, he strained to reach the nearer of the two bales. "Let me," I said. With a heave I had the entire bale over the side.

"Thankee, Mista Benton," he said. As he plucked mere handfuls free, I knew I had done far more than was called for. What's more, his gentle smile seemed to reveal he sensed this too. Was I making poor amends for that night at the inn, I asked myself? If so, justice was served by my standing there, arms loaded, feeling the fool.

"My, aren't we generous with Eli's feed," Heman joked.

"Perhaps our friend intends fattening my ox so that the poor beast can better haul his timber." Eli it was who had spoken. Heman arched both eyebrows - surprised once more by Eli's humor, and the fact that this acquaintance-turned-friend would strike with a jibe that bordered on insult.

"I confess that was my devilish design," I said. Relieved I was at their laughter, for it offered me escape and at a small price - a deserved lash at my pride.

Within minutes we were underway. "I do pity Noah," Heman said. "A few miles in that spring-less contraption and he's like to sell his ankle to Lucifer himself if it'll save his spine." Grasping his own in sympathy, he fell back towards the cart. "Pray we never need to ride in the rear of one, Elisha."

"Amen to that," I called. Azariah had resumed the point, so I walked alone with my thoughts. Though I reveled in the warmth of my companions' affections, my brother's words had cast my fears in pictures. I saw them now, each time I blinked away the rain. King George's troops marching to and fro upon our green. Scarlet sentinels stationed in every doorway. One even barred entry to Jemima's door. Feeling a presence beside me I turned. "Eli..."

"Did I disturb?"

"No, not at all. Join me." We walked together, the wet now dripping from the open sides of our tricorne hats.

"Do you intend to come into town? If Captain Willes calls a muster of the company?"

I busied myself with tipping a small pool of water from my hat. He knew the answer to this, of course. Knew that I would report, as must every member of our militia. Why ask? To our collective surprise I reached out and shook his hand. He smiled broadly, as gladdened I thought by my form of answer, as I had been by his query.

Within hours our path forward more resembled a muddy stream than a road. Only a few riders had passed us throughout the morning. Now no others came or went. The Captain instructed Newport to guide the cart beneath a towering pine. The spot afforded Noah shelter, as did the oilskin Heman had draped over him. The Captain stood beside Newport there at the ox's head. Azariah, Eli, Heman and I lingered beneath the longest of the branches, gazing out at the steady rain.

"Do you men wish to press on?" the Captain asked. "You could make better time without this cart to slow your progress."

He had guessed our sentiments once more. But to divide our party now would not be right. "You had said, sir, that it was your wish that we return as we left Tolland. Together."

"I agree with Elisha," Eli said. "Our success should be yours to report, Captain."

"Events may have overtaken the outcome of our charitable mission," he replied. "Eli and Elisha, come, I would have a word. The rest make up your packs with whatever provisions you will require." And so it was that Captain Willes confided "You men will have to deliver our message to Colonel Chapman and the town selectmen." Within the quarter hour we had bid farewell to him, Noah, Newport, and even our four-footed companions, though the dogs had to be sent back time and again.

Without the ox and cart to slow us, we surged past the mile markers at a remarkable rate. Heman and I were blessed with long legs and strides to match. We now employed them to the full. Eli too covered the ground at a good clip, accustomed to walking as he had become during the outgoing trip. Being the shortest, Azariah must have taken three steps for every two of mine. Observing us from afar, however, one would hardly make note of it. He loped along with the ease of any woodland creature that one could name. What's more, that 10 pounds of musket seemed but an extension of his arm. My own weapon I shifted from hand to hand, and palm to shoulder, seeking in vain a convenient place to tote it.

That night to our collective relief we slept on Connecticut soil. Our feet throbbed and our shoulders ached but home was no more than a day's hike distant. Azariah had found a rock ledge under which we now stretched. A fire coaxed from damp kindling outlined him as he stood guard.

"Be sure to warm that bedroll, Brother," he called as I drew my greatcoat over the woolen blanket.

"Not only must I carry it," I protested to Heman and Eli, "but the brute wants me to warm it for when his turn comes."

"A poor bargain you made of it, Elisha," Eli said. "For shame! A man of your experience in business."

"Aye, poor indeed, my friend," Heman agreed. "It'd leave a surprise for the little rascal. Any serpents about, perhaps."

General laughter gave way to sighs as each man settled into what he'd brought to keep the damp at bay. The idea to pack one of the oilskins, and to take turns lying upon it when off watch, had been Azariah's. That I carried the bulky thing had been my own doing. I felt it only proper as he sallied forth as scout the long day through. Besides, I harbored the belief that he only suggested this protection from the cold, wet ground for one as unused to it as I.

A few raindrops continued to fall even as I glimpsed patches of stars, exposed in the vault of heaven above. The gentle breeze that shredded the clouds also stirred the thinning leaves of an old oak leaning just beyond our shelter. Off to the east, the veil of black succumbed to a dull gray. Dawn at last, I thought, stomping my feet and shifting my musket to the opposite shoulder.

Once I could make out individual branches of the oak, I stepped amongst my companions, rousing each in turn. Still below the rolling hills that marked the horizon, the sun bathed the remaining clouds with all manner of bright color.

"Will you look at the red just there," Eli said, rubbing his eyes.

Azariah had already begun rolling up our bedding. "Puts me in mind of the regulars' coats," he said.

"You have to admire their drill," Eli replied. "Good heavens, such precision." He, too, turned to me. "Cannot help wondering how our company's movements pale compared to that."

"They are professional soldiers, Eli," I said. "They drill for a living."

"Whether a man can hit what he aims at is what matters." Azariah handed the bedding to me as he spoke. "I'll reconnoiter the road, shall I Brother?"

I nodded. Whilst packing our gear I watched him go.

"Anger still burns in him," Eli said to me. "If I can speak so freely?"

"I do not mind you doing so, Eli. And yes, he cannot forget. Nor can I." Images of those densely-packed lines of marching men stirred anger, and admiration; fear, too. Eli lapsed into what I took to be a respectful silence. Heman's failure to speak was unlike him. Especially so was his refusal to make eye contact whilst he made ready. "Heman?" I whispered, when Eli had stepped apart to relieve himself.

"What will happen now, do you think?" he asked. "Will anything be the same?"

Before I could think how to respond to such a question, Eli rejoined us. Yet now I understood Heman's mind in this. And he was right to worry. Could he expect to return to avail himself of his father's gift of land? Would I help Daniel prepare for winter's coming? What would all that we had witnessed mean for each?

"Are you unwell, Elisha?" Eli asked.

"I am thinking we must hurry." And so we did.

Chapter 18

October had vanished like a morning fog. And November I experienced as but a blur of drill and chores; precious little of either orchestrated by me. Most recently a gale had swept the bleak, white landscape surrounding Father's house for two days and two nights running. December had thus arrived, borne in upon us by winter's fury. Its coming buried any lingering remnants of autumn. Azariah had gone off to Tolland center just before the onslaught. Though Mother worried, I reassured her often that he had enough sense and friends to find shelter in the town. I could not help but wonder if counted amongst those friends might be the Barrows.

The rest of the Benton clan spent the better part of each day within the warm confines of the kitchen or hall. I had assumed responsibility for feeding the fires in these rooms, just as I did for Grandsire's home. Common sense dictated I do as much, for the winds nearly swept slight Jacob from his feet. Additionally, the trips to the woodshed afforded me reasons to vacate Father's house with regularity.

This morning, I had already managed to sally forth on three occasions. The first when I restocked Mother Sarah's indoor supply; the second when I served as an anchor for both Jacob and Hannah - that they might gather milk and eggs from the cows and chickens snug within Father's barn. The third came when I ventured out alone for the fuel stacked beside me. Seated thus before the kitchen fire, I watched as the hungry flames consumed this latest offering, and were in turn sucked up the chimney as though devoured by a howling beast that dwelt therein.

I avoided Daniel's eye for he watched me close. When last I had braved the elements I hurried my departure lest he offer to accompany me. He meant to have a private word, and he would seize the opportunity if I showed the slightest inclination. Cowardly I may have been for denying him. It could not be helped. His entire being was bloated with what he meant to say, and had swelled further each week of my return. My brother had missed me sure, but he had also benefited from my absence for I had come back a changed man. He had flourished under the weight of bringing in the crop and of preparing the fields for their winter rest. Despite Father's impossible expectations, and what must have been near constant slights, he had stumbled upon a thing he loved, and in the process had ceased striving to become a reflection of me. He had discovered, I sensed, his own worth. I did feel joy for him. But so great was his eagerness in what he'd done, and it so near to gloating, that sight of it choked any expression of thanks I owed him. Besides, had he no comprehension, no regard at all for the fact that his elevation must surely seal my fate. With Father it would force my hand. I must ask what he intended for me, if anything at all; and soon.

"Mary!" Father called from the parlor. "Wife!"

Mother set down her sewing, and after instructing Hannah concerning a tricky stitch, she rose. "He will probably ask for tea," she whispered confidentially to me. "Coffee will have to do. Might you care for a cup, my son?" Politely I declined, but I did rise and swung the iron pot from within the hearth so that she might draw hot water from it. A moment more and she left me with a tap and a smile.

Her departure brought to a sudden end the soft murmurings that had passed between Mother and Hannah. Now there was only the crackle of burning embers and the spinning of Jacob's top upon the floor. At any moment Daniel would rise to fill this vacuum. I busied myself with the repositioning of the pot, my back to him the while. Father's voice reached my ear. The tone was strangely flat, as it had been for many weeks. Perhaps he, too, sensed the change in my brother. Father had begun to choose his words with Daniel; much as he was able. He did not appear to trust my brother, not fully at any rate, but he had glimpsed something there in him. He treaded lightly, so as to not crush what Daniel may yet become. When dealing with me he harbored fewer reservations. We were to be played off each other, it seemed to me; as might a gambler hedge his bets.

Safe within the confines of the hall, I squeezed my eyes so that I might block out such hateful accusations. How I detested the fear and confusion that gave rise to such unworthy thoughts.

The scrape of Daniel's chair startled me. He had followed and taken a seat at the table. Thankfully, Jacob wandered in to join his older brothers. I, too, then sat. The tabletop separated Daniel and I, which served as a river wide. Into the dancing flames I stared.

How had this state come to pass? We of the Boston party had returned, full of expectations, leavened with doubts. The reception brimmed with an anxious gaiety. Citizens, inhabitants, it mattered not. Every living soul in Tolland had turned out. Despite this acclaim only Eli's wishes had been largely fulfilled - for the very day of Captain Willes's arrival, each boy and man between 16 and 60 was assembled. The Captain nominated Eli and me as corporals, and our neighbors had blessed us with their ringing votes. Eli beamed at the honor, but the rank merely served to deepen the odd melancholy that had taken root within me. Each afternoon thereafter, while the weather held and excepting Sunday, we drilled. Each inhabitant possessed a musket in sound working order, but many mere residents had naught but a fowling piece or some other ancient weapon to practice their shouldering of arms.

In our absence, Lieutenant Parker had somehow managed to procure the allotment of powder per man that Captain Willes and Colonel

Chapman had decreed. Prudence dictated that this precious supply be husbanded and hidden safely away. Prudent a course, yes, but as a consequence, the practice of aiming and firing consisted mostly of leveling barrels at straw targets, and causing hammers to strike empty pans. Dumb show is what it amounted to. Raw recruits learned little to improve their accuracy and more importantly, to experience the shock of stocks leaping against one's shoulder, and smoke and flame bursting about one's face. For marksmen such as my brother, the charade as he called it induced sheer boredom.

Heman, like me, fell somewhere in the middle of our company of citizen soldiers. The call to muster had thrilled us in years gone by, but the memories of our last journey, so unsettling and so fresh, whetted any spark we felt. Nor, we soon found, could we share what we had experienced without stoking the passions of men prone to strong emotions, like Azariah, or planting the seeds of dread in fellows of more placid stock. So we went each time called, and went when called again.

I did repeatedly journey to the northern part of Tolland so that I might lend Aunt Sara a hand. I also rode west on those rare yet precious occasions that Heman asked me to help clear the land gifted him. Rarely when traveling north or west did I stop in town, and not once had I sought a private word with Jemima Barrows. For this, Azariah called me a fool, and only God could guess at what Jemima herself thought.

In my father's home or on my father's land I remained, though seldom did I speak with him. No, I spent my time thinking on Boston, and once Father and Brother Daniel determined what tasks needed doing, I did my allotted share. And now winter had come. It brought with it bone-aching cold and white landscapes, and the end of news from up Massachusetts way.

I snatched my coat from where it hung drying and made straight for the back door. Four pairs of eyes pinned me and I ignored them all. Outside, I welcomed the icy blast that near tore the shirt from my chest. I'd reached the deep lean-to where we stored the wood before

I'd managed to fasten the last of the buttons. By then my fingers protruded from my hands like bent nails from blocks of wood.

The bang of a door behind me proved that my haste and shivering had been in vain. Daniel's huddled form leaned into the gale as he crossed over. I moved to the far end and began brushing snow from the stack. A bank of the powdery stuff curled 'round the corner post like a crystalline bowl, three feet deep.

Mother Nature paused in her ferocity. There had been a time I would have viewed this as one of her small favors; a kindness returned for how I endeavored to care for forest and field. Now I could only think she aligned herself with my brother, intending by her sudden forbearance that Daniel should be heard. "Elisha?" he called out quite plain.

I replaced the log and turned to him. My God, how earnest was that face I loved so dear. "It must be important indeed," I said, "for you to follow me into this."

"Yes, Brother. For me it is."

"Then let us seek better cover than this." Touching his arm I forged a path through the drifts into the shelter of the barn. Here our labored breathing burst in great clouds but at least the renewed gusts were kept at bay. Somewhere a loose board banged. April whinnied from her stall. "In a moment, girl," I said before giving Daniel my full attention.

"I have," he began. "I have wished to speak with you. Almost from the day of your return."

"I know this, Brother. I should have given you the opportunity. Long ago."

His shy smile came and went. "No matter. I do not mind it. It is just," and he took in the shadowy outlines of the cows with that soft gaze of his. His eyes fixed next on me, with an expression that mixed hope with fret, and always, his innocent sincerity. "Just that, Elisha, are you disappointed in me?"

"Disappointed?" I repeated in dumb confusion, much as if I'd been tethered within a neighboring stall.

"Father speaks little to me; since the harvest days. But with him this only means I am stung less by his barbs. That you would keep silent, Brother, well, I have wracked my mind, but can only think that matters are not to your liking. The fields are turned. They lie quiet for the winter as you had instructed. Was it the bringing in of the crop? Mister Stimson did take a goodly portion of the profits, but not a barrel more than you and he agreed. Perhaps you..."

"Sssh, Daniel, no more of this I pray you." I had fastened one hand upon his shoulder, the other against his chest; and all in hopes of quelling his upset. "I am," I told him, "truly one of God's most contemptible creatures. No, Brother, hear me out. I am contemptible indeed that I would cause you such grievous self-doubt. You who have borne an unexpected load so well, and with your nature unaffected."

"So, Elisha. You are not, then, not disappointed in me?"

I clasped him to me, and squeezed his stout frame till his gasp caused me to let him be. "Do not think it. Perish such thoughts. It is I who should fret for fear of falling short of the mark set by you." I could see in his face that he harbored doubts, but his features had relaxed; and I lacked the strength to further explain or convince. "Go back inside, Brother. Before I make an even greater fool of myself."

"What will you do out here, and alone? Is there a chore I might..."

"Go," I said. "Get thee inside and warm. I will join you, Mother and the others, bye and bye." When he had gone at last, I wandered over to the mare. She greeted me with a soft whinny, then swept the hay from my palm though a mound of it lay before her. "You would not eat from my hand," I told her, "if you knew what a shite I truly am." How could I have thought ill of one such as he, I wondered? "What has become of me since Boston?" I said aloud. No response came forth from the beasts on either side, nor from the rafters high above. No, none here could answer me.

Chapter 19

Another hour I spent in the barn, alone with my thoughts. Though I succeeded in mucking out each stall, I resolved none of that which tormented my mind. Satisfied that I could not, I returned to my father's house. Something drove me to enter by way of the front door.

"Must you come through here?" Father bellowed, before ever I entered his parlor. "I'll see those boots off your feet first," he instructed from around the corner. "Do not think for a minute I intend to ford wet puddles of your making."

Thus he spoke to me though I had not planted a foot within his cozy sanctum the morning through. Nor had he budged judging by the empty cup and plate that had been brought in to him. I approached with my boots held on my opposite side. Though he would not deign to nod, I paused and accorded him the courtesy. Was this what our relationship had come to, I wondered? He abused me for prospective wrongs, and I goaded him with my unwanted presence.

Neither one of us had much to recommend us I decided by the time I entered the kitchen. Mother approached at once - her skirts rustling about her. On tip-toe she pressed her fire-warmed cheek against mine. "Why you are frozen half to death. Come. We kept your place by the fire. Hannah, more coffee for your big brother."

"Yes, Mother!"

They both hovered about me. Mother handed me the steaming cup whilst Hannah knelt and rubbed my feet 'till the blood flowed free once more. Though Sister's ministrations brought a surge of burning deep in my toes, I smiled in thanks. When she had rejoined Jacob at play in the hall, I asked Mother where Daniel had gone off to. By way of reply she hugged my neck and kissed my head. "What is that for, Mother?"

"You should have seen his face when he entered that doorway. Thank you, my son."

"I am owed no thanks, Mother. If you knew what I had accused him of, in my mind, why then..."

She placed a finger to my lips. "You have restored my Daniel to us, and that's enough. He is upstairs, sound asleep. His worries, and I have told him time and again they were needless, have exhausted him. I promised to wake him for supper." She patted my knee, and with a quick wipe of her eyes, busied herself at the table.

So Daniel had been so upset he sought Mother's counsel. Until today he had not dared approach me. My father's son I have become, I thought. Before the hour was up, I excused myself so that I might check on Grandsire.

The wind no longer set the bare branches clacking together in the trees that arched over my head. In the relative calm, the drifting of snow had also eased. I could still make out the path I had stomped through at daybreak. This I followed to my grandfather's doorway.

Mother Sarah greeted me at the door. "Is Grandsire well?" I asked.

"Come in, Elisha, come in." She helped brush clumps of white that had dropped upon my greatcoat. "Do not be alarmed," she said as she took the heavy coat from me. "He has felt poorly since you saw him last. I do not like his color, but it is that cough that worries me."

"Is it all right that I see him?"

"Of course, Elisha! He is awake and sight of you will cheer my dear husband. Come! I brought him into the kitchen bedroom to warm his bones."

The closet-sized space in one corner of the cooking area served as extra storage most times. But when a family member took ill, it served as the sick room. From there the patient could most readily be observed and ministered to. What's more, no room in the house had a fire better tended.

"Grandsire!" I called out as I squeezed in beside his prone form.

"My Boy, My Boy!" he exclaimed, coming fully awake. I bent awkwardly that he might kiss my head. The effort drew a cough and then another. They rasped from deep within his chest. Mother Sarah's gaze met mine before she hurried off to bring a promised cup of coffee.

I re-arranged Grandsire's pillows so that he might see me without straining his neck. The room offered only enough space for one to lie prostrate, and for a visitor or two to stand. I chose to perch upon the side of his bed. A broad smile graced his haggard face. He must have slept but little of late. Mother Sarah had prepared me for the paleness of his skin, but not how thin it appeared - for tiny veins ran riot across his cheeks. "How do you feel, Grandsire?"

"Only my age, My Boy. Or should I greet thee now as Corporal Benton?" Knowing his dislike of martial matters, I had not told him. Seeming to read my thoughts, he said, "By unanimous acclaim were you chosen. So your father acquainted me." That Father had ventured out to convey the news surprised me more. Grandsire patted my knee. "Men can lose a son, or a brother, to war, My Boy, and still feel pride. Your Uncle William was both brother and son to your father and me, but we are proud of his service, and his rank, to this very day. He preserved us from the French. Sergeant William Benton and others like him." He coughed after this speech, and let his head sink back for a moment.

I had not the heart to relate to him my fears about the threat now posed by our own sovereign. I rubbed his hand, so large yet grown so light. When I lifted my eyes I found him studying me.

"Enough of this talk of war," he said. "What's past is past. Now. What troubles you, My Boy? Come, out with it, for I know of it from your Mother. My Sarah winkled it out of her on her last visit."

"Must all women gossip?" I muttered aloud without thinking.

"Fie! Elisha Benton! I will pretend I heard you not, and this once will tell neither the one nor the other what you spoke."

"Forgive me, Grandsire. I had no right. I, well..."

"Your words and stumbling are proof that they are correct. Do not be angered of them for caring. Consider, My Boy that most talk amongst women serves to better the lot of children, or us menfolk. It is grateful we should be and not resentful."

Despite my being proved wrong, and unkind in the bargain, his smile drew forth my laughter. "Which also proves I know nothing of the fair sex, Grandsire."

He chuckled and coughed at the same time. "It is a sage man who can admit it," he managed to get out.

Mother Sarah appeared and set down a pair of steaming cups. "I see the two of you are up to no good. Again!" she added with a pinch of our cheeks.

"Pinch mine harder," I begged her. "For your wise husband has exposed me in all my wickedness and folly."

"Though he be my dearest friend, I refuse to believe it. Not of you, Elisha." With that she clasped me tight, and with another of her deep, infectious laughs, went away once more.

Grandsire lay still for a bit, recovering his wind after all that talk and laughter. I sat quietly beside him. I discovered that the woman who occupied my thoughts was not kin to me. What did I comprehend about Jemima, after all? She had been known to me her entire life, but only as Azariah's little school friend or as the always carefree, sometimes irreverent daughter of Jon Barrows; and he a mere resident, no matter how charitably I wished to view his station. What possessed me to contemplate such a one as she, and why? Defied me in public, she had, and shared with another the sole private moment between us. Even so, the blue of her eyes and the wisdom of her words refused to leave me be.

"I will keep at you, My Boy," Grandsire insisted. "Until you confide what disturbs you. Tell me true, does my son play a part?"

Despite the seriousness of his expression, to say nothing of the implications, I could not help myself. "When does Father not," I replied with a grin that split my face.

"Indeed. My first born does have that effect."

We sat for a time; his hand held in mine. I had neither plan nor wish to pass my troubles on to him, especially given his state, but he had always drawn the truth from me. He did so now. "What you told me once, Grandsire, about there being an anger in the land. 'Tis true, or at the very least, a deep suspicion that infects men of every political leaning."

His white head gave a nod. "So it was that visit to Boston then. It troubles you still?"

"There are other things, sure. They existed well before I went away. But what I saw in that city o'ershadows all the rest. It seems I can make no sense of the matters at hand, when this greater ill hangs over me."

He took his hand away to cup his coughing. "Would it help to talk it through?" he asked.

"Thank you, Grandsire, but I wouldn't even know where to begin. Actually, I was thinking of going into town. Perhaps some word has come now that the roads are passable. Besides, it's high time I go regardless."

His bleary eyes seemed about to close. "If you think it best, My Boy. A word of advice, ere you go. Address what you must, and what you can; fret not over that which is beyond your power."

"Thank you, Grandsire. Now sleep." I bent to kiss his thin, white locks. "I will look in again before nightfall."

Mother Sarah waited on me in the kitchen. "Thank you, Elisha. For bringing laughter under this roof. He always longs for your coming."

"If you wish it, Mother Sarah, I can spend the night. A few nights together, perhaps, to help you with what needs doing?" She nodded and hugged me tight. "The doctor visits Father tomorrow," I said. "He means to check on Father's arm, and general well-being. I could ask that he come 'round."

"Bless you. My husband will resist us so we must be firm."

"A united front," I agreed. "Mother will come up I'm sure. Grandsire can never refuse the two of you." I left her with the promise to return. Meanwhile, I had a long trek ahead of me if I was to reach town and back in the hours of daylight remaining.

Chapter 20

I made an attempt to reach town that day and the next. Both proved to be in vain. The first led to my mare and me floundering in a bank of snow that surpassed her withers. The next provided no sound footing due to a sudden melt. By noon of the third day matters had changed on many fronts. Most importantly, the doctor had finally been able to complete his rounds south of the village. He had called on Father first, who received him with little more than civility despite the disheveled state in which the doctor arrived. I ascribed the coolness of the reception to two factors: that given the elements Dr. Cobb had dispatched his young and active apprentice, Jeremiah West; and that Father had always been reluctant to have anyone other than Mother view his wasted limb. Anticipating his sensibilities, I busied myself with rubbing down Jeremiah's horse. The poor, lathered beast required attention and doing so kept me out from under foot. Daniel emerged from the house a moment later.

"May I lend you a hand, Elisha?"

"Thank you, Brother, but I believe I can manage." Seeing his disappointment I added, "You could render a service, however. If you would bring word to Mother Sarah that the doctor is come..."

"At once," he replied. Back inside he went. He re-appeared and trotted past despite the still ankle-deep snow. "Perhaps she or Grandsire will have other chores as well," he called.

I shot him a wave, for in the next minute he had carried on into the tree line. Grandsire's cough had lessened during the days and nights I had stayed with them. Even so, Jeremiah's arrival was more than welcome. His presence would bring peace of mind if nothing more. I smiled at the thought of what my brother would soon be up to. He would ferret out some task or other, despite my best efforts of recent days.

Mister West departed leaving a smile on all our faces. And Mister was how we Bentons referred to the young man after he rendered favorable diagnoses for the family's patriarchs. I resolved to follow his footsteps into town. Mother insisted I pack provisions, lest I be caught out in the weather. I accepted, though the cold assured good footing at last, and the fierce blue sky forecasted more of the same come nightfall. I also promised to persuade Azariah to return home; though Mister West had reported seeing the wayward son about town - looking fit as a fiddle. Despite all this being arranged, Mother hung at my elbow as everyone made their farewells. Even Father gave me a nod of his head, though his liberality may have had more to do with the medical tidings than with any change between us. At any rate, I walked outside under a cloud of pleasant surprise that blossomed further when she accompanied me. "You'll catch your death, Mother!"

"Nonsense," she replied. "I trust, my son, that your search for your brother will take you to the door of the Barrows family." The name had hardly left my thoughts ever since Grandsire counseled me to address matters within my power. Even so, to hear it upon my mother's lips proved shocking. "I thought as much," she said. "The girl Jemima..."

It could have been a question, or simply Mother guessing aloud. The name bound us in silence. Not wishing to give vent to the muddled emotions churning within me, I loosed a petty but rising resentment. "Did our youthful medical man mix rumor with his learned verdicts?"

"Fie! Elisha Benton! As far back as the harvest a friend confided in me. Whilst you and Azariah were away this was. Jon Barrows' daughter was said to be overheard arguing with a son of mine; in the street. With you, Elisha, and as concerns hired hands." I had no defense, so I said nothing. "'Tis true, then," Mother said. "And did this girl sway you? I know her to be a high-spirited creature, but to influence your thinking and on such a matter. Consider if your father were to learn of it..."

"She did not lead me astray, Mother. We merely viewed the issue with like minds. Time and again I've pondered over it, and I would act as I did that day."

Mother studied me for such a prolonged moment I nearly spoke just to break the awkwardness. "The young woman must be strong," she said at last, "to speak up as she did, to you."

"She is that and so much more. More than I fully comprehend," I added, forgetting for a moment that I stood before her, and just beyond Father's door. Mother had hold of my hand by this point. Her skin was ice cold. "You must get inside," I said.

"Listen to me, Elisha. Go to her. Go to this girl."

"What?"

She wiped at my cheeks, although it was to her eyes tears had come. "It is high time you think of yourself, my son. Follow your heart." With that she whirled about. The door closed. I stood for a full minute staring at it before I set out.

The road had improved markedly. April had no trouble keeping to it or stepping 'round the few drifts that narrowed its width in places.

After a time I hardly bothered keeping to the tracks left by Jeremiah's carriage wheels, for nowhere did even a foot of snow remain.

The ease of our transit left me with plenty of time to contemplate the advice given me. That of Grandsire, who had urged me to act upon matters of direct import. And then there was Mother, she who had always strived to not contradict Father, telling me to follow my heart. Whose words could possibly mean more to me than this parent and this grandparent? What dictate did my heart intend for me to follow, however? Would I know when I saw her again? That at least I must do - I must insist on an audience with Jemima. I sat upright in the saddle. Only now did it occur to me - that I might dare all this; only to discover she cared naught for me...

The road rose as it entered the town, presenting itself fully to the south. Even in its weakened state the sun had done its work; drying the length of the incline right down to the packed earth surface. I glanced beyond to where it bordered Meeting House Green. Just opposite, set back and appearing impossibly small under its veil of snow, stood the home of Jon Barrows. A gentle tug on the reins brought April to a halt. She turned a wide, luminescent eye towards me, for this was not a normal stopping point. "I know, I know," I said, in an effort to comfort the both of us. "We've not come for an age." Soon I would have to dismount and approach their door, or walk on, lest I languish here in the road looking the proper fool.

That very instant Azariah yanked open the Barrows' door and stepped forth. "Brother! Join us!"

April skipped sideways a few feet at his shout and sudden appearance. I, too, was shocked, but equally with the breach of etiquette that led him to invite me, and so boldly, to another's home. Yet Azariah being Azariah, such behavior was not wholly unexpected. Besides, I had to admit that the sight of his smiling face was welcome.

And then Jemima squeezed in beside him. She wore a simple frock; her head uncovered. The breeze toyed with her auburn hair. When she waved to me, I dismounted so quickly my left foot nearly caught in the stirrup. The mare followed along behind me.

"For a moment it appeared you might stumble," Azariah said. "In your eagerness." His chuckle widened her smile. "Or have you been so long away, Brother, that you've forgotten the lay of the land hereabouts?"

Devilment lit his eyes, but with hers watching my every move I could hardly defend myself. Ignoring my impish brother I smiled for her. Her father stepped into view, catching the exchange. "Mister Barrows! Good day."

"Why, Mister Benton! Greetings! Come in, come in." He turned away. "My dear. Both of the Mister Bentons join us this day."

Azariah had hold of my arm and ushered me in. He, however, stopped at the entry. "Are you not coming in?" I inquired with far too much urgency.

"Step along, Brother," he said with a laugh. "Fret not. I'll see the mare to the livery and return before ever I am missed."

At this last he gave me a shove forward that pressed me right against Jemima. I caught her with one arm lest she fall. She gasped, then recovered her balance. I released her at once, but not before her parents had taken note. Their eyes met, then the father set about arranging benches. The mother busied herself at the hearth. My fingers insisted I pay them heed, for they had clasped the very small of her back, so far down that...

"Elisha," Jemima was saying to me. "If I may..." Snatching my hat from my head, I stepped farther into the home. She smiled and closed the door. An entire clump of my hair, dislodged by my haste from the club at the base of my neck, now spilled across my cheek. Standing directly beside me, her face upturned, Jemima could scarce avoid it. In fact, she did just the opposite. Smiling fully, she peered at me from first one side of it, and then the other. I seemed powerless to brush the hair away. She giggled. Her pale hand rose up, gathered the wayward strands and slipped them behind my ear in one motion. At her touch all the power I possessed surged, and at once. Only barely did I refrain from snatching her right off the wide, pine boards. Roses bloomed in her cheeks and her eyes fell.

"Daughter," her father intoned. "Perhaps our guest would care for a cup. Something to ward off the chill of his ride."

I faced him abruptly. "Aye, Mister Barrows, I would. Thank you." Her parents exchanged glances once more. I was in deep waters here. I knew it, but had no defense.

Jon Barrows invited me to sit, and so I took the edge of a bench closest to the door. Jemima set a steaming cup on the table before me. She curtsied without making eye contact, and rejoined her mother at a counter that also served as a sink along the far wall. I began a scan of the layout and furnishings if only to distract myself. The kitchen, I saw, doubled as a hall, for it was both cooking area and a place for the entire family to dine. Unlike Mother's wide hearth, complete with swinging hooks, heavy iron pots and boasting width enough for a baking oven, this one accommodated but one middling pot that dangled by a chain over a meager fire. And whereas Father's table easily accommodated eight or 10 diners, with plenty of room to serve all about, here perhaps four people could fit. Beyond a doorway was a room in which Jemima's parents surely slept. Just to my right, a small trundle bed filled the corner. At the sight of a discarded shift I turned away. Not fast enough, for her father had seen what caught my eye.

"What brings you into town, Mister Benton?" he asked. "If I might inquire? Our daughter tells us you've been seen but little of late."

"Is your family well?" Mrs. Barrows asked, with a raised eyebrow for her husband. "Your parents, and grandparents."

"All well!" I proclaimed in happy relief. "Thank you, and might I inquire after your health?" What would I reply if he asked my purpose here once more...

"We are as you find us," Mister Barrows replied. "Well, despite the storm."

"Aye, you are all of you looking quite well," I replied, unable to keep my gaze from alighting upon Jemima. It lingered there, though I felt her father's stare. Finally, her eyes lifted; met mine. I thought for a moment another giggle might ally itself with the blush of her cheek. It did not. Instead a smile appeared, so slight I was sure that only I could make it out from where I sat.

Azariah burst through the door at the same instant that his knuckles rapped the wood. For the first time I noticed the finely worked panels. Jon Barrows must have fashioned it himself. I turned to find him studying me, intently as if by so doing he could make out my character.

My brother plunked down beside me, cascading a wave of cold air across my face. "Jemima," he called. "What say you join us? Can you spare your daughter, Mrs. Barrows?" he asked, and it was clear he had charmed the woman of the house. "Here, Jemima. Sit here beside my dumbstruck older brother."

In that instant, before any other could speak, I stood. "Sir," I said, addressing Jon Barrows. "Might I speak with your daughter? A private word if I may."

Chapter 21

Jon Barrows stood slowly. His chest expanded and his shoulders squared. "Perhaps, Mister Benton," he said, "you and I might first..."

"Nonsense, Husband," Mrs. Barrows interrupted as she came across and took him by his heavy forearm. "There's no need of that. Why don't you two young people run along?" Only reluctantly did Mister Barrows yield his hand to her. "Mind, now, Jemima," she said. "Wrap up snug with a shawl. Oh, not that one. Take mine, for it's heavier by far." She smiled at me as if so doing might encourage haste.

Azariah had remained silent through all this. Keeping his peace, he simply lifted my greatcoat from the hook beside the door and handed it to me. His arched eyebrow said quite enough.

A moment more found me outside, with Jemima at my side. Not knowing what else to do, I extended my arm. "After you, Miss Barrows."

She stepped lightly along the well-trod path. With a glance back she said, "As you requested a private word, perhaps it is fitting you address me as Jemima."

"Of course," I replied, trailing after.

She faced me at the road. "Try it," she challenged me. "Jemima. It is a common-enough name."

"Do you mock me?" She looked around my bulk; searching the front windows of her home I presumed.

"If I do," she replied, "it is only because I am nervous."

"Are you?" My next breath came more easily. "Well then, I suppose there's no shame in admitting I am too."

She flashed a smile and spun about, sending her auburn locks cascading across the shawl. "I saw you when your party returned," she said.

I came abreast of her. "Did you," I replied, clearly recalling how she had preceded her parents as everyone swarmed to greet us.

"You looked as I imagined soldiers might, returning home from war. A great pack you carried, and your musket." She stopped. "I came to the muster, too. Yet as on your return, you traded nothing more than civilities with me."

I found my words lay thick within my throat, with this day's emotions choked by memories of yesterdays. "Boston," I somehow managed to say. "It had an effect on me."

"A lasting one, too, I think." One step closer she came and tapped my chest. "Compared to Eli's bluster, and he by your side that afternoon, you seemed suddenly humble."

Awoken by her light touch, I chuckled. "Unexpected behavior indeed, for one as arrogant as I."

"You have not behaved as badly as that," she said, smiling. With a half turn that held me in her sight she started for the Meeting House. "Almost, but not quite."

With a single stride I caught her up. Just then Azariah emerged and quickly fell alongside. "How are the two of you getting along?" he asked. "Both smiling - good, then," he continued, thus answering his own inquiry.

"Did the Barrows tire of your company so soon?" I asked him.

With a wink for Jemima, he said, "Methinks Mrs. Barrows wished a word with her husband."

"And Father will listen if he knows what's best," Jemima replied. The way her head leaned back when she laughed, and how her joy seemed to flow from her eyes as well as her lips, captivated me in a way...

"Well, in that case," Azariah announced, "I'll be off. See if I can stir up some trouble somewhere." With that he left us.

"He holds you dear," Jemima whispered to me.

"He dearly loves to tease me," I replied.

"As do I. Don't look at me that way Elisha Benton. The fault is your own. You make at times such an easy target."

"Marvelous. More mocking."

"I am sorry, Elisha. But this is one of those times."

At that very moment Dr. Nathan Williams emerged from the Meeting House. On his arm was Mrs. Williams, and she as proper as any minister's wife should be. My feet stopped without being told to do so. Jemima followed my gaze. A few other couples passed through the solid, double doors - prominent citizens all. As we stood but a few paces from the wide steps, I saw no choice but to remain where we were, and greet them two by two as they passed. A steady chorus commenced: "Good Day, Mister Benton" followed by a sidelong glance at my companion. I returned each greeting, my hat crushed in my hand. Finally they had all gone about their various business, though the road was now more peopled than before.

"We might wish to turn back the way we came," I suggested to Jemima.

"If you fear you may have escorted me too far from my parents' home, you need not, for would-be chaperones surround us."

"A man would have to be blind not to notice," I said, more as an observation than to Jemima, as I scanned the meaningful glances cast our way.

"Does it shame you, sir, to be seen thus with me?"

I faced her as she now faced me. "Jemima Barrows, I would not leave your side if a thousand such stared so. I will not, unless it is you who asks me to."

Her hands abandoned the shelter of her encircling shawl. Through the icy air they moved. Against my chest she placed them. And upon my cheek did she press her warm, full lips. My eyes met none other than hers.

"It is not to be borne!" Azariah proclaimed, standing on the steps above us. His arms stretched skyward as though he'd been martyred.

"What, Brother?" I asked. "For the sake of Heaven!"

By way of answer he leapt the four steps, showering us with snow, and landed between us. "I just left the Captain's side. There's no moving him."

"The Captain? Has he taken ill?" Both Jemima and I stared past and along the central aisle.

"Him? Never. He's like an old goat."

I clamped my hand over his mouth at this remark. "Settle yourself, Brother. Talk reason, and with respect."

He yanked my hand away. "Word is come this very day. The Sons of Liberty, Warren and likeminded men; they've taken to patrolling the city's streets at night." I refrained a moment from asking why, as I was certain he would soon reward my patience, and perhaps calm himself further. "They patrol," he whispered to us, "to learn whether the Regulars march out."

"Out where?" asked Jemima.

"For pity sake. To wherever likeminded men have stored powder and cannon."

Clearly things had taken another turn for the worse if the men of Boston violated curfew to spy on the movements of the King's troops. "This news is bad, Brother, but why does it anger you with Captain Willes?"

"Why! Because even this will not convince him to establish a detachment of minutemen in Tolland."

"You, Eli, Heman, we all of us discussed this before," I said. "Think of the distance that separates us; hard miles that are now near impossible. To respond to such an alarm we will need a day at least to gather and provision ourselves. There is no sense in a body of men that can respond in less than..."

"Bah, what do you know of it? A battle could be lost before you'd have us pick up a weapon." He swatted his leg with his own hat. Jemima took hold of his arm. Crestfallen, he stared as if seeing her for the first time. "Oh, yes. Jemima. He did ask for you. The Captain. A reply is needed, or some such. More words..." Muttering still he walked away.

"I should see to Azariah," I said.

"And I the Captain." She climbed the first stair before I caught hold of her hand.

"Jemima. I am sorry we part this way." She smiled. "Words do matter," I said. "And I meant every one I said."

She leaned down.

I stepped beneath her and received another kiss. "As did I."

I wandered Meeting House Green only vaguely aware of neighbors hurrying past. Of the random gusts that buffeted my collar I was completely oblivious. At one point they bent a stand of pines off to the west, spilling an avalanche of snow. I made no effort to tuck my chin as it swirled along the road and engulfed me.

In its wake I turned in a full circle, lost in contemplation. To my left stood the Meeting House, and inside of it Jemima. I felt a smile spread, and warmth to keep it company. The Captain was housed within as well. Before leaving I must see him. But not yet, not whilst they had business to tend to.

Along the entire street, snow blanketed every roof. And from every chimney smoke poured. My gaze lingered on one particularly fine, two-story structure on the far side of the green. Here Rebecca and her family lived. Father would have had me entwine my life with hers. Those fawn brown eyes had attracted me, but therein lay the trap, for softness and shyness was all that cowered there. I could not love a mouse, though it was cruel to think it.

"Oh, Azariah," I said aloud. "Where have you got yourself to?" I started for the livery, then abruptly reversed course. There was a place I must go first.

On the way, Jemima's eyes, so blue and speckled with gold when found by the sun, appeared in my mind. None others outshone them, and they were but one of her many attractions. The curve of her lower back was another. Given my destination, however, dwelling on such enticements would never do. Besides, Jemima meant so much more to me than the appeal of her person. Amazing it was, that she cared naught for men's conventions, yet time and again exhibited the utmost care for her fellow man; that despite my failings she professed her feelings for me.

The doorway loomed before me. How strange to approach this hovel of a house, and its master, with hat in hand. Yet how many times had he stood before me, his hat twisting in his hand; whilst mine sat comfortably upon my head. "What a conceited ass am I..." I muttered. The door yanked open even as I raised my fist to knock. "Mister Barrows!"

"Mister Benton. My wife saw you come up." His eyes swept past me and back along the route I'd come.

"Of course," I stammered. "Well, I thought that you should know. Would want to know, that is, that Jemima was called to the Meeting House. By Captain Willes." Her father seemed about to thunder at me for not returning his daughter when Mrs. Barrows squeezed her small frame beside him.

"So kind of you to think to tell us, Mister Benton," she said. She glanced at her husband, who nodded, late. "Would you like to come in?"

"Thank you, but no. I really should find my brother." Jon Barrows' broad hand had never relinquished hold of his door, and now he moved as if to close it. "Mister Barrows!" I blurted, surprising the three of us. After a moment, in which I gulped a lungful of air, I resumed. "I imagine that, well, me coming here this day, unannounced and all. It must be awkward, or unexpected at any rate. I am sorry for that." I felt my hat go about, by the corners. "If I may," I said. "If you both approve, that is, I should like to call on your daughter again."

With a quick step not unlike Jemima's, Mrs. Barrows stretched up and pecked my cheek. "We would love to see you back again. Would we not, Husband?"

A slow, sincere smile split that square face. His suddenly free right hand extended. "So good of you to state your intentions. And aye, you are welcome under my roof, Mister Benton."

I took his hand and met his strength with mine. "Please, sir. Call me Elisha."

BOOK II

Boston, Massachusetts - 1775
Battle of Breed's Hill

Chapter 22

The winter solstice came. It went. And though the calendar told us that the tide had turned in the perpetual battle between day and night, the snow piled higher, the northwest wind whipped beast or man who risked the out of doors, and the cold sealed all - whether it be the well with a nightly sheet of ice, or one's nostrils within mere minutes.

Yes, bone-chilling cold was our constant companion. Even seated directly before the fire, only one's front reveled in wondrous warmth whilst the icy legions retreated no farther than the back of your neck, your torso and your legs. Nevertheless, those moments of uneven bliss were treasured. While trudging to or from Grandsire's, or splitting logs, or salvaging the carefully stacked cords from the creeping banks of snow as I did this day, I envisioned gazing into the hearth's dancing glow. Such flames belonged to Father, sure, but when I had stared into them long enough, my own hopes assumed a pleasing shape therein. This coming spring I might be felling trees, on my land, and milling planks for my very own house. And before the hearth in that new home I might sit with another beside me.

I realized young Jacob stood at my elbow, and he too polite to interrupt, for I had been talking out loud. "Were you eavesdropping, little man?" I asked.

"No, Brother Elisha," he promised with a vigorous shake of his head. When I frowned at this, he added, "Well, at first I thought you spoke to me, so that is not eavesdropping; is it?"

"And what did I have to say?"

"Something about planting your own crop. Just the two of us?" His hands had come together before him, as if in prayer.

"Excellent, Jacob." I placed a hand on his shoulder. "For you see, little brother, I had been reciting nonsense to myself, and completely lost my place. Now you helped me find it."

He giggled. "Were you really talking to yourself, Brother?"

"Of course. But no more, I promise. Not whilst I have your company. Here, take these, and these." I loaded his long, thin arms with kindling. "Now, let's get ourselves inside and warm."

January was a mirror image of December, if only colder still. While unfortunate, such weather was to be expected in the midst of a Connecticut winter. Besides, we Bentons had succumbed to the seasonal routine. And even an always numbing, often boring reality yields a sense of comfortable familiarity. Mornings I spent fetching water and splitting wood sufficient to both cook the meals and heat the rooms of two households. Daniel often assisted me at these tasks whilst the children gathered eggs and milk, and saw to the feeding of the chickens, cows and horses. Of Azariah, well, we saw precious little of the impetuous one.

On this particular morning Jacob and Hannah had just staggered from where I stood in the barn, laden with plenty for Mother's table. She would be pleased, especially as Grandsire and Mother Sarah had agreed to join us once the sun had warmed the air a tad. Not since his illness had he chanced a visit. To enable their safe transit, Daniel had gone off to ensure that the night's winds had not compromised the path connecting the two houses. I, meanwhile, decided to muck out the stalls of the larger beasts. Surely the animals suffered from being cooped up inside the barn. The mare alone ventured out of doors, and she only when I traveled as far as town, or rarer still, out west to the Baker lands.

Just one week had passed since I had last journeyed to where Heman's clan resided. Their greeting was raucous and warm, though I had visited a fortnight prior. Heman and I had been able to reach on foot the acres now marked out for him - so near were they to his father's house. Together we worked to fell a half-dozen more of the trees we had selected earlier. First his ax rang out, biting into the hardwood. Then my blade struck, the blow echoing throughout the copse. Despite the chill, we had already stripped one layer of clothing before the first oak fell.

I smiled at the recollection, and leaned on my pitchfork. Smiled and laughed at the barrow full of cow flaps I had sifted from the straw. This work made similar demands on the back, but how unlike the feeling of standing there beside my friend, in that still woodland he could call his own - dreams dancing in both our heads.

Daniel eased the door open and stepped inside. "Brother," he said. "So glad I am to find you here. And alone. Might we speak again of the plans for the coming spring?"

That he would ask this of me came as no surprise. Stifling a groan, I smiled and nodded. "Let us move indoors. It's frigid as death in here."

"As you think best, Elisha. But what of Father. Might he not overhear us?"

"Ah, yes. Father." It gnawed at me. There was no denying it. Each private talk served to augment Daniel's knowledge even as it widened the gulf between Father and I. It could not be helped. If ever I was to strike out on my own, Daniel must be made ready. Besides, what was this distance between father and son compared to the deceit I practiced concerning his ignorance of Jemima?

"Elisha? Are we to go inside?"

"Why ever not?" I patted the rump of the nearest cow. "The beasts and I have seen enough of each other for one morn." Out of the barn and across the cleared space that led to the woodshed we went; circling it in turn to reach the kitchen door. "We will go up to the loft," I told him, then stepped within.

As we slipped out of our coats, the only sounds I heard were the soft voices of the children playing a game of jacks in the hall. Mother entered from the parlor. In a single look she deduced what we were about. "Your father is sleeping," she said in a near whisper. "If you keep your voices low, you can make your plans here, by the fire."

I sat, as did Daniel beside me. So, I had managed to make Mother a willing accomplice in this deceit. My brother unfolded a lone page and laid it between us on the table. "Did you draw this?" I asked. "Are these Father's fields?"

"Aye, I did." With care he smoothed the creases flat. "When last we spoke you asked me again about what crops are to be planted, and why, and in which field. I thought this sketch might aid me in answering you."

I shifted it about, that I might better appreciate its accuracy and detail. So much logic did the notes convey; and all compressed onto a single sheet. With such a tool my brother might prove himself up to the challenge of Father's doubts and mockery. He would need such a weapon to hand to Father, when we revealed that this year's planting season would be Daniel's charge and his alone.

A question or two unleashed my brother's enthusiasm and budding knowledge. I smiled occasionally to keep him talking, and because I could not help myself. His eagerness and competence were a pleasure to behold. After a time, however, a seed of guilt sunk its fibrous roots. Daniel's ascension would relieve me from the role into which, as the eldest, I had been born. Such a short time ago the prospect filled me with doubt and resentment. Now it meant my freedom. I would be free to begin a life of my own, free from Father and his suffocating expectations. Free to...

I rubbed the frown from my face, lest Daniel think it was meant for him. Yes, this other aspect served only me. Selfish it was, but fraught with challenge too. I must ask for my inheritance to see it come to pass. Demand it if necessary. And when Father had granted it to me, the very next day I would seek Jemima's hand.

"Will it serve, Elisha? Was anything left out?"

"You know it by heart, Brother. Thus my final question to you is this. Do you believe it to be a good plan? Is it the one you would employ to guide your course, and the work of many hired hands?"

"Truly it is!" he replied.

I cannot say what made me do it. For I did not know. Perhaps it was little more than guilt. Whatever the cause, I found myself alone with Father in the parlor, and he sound asleep in his chair.

Mother and the children had brought fresh baked bread up to Grandsire and Mother Sarah, whilst Daniel labored in the barn. For the life of me, I could not remember when Father and I had last been alone together in his house. One or the other of us always seemed to contrive to avoid it happening.

The fire had nearly died away whilst I'd been outside sharpening axes. Rivulets of cold streamed through the room. They chilled my stocking feet as I stood silent with my boots held in one hand. Carefully I set them down. Father did not stir.

I moved quietly as Azariah had taught me, weight rolling from heel to toe; heel to toe. Split logs lay stacked before the hearth. I selected one near as thick as my upper arm. Studying his tilted head once more, I set the wood upon the glowing embers. A second log was laid beside the first. The middle space I filled with kindling, and built upwards from there. Within a minute the reborn fire licked hungrily up through the stack. The warmth reached me, and spread to him.

Father's bible perched on his lap. I wondered for a moment what passage he had been reading. I abandoned this notion, for fear of mocking his failure to practice what he studied and preached so ardently. Who was I, after all, to cast a stone?

The quilt's many colored pattern folded down within my grasp. And so what I did, I did without thinking. I lifted it gently clear and fanned it out; it enveloped his lower body in its soft embrace.

"What are you doing here?" he demanded with wide, angry eyes. "What are you about?"

I stood abruptly. My anger shot up faster still. "Your covering!" I shot back at him. "Nothing more!" With that, I snatched up my boots and headed for the kitchen.

"Elisha," he said. His voice had been loud, but he had not shouted. "My son." This was softer still. Though I had reached the arch dividing the rooms, and did not turn, I did stop. "I thank you," Father said. This he said, and nothing more. It was enough.

I do not know if I would have turned then. If I would have shared with him what Daniel and I had worked out in stolen, secret moments. Told him, too, of my love for Jemima Barrows, and she, daughter to Jon, the cabinet maker. I don't know these things for Mother and the children burst through the front door at that very moment, bearing news of their visit and pushing a wall of cold air before them that engulfed us both. I made for the loft directly. And there I lay on my narrow bunk, as tears came into my eyes and my limbs went frigid, one by one.

Chapter 23

I rode into town not long after, in February this was, citing the need to procure nails from the smithy. I might have made a pretense of the urgency, but after my string of deceits this winter, such falsehood came easily to my tongue. There seemed now but little hope for my character. If any chance remained, it rested upon Jemima. And so visiting her was my real purpose. Perhaps the mere sight of her might cheer me...

"Oh for the sake of heaven!" I blurted out, startling a jay into a squawking departure. Again with this business of me. What of Jemima? If her need for me was but half of mine for her, well then I'd done her a disservice worse than that done by Father.

How could so many weeks have passed since I asked Mister Barrows for a word with his daughter? And how many times had I returned to their door? All these, and yet I had not confessed to her that Father knew nothing of she and I. Yet here I came seeking succor, when I should be begging forgiveness.

April hopped sideways and shook her head as if so doing might expel the taut bit. Patting her neck I draped the reins loosely over my fingers lest I yank it tight once more.

After services on Sunday next I would speak with Father. Aye, the end of this very week would see all revealed - Daniel, my inheritance, Jemima, all. And today Jemima would learn of my cowardice and deceit. My mind was quite made up. I clucked and touched the mare's sides with the heels of my boots. Her ears pricked, and she leapt forward with a powerful thrust. Great clods of earth and clouds of snow marked our wake.

By the time we trotted up into the center of town, my resolve had weakened as though susceptible to the relentless cold. April paused at the path to Jemima's door, but I urged her on. The mare served as justification for the postponement, for in truth she must be stabled during my stay.

Once more afoot, I started back along the far side of the common. As the smithy was on my way, I glanced within. One door had been left ajar, as if to advertise that he was open for business despite the weather. Titus Baker, blacksmith and relative of my friend Heman, gave me a nod. I went in. The heat of his furnace lent a toasty warmth to the interior. His hammer beat in time upon a glowing rod snared by stout tongs. He paused, examined the curvature of the piece, and set it upon the anvil once more. "Mister Benton," he said. "I have your nails just there."

"At your leisure, Titus."

With another nod, he resumed the echoing dance performed by a heavy, iron head upon yielding metal. His labors, the sounds and scents of the air, the bed of shimmering coals behind him, cast a spell on me. I could nearly forget all that I must soon do. "Eli!" I exclaimed, somehow shocked at seeing a familiar face in a familiar place.

"Elisha Benton, as I live and breathe! Greetings, friend!" We advanced and grasped hands and arms.

"What news?" I asked.

"Precious little." I knew then that his head, like Azariah's, remained stuffed full of Boston and its troubles. The images I had jammed in the recesses of my mind now flooded forth. Chronologically he recounted various correspondence received by the Captain, and shared with his uncle, the Colonel. Though letters had conveyed much throughout the winter months, clearly the punishing occupation persisted. At length he drew breath.

"Is it not possible this shared suffering may bring about a favorable outcome?" I interjected. His face sagged at once. For his sake I prayed his reaction was due to a differing opinion of matters up north, and not thwarted personal ambition.

"Do you truly believe that, Elisha?"

"So I hope, at any rate."

"Aye. Let us all hope thus. But what of you, Elisha. How fare you?"

Names swirled in my head and I owed each an explanation. "There is much that I must tend to."

"Of course, you are busy," he replied, misreading my intent. "It is the curse of first-born sons. Like you, I have much that occupies my mind."

By confiding no more than this, all that troubled me nearly tumbled out and at once. If Heman had stood there before me, it would have. As it was, an awkward, bottled up silence fell upon us. His eyes suddenly alit on the Barrows' home directly across the common. His single glance convinced me that he knew of Jemima. And if he had learned of our walks together; he who few approached with idle gossip; why then how much longer would Father remain unaware.

Shifting under the weight of my scrutiny, Eli motioned towards Titus. "As you await the smithy, I shall return at a later time."

"You will do nothing of the kind," I insisted. "I only wait to settle accounts for some nails. When you take up your business with Mister Baker, be so kind as to tell him I will return within the hour."

"I will of course. Be well, my friend."

I bid him the same, and gave a wave to Titus.

Only when keeping to a footpath that crossed the green did I realize I had failed to ask either my friend or the smithy whether my brother had been sighted of late? I kept my eyes peeled as I continued along. My thoughts operated independent of my feet, and they were in complete turmoil. Even as my frozen knuckles struck the Barrows' finely wrought door, I knew not what I would say - other than that I must speak at last.

I found the entire family hard at work. Out of courtesy I bid them continue. After seeing me seated and served with a steaming beverage they regrettably did as I had suggested. Jon Barrows bent by the south-facing window. Seated there he painstakingly sharpened one chisel blade after another. Between each we offered up bland commentary, much of which concerned the depth of snow or bite in the air. As he typically made an attentive host, I should have noted this change. My own internal ramblings left me blind.

Jemima and her mother were equally absorbed. Their candle-making occupied nearly all of the area that encompassed the hearth and table. I had folded myself as much as possible into a corner. I tried to not contemplate that Jemima's bed frame pressed against the small of my back. Much of their conversation could have passed between Hannah and Mother, with instructions and soft banter passing to and fro, much as the candle wicks that thrived on each dip within the heated vat of tallow.

"'Tis late in the season for this work," Mrs. Barrow said to me. "But when my husband was offered partial payment in a quantity of animal fat, why, we could scarce refuse."

"One can never have enough candles," I offered. Jemima glanced at me over her mother's bent back. She wrinkled her nose and smiled.

Barely did I wipe off my grin before Mister Barrows agreed with me, especially given February's long nights he pointed out. Jemima followed his remarks with a somber, significant nod, overtaken by another smile.

My heart stuck high up in my throat just then. I could not go on this way - leading them on so. Jemima studied me for a long moment, then stood. She strung her candles by their wicks over a rack set well back from the hearth. After wiping her hands on her apron she said, "Mother, may I speak with Elisha a moment?"

"Oh, yes, Daughter. We have more than enough of these at any rate."

A minute more and Jemima, her fat-splattered apron off and folded, sat beside me. Beneath the table her fire-warmed fingers found mine. "What ails, Elisha?" she whispered.

I shifted my body towards her. No half-measures would suffice at this late date. "Forgive me," I whispered in turn. She made to protest but I gave her hand a gentle squeeze. "Father, my father," I said, "he does not know. About us!" Her mouth that had begun to open in question now closed, like a vault sealed of a sudden. "I meant to," I went on. "And I shall." She turned towards her parents. I blundered ahead. "Daniel and I had to first plan, you understand, how to approach him."

"Daniel? Your brother?"

"Aye. You see, he has to assume my role. That is, if I'm to inherit..."

Her parents now stared at us. I could not read the expression on either face. Mrs. Barrows set aside a half-formed candle, and gestured to her husband. Immediately, he put down his whetstone, cleared his throat and stood. "Mister Benton," he said. "If it pleases, my wife and I would have a word with you."

At this, Jemima withdrew her hand. "Father," she said. "Do not, I beg you. Now is not the time..."

"Now is high time, daughter. We, I, have delayed speaking on this subject far too long."

I stood up, nearly upsetting the bench, and I would have too if Jemima had not remained on it.

His large, calloused hands wrestled with each other. "It is about Jemima's dowry I must speak, Mister Benton."

"Father, no..."

Mrs. Barrows shushed her daughter. Her husband carried straight on. "There is not much to speak of, and that is the simple truth. Some linens and a few pieces of furniture there'll be." He aimed his square chin at the bed behind me. For the first time I looked straight at it, and noticed that birds on the wing had been carved into the sideboard. "Cooking implements, and such," he was saying. "Not what your father might be expecting for you to have, by way of dowry. That's the point, and that is what I mean to say. And so, the mistress and I have decided, it is past time when we should have a talk, your father and I that is. So he knows, well, how things stand. Whilst all parties still have time."

This last must have hurt him dear, for he looked at Jemima seated beside me as though his heart would break, for fear of breaking hers. "Mister Barrows," I began. "Mrs. Barrows. First, before we talk of dowries, there is a thing about which I must acquaint you. I must tell you, as I've been telling Jemima..."

Jemima stood. I exhaled loudly for I could use her help in what I must say. "Mister Benton will be leaving now," she said.

Her parents ceased movement. As had I. We three had lost the power of speech as well. Without another word, Jemima took down my greatcoat and hat, and handed them to me. "Jemima?" I managed to get out. She opened the door. A frigid blast struck my face. What choice had I but to take my leave?

She followed me, but only far enough so that the wooden slats prevented her parents from hearing what might pass between us. "What kind of man are you that you would lead us on in such a way?"

"Please, Jemima." My entreaty drew such a glare of hatred that I risked not another word.

"Care you nothing for the pain of others? For a fortnight my parents have used up each evening in worry over this horrid talk of dowries. Heartsick and ashamed they are, and why, over how little they have to offer such a one as you - a Benton! You who would play them, and me, for poor and ignorant fools."

I was innocent of the motive ascribed to me, but I was guilty of so much else. The wind whipped my shirtsleeves and lifted high her hair as if it might smote me where I stood. I offered no defense.

"How could you, Elisha? How could you have?" Tears flooded her eyes, washing out the deep blue. She swiped at them quite as if they were detested near as much as I.

"Forgive me," I said, and turned away.

Chapter 24

The remainder of February passed as a blur. That fateful visit, to the home of the cabinet maker, had been my last. I cared not to see a single soul in the whole of the town. My indifference finally reached the point that Mother sent Daniel off in search of Azariah, in hopes of jolting me free of whatever ailed me. Daniel found the youth and returned forthwith. Azariah baited me often as only he could, but not even his biting, accurate jests could rouse me. His task was impossible, for I had nothing to be indignant about. Not anymore.

Oh, I had not forgotten what I had promised Daniel. The spring planting was to fall to him, regardless of whatever else came to pass. Only the context had gone, and this meant everything. I cared not for an inheritance, for what was it to me now? To Daniel I would cede my place, and come summer move on. Perhaps I would journey to the rugged, still sparsely settled lands to the west. I could never be free of myself, but I could gain separation from all those I had so disappointed.

As to Father, I could fathom not what he made of my present self. At times he railed at me, as he did that Sunday when I refused to attend services. Scandalized, we Bentons would be, he had shouted; but I cared little now for a name that marked me so. And when I declined to argue, it seemed he could not choose between raging more or speechlessness. Trapped thus, he merely sputtered, in a manner alien to us both. He sensed, too, his hold on me was forever lost, though he guessed not the reason why. From then on he watched me close, though said little, like a card player left to ponder the hand of another.

My present course was a selfish one. Of that I could hardly deny. The painful truth of it was most vivid in Mother's glances, when she thought I hadn't seen. She tried to draw me out, regardless, but I had grown skillful at putting her off. Only Grandsire could tumble down my many defenses, but the constant cold and damp had reduced him to his sick bed once more. God forgive me that one impulse of gratitude I had felt, as I knelt there beside him, and realized he could not soon question me.

Such was the sorry state of affairs that my presence and behavior had called down upon my parents' and grandparents' houses. And so it was late one morning in March when I had completed my chores and retired to the twilight solitude of Father's loft. From the stairs to the kitchen I overheard Daniel trying, in vain, to engage Azariah in a discussion of his notion for re-arranging the house garden. On occasion, Mother assisted him in this, for the garden was her province, and she had armored Daniel's plan with ideas of her own. She had no more success than he, however. Despite myself, I felt a smile crack the somber facade of my face, as I lay there in the dark. Their voices wrapped round me, quite as if we sat together, as in days gone by. If I had known then, that this was to be the very last time I was to find refuge in this place, I might have studied more closely the thick, knotted rafters joined above me, or inhaled more deeply the bound bundles of herbs suspended there, or drunk in, then savored, my family's every word.

Far below a faint knock echoed at the front door.

"Mary!" Father called from the parlor. "Wife! Will you see to the door?"

"I'll go," Azariah sang out, for our unknown visitor signaled his escape. Even his hurrying tread produced no sound. What I heard next was the door being pulled inward. "Jemima!" my brother exclaimed. "Come in, come in. You look half-froze."

Both blanket and boots I left behind. So swiftly did I descend the staircase that I caught up to Mother, Daniel and the children as we jammed within Father's parlor entry. From the opposite side came Azariah, then Jemima Barrows.

Like a fool, and a childish one at that, tears brimmed in my eyes. They blurred my vision, though I blinked them back. None noticed; no one that is but her. All stared at her, whilst she studied me - searching, it seemed.

"What in heaven's name is this about?" Father demanded of Azariah. "Who is this young woman, and what is she doing at my door, and in such a state?"

I paid no heed to Father's tone. Her disarray I could hardly deny. The wind had dislodged her mother's shawl from about her head; her sopping hair hung in dark strands. She endeavored to brush away those that clung to her face.

"Jemima brings news to us." Azariah's words were addressed to Father, but it was to me he now looked. "News of the King's troops. They are out." I tried to fathom the implications of this, but could not break from her. "Tell them, Jemima," he implored. "Tell my family what you began with me."

Father glared at the pair marooned at his parlor door. His mouth hung open the while. At last he demanded, "Speak! One of you speak up!"

Despite her utter dishevelment, Jemima's eyes were clear as she took a half-step closer to Father. "A letter arrived this very day. From the Committee of Correspondence in Boston. A regiment of the King's troops sailed to Salem, a town some 10 miles or more north of the city. They sought cannon and hidden stocks of powder. What they encountered were militia from the surrounding villages."

"Were shots fired?" Azariah demanded.

"None. An agreement was reached it is said, between the various commanders. The militia lowered a bridge, the soldiers marched across, thus setting foot on their objective, and marched away again."

"What idiocy," Azariah cried. "That is no outcome…"

"No blood was spilled," she replied. I nodded. Thus encouraged she continued. "These actions took place back in February. Then, just days ago, an event occurred more serious still. Four regiments, numbering far more than one thousand men, marched out to drums along the causeway linking Boston to the mainland. They swept through Roxbury, Brookline and all the way to the Great Bridge over the Charles." Azariah caught my eye. "Here again, the militia stopped them, but with cunning, for they had taken up the planking to prevent a crossing. The King's men had no choice but to retrace their steps. They destroyed rail fences and stone walls along their line of march."

"Then they plan to come again," Azariah said. "Do you see, Elisha? They have stripped away what cover the roadsides might offer." My brother's reasoning in this was not to be faulted, but the fences of Massachusetts towns mattered little to me at that moment. Behind me, Jacob stood tall whilst Hannah had slipped within Mother's embrace.

"The report concludes," Jemima said, "by suggesting that General Gage commands five thousand troops within the city. And that he intends to send them forth again. That these forays," and here she paused as if remembering the language she had heard, *"were meant solely to test the abilities and resolve of the Provincial forces."*

Something about Jemima's struggle to command the essence and verbiage infused the report with sudden life. I pictured Captain Willes reading it aloud in the Meeting House. The elders would have been in attendance; Eli too. And I, I should have been among them.

Father shocked us when he slammed his cane upon the floor. "Enough! I have heard enough. What is this to the Benton family? We have helped Boston, and more than most I hasten to add," This charge he leveled at me. "And who are you, Miss, to show up uninvited, and burden us with such tidings."

Azariah boldly took her hand. "Jemima is my friend, Father, and has been many a year. You know this."

"Aye, I mark her well, for I know her sort. The cabinet maker's offspring you are. Well, out with it," he demanded of her. "You darken my door for more cause than this marching about of the King's men. Which of my sons do you have designs on?" At this insult Mother hurried the children into the kitchen. "Draped you may be on Azariah's arm there, but it's my eldest you cannot take your eyes from. Do you think being crippled makes me blind?"

Azariah's jaw worked convulsively. For her part, Jemima weathered Father's verbal assault, though perhaps by clinging tightly to my brother, her eyes never leaving mine.

Daniel moved closer to Father. I stopped him with one hand. "No, Brother," I said, my voice strangely mild. "It is I who must speak." Father stood as I stepped within reach of his stout stick. "Jemima Barrows comes to us as Captain Willes' trusted scribe," I said. "As such, her news is true, and must shock all men of heart to the very core. I find it shocking, and will proceed to town and ask the Captain what he requires of me. If Jemima's visit has another purpose, it is likely a concern over what this news might mean for my brother, her lifelong friend. Yes, of this I'm certain. I am much less sure, but I do fervently hope, that her concern extends to me."

"To you? What hold can such a one have on you?"

My gaze had shifted from him to her and back again as I spoke. It now settled upon Jemima Barrows. "If I possessed courage, even a fraction of what I ought, she might this day stand beside me as my betrothed."

Mother gasped. She stood in the parlor entry, tears flooding her eyes. "My son! At last!"

I smiled quickly for her, and turned back towards Jemima. I never saw Father's cane coming. Someone cried out, Daniel, or Azariah, or both. Then the blow struck. It connected with my head and thankfully my shoulder too. It staggered, but failed to drop me where I stood. I saw the cane rise again, and wrenched it from Father's hand. In an instant my brothers set upon him, driving him onto his chair and pinning his arms. Screams split the air – Mother's or Jemima's I could not tell. In the other room Hannah was crying.

"Deceiver!" Father spat. "Did you bed the wench? Is that what this is about? Is she with child?" He seemed oblivious to the grunting, sweating efforts of my brothers who struggled to contain his rage. Oblivious, too, to the women who stared at him in horror, their arms now entwined. "Sleeping under my roof all the while. Eating my bread..." Spit flung off his lips at each utterance. "Did you know, wife?" he demanded of Mother.

A full minute more it took to vent the vast vat of bile that boiled within him. It seemed an age. The end of it saw my senses restored to me, and Father panting with exhaustion. Trapped now between my brothers, Father glared at me. "Not another night; not one more; will you spend beneath my roof."

"No, Daniel!" Mother shouted, her voice strong. "I will not have it. Elisha is my child too and I won't..." the rest of it died within the sleeve of my shirt. She lifted her head only to glimpse the blood that coursed warm along my cheek. "My son! You bleed!"

"It comes to nothing, Mother. I assure you." She wiped at it a moment with her fingers, and then hurried off for something, I imagined, to mop it with. Jemima followed suit.

"Release him," I said to my brothers. They hesitated. "Daniel. Azariah." With that they stepped back, though watchful they remained. Father budged not from the awkward posture they'd left him in. "You are correct in one aspect, Father. I did deceive you, though I did not set out with that end in mind. I wanted to prepare things, as always I have done, so as to please you. But there is no pleasing one such as you. Not as regards the harvest, nor the planting, which Daniel is to oversee come spring."

Mother and Jemima returned. One held a dripping cloth; the other a steaming pot. I bid them pause a moment more. "What became of you, Father? You who taught me the plough and the scythe? The ways of right and wrong. And what of me who should have come to you. Should have asked your blessing, of she whose hand I sought. What's become of me?" Mother shook her head no, but I went on. "I will leave, Father. Because you ask me to, and because I would have it so."

I went to Mother and Jemima. They could not return my embrace, their hands being full. This was somehow just. I turned to my brothers. "Azariah. Though I journey to town, it is more seemly that I do so alone. Will you, therefore, as her friend, see Jemima safely to her parents' home? And only once she has warmed herself?" He nodded. "Well then, Daniel, the farm is yours to manage. I know you will make our elders proud." I discovered that I still clutched Father's cane. "Despite the use you found for this," I said to him, "you will have need of it." With that I rested the bloodied branch against his chair. He turned his head such that he could not lay eyes upon it.

In the kitchen Hannah huddled close to Jacob. I kissed their heads and hugged each in turn. "All will be well," I promised, then retrieved both my boots and greatcoat. No one spoke and I dared not risk my own voice as I strode between the men and women most dear to me.

Neither woman would allow me to leave so easily. Both followed me outside. Jemima spoke first. "Elisha. I will return home with Azariah, if I have your promise. That you call on my parents at our home."

I breathed more freely than I had in a fortnight. "It would be my pleasure, Miss Barrows."

Mother touched Jemima's arm before approaching me. In her hand she still held the cloth, now somewhat stiff from the cold. She tried, once or twice, to clean my cheek. "I will speak to him," she said. I shook my head only to have her fingers press against my lips. "You do what you will," she insisted, "and let me do what I must. Now, I too, will have your promise. You will stay with your Grandsire this night and all those to come, until this is resolved. No, I will broach no argument. I do not insist on a particular resolution; only that you wait until such time. Good. Now then. Mother Sarah tells me your Grandsire sleeps in his own bed once more, so the small bedroom off the kitchen awaits your return. Can I tell them it will be so?"

"Aye, Mother. This I can promise you."

My smile earned her kiss. Taking Jemima's arm in hers, she said, "I am proud of you, my son, as ever I was."

With that I took my leave and turned towards town and Captain Willes.

Chapter 25

To walk into town was a conscious choice. I did so only upon setting eyes on the mare, and realizing that she may not belong to me - despite my having contributed to her original purchase and nearly all of her upkeep since. I whirled around fast but she had caught my scent. Her whinnies pursued me from within the barn. My hurried steps from Father's homestead soon had me turning left onto the main road. Perhaps it was more fitting I soon thought, that when I should appear at the Barrows' door, that it be by foot.

The freezing rain had stopped, having darkened every tree and branch, and turned the snow to slush. The going would be muddy, but this changeable weather promised that spring might soon arrive. My heart dropped. Spring... The renewal and promise of the season to come had always made of it my favorite. Not so this new month and year – April 1775.

The farm was Daniel's responsibility now. 'Tis sure he had earned it. I recalled his eagerness in outlining his planting scheme; the steadfastness of his step when he had moved towards Father. Father! No, of him I could not let myself think. Not anymore; not this day at any rate.

Here and there buds swelled the tips of otherwise barren shrubs adorning the forest edge. Would I still be here when they opened?

Or would the next ill tidings from Boston draw me north before then? How that thousand strong column must have shocked the good folk of Massachusetts. Surely it had smothered the length and breadth of that narrow causeway linking occupied city to open countryside.

I paused alongside the marsh that I had known as boy and man. The thickets along its reedy border were alive with the quick movements and competing notes of songbirds. How far would such a column of soldiers extend in this place? One thousand infantry; 2,000 booted feet, pounding out a cadence in time with the drums. Such a demon might rear its head at our common, whilst its tail encircled Benton lands and lives. The horror of it drove me up the rise and into town.

First the home of the Barrows must be passed, just off to my left. Part of me wished to drive on, as might a horse with blinders. That would not do. Jemima's arrival at Father's door had granted me another chance. I would not squander it by concealing my shame. Boldly I glanced sideways. Jon Barrow's stocky outline in the front window tested my resolve at once. He observed me close. He did not lift a hand in friendship, nor recognition even. I carried on to the Meeting House and Captain Willes, knowing with every step that surely I would be made to suffer upon my return. The knowledge of it failed to alter my intent.

A few inhabitants passed to and fro on the main street. I exchanged polite greetings but felt their eyes upon my back. Walking the public way in a maid's company would hardly have earned me these stares. Subsequently avoiding her door and then skipping services likely had. I strode up the building's wide steps. One couldn't help but note that the double doors had been left ajar, and this despite the lingering chill in the air.

Only two souls occupied the interior: Captain Willes and Lieutenant Jonathan Parker. Some of the elders' chairs that typically stood along the wall opposite our family box had been taken down and grouped in a semi-circle. An impromptu meeting most-like, and those who had sat here had dispersed of a sudden.

"Ah, Corporal Benton! I've wondered what's become of you." Captain Willes followed my every move as I approached. "You remember Lieutenant Parker, of course."

"Most certainly, sir. How do you do, Lieutenant."

The slender, well dressed officer bowed. Upon rising he appeared to study me as intently as did the Captain. "Your commander has filled me in," he said. "On your successful relief of Boston. And of more recent events."

"I see," was all I could think to reply, as I searched the men's face for clues.

The Captain revealed nothing. "Mister Benton," he said, in his formal, public voice. "May I understand from your presence here that you are made aware of the messages we received today?"

"I am, sir. Jemima Barrows brought them to my father's home. Azariah will be here directly. We come to learn what is to be done."

The Captain gave a knowing nod to the Lieutenant, as if to say that a lingering question had been answered. I could only assume it dealt with me; my character perchance. "Miss Barrows made such a warm appeal for permission to seek you out that I could hardly refuse her," Captain Willes said. "And despite the fact both Corporal Chapman and Heman Baker had volunteered to ride to your farm. You are much sought after, despite how little we have seen of you of late."

"So it would appear," the Lieutenant agreed.

"Gentlemen, perhaps an explanation would be best." I took a deep breath, prepared to state my private affairs in the briefest possible manner, and reassure them of my loyalty to our common cause.

Captain Willes cleared his throat most emphatically. "Thank you, Elisha, but neither the Lieutenant nor I think that necessary. We know you. I, for one, know all that I must. I've but one question. Should it prove expedient for our company to hasten back to Boston, and under arms, will you be among our number?"

"You have my word on it."

"Good, good. That's settled then. Well, Lieutenant. You have your orders. I shall expect you to report back by week's end, or to be in receipt of your sealed message before that time."

"And you will have either me or it, sir. Corporal Benton." He bowed. And with that he hastened away.

"A fine, young officer, would you say," Captain Willes observed. "He expects to contribute as much as a score of men to our company. The village of Coventry being too small to muster a trainband of its own you see."

The numbers I certainly understood, but not why our company should be augmented so. As if reading my mind he drew a folded sheet from the pocket of his vest. "Allow me to read this out to you. I'm certain it will resolve the confusion you must suffer. From the Provincial Congress this is. It is a standing order to all Massachusetts militias, and as I told our community's leaders, we in Connecticut intend to honor it. So says the governor himself. Allow me to read the passage.

> *'Whenever the army under command of General Gage shall march out of Boston, it ought to be deemed a design to carry into execution by force the late acts of Parliament, which ought to be opposed by the military force of the Province.'*

He refolded the note. "One could hardly demand more clarity of purpose than that," he said.

"Captain. That amounts to, to what; a declaration of war? And civil war no less?"

"Not so rash as that. No, it is more a statement that free men, if threatened, will defend their freedoms. Even if in the unfortunate and perverse instance that the threat looms from the very Parliament that should afford those subjects its protection."

"And I agree with its language!" Azariah declared from the entry. "Wholeheartedly." He advanced on us. "Captain. Does this mean we're to form a minuteman detachment at last?"

"You will be happy to learn, Azariah Benton, that we will be building up a store of provisions that will enable the entire company to move within a day of receipt of an alarm. There will be foodstuffs, clothing and, of course, the powder and flints we have already provided for."

Azariah's jaw twitched as he contemplated this development. I spoke up. "My brother is not typically fond of the intricacies of packing smoked-meats, flour and cheese, Captain, but in this instance he might relish the notion of playing a part. Knowing full well that the readier the supplies, the faster we might march."

The coupling of speed with marching had the desired effect. Azariah smiled. "Aye, sir. I am prepared this instant to do as you and Elisha suggest. When might I start? What would you have me do?" The Captain obliged him with the particulars. My brother whirled about, but paused at the last. "Elisha. Shall I linger awhile? Might you wish a word with me, Brother, about...?"

"Thank you, Azariah. Later I would, yes. I would treasure it." He nodded, and left.

"He is a likable lad, your brother," Captain Willes said. "A tad headstrong at times, but likable nonetheless."

"He is all that," I agreed, staring at the very air into which he had vanished. I turned. "What of my orders, Captain?"

"I intend drilling the men right outside. Tomorrow morning this will be, for word will have circulated by then. I have a list for you. Here it is. Noah Grant and half a dozen others to the southwest. If you can contact them, and return on the morrow with them – the very moment critical chores are seen to."

"Very well, sir. Will there be anything more?"

He smiled. "If you were to offer a freshly slaughtered lamb, or a hindquarter of smoked meat, I am sure it would be eagerly accepted by those charged with provisioning us." My expression must have been transparent. "Forgive me," he added immediately. "The Bentons have given so much. It was impertinent in me to presume that..."

"Sir, please. It is not that. It is just, well, as it stands, with me and my family just now. Truth is, I cannot speak for them."

"I do apologize, Elisha. It was certainly not my intent to interfere. Or cause you discomfort in a family matter."

"You are too kind, Captain. Long have you known my family. It comes as no surprise to you, I'm sure, that there are, well, sensitive matters between my father and I."

He shifted his weight, quite as much as I longed to. "I have known the Bentons for as far back as you state, Elisha. Generations of your family I am acquainted with, to varying degrees; your Uncle William, for instance, with whom I served." He paused at the remembrance. "Suffice to say, I believe I understand the general situation full well. Might I be of some service in this regard? A private audience with either your father or grandfather? I would be happy to speak with either or both on your behalf."

His look probed deeper than I had expected. I swallowed hard. "The sad truth is that I did not act as a son should, and so played a part in our descent to the current state of affairs. Though I most sincerely thank you, sir, for your kindly offer. Will that be all, Captain?"

"It will Corporal." I left him then. He called out before I reached the door. "Elisha. I am pleased that you have come back to us. Quite pleased."

Chapter 26

As I made my way past the house fronts, I noted the urgency in the movements of my neighbors that I had not grasped on my way to meet Captain Willes. So consumed had I been with my own troubles that I had failed to sense the prevailing mood. Certainly their hurried steps betrayed no panic. In the eyes of more than one, however, I thought I detected a hint of fear. I missed the mare just then, for with a shake of her mane she could confirm my mere speculations.

She would certainly toss her head, and flare her nostrils too, at the scent I must exude; standing now before Jon Barrows' door. Once again I had been detected coming up the walk. And for a second time this day I was to be ignored. There could be no talk of roads or weather. I must address this from the outset. Even as my knuckles grazed the wood it occurred to me - that with Azariah in town, Jemima had come home.

The door opened. Mister Barrows barred the entrance. His expression was set, and it bore no welcome. "Mister Benton."

"Good day, sir." Peering over his shoulder, and it as squared off as his head, I glimpsed Jemima seated before the fire. Her mother dabbed at her still damp hair with a cloth.

"What brings you to my door?" he interrogated.

That he would make such a demand of me, and in such a tone, brought a reflexive surge of heat welling up inside my chest. Knowing that it stemmed from an arrogance I could no longer afford, and now detested, I choked it down.

"I have come to apologize, sir. To you, to Mrs. Barrows and to Miss Jemima."

The only move he made was a turn of his head. Whatever look that passed between the master of this house and his womenfolk was unseen by me. The result was that he sighed, and stepped back that I might enter.

As I did so, my body tensed at the possibility that, like Father had, he might strike me. He did not. I exhaled quietly as possible and took the seat pointed out to me. I had unbuttoned my greatcoat in the street, but had not removed it. As no one bid me do so now, I sat directly opposite the fire, encased in heavy wool, sweat trickling beneath my arms. Jemima had not once raised her eyes. Her parents more than made up for this by studying me the while. No one had said a word since I entered. I need not have worried about being delayed by civility for I was to receive none. Resentment I vanquished, but such treatment most certainly induced embarrassment; and more sweat. I stood, but kept my coat for fear of taking too great a liberty.

"Sir. Madam. I am confident that Jemima, pardon, that Miss Barrows, has, by this time, acquainted you with, with my earlier failure to have informed my father of my intentions. That is, as concerns your daughter." Jemima offered me not even the support that a single glance might provide. Nor did her mother's face soften in the least, though she had always looked kindly on me before. Her father's expression kept me in mortal fear. I was left with nowhere to go but forward. "This is no longer the case. Father is aware, and fully. But the unhappy consequence is that I am to have no inheritance." This announcement, though it caused me pain, produced no more effect on them than what I had related previously. Despite

Jemima's current silence she must have spoken to them a good deal, and hastily too, since her return from Father's house.

"I forget myself," I blurted out. "Before I speak of inheritance, or a renewal of intentions, if that notion is not abhorrent to you, I must offer my apology. And I do. I apologize most sincerely for allowing you to believe, for behaving as if a courtship existed, when my father was not informed. You see, I thought he would, approve, in time. Once certain other matters had been resolved. Matters that..."

I stopped then. Not because I was breathless although I was. It had more to do with a note of disgust creeping into Jon Barrows' face, and a slumping of Jemima's shoulders quite as if my words were disappointing her, and deeply.

"Mister Barrows," I tried anew. "When first I came to your door, I appeared as Mister Benton, first-born son of Daniel. As such, my courtship was false, for I lacked my father's blessing. I stand here now as mere Elisha. I am poorer, yet richer too. No longer can I offer your daughter that which as a Benton I might have. But unencumbered as I now am, I can freely state that I do love Jemima and seek your permission to court her." My heart and breathing raced. Jemima's moist blue eyes upon me were all that kept the words flowing. "I possess many skills acquired through years of hard work. I am certain that in time I will acquire both land and house sufficient to keep her in a type of comfort that would not displease you. If she will, at the proper time that is, have me."

"I will. I mean I would," Jemima said. She had stood, spilling the cloth to her feet. A smile spread on her mother's face as she pulled her daughter close.

It had more to do with the evident joy and relief on the women's faces, I'm convinced, than any eloquence on my part, but Jon Barrows did then extend his hand. I strained to meet the pressure there in his grip. "I'd not wish to see her disappointed once again," he said.

"I will not be the cause of it, I assure you."

"Very well. In that case, Elisha, yes, you may court my daughter."

If I thought my apology would see an end of it, I was sorely mistaken. With but a cup of coffee and a few civil exchanges, I was ushered out the door. The excuse put forth was that traipsing about the countryside had done Jemima in, but the color in her cheek put the lie to that. She longed, it appeared to me, for a moment in private near as much as me, but in this we were to be disappointed. So outside I found myself, with no clear destination in mind.

Unlike every soul walking by bent on some errand or other, I had no roof for the night - not one at least I could call my own. I begrudged them not their stolen glances. This was the reality I had fashioned for myself. It was also up to me to do something about it.

Entering the tavern, I removed my hat. I stood quite still so that those at both bar and tables could have a good look. They nodded and turned away, though those in the company of others likely also bent their conversation to my dimmed prospects. With a tankard of hard cider in hand I made my way to one who alone had not taken note of my arrival. With his back to both me and the door, he had continued to scratch away at some document or other.

Seeing me step beside him, Eli Chapman set down the quill and stood at once. "Elisha! A good day to you, my friend. Here, sit! Join me." He blew on the sheet upon which numbers ran in columns and rows. "That will keep," he said. "How have you fared? It has been what, weeks?"

"A fortnight and more, no doubt. I have been well, all things considered."

"Ah, yes." He dragged his chair so that it butted up against mine. "And are, things as you call them, are they set to right?"

His earnest, open expression put me in mind of Daniel for a moment. It was enough. "Let us speak plain," I confided. "It was affairs of the heart that kept me away."

He leaned in close. "Relieved I am to hear it. I had grown concerned, what with planting season so near at hand and there had been no sign of you. Uncle worried, too, but likely only with the prospect of forfeiting your rental of our oxen." He grinned somewhat sheepishly at this confidence. My only reaction was to wonder whether I should remind Daniel to meet my friend forthwith. "For my part," Eli said, "I could only think on how you looked when I saw you last. At the smithy, you'll remember. I wasn't quite sure what to think, though rumors had circulated for some time." He laughed, then whispered. "I must have been the last in town to know the truth of it. Only at the service, when all saw you absent, did I finally see the way of it."

"See what, Eli?"

"Well the entire congregation casting those looks of theirs. First at your family, and then towards the Barrows in the rear. Surely I was the last to appreciate that your father had forbid you to return until you ceased your pursuit of Jemima." I sat back. So, I had managed to shame not only myself, but both our families as well; and remain ignorant in the bargain. "Seeing you here," Eli went on, "I must assume the fires have cooled as regards her, despite her evident attractions. Your father has, I take it, made you see the folly of such a mismatched entanglement. And now, you are free to come and go as once you did." He clicked his glass against mine. "A toast! To the tribulations of first-born sons. And to the women we may not pursue, whatever our hearts might wish, and all for the sake of the ladies chosen by our families."

I never did raise my tankard. Seeing this, and comprehending something about my expression at last, Eli lowered his glass. "What have I said?" he asked. "What have I done?"

"I seek the hand of Jemima Barrows still. For this Father has disowned me."

"Oh good God! Elisha. Please forgive me. I am a dolt. It is inexcusable..."

"Listen," I said. "There is a favor I would ask of you."

"Anything! Yes, of course, it is agreeable to me whatever it is."

"Allow me to finish, Eli. I do not ask it in the belief I've ensnared you in my debt. Quite the reverse. If you grant it I will be in yours." He nodded vigorously but he had regained sufficient control to keep his peace. "Now then," I continued. "As you say the time soon comes when all the landowners will seek to rent your oxen." Again, the nods. "And is it not true that many also seek experienced hands, at one and the same time."

"They do, most do. Often do they complain to me of the lack of steady men."

"Then would it be too much to ask if you gave out my name? If in discussion these farmers conveyed a need."

He sat back suddenly, as if I'd whacked him with my hat. "You would have me give out your name, Elisha? As hired help?"

"Just so," I replied, with as much assurance as I could muster, which was not great given the shame his shock inflamed within me. In his eyes I saw clear what favor I asked - that I be rented, alongside Ben, his ox.

"Of course I would." He leaned forward and patted my hand. Then stopped abruptly once I stiffened at the gesture. "I will, Elisha. If that is your wish."

I stood. "Thank you, Eli. I regard it as a kindness."

"I will see you on the green tomorrow, will I not?" he asked. "For the drilling?" At my nod he smiled. "A fine pair of corporals we shall make, eh?" I did my best to return the smile. Though he seemed intent on saying more, I left, for his embarrassment surely made it awkward for him, and my bitterness and shame prevented me listening further.

Chapter 27

I nearly reversed course on the tavern steps, driven by a sudden bout of loneliness to reclaim my seat beside Eli. Instead I forced my feet to find the road. Estrangement from former companions would be my lot; for the foreseeable future at any rate. And when fortunate to be in the company of friends, I must learn to bear their awkwardness in my presence. How else would I ever learn to cope with the harsh judgments of mere acquaintances?

Stopping, I breathed deep of the air. A hint of spring there was, in the eddying pools that carried scents of damp earth, freshly emerging from a blanket of snow. On the far side of the green I spotted Azariah. We should speak of what transpired, but at present he hurried along in the company of another. I was shocked to realize that the squat fellow at his side was none other than the butcher. Never in life had I seen the two together, yet now they carried on a conversation so animated that neither had eyes for me. Such unlikely comrades were already being joined by these martial preparations.

I went about in a circle, conscious at the end of it that my actions were drawing stares. I needed a direction. "Southwest," I said aloud, and set out to inform the men who would comprise my squad. And after that, to Grandsire's; and with his health recovered, I could expect a good deal of scrutiny for certain sure.

Each man, and his family too, had been stunned by the news I conveyed at their door. In each re-telling, I eventually found both composure and acceptance that supplanted the sense of impending doom I had first felt. Salem and Brookline were, after all, Massachusetts towns, and within easy hail of Boston and the King's troops. No such danger existed in far-off Connecticut, and was unlikely to ever extend so far. Having dispensed so handily with the threat to the homes and hearths of both family and friends, I made my way towards Grandsire's, footsore and chilled, but calm, as the sun slipped behind the western hills. Along the lane I passed Father's house with quickened steps and a lingering look.

A few minutes on and a glow from Grandsire's front windows guided me, for dusk succumbed quick to night. I paused to consider what he might ask, and how best to respond. It was easier to speculate on possibilities in Boston than to relate the argument with Father. In this vein, not even the imperative to respond to a provincial alarm need lead to upset. In the retelling this could be fashioned to conjure nothing worse than another hike to Boston. Not a single ball had been discharged after all, per any of these reports. With this comforting thought foremost in my mind, I knocked on my grandfather's door.

"Elisha! Dear boy," Mother Sarah announced, wrapping me in more than her customary exuberance. "You've no need to knock to enter here!" She hauled me not into Grandsire's parlor where I glimpsed his empty chair, but rather into the hall where he sat; his back to the fire and a quilt upon his lap. The table had been set, and for three. Grandsire's smile conveyed nearly as much as his wife, who happily described holding supper for me till the very last, and expressed concern as to where I'd spent the afternoon and evening too.

I did my level best to acquaint them both with the messages from Boston, and my travels since. I pointedly made no mention of the morning altercation with Father, and for all her talk, Mother Sarah dropped not a hint she'd learned of it. Throughout these exchanges, and the serving out of the stew and bread, Grandsire said not a word. His gaze, however, had hardly settled on a thing other than my face.

"How do you fare, Grandsire?" I asked, at a moment when Mother Sarah busied herself in the adjacent kitchen.

He held his broad, thin hands apart and above his lap covering, as if to say, 'as you behold me'. His honest and silent acceptance of his frailty, both too sudden and foreboding, touched me to the quick. "I might ask the same of you, My Boy," he said.

So he did know. He must. "Am I welcome here?" I asked. "Truly? After what I have done."

His lower lip quivered. That familiar hand settled, light now as a bird, upon my knee. I covered it with my own as if I might hold onto it, and him, forever. Mother Sarah bustled about us, refilling our bowls. She touched each of us on the shoulder in turn, but said nothing that might break the spell. After a decent interval, she inquired as to the state of the roads. Such mundane topics occupied us through the remainder of the meal. After I had thanked her for it, and she had refused my offer to help her clear the table, Grandsire caught my eye once more.

"And so, My Boy, you intend going?"

I knew he referred to the occasion of an alarm. "My duty requires it."

"With you it is far more than that," he replied. "So it was with William, my son. It will be as it must be. I will not seek to change your mind in this." We spoke then of other matters, though nothing of real import. Within the hour Mother Sarah and I assisted him to bed.

When she went off for his chamber pot, he took my hand. "Will I see you come morning?" he asked.

"I aim to rise before dawn. I will tend to a few chores I have promised Mother Sarah, then straightway to town for the drilling."

"Of course. Well, then, best I speak now of it..."

I knew he meant to have his say regarding Father. A revulsion seized me so strong that I could not bear to hear my father's name, whatever the attending advice might be. "Is it not best, Grandsire, that you get your rest? After all, I shall return before sundown..."

He gave my hand just enough of a squeeze that I understood he meant to continue. "I am acquainted with all," he said, "as I am certain you surely realize. You had a part in this, I am led to understand." To this I dropped my eyes. "Yes, and I see that you are sorry for it. Whilst I condone your behavior not, I..."

"Grandsire! I did deceive Father, yet this was not my intent. You must believe me."

"Sssh, now. Enough of that. A man may find fault in another's action, but no more than that. Your heart, My Boy, I have never questioned. I never will." The pat, pat of his feathery hand quieted me. "It is your father's role in this, this thing that threatens to tear my family apart that I find abhorrent. I pray that I might forgive him, for despite what he has done, it is not my place to judge. That is God's province, and his alone." Grandsire's eyes drifted, for a moment, to the still swollen gash at my hairline. I shifted the angle of my head as to conceal it from him.

"My Boy. There is a parcel of land that you and I have often walked together. In happier times." I knew at once the place, but not why it would come now to his mind. "It is modest in acres," he continued, "but happily situated to the southeast. The soil is good and unspoiled, other than its present use as orchard. It even boasts a stream, narrow and shallow 'tis true, but the water runs clear. You know the one I mean."

"I know it well, Grandsire, yes, but why concern ourselves with..."

"I would that it be yours."

"No! You do not understand, Grandsire. Father intends to withhold anything that might have formed an inheritance for me. Land, coin, even my horse I fear is no longer mine!" I heard Mother Sarah behind me, and then the swish of her skirts as she went away.

"Elisha. Listen to me. This piece is of my own land. I intend that it be held for you and no other purpose. Before I gift it to you, I also mean to speak to my son. I will give him every opportunity to relent in his decision as regards your fortune. If he refuses, this land I describe will pass to you, and at once. Do you understand me now? This is my fervent wish and I will have it so."

"I do not deserve it," I whispered. "I do not deserve you."

That night I slept as I had not in weeks. The crow of the cock it took to rouse me. I woke with a sense of relief and purpose, and cared little for how my long limbs ached from the cramped quarters. With difficulty I sat upright within that small closet of a room off Grandsire's kitchen. Mother Sarah already knelt at the hearth, setting dry sticks within it in such a way as to cause no sound. What a debt I owed her and him both. One such that I could never hope to repay. "Leave that, I beg you," I whispered. "I am up. In a thrice I will have such a fire for you. Why," I said, jamming my feet into my boots, "it will fairly roar at your command." Within a minute I had her laughing so, that I had to help her find her feet.

I had gathered up a good many men of my detachment by stopping at their homes along the road. We walked into town together, burdened with rucksacks. These had been stuffed with whatever each man intended to take on a march, for that was what the Captain had commanded. Each also carried his musket, for as farmers one was ill-disposed indeed to be without a modern firearm. I hefted mine with the knowledge that as my Uncle William's, given me by Grandsire, I could not be asked to relinquish it.

Nearly three score of our company already milled about the common by the time we arrived. They were similarly burdened, though many of the townsmen toted lesser weapons, such as fowling pieces or near ancient, heavy blunderbusses. Two men off to one side had stuffed their empty hands far down in their pockets. The Captain, on behalf of the elders, would have to provide weapons for them and they appeared to feel the obligation most keen.

Heman made a straight line towards me. We shook hands warmly. His lips worked as if containing a mouthful of tidings and inquiries, but he managed to simply smile. Likewise, there were so many things I ought to tell him, and so much I wished to learn about the progress of his lands. "I have been remiss," I said. "In not returning."

"Think nothing of it, my friend. I am made aware how engaged, how busy that is, you have been." His freckles shown in his sudden embarrassment. He looked towards a mutual acquaintance. So it's Eli who's his likely source of information. "I do bear glad tidings," Heman said. "Corporal Chapman yonder has given his permission for me to join your band of fellows. If you'll have me that is."

"I would be honored." I shook his hand once more. "Of course, you will have to tolerate my little brother." I said this last loud enough for Azariah to hear me as he approached.

"Do my ears ring with more deserved flattery?" he asked, stepping directly between us. We each cuffed him from opposite sides. He made no move to protect his midsection. Instead, he looked directly at the egg-sized protrusion on my scalp. Heman followed his gaze, then looked away. "As shocked as I was at the blow, Brother," Azariah declared, "the more amazed was I that you refused to return it." Heman continued to stare at anything other than me or my head. In disbelief Azariah added, "He is your closest friend, yet he does not know?"

Even with the luxury of time, I was hardly likely to boast of being set about the skull by my own father; though if I were so disposed, it would be my oldest friend to whom I would confide such an affair. "Your prompt arrival, Brother," I chose to reply, "precluded saying much more than good day to you, sir."

The unintended formality of my tone elicited a guffaw from Azariah that at once caused Heman to join in. And so I simply turned away until they saw fit to regain whatever composure they may. That simple wheel to my left brought Jemima clearly into focus. She stood at the edge of a crowd, for the entire population seemed assembled with the same expectant pulse as the company. Her parents flanked her. All three stared in our direction.

Clearing my throat, I marched away from my companions, and straight towards the threesome. The closer I came, the nearer her father seemed to crowd her. The closer I came, the more eyes I felt following my progress. I stopped before the Barrows. My hat came off my head and tucked neatly beneath my elbow in one sweeping gesture. "Mister Barrows. Mrs. Barrows. Miss Jemima." Even as her parents returned my salutation, I reached for her hand. Jemima blushed beneath her cap, and lifted her limb to me as she had that day along the road. And as I had then, the two of us alone, I kissed the back of her hand. Her lips moved but no sound came forth. They moved again and no one saw but me. And this time I realized that she had mouthed my name. My own blush, if I could but have seen it, must surely have rivaled her own.

The beating of the drum sent feet scurrying from every corner of the green. Mine likewise obeyed as they must. "Your servant, sir," I called over my shoulder to her father by way of parting, and rushed to my fellows. My heart hammered so in my chest that I could scarcely breathe. If I was to die I thought, let it be from joy such as this.

"Well, Brother," Azariah proclaimed, "there can be none in the town who now doubt your intentions."

I glanced about and found innumerable eyes following me. Heman merely beamed. I took each of my companions by the elbow and directed them to where the company had begun to assemble. "Strange it is for you of all people, Azariah, to chastise me over a display of honest emotion."

"Oh, trust me, Brother," he countered, as I hurried him along, "I find no fault whatsoever in Jemima becoming soon my sister. Even if it must therefore bring happiness to you."

They both enjoyed themselves at this turn of phrase that managed to insult me whilst complimenting my Jemima. "My Jemima," I murmured aloud, just before Captain Willes' voice commanded our silence.

Chapter 28

We then embarked upon what the Captain termed a good stretch of the legs, which consisted of our company marching to the Benton farm and a few miles farther to the southwest. This brought us to the intersection with Boston Post Road, which carried the mails, freight, and travelers of all descriptions and means from the city bearing its name to Hartford, as well as to New York if one remained on it. Here at the junction he stopped us, and allowed us to take our ease.

The crossroad also marked the northern edge of Coventry, of which village Lieutenant Parker and his group were residents. He and the Captain now conferred off to the side for a few minutes. The Lieutenant and his contingent of a dozen men, not quite the score he had hoped, but a significant turnout just the same, then left us for their homes and fields. Our four score shouted 'Huzzah!' at them, and twice again to see them off. They returned the compliment, doing their best to match the happy bellow from our 80 throats.

"So many fine acquaintances," Noah Whipple said. "All to be met on the same day." Our fifer was among the youngest of our company, and nearly as thin as the musical instrument he played. He glanced about now in hopes of spotting someone among us who might agree with him.

"A fine lot of men, indeed," Noah Grant replied with charity and sincerity. Heman nodded as he stuffed tobacco into his pipe.

"And well led," Eli Chapman made note. He had worked his way from the head of the column and now lingered on the edge of my group. As he glanced at me, I made a polite bow. I regretted that our discussion in the tavern had caused a slight rift in our relationship. However, his awkwardness concerning this matter, and my lingering resentment about his inferences towards Jemima, prevented an easy means of healing it.

"The First Corporal deigns to offer a compliment," Azariah said in a whisper not near low enough. "Perchance he hunts one in return. Some recognition of his recent elevation in rank I'd imagine." Eli looked away and then turned away. "Ah, there he goes. Back to the head of the column. To lead!"

I shook my head at my brother who, in what constituted an apology from him, gave a shrug of his shoulders. The damage had been done, however, for a few barely stifled laughs pursued Eli in retreat. I felt badly that Azariah had spoken, especially since my stiffness towards Mister Chapman had likely contributed to the heedless barb. However, I could not help but notice the polished, London-made fowler that the First Corporal carried. A graceful and lightweight piece such as that was worth twice what I was fortunate to carry, and far more than that of some others. "All right then," I said to one and all. "Best tighten the straps of your packs. Seems we're to be off once more."

The men did as suggested and a minute's duration witnessed us form up in ranks of four abreast. With an about face, the road before us led home, to Tolland. The Captain was alone in front now that the Lieutenant had departed. Our fifer and a drummer walked just behind! But unlike the heralded onset of our march, the return was to be silent. Eli came next in the column. As First Corporal, he and his men had precedence in the line of march. I followed with my men. Sergeant Comfort Carpenter outranked both Eli and myself, but he came last for he commanded the rear guard and what would constitute our baggage train should a real alarm reach as far as Connecticut.

All aspects of the homeward journey unfolded with less formality. The Captain even agreed to a suggestion that allowed men to peel away so that they might aid their families' late-day chores. And so it was as a diminished command, in numbers though not spirit, that we skirted the marsh now speared with the shadows of trees that dominated the higher ground. Ranks had dissolved into knots of comrades tied close by friendship or kinship. Azariah breezed along beside me as though we had just set out moments earlier. For my part I minded the unaccustomed weight of the musket far more than the miles covered or the bite of the pack's straps. My brother and I had agreed to continue into town, though for different reasons.

"So what was the point of all this?" Heman asked. "Slog one way on muddy roads, only to slog back again."

"I could hazard a few reasons," I replied. "If Mister Parker and the Coventry gentlemen are to be counted among our company, the Captain and he likely thought to throw us together."

"A sort of courtship, you mean?" Heman winked for Azariah and inclined his head.

Always rising to such bait, my brother quickly added, "And if any would know of the etiquette required, it would be Elisha."

They shared a laugh. Then Heman asked, "Why this road, in particular?"

"Oh wise one..." Azariah added.

A sudden thought erased my smile despite all their jests and making of faces. "Perhaps so no man among us will panic, should we take to this way in earnest." Though I had not meant to do so, my remark quieted ourselves and those within hearing. And so we remained until we reached the green.

The moment Captain Willes had finished dismissing us, Azariah hustled off. I could only assume that he intended to ensure that the provisioning had proceeded apace during our absence. My gaze wandered to the door of the Barrows, closed now against the evening chill. Smoke curled from the chimney and a light shone in the lone front window. Like other houses lining the road, it gave every indication that the family had retired within to share the evening meal. I would call on her, but with apology and dispatch.

"A word before we go," Heman said, taking my elbow. Before I could reply, the Captain hailed me. Eli and Sergeant Carpenter already stood beside him. "Go to him," Heman said. "I will wait here."

The three of us surrounded our Captain and listened while he praised our efforts and that of the men. Knowing such words ushered seldom from his lips, yet with utmost sincerity when they did, my head bowed in grateful acknowledgment. When he finished I was surprised to find Eli choosing to ignore such high praise, so that he might catch my eye instead. My surprise was such that I nearly missed what the Captain detailed about how any forthcoming alarm would be spread, and expectations he harbored of us. When he finished, and bid goodnight, I lingered, despite seeing Heman's dimly outlined form some 30 yards distant.

Captain Willes and the Sergeant walked off leaving Eli and me alone. "Elisha. I am glad to have this occasion to speak with you." I nodded. "I must apologize once more," he said. "I speak of what passed between us that day in the..."

"There is no need for this, Mister Chapman. My own behavior..."

"The thing is, Elisha. The thing is I had no conception of the strength of your attachment. If I had but known then, what I now know. ... And if I was not such a complete blockhead..."

His contrition was clearly powerful and sufficient to overcome any residual resentment I might bear him. "Enough, Eli, please. You do yourself an injustice." I extended my hand. "As your friend I will allow no more such talk." We shook, and warmly too.

"Good night, then, friend Elisha."

I left him and made my way to Heman, hoping he did not have tidings that would dissolve the pleasant swell of my chest.

"I wager you have one more stop to make," Heman said before I reached him. "Ere you head home."

"If I dare," I replied. So close had I stopped beside him that our shoulders touched. Together we surveyed the Barrows' light. Standing thus, I determined it would be easier for him to raise whatever issue troubled him. I had not long to wait.

"My friend," he began. "I am acquainted with the recent unpleasantness; between you and your father." I did not have to guess the source of whatever details he now possessed, for Azariah had announced quite enough within my hearing. Nor did I resent my brother confiding in him, as I had meant to, though not so soon. "Elisha. It is rude, I know, to recall the matter to your mind. I only do so, well, in truth I have a proposition to make." I faced him now, for his comments had taken an unexpected turn. "As you helped me fell my trees," he stammered, "why, you can hardly deny comprehending that I plan to raise a house. Soon, too. Just as soon as the milled planks are seasoned."

"Heman. I promised to aid you in this and so whatever else needs..."

"Let me finish, will you. Pray, do not trouble yourself in remembering your words for already have you exceeded them. 'Help me select trees,' you said. This you did. And side by side we cut them down though never did you promise this. And so my proposition is thus. Should you now agree to clear fields or assist me with other tasks that arise, you should be paid for your labors, and in felled timber. You shall be. My father has already drawn up a contract. I have it here."

A folded page hovered between us. "Paid? In timber." My mind raced as I blurted out these words. I looked at him; at the Barrows residence too. Anywhere, in fact, but at that white rectangle suspended there. A larger portion in hardwoods was all that could be said to be lacking in the parcel Grandsire had described. But to be offered a solution to this deficiency by my dearest friend, as payment in kind, I simply could not grasp. "What makes you believe I have a need for wood, of all things?"

My question was lame indeed, and meant only to grant me a moment more to think. But the effect on Heman was immediate. "If you have no need for lumber," he replied, "it could just as easily be sold." He resorted to studying the ground between his feet but there was resolve in his words.

"Heman? Did the same little bird who spoke of dealings with my father; did he sing to you of a confidence between Grandsire and myself?"

"Azariah had it from your mother, who was told it by your grandmother." He met my gaze then, his sincerity evident even in this light. "He said all were overjoyed for you, but that no one was to be told. Not yet."

"I see. And with whom have you shared these strange, joyful tidings?"

"Why no one, Elisha. 'Cepting you."

I could not help but think, for a moment, that if ever my brothers Azariah and Daniel were to be joined in a single person, the result would be Heman Baker. And I had the utmost good fortune to count him my friend. I received the page from his hand. "I accept your proposal."

"But you have not read the terms."

"I accept them, whatever they be." I took his hand. "You honor me, my friend."

"And I wish you the joy of your land, Elisha. Your own land!"

Thus buoyed, I appeared at the door of Mister Barrows. I set both pack and musket against the wall before knocking. Though surprised to see me, he did step aside, revealing his wife and Jemima seated at the table. "Forgive the intrusion," I began. "The company is returned from its march, and I was uncertain whether it was more rude to risk an interruption, or to leave town without calling."

"Please do come in, Elisha," Mrs. Barrows said. "We have more than enough to set a place for you." Jemima hopped up and set her hands upon a bowl.

"So kind of you," I replied, "but truly I cannot stay. I did hope for just a word, with Jemima."

"If you keep to the path just here," Mister Barrow said. "My wife nor I have any objection."

Relief mingled with surprise. "Thank you, sir." Jemima snatched up a covering and scooted between us, pausing only to peck her father's cheek. The door closed behind her, but not entirely, I noticed.

I stepped down onto the walkway. She remained on the granite entry stone and from this perch could nearly meet me eye to eye. Standing this close and with her lively features at my level, lit by the light slanting through the opening, created all manner of sensation within my being.

"What is so important, Mister Benton?" she asked, with her nose uplifted, "that you deign to disturb my family at such an hour."

"Jemima, I..."

"Oh, I tease you, Elisha!" Both her hands came to rest upon my chest. For a second I thought she meant to kiss me. "See!" she said. "I told you once before how easy a target you make."

Her hands fell away just before I could screw up the courage to kiss her instead. "I came by to relate to you, Jemima, some news that I hope is welcome to your ears." Suddenly I wondered if it was taking a liberty to speak so soon of land, and timber for a house...

"How somber you look," she said. All at once the merriment in her eyes and mouth gave over to a seriousness of her own. She touched the knob and pulled it nearly closed. "Does this concern your Grandsire's gift?"

"What? Azariah told you too? Damn him! He had no right!"

"Sssh! Elisha. My parents will hear. I've told them nothing of this." My breathing slowed and I became aware both her hands were back, and this time I could sense her individual fingers upon my waistcoat. "Do not be angry with Azariah," she pleaded. "He was so happy for you. For us perhaps." She blushed at this. "He came to me fairly bursting with what he longed to say. The fault is mine, for I asked him the cause."

"Even so. These tidings were mine especially to tell. How I did so, and when..."

One hand, her right, rose up and stroked my cheek. It took all my self-control to not snatch her directly from the step. "He loves you so. More than ever he would reveal to you. Pray you, do not be angered of him. Through all, well, all that went before, he was your constant advocate - to my parents. And to me."

I understood then how close a thing it had been. How my failure to speak and act for myself, and what sins this had led me to commit, had nearly sealed my fate and caused such doubt and pain. Yet now she stood right here, before me, with me, mine. And I hers. I kissed Jemima then.

As kisses go, it was precious short. I had stolen it, I realized, and so no sooner had I begun then I released her. This in turn was too soon, for she had returned the kiss once started. I moved to take her up again when the shaft of light grew suddenly brighter. Her father, I am convinced, meant only to seek out where we stood upon the path, for he seemed as shocked as we, to find us at his door. "Well then, goodnight, Miss Jemima," I said. "Your servant, sir." Jemima uttered not a word, but with fingers to her lips and a sidelong glance at me, she slipped 'round her father.

He followed my progress along the walk but I turned back once, and found no censure in his gaze. Back on the road heading south, with the mild, dark night my everywhere companion, it was my fingers that found my own lips.

Chapter 29

At last the mild weather persisted for two days, back to back. Within Grandsire's barn not a blade needed sharpening, nor a harness mending. Wood had been split for a month of fires. I had even resorted to troubling the hens for their eggs, and the cows for their milk - tasks normally attended to by Mother Sarah. None of these labors diminished my agitation for spring had come, and for a fortnight barely a foot had I placed on Benton fields. Had Daniel so usurped my role that he sought neither my help, nor my advice? A sudden doubt seized me. What if the opposite were true? What if the weight of responsibility had robbed him of the will to act, and even now, the 19th of April, he had rented not the oxen, nor hired a single hand. This would not do. I had vowed to not reclaim what I had relinquished, but neither could I allow a calamity to befall the family. I must speak with my brother on this subject so dear to both of us. I must.

Along the path towards Father's the leaves of the birch trees had already begun to turn light-green. For more than a month I had come this way with no intent other than continuing on to town, and thence to Aunt Sara's or Heman's parcel. Not once had I directed my steps to Father's door. Nor would I this day. I had no invitation from him, and would certainly not entreat him for one. The barn doors stood wide open and there I went.

"Daniel!" I called a moment later, on finding him alone. "The very one I seek."

"And I you, Brother!" He greeted me warmly, then blushed and would say no more.

I discovered that after such a promising beginning, I felt no more inclined than he to broach what was on my mind. The mare smoothed over this impasse with a whinny that drew me to her side. Daniel accompanied me. "So," I undertook at last. "I find you inspecting the plough blade. You must be near to turning the fields."

"Oh, yes, Elisha! Just as we had planned. I have been into town, and met with Eli. He confirmed the availability of the oxen. As you had arranged in the fall."

"Ah, good. I did not know you had seized the initiative."

"Yesterday this was. I, I rode April. I hope you do not mind."

I had been stroking her muzzle. I stopped. "No, of course. It is not my place to mind."

"Forgive me, Elisha. I should have thought to ask."

I shook my head to affirm I minded it not, though I could not manage to say as much. I stepped away from the mare I still held dear. Outside, the day seemed to grow finer by the minute. Well, I had my answer. Things were both better and worse than I had wondered. The many facets of the planting season had been set in motion, and this was good. Yet I was not required; not my hands nor my head. I faced Daniel with a fixed smile. "Well, you have matters in hand, it appears. I should leave you to it."

"Elisha? Are you upset with me?"

The earnestness and fret so at home on his countenance bloomed in full measure. "I admit to being somewhat out of sorts, Brother. But not with you."

"I'm so relieved to hear it. More than once I set out to find you. To seek your advices. Oh, if you only knew how I agonized over sitting across from Eli Chapman; desperate to come to terms. He made it easy for me, and was generous too. 'For Elisha's brother', he said, 'whatever I might need'."

"He is a good man. And fair."

"About the ox and the seed and so much else I worried, but I did not want to trouble you."

I touched his arm. "It would have been no bother, Daniel. It is none."

"But you entrusted me with this responsibility, so I set out to accomplish it on my own. My only wish is to please you in this, Elisha. Of Father's expectations I care nothing; not after what he said and did to you, to you and Jemima."

"You are kindness itself," I told him. "And you have done well. But Father is the family's patriarch. Especially now that Grandsire is confined so often to his bed. Keep him informed at the least. And remember, whatever I taught you of the land, I learned at his knee."

His only assent was to nod, which signaled his keen distaste for the prospect. Yet he would do as asked. It was for the family's betterment that he do so, though I was a poor source nowadays for such advice. "Elisha? I can acquaint you with the particulars if you desire?"

"There is no need, I see that clearly. No. Your time is far better spent attending to the work of the farm than describing the labors to me. I am off to town at any rate, as I have business with Eli myself."

"Before you go. There is a thing I would ask." I paused that he might speak. "You, you and Azariah too. You drill with the militia. Am I not of a more suitable age than he? Is this the way of it, or should I..."

"Perish such thoughts, Daniel. No man is more suited for the role of soldier than our brother. You know this as well as I. And as for me, why, I believe the good Captain has an esteem for me that I once enjoyed here. I shall endeavor to not disappoint should the time come." I squeezed both his hands in mine. "Please, do not mention this again. Is it not enough that two of us might be called away? Think on it,

Brother. Of what use is the protection of our family if the table stands bare come summer. No, Daniel, yours is an absence we Bentons can simply not afford."

"As you wish, Elisha."

Before I went away, Daniel insisted that he be allowed to fetch Mother from the house. As I had not seen her during this spell of pleasant weather, and as I had no fixed appointment in town, I readily agreed. She immediately gave me every assurance that progress was being made with Father, though I solicited nothing of the sort. The children soon joined us, and so we made merry, despite remaining on the side of the barn out of sight of the parlor windows.

The smile borne of those stolen moments lingered as I walked along the road into town. Daniel had insisted, with astonishing persistence for one whose temperament was so mild, that he be allowed to saddle the mare for me. I had just as steadfastly refused. An unexpected benefit was the chance to admire the brilliant hue of the daylily plants along my route. The yellow flowers clung to long stems sprouting the length of the ditch just opposite the marsh. Their beauty and wild state put me in mind of Jemima, though my intended business was with Eli, and that as off-putting as the intended rental of one's being could supposed to be.

The precise moment I thought of Eli Chapman, my eyes discerned him astride his favorite mount, and both bearing down upon me. They came on at a gallop, dragging a whirlwind of dust. I yielded the crown of the road lest I be run down. Even as he hauled back, reining in the lathered stallion, I hollered up at him. "Eli! For God's sake, what's amiss?"

"A rider is come, Elisha! From Boston!"

"What tidings?"

"We're to gather at the Meeting House. On the instant! Come up, come up! Not a minute's to be lost."

He managed to guide his frantic mount beside a convenient stump. Thus aided, I clambered aboard, just behind Eli's saddle and with my hands at his hips. As he was near as agitated as his horse, and just as winded, I got precious little from him. A post rider had come; of this alone could I be certain. A Mister Israel Bissell, he was, though the fellow's name seemed of little consequence when the express he carried remained a mystery. Only Captain Willes and Eli's uncle, Colonel Chapman, had thus far been informed of the contents; and the latter had ridden off to Hartford at once. Never had I known the Colonel to travel without his carriage. Within a minute the common came into view. In such a short span my state now rivaled that of my companion.

The door to the Barrows stood ajar as we cantered past, though not a soul could be spotted within or without. This alone would have heightened my anxiety but there was much more besides. Every man, woman and child seemed to be converging on the Meeting House.

We dismounted. Without pausing to secure Eli's horse at the hitching post, we practically leapt the steps. A logjam of people of all sorts blocked the entry but those who caught sight of us did their best to make way. The center aisle was likewise crammed along its length, though principally by men. Gentlemen filled the space 'round the pulpit, with the elders closest in. At the center stood Captain Willes.

"Come to order!" he bellowed in a voice that reverberated off the walls of the loft as well as the ground floor. "If you please. Thank you," he said in his normal speaking voice, for the hall had fallen silent. He set eyes upon us, for we were difficult to miss even in such a throng. "Mister Benton. Mister Chapman. Good, good. Welcome." He waved us forward. "Good people of Tolland," he continued, with us now alongside him. "News comes this day to our town, from our neighbors and friends in Massachusetts. The news is grave, I warn you." With that he gestured towards the pulpit.

There, draped upon a chair, we discovered a stranger. A wig rested atop the fellow's head, but at a rakish angle that seemed quite out of character judging by the cut of his fine coat. Sweat streaked his face and dust obscured the color of his clothes. As he struggled to stand, I bent to his aid. He nodded thanks. Then, at the Captain's bidding, addressed us. "To arms!" he cried, in a voice near as spent as his limbs. "The Regulars are out!" With that he sagged; Eli and I set him once more upon the seat.

"What's that he says, Solomon?" called our minister.

"Patience gentlemen," the Captain replied. "If you please I will read out the message our friend bears.

> *'To all friends of American liberty be it known that this morning before break of day, a brigade, consisting of about 1,000 to 1,200 soldiers, landed at Phip's Farm at Cambridge, and marched to Lexington, where they found a company of our colony's militia in arms..."*

"How far is this Lexington, Captain?" a voice cried out. Others hushed him.

> *'...upon whom they fired without any provocation, and killed six men, and wounded four others.'"*

"The King's men fired?" the minister said. "It cannot be..."

"Sheer butchery this is!" Captain Willes announced to those in the farthest corners of the chamber. The note crumpled in his hand. "Fathers, husbands and sons. Gathered together, within their rights as fellow Englishmen, on their own town green." At this he pointed outside. Heads turned to view our own common. "And there were they shot down! And there they fell in pools of blood. And died! Mere steps from their homes, mind you, and in full view of their wives. Their children, too, no doubt."

Often had I heard the Captain's voice raised in solemn oration, but never on the verge of breaking. Silence hung for a long moment, followed by a guttural roar that rose up, churning louder and louder until men's fists punched at the very air.

Chapter 30

By craning my neck this way and that, I discovered Jemima seated on the far side of the pulpit.

I confess, I relied on more than one well-placed elbow to make my way beside her. Men shouted into each other's faces, all at once and in violent agreement over what must be done. The company must be made to march. As yet she had not made note of me. Her body bent dramatically to one side as she endeavored to use the elders' raised platform to scratch away with quill and ink. A cap she wore, but it had been donned in haste. At a pause in her writing, I touched her shoulder. She rose at once, the feathered quill brushing my sleeve as she pressed hard against my chest. The intensity of her embrace, the shudder of her shoulders, caught me unawares.

"All will be well," was what I could think to say. Men shoved against me. I wrapped her tight to shield her from this.

The Captain shouted out commands. My name was among those that rang from his lips. Men began to force their way towards the wide flung doors. I spied Azariah among the first to depart.

"Jemima," I whispered into her ear, my lips touching her neck. "I must go." She clenched at me; then released me. Her eyes, wet, roamed my face. Her sadness stole my voice away. And so I left her. At the door,

I was rewarded with one more sight of her, standing, a steadying hand up on the stout pulpit.

Azariah was nowhere to be seen in the crowd. The Captain appeared alongside me on the steps. He gave orders to a mounted courier, who wheeled and urged his skittish horse through the throng. "Make way!" the fellow shouted to people in the road, heedless of their station. "Make way at once!"

I could locate but few of my nearest neighbors despite the swell of the crowd. As the Captain had commanded, I must alert them and at once. Eli had recovered his stallion upon the common. Mounting, he struggled to advance as had the courier moments earlier. "Eli!" I hollered. "Heman must be told..."

Keeping the reins tight in one hand he waved his hat to me. "I will stop at the Bakers. Have no fear on this account."

"Godspeed!" I said, waving my hat in turn. Breaking clear at last, he galloped north and west, to the Chapman and Baker homesteads.

"Corporal!" Captain Willes called out, even as he grabbed my sleeve. "You must depart at once. Have the men pack what provisions they can. Three days and nights worth should see us there. But at all costs they must be at your side come sundown this very day."

"Are we to meet you here, sir?" I asked, wondering how all this could be accomplished by sunset.

"No time for that, Elisha. No, gather the men to you where your family's lane intersects the main road. I shall march the company to you, or whatever part of it I can assemble in such time." It took a few seconds before I understood that I was not to return to town. From where we stood on the steps I searched the confines of the Meeting House. Perhaps I might catch Jemima's eye.

"Now, Corporal! You must set out."

"Aye, sir." And with that I left his side, and hers.

With a flood of apologies I worked my way. The initial outpouring of folk from the Meeting House had subsided, but this only opened more space through which those remaining could heighten their harried pace. Every person, it seemed, had an urgent purpose. Mine could certainly not be denied. My family must be acquainted with these tidings, and oh, how ill such news would be received. And my comrades must be fetched. "Pardon," I begged the cobbler's goodwife after nearly knocking her down.

Finally I broke free. Here my long strides would serve me well. Instead I abruptly stopped. Mister and Mrs. Barrows had spotted me, and now advanced along their walk. So hurriedly did they come that the mistress' feet found more mud than stepping stone. I moved to remove my hat, but realized that I had held it in my hand all this while.

Mrs. Barrows continued straight on, wrapping her slender arms about my neck, best as she could reach that is. Not expecting a reception of such tenderness, I had not bent down. I looked to her husband for guidance, but his eyes held all the sadness that I heard now in a muffled sob upon my chest. With my embrace I endeavored to make up in warmth what I had forfeited in tardiness. "All will be well," I said for a second time, believing it less.

In time she relinquished her hold of me. Jon Barrows extended his hand. "Do take care," he said. "The utmost care. Both you and your brother, Azariah."

I pointed in the direction of the Meeting House, but thoughts of her and the sight of her worried parents kept words from coming. I bowed, and left them then. Only when I had covered 50 yards or more did I collect myself enough that I turned back. They were gone. In the road I murmured aloud my promise: to return to her, their daughter.

Stops at the Skinners, Luces and Wests had drained me of emotion. In my wake did the cries of women and children follow me, whilst men had rushed to prepare their kit and themselves. A few hours' time saw me heading up the lane towards my parents' home. Shouts of "Elisha is come!" rang out before ever I saw Jacob rushing forward through the trees. So now I knew to whence Azariah had scampered.

Mother clutched Hannah, together there before the entry. Jacob and I went up to them at once, Hannah nearly getting crushed between us. "What does it signify, my son?" Mother asked. "Azariah told us so little. We know only that shots have been fired. Men killed." At this she covered Hannah's ears to what end I could not discern, nor she, I suppose. "Must you go?"

"You know that I must, Mother. And at once, for I have more visits yet to be paid our neighbors."

"Oh, you and Azariah are not enough to risk!" she cried out. "Must it be our neighbors too?" Never had I seen her thus. Jacob tried to calm her.

"All will be well, Mother," I said, hating myself for lying, for the words had lost a degree of truth in each telling. Suddenly, I felt Father's gaze upon me, though I saw him not. "I will stop on my return from Grandsire's," I promised her, and broke away so that I might gather my things, and say one final farewell.

I knew not how long Mother Sarah had stood in the doorway, keeping watch for me. But her reception could not have differed more than I had experienced at home. Her cheeks were streaked from tears, but she met me with a dry eye. "Elisha," she said simply, then held me tight. "Come, he awaits you."

"Forgive me but I can only stay a moment," I confessed. "I must gather my belongings and be off."

"As to that," she replied, "your brother has come before you." She pointed and there just inside the entry leaned my pack, quite stuffed, and beside it Uncle William's musket.

She ushered me to the parlor. My grandfather's health had buoyed of late, but this fact could not be discerned in the pale countenance he turned towards me. "Grandsire..."

His dry hands drew me down to where I could kiss his forehead. This time he released me not, but rather held my face against his own. "My Boy," he whispered. "My Boy."

"Grandsire, there are things I would say to you..."

"Sssh. We need no words, you and I. Not now." Finally, he released me, for I could never have let him go. As I turned away, his thin voice spoke my name. "Elisha..." he said. "Come back to us."

"I promise," I replied, without looking back. And so I left him, left them.

I was still settling the rucksack upon my shoulders as I emerged in the clearing to Father's house. He was the first I saw. His good hand had hold of the door frame. Of his cane there was no sign. I slowly continued my approach.

Mother had regained the composure that I had come to rely upon. "My son," she said, and kissed my cheek before surrendering me to Jacob and Hannah. As I was hugging them, Daniel ran to us. Apologies flowed from him. Azariah had come to him in the fields and now that he knew all; asked what he might do. I held him in a long, hard embrace. Father neither advanced nor relinquished the grip on the frame. His eyes, however, had not left me the while.

"Father," I said, removing my hat. "I must leave now. I have many calls yet to make."

"You will make far better time mounted. Take the mare."

I was shocked to hear his voice, and more so to have it address me in a civil manner. "I, we, we are meant to march to Boston."

"Of course you are," he replied. "Ride to gather the men. Jacob can follow. He will see the mare safely returned."

"As you wish, Father."

"I will saddle her," Daniel announced. "Let me help!" Jacob shouted as he hurried after.

In the silence that followed, Mother took hold of Father's sleeve. Hannah nestled in beside her. There were so many things I might have said. I suppose the same could have been true of Father. Yet neither of us spoke another word. When April, whinnying and prancing, was brought to me, I secured the pack to her saddle. "Jacob," I said. "I will leave her to graze where our lane joins the road." With that and nothing more than a last glance at them together, I mounted and trotted away. The voices of my entire family, save one, cried out their farewells.

Chapter 31

The trill of the fife reached my ears long before I could see Tolland's militia. A dozen of us crowded together on the road, facing the way that they would come. Captain Willes was first to appear, and even he on foot. In place of a drummer he had selected both Noah Whipple and Steven Steel as fifers. Eli followed and, behind him, scores of men, in ranks of two abreast. All of us were to walk to Boston together.

The Captain shook my hand but he was in no mood to tarry. The column paused only long enough for my neighbors and me to augment its midsection. As it was, I had to hasten greetings to Azariah and Heman. To others like Jeremiah West, who was to serve as our surgeon, I had to confine myself to mere nods. The trilling of the fifers set us in motion once more. April trotted beside me until I heard Jacob's faint whistle from somewhere behind us. She peeled off at last and we continued southwest.

"You missed a fine sendoff in town," Heman said. "So grand as to be almost gay." His light-hearted tone planted smiles on the faces of some of the younger men. We must all wear happy expressions if we are to see this through.

"None had a finer farewell than Azariah," said one of these youngsters, he of the Cook brood, I recollected. "Miss Jemima clung to his neck so," the youth exclaimed, "I thought her to be coming with us." While a few chuckled at this remark, those who knew us Benton brothers best glanced my way. Though sorely tempted, I refrained from studying my brother's face. I trusted him as I did her. Nonetheless, envy I did feel.

The Captain had judged right in taking us previously along this route. Having traveled it so recently, and without urgency, the men now spent their time recalling the well-wishes of kin and acquaintances alike. And so any anxiety that might have attended the purpose of our quest, succumbed to a tranquility both immediate and mundane. Commentary turned to the dry state of the road and the clear, high sky. Each man adjusted the unfamiliar weight of the pack upon his back, or arranged the straps of his canteen or powder horn as he saw fit. With but a few adjustments I managed to settle my cumbersome load such that the bouncing at my hips would not raise bruises 10 or 20 miles hence. In this I surveyed the arrangement of Azariah's kit, for no other among us proceeded with as much ease and dispatch. Having seen to my own comfort, I offered help to those who struggled.

Most had been straightened away by the time we emerged from the forested stretch running nearly unbroken from Tolland to Coventry. The junction with Boston Post Road lay before us, and people clogged the entirety of it. As we approached, the cheering mass parted revealing Lieutenant Parker and at least as many men as had accompanied him before. The officers joined in hasty discourse while the good folk of Coventry milled about the reunited column with happy tidings for all. The joy it brought us could not, for me at least, mask the many tear-stained cheeks I saw. My heart seized at the sight of one such face. A young woman, her dark hair shining in the slanting rays of the late-day sun. She smiled for me, and though I smiled back, her comely features only visited sadness upon me.

"Brother," Azariah said, suddenly at my side. "I see you found your kit."

"Thank you, yes. You came and went so fast to Father's house. I thought sure our paths would cross on the road from town."

"I took to the woods. So much faster, you understand."

I returned his grin. "For you, perhaps."

"Do not short yourself, Brother. You possess a light tread, for such an oaf of a fellow." I laughed at this. Heman joined in, though he had done his best to pretend to not eavesdrop. "By the by, Brother," Azariah said, "I am become the older brother it would seem."

"How is that?"

"Jemima would have it so." I stared at him with a confusion so profound I found my mouth had fallen open. "'Tis so," he insisted. "She would not release me until I promised to look after you. And so I did. Little brother."

At that moment a rider came round the westward bend at a gallop. Such were the carryings on in the road that none had heard his approach. He reined in hard and then proceeded to the Captain, identifiable by the very uniform coat he had worn whilst fighting the French. A minute more and Captain Willes had assembled me, Lieutenant Parker and all the sergeants and corporals beneath an upright maple, newly clad in brilliant green.

"We have our orders and about them there can be no mistake," the Captain said. "We are to proceed at once to Roxbury."

"You are proven quite wise, sir," Eli said, "in marching us to the road to Boston." Such a remark, which purpose could only be condescension or so nakedly ingratiating as to offend, awakened that resentment I had once felt so keenly for him.

Captain Willes reacted with similar disdain. "Colonel Chapman," he continued, waving the message he held, "has met with Governor Trumbull himself. Our governor is said to be outraged. Allow me to read his very words: '*...the actions of Gage's troops would disgrace even barbarians. The General is guilty of a most provoked attack upon the lives and property of His Majesty's subjects*'."

"If I may, sir," the Lieutenant asked. "What would the Governor, and Colonel Chapman have us do? In Roxbury."

"Gentlemen, we must prepare ourselves, so that the men in turn are made ready. For if we find the King's troops in Boston we are to lay siege; and if they are attacking the countryside, we must repel them." To these remarks no one had a rejoinder. "If there are no questions, let us make haste. I will have us encamped on the eastern side of the Willimantic River this night."

We made good on our commander's wishes, though weary we were. Azariah had scouted to our rear and reported that the pair of horse-drawn carts bearing our tents and sundry provisions should catch us up no earlier than two hours post full dark. Given that predicted late arrival, and the star-studded sky that foretold no rain, Captain Willes opted to have us bed down on the bare ground in a clearing within sight of the road.

My brother insisted that he be allowed to volunteer as a guard, but I overruled him explaining that to continue in the role of scout he must also rest. So it was I saw him lie prostrate and fall asleep at once. Heman needed no inducement to retire. After contributing two men from my squad as sentinels, I wandered the huddled forms, offering advice drawn from what I had learned during our recent journey over this same ground. I did insist that each man refill his canteen before retiring.

I was doubly glad I accompanied them, for at the stream's bank I encountered Private John Lewis. As he was in Sergeant Carpenter's platoon I seldom saw him, but was always glad of the opportunity. Though not of Tolland, he had mustered with us often and glad was I that he had enlisted with our company. He was my father's age, though with Grandsire's ways. A veteran of many campaigns, he lent confidence to the younger men. In his presence, I felt thus too. "John Lewis," I said. "How good to see you."

"Young Mister Benton. Pardon. Corporal Benton it is now. Congratulations are due."

"And how are your feet bearing up?" I asked.

"A tad sore, I confess. But if you need carrying on the morrow, I'm your man."

It took a summons to draw me from his side. At the fire prepared for our officers, Lieutenant Parker detailed our line of march and intended stopping places. I noticed that like me, Eli listened with but one ear, for these towns and rivers and the mile markers separating them were fresh indeed. Rather than the journey, I found my thoughts scudding along to what lay at its end. And of those whom we'd left behind.

When we were dismissed a few minutes later, Eli kept to my elbow. As his squad was bivouacked beside mine, I should have expected his company. Much as I tried to like him, and ofttimes did, he had the knack of riling me with one inopportune statement or another. I disliked him this instant, if only because he had awoken in me a meanness of spirit that I would rather have denied.

"'Tis a pity," the First Corporal said, "that the tents did not arrive more timely."

I could not help but wonder if he desired them for the men, or for his own comfort. I nearly remarked that the Brigham Tavern stood a mere mile in our rear - should he wish to walk it. To prevent speaking in so uncivil a manner, I bid him goodnight.

"If I may impose a moment more," he said. Taking my arm, he led us to a fallen log some little ways apart from the others. "Do not think me callow for asking, Elisha, for I must." At this preamble I had no notion of what might follow. "How do you do it?" he asked. Before I could say, "Do what?" he explained. "The way you lead your men astounds me. How is what I seek to comprehend?"

Never was I so unprepared to answer what was clearly a most genuine inquiry. His earnestness utterly disarmed me. "Truly, Eli, I have no conception of what you speak."

"How can you deny it? Whatever you advise, they do. Whatever you ask of them, they attend to, at once and cheerfully." My eyes swept across the sweeping forms of our companions, yet nothing could I find there which might satisfy him.

"Oh, my men do what I tell them," he lamented, "but I discern no real willingness. Yours laugh and make merry, even while they sweat for you."

"None sweat for me, Eli. We are all of us in this together. Each does what he must. As do I."

"So that is your secret," he murmured. "They follow not your lead, but rather your example."

"Eli..."

"No, I see it now. That may work for you, for you are that type of man. For better or worse I find that I must lead by issuing orders. That at least I can do, for I have been reared to it. Tell me though, friend Elisha, and I hold your friendship dear though we have known, truly known each other such a short while. Will your way bear up in what's to come?" It dawned on me that here sat no one's fool. He had contemplated what lay before us far more than I. "The courage of a leader such as you," he said, "must, it stands to reason, far exceed mine." He spoke on, quite as though he sat alone, thinking aloud. "When the time comes, I need only order men forward; whilst you must plunge ahead if they're to follow."

Only then did I understand what we were doing here; squatting on this decayed log alongside the road to Boston. The First Corporal and I had been appointed to lead, or order, the brothers and friends and neighbors of our lifetimes, into battle. And against whom: the soldiers of our King; the finest professional soldiers in the world. And we would do so within three days, or two if our feet could carry us to the fray quick enough.

"Do you hate them, these Regulars?" I asked. "Enough to level a barrel at their heads?"

"Are you serious, Elisha? Of course. Do you not?"

The immediacy of his answer, as well as its coolness, took me by surprise. "I resent them, yes. Loathe them, too, I believe, after our last visit there. But to kill another seems to demand, I do not know, a depth of hatred that I'm not convinced I feel."

Eli leaned in so close I could feel the warmth of his breath as he whispered. "You must not let the men hear you speak thus, Elisha." His hand took hold of my arm. "I understand what you say, but they must not hear this from your lips. No. They mustn't even sense your doubts. If I have learned one thing from a decade of ordering men about, it is this." He was right, I knew, for in so many endeavors of my own life, I had come to accept that when I believed in a thing, so too would those who labored beside me. If this was true of work, so too must it be of killing. I shuddered at the comparison.

"Consider, my friend," he went on. "Such tales I have heard from my uncle the Colonel, lo these many years. Since the massacre in Boston it has been so. Why, I have practically been weaned on the dastardly acts by which the King's soldiers have revealed themselves. This has not, perhaps, been your fate, Elisha, but take me at my word in this. Far too many of them are bastards, and if we can only preserve our freedoms by taking their lives, why then they are dead already."

Suddenly I understood that I had misjudged Eli Chapman, and always had. A self-absorbed and vain man I had marked him, a veritable font of personal ambition. Oh, awkward he might sometimes be in manner of expression, but that relentless ambition he harbored was to serve his countrymen, onto death. If any had been absorbed it was me, and by petty local politics. So much so that I had failed to see what was undeniable to him. War had come, and he was destined to lead us. Whereas with my selection the Captain, I now feared, had made a grievous error.

Chapter 32

Through the towns we went, near as quickly as we passed the mile markers, set like stone watchmen along the side of the road. Mansfield and Ashford, then Pomfret - thus departing our Connecticut homes and setting our feet on Massachusetts soil. We had acquired volunteers from towns along the way, a few of whom now became my responsibility.

Men these were who knew not the route, nor the geography of the province. Some expected to encounter redcoats behind each tree. I took pains to explain that we were but halfway to our destination. Besides, I had not the heart to tell them that should we encounter the King's army, a stealthy approach mattered not to this colossal beast.

During a respite in which the men drank and the horses were fed, the Captain gathered his platoon leaders together. "Some," I said, in response to his question about how the men were getting on, "are become jittery. The younger ones more so than the rest." When asked the same question, Eli agreed. I had discovered, in the last day and a half, that he disliked volunteering any news that might shine a less than favorable light on his charges. The men's state of mind he would not, however, deny.

Our commander must have made a similar discovery, for no sooner had his First Corporal spoken that he stood and surveyed the 100 men. "Perhaps they are right to be," he said. "You have noted, to be sure, the increase in the number of express riders." Truly what I had observed was the need to hurry the column to the shoulder whenever these fellows came galloping through, demanding the right of way. "And whereas we received cheers and bread from Connecticut townspeople," he said, "the people of Uxbridge watched us from within doors near closed."

This reception merely two miles back could scarcely have been forgotten by me, for I'd had to speak to one Amasa Allen. He had fallen in with us as recently as Stafford, Connecticut, but given the wary reception by the good folk of Uxbridge, had somehow determined that it fell to him to reply with foul oaths.

"Why the change?" Captain Willes asked. Thankfully, he provided a prompt answer to his own question. "Because their militia has already marched on Boston, leaving them quite unprotected. Yes, I believe we will double our guard beginning this night. And from this point on, we shall fan scouts ahead of us." He turned to me.

"Shall I send Azariah to you for instructions, sir?" I asked.

"If you please, Corporal."

"Captain?" Eli said. "Perhaps a second man would prove useful."

"And I presume you have such a one in mind. His name?" This was eagerly provided by the First Corporal. His satisfaction dimmed somewhat, however, when the Captain stated that the fellow would be under the nominal direction of Azariah whilst on patrol. We were then dismissed, with orders to resume the march.

Heman and Azariah waited on my return. Noah Grant and Jeremiah West got to their feet beside them. "Are we off?" was all my brother wanted to know. "What says the Captain?" Heman asked.

I had the others join us. "We should expect that from here on, most Massachusetts towns will be stripped of their militias. We will take utmost pains, therefore, to not alarm the residents in our passing."

I lingered on Mister Allen, whose pipe soon fumbled in his gapped teeth. "With this gathering force of like-minded militia on the road before us, there is little expectation of encountering the King's troops. However, as a prudent measure, Captain Willes has ordered a doubling of the night sentinels, and that a pair of scouts patrol to our front." Azariah's hand shot up. "You are already chosen, Brother." He went forward to receive the Captain's instructions. As he was popular, his smiles now brought far more comfort to his companions than anything I might have said. I repressed the urge to tell him to take care, for this would surely reverse the reassurance his good humor and confidence had wrought.

"Not to fret," Heman whispered in my ear. "That lad will be just fine."

We made it all the way to Mendon that evening. The Captain had been eager that we reach this destination, if only because he recalled the warm reception we Tolland men had so recently received. Not more different could the town have appeared. The inhabitants did come out doors as we marched in, but there the similarity ended. Not a man did we glimpse younger than 60, nor a boy older than 15. The alarm, an elder confided, had been received the previous morning, Wednesday the 19th. Within the hour a Captain Nelson had hurried off towards Boston with their detachment of Minutemen, some 40 strong. Before noon, two other companies had followed suit, dragging with them the two cannon that they prized so highly. By this point in the retelling we were surrounded by white-haired men and women of all ages. Candles were shielded in many hands. The Captain suggested that he and the older gentleman, and the Lieutenant, retire to the tavern to hear the remainder of the tale.

As the womenfolk dispersed to their homes, Eli, Sergeant Carpenter and I saw to the needs of the men. The older townsmen were generous with whatever accommodations could be offered in the livery, smithy and even a barn within a short walk of the common. Fearing no danger from the west, Eli and I saw to the posting of a roadblock to the east. This consisted of four men arrayed about our supply wagons, drawn across the road. Azariah insisted on being among them. Eli did not try to dissuade him, though he immediately sought volunteers from within his own group. Seeing his agitation I suggested that he alone be the one to report to the Captain that all had been made safe. This our First Corporal was pleased to do.

Friday morning bore witness to our company passing through the settlement of Milford, and after crossing the Charles River, the town of Medfield. The river remained our constant left-hand companion as we marched ever north and eastward. Once more our commander broached no half measures. Onward we pressed though the sun had long since shifted from our right sides to full upon our backs.

"Elisha," Heman whispered. "How are we to fight, if we arrive at last but cannot stand?"

Dirt and fatigue marked each face. With downcast eyes, the men stared at the heels of the man directly ahead. "We are to pause in Dedham," I replied. "I will speak to the Captain then."

It was at a tavern in that town that the various leaders were called together. We sat silent, a beer in hand, whilst the Captain read through a dispatch that had been sent from Hartford. Eli looked as worn as any. So tired in fact that he made no effort to smooth his rumpled coat nor to affect the air that so often sustained him. Lieutenant Parker still sat straight, though his strained features revealed his pain. Sergeant Carpenter concealed not his distress. Rather he bent low; rubbing at his legs. Like the Lieutenant, I tried to await the Captain's pleasure with whatever grace I retained.

Outside the window a mass of people surged past. These were principally family groups, though sorely lacking in men of militia age. The shoulders of each were heavily burdened by whatever had been jammed into packs or suspended with rope. More and more such refugees had we encountered in the last few miles. It tore at my heart to see them stagger to the roadside as we drove incessantly forward along the road's center.

"Well, then," Captain Willes said. "I have the name of the officer to whom I must report in Roxbury. Good! He will instruct us as to our posting." With that, he folded the message and surveyed us one by one. "Tell me, how fare our men?"

He had started with me. "They are footsore and more asleep than awake, sir." The others glanced at me. "Even so, sir, in my opinion the unfortunates beyond this window argue for our continued haste."

Captain Willes sighed and turned to my companions. "Elisha has provided an answer far superior to the question I asked. The simple fact of the matter is, gentlemen, that we must find a way to go on. You must find it in yourselves, and convince the men of the necessity. Our orders are to proceed post haste. The King's forces, I am told, are bottled up within the city, and there they must remain. Under no circumstance can they be allowed to break out and terrorize the countryside. Every man, every musket must be brought to bear."

Back outside we stepped. The milling citizenry dodged our prostrate comrades. Eli took hold of my elbow. "I was wrong, Elisha," he said. "A man such as you will always find a way to lead by example. And I am grateful for it." With that he walked away.

The men received the news that we must proceed directly to Roxbury with silence. I glanced first at Azariah. When my brother turned away,

I realized how poorly I had judged the men's state. Heman met me with a stony stare. Mister Amasa Allen waited till my eye fell upon him, then spat. A few cast looks at him. Then me. At once I hated the gristled, little rooster of a man. Stringy and combative he was, and with this act he had defied me.

Along the street, Eli, Sergeant Carpenter and the officers themselves were encountering similar difficulties in rousing our company. "I will not deny your exhaustion," I said to all in my platoon. "We have covered a good 60 miles in little more than two days. As for me, I feel every step of it. The Captain and Lieutenant Parker, they are amazed at you; at what you've accomplished."

Azariah and Heman glanced my way. Amasa muttered something to the effect that them officers should bloody well give thanks, but the men were listening to me now, not him. "Even so, we must press on," I told them. "You need only look about you to understand why." As if delivered by providence, a frail, white-haired man collapsed on the periphery of our group, spilling his bundles at our feet. What we took to be his daughter and grandchildren dropped to the ground to aid him. The men of the Tolland militia had him up and dusted off in no time. Water was poured for the family from three or more canteens and all the items were recovered and doled out and made secure. When the family had moved on, my men faced me once more. "Think on it," I said, "what horrors they flee to end thus."

"When do we make a start, Brother?" Azariah asked.

"Aye, Corporal," Heman said. "Let us be off." A chorus rose up, ragged, yet with more zeal than I had thought possible. We fell into ranks then, and so too did the entire company.

The sun barely clung to the western horizon when we trudged up the hilly ground into Roxbury. Captain Willes had looked close at our fifers, but in the end had taken mercy on their chapped lips, and thus our blistered, bloody feet. We came on loosely, and in silence, more as a narrow mass that crept up the slope than as ranks of fighting men. Still, we had fulfilled our leader's every expectation. As proof, he and the Lieutenant stood off to one side at the top of the rise. With drawn swords they gave us three cheers as we came abreast. Their tribute rediscovered our marching legs, and with huzzahs we paraded by.

We halted outside the parsonage that served as General John Thomas' headquarters. Muskets were stood in stacks, and canteens and pipes encouraged. Our raucous arrival had drawn forth residents and militia alike. Of the former, there remained but few, despite the many houses, most of two and even three stories. Noah Whipple whistled at the size of the Meeting House steeple. Of the latter, we had never seen so many armed men, not since hurrying along The Mall in Boston. Whereas the King's troops had been all precision and outfitted in fine-cut, red cloth, these drifting knots of men sported all manner and degree of clothing and equipment.

Upon learning that we hailed from as distant a place as Connecticut, a series of cheers reverberated that made our earlier shouts seem pale indeed. We shook hands roundly - meeting fellow militia troops from Massachusetts, most certainly, but also from New Hampshire and Rhode Island. We numbered in the thousands it was said, and comprised a ring that ran from Dorchester and Roxbury in the south, through Cambridge to our north and west, and dead north, encompassing the peninsula on which Charlestown stood; and it recently abandoned by the Regulars. Many of our company thought that given this intelligence, the fighting must certainly be won. Disappointment registered in my brother's eyes, whilst Eli's seemed to reflect grave doubts; and these I could not help but share.

Chapter 33

That night we were assembled on the Roxbury common. General Thomas himself addressed us. His thanks concerning our speedy transit and timely arrival were genuine enough, though the growls of my stomach and the lightness of my head prevented me from drawing any true assessment of the man. I did note his white wig, his long face and longer nose, and precious little else. I feared one of my companions might collapse before he finished. As it turned out, he was no stranger to brevity, and so none of us disgraced the company.

We were then excused to be feted. Iron tripods had been erected. From them massive pots hung over open fires. Without ceremony we found places to sit. A piping stew thick with fish and potatoes, and accompanied with that day's bread and copious quantities of hard cider, were served to us as though we were visiting royalty.

After seeing that my men were comfortable and sated, I joined a circle that included my brother, Heman, Noah Grant and Jeremiah West. Heman raised his glass. Jeremiah handed me a tankard; I in turn toasted all of them. Nearby, I saw Eli making similar rounds.

"You are being mimicked, Brother," Azariah suggested.

"Like proper horsemen," I replied after a moment, "we corporals understand that we must see first to our mounts." I had judged my audience well, for Heman chortled at once, and Noah, caught mid swallow, guffawed till cider trickled from his nose. Even Jeremiah, who did his best to retain the dignity of his newly won office, covered his grin with the back of his hand. Azariah simply raised his glass to me.

Eli approached. I invited him to join us. Next to me he sat. All welcomed him, though with no more than a touch of their brims. His presence would detract, no doubt, from our joviality, but I found I did not mind overmuch. In the First Corporal's solemn expression I recognized my hidden feelings.

"Eat and drink hearty," he said as an aside meant for me.

Aye," I agreed, for we both had been informed that come the morrow our company was destined to descend Meeting House Hill.

At the cock's crow Captain Willes assembled his company's leaders. We stared as one along the single road that sloped downwards, dwindling at last to a flat finger of land that formed a causeway. It pointed straight into the heart of Boston. Water surrounded the city, with the Atlantic Ocean hugging the wharves along the right shore, whilst the mud flats of the Charles traced the opposite coast. Midway between the city and where we stood lay our immediate focus and concern - for here loomed that low yet stout fortification that stretched from one body of water to the other. Handed the Captain's spyglass, I could detect the black, iron muzzles of cannons protruding from triangular embrasures that had been cut into the thick walls. When last here the insults of the red-coated sentries had occupied my attention. Now their presence paled beside the menace of these squat brutes. May they remain mute, I silently prayed.

"We must not tarry," Captain Willes warned. "General Thomas says the twenty-four pound balls those guns hurl can reach this place, and have. A group such as ours will make a convenient target as the light comes up." We followed him to a slight promontory shielded somewhat from the bastion. "There, down on the left of the road, and bordering the salt marsh. That is to be our posting. Another force arriving soon from Connecticut will defend the far side."

"We are to be thrown directly into the fray it would appear," Lieutenant Parker said, speaking for us all.

"The men will have precious little opportunity to prepare for what may come, 'tis true," the Captain replied. "But the need cannot be denied nor delayed. The Massachusetts companies that first responded to the alarm arrived without food, tents or equipment of any kind. As other units arrive, these minutemen detachments are being rotated back to be outfitted properly."

I focused the glass once more. A sort of moat had been dug before the bristling wall that had not existed before. The rushing tide poured through it. Little more than a patch of marshy ground of some hundreds of yards separated these formidable obstacles from a thin line of crouching provincials fronted by piles of brush. "So close..." I murmured, and handed the glass back to Captain Willes.

"I trust, Corporal, that your study of the terrain confirms this to be the only feasible position by which the left flank may be anchored." Humbled by his tone I kept mum. "General Thomas frets that the Regulars might row across the bay. They might thusly skirt the marsh and bring boats up Stony Brook, the stream on our left, and so attack Roxbury from the rear," he continued. "A successful foray of this ilk would spell disaster for the troops assembled here, and the citizens all about."

"As I understand it, then, Captain," Eli said, "we are charged with stopping such an assault."

Our commander offered a tight-lipped grin. "Stop them, First Corporal? May heaven be so kind. No, our task would be to give warning of their arrival."

"How are we to signal the General?" Lieutenant Parker asked.

"With the sacrifice of our company, Mister Parker." The Lieutenant appeared shocked, but he recovered quickly. Faster and more completely than the rest of us, if my comrades' expressions and my thudding heart were proof. "Gentlemen," the Captain added, "I trust you will make pains to conceal the extent of our potential predicament from our men. As for you, however, you have proven your worth. So much so that I entrust you with the truth. Keep each man on his guard, without panicking the whole. Am I clear? Have I judged rightly?"

"Yes, sir!" Eli said, overly loud I thought.

Lieutenant Parker touched his cap with a crisp movement. Sergeant Carpenter hesitated, then blurted out, "Aye, sir."

That piercing gaze found me last. For a frantic second I nearly confessed my doubts - about the insanity of what he and General Thomas proposed, and about how unfit I was to lead men to kill or be killed. Strangely, only when worry appeared in his look, did I calmly answer him. "There seems little else we can do, sir."

"Then we are of a like mind in this. Good! Now, when we emerge from between the buildings it must be a massed movement. Come at a run down the road. At the small orchard, divide into columns. Lieutenant, you command the center, to be comprised of the Sergeant and his detachment. Lead them to cover in the scrub pine on the flatland. First Corporal, take your platoon to the right. Keep your spacing from the Lieutenant so as to make it difficult for the gunners. Corporal, you do the same, but break left."

"What of you, sir?" the Lieutenant asked.

"I shall bring up the rear; should panic or accident lead to stragglers. Now, let us begin for the light improves far too fast for my liking. Corporal Benton, a word." As the others trotted away only Eli cast a look back. The Captain faced me. "Corporal. Your honesty I appreciate, as ever I have. Few men can speak thus. Especially when doing so demands utter indifference to appearances. But I must know if in this instance it masks more that you would say? Is it my order that you think ill-advised, or do your own feelings give you pause?"

Here he had handed me the chance. Should I bare my soul to him? Did I comprehend it myself? "It seems a hard thing, sir, to order kin and dearest friends down into such a place as that. And, for no purpose other than to fire upon other men."

His hand came to rest upon my arm. "Search your recollections, Elisha," he said, in a low voice. "Have you not long known that we were fated to return to just such a place; for precisely this purpose?"

Visions I had had, yet none as dark as this. Nonetheless, there could be no denying his apparent faith in me. "I will follow where you lead, sir."

We plunged downhill. Not a word was spoken, yet we smote the silence with the clanking of our gear, the pounding of our feet, and before long our sucking gasps for air. The slope threatened to tip our overloaded bodies headlong. Just after we split from one group to three, somewhere to the rear a shell concussed the ground and a crash rendered the air. A glance at the bastion below us and off to my right revealed a drifting puff of smoke. One of the monstrous guns had fired. My foot found a slick patch; I slid sideways, yet somehow I kept my balance.

Finally we reached the relative safety of the far side of a low hillock. Some of the men collapsed, panting, upon all fours. I quickly surveyed the sweating faces about me. Azariah, good, and he with a grin no less, for me. Heman too, retained his feet. Noah, Jeremiah, Amasa and the rest all accounted for. I made my way to the Captain to report.

The rest of that day was spent gaining familiarity with the patch of ground we were to defend - with our lives if need be. The tour was of a stealthy nature, so as not to awake the gunners' interest. Conducted it was by the officers of the Massachusetts Company, who seemed anxious to cede the responsibility for this position. The entire left flank consisted of a shallow bay. From this quarter an attack was roundly feared. We learned the nature of this peculiar landscape in the hours that followed. The tide slunk silently away throughout, exposing vast stretches of mud broken by rivulets and isolated pools. The rising sun cooked the mud, strewn as it was with seaweed, smallish stones and the shattered remains of clams. This concoction soon raised a stench.

The line itself amounted to little more than a ragged, shallow trench. It ran from the flats to the causeway road - a span perhaps 100 yards wide. The dug earth had been thrown forward, acting as an earthworks of sorts. On top of this the chopped remnants of apple trees had been piled. We stepped down into the trench, making our apologies to the crouching Massachusetts men who shifted about to make room. For a man of my height, the breastworks offered certain cover only if I dropped to my knees. As water puddled in the bottom, and as the bastion was too far off to put me at risk from musket fire, I opted to risk my head to save my breeches.

The Captain attending us regarded my exposed upper body. "On occasion, Corporal," he pointed out, they post riflemen on the ramparts yonder. These marksmen can and have found my unwary soldier."

"Down, Elisha," my own Captain ordered, though I needed no further inducement. With wet seeping into the cloth at my knees I noted that my comrades had all pulled their heads lower. Like a line of startled turtles clinging to a single branch, we waited.

We had not long to wait. The Captain pointed out stout shapes dotting the bay beyond the ebb tide mark. They appeared as might an especially orderly beaver dam, but were said to be floating batteries. A moment later the Captain advised that these gunners, manning as they did much smaller cannon, occasionally loosed a gun at whatever captured their fancy.

Our host next pointed across the expanse to our front. He estimated the fortifications at considerably more than 200 yards. As I had thought, muskets posed no danger, but a rifle in the right hands most assuredly would. My brother was one such man. The possibility that he might be tasked with making marks of his fellow men loosed a shudder across my back.

"The cannon are 24 pounders," our host went on. "Though they fire a fearsome ball, such objects are too precious to be wasted on a lone man, or even a pair of sentries. So long as you present no grouped targets, you have little to fear from them." Captain Willes tipped his cap in acknowledgement of this sage advice.

I stared at the vast stretch of nearly flat, marshy land. The farmer that I was could not help but dismiss it as miserable stuff; incapable of sustaining any crop of which I had knowledge. In low spots, waist-high stands of stiff-looking grass sprouted. So this was the saltmarsh that on earlier transits of the causeway I'd never paid heed. I could almost hear Azariah whispering to me, as hunter to farmer he often did, that from places such as these, ambushes could readily be sprung.

The road, Orange Street as it was known, marked the extent of our line. A second company of Massachusetts men held from there to the opposite side of this narrow peninsula. These were the fellows who would soon be replaced by a newly arrived unit from the shore of Connecticut. We would all of us be new to this siege of but a few days duration. How long might it last, I wondered, and what would its outcome be?

Chapter 34

There you have it, gentlemen," the Massachusetts Captain said, once he had led us to a place where we could safely gather. "You are charged with defending what the local populace call Boston Neck. Can I answer any questions?"

As did my comrades, I deferred to Captain Willes. "Have they made any forays towards your line?" he asked. "By land or sea?"

"Nothing of consequence. Nothing that is, beyond the occasional firing of their batteries, or the big guns. That and the harassing fire of their riflemen."

"And no attack upon their positions, I take it, has been attempted by us."

The provincial officer raised an eyebrow at the mere suggestion. "The field is as you saw it Captain. Hundreds of yards of soggy ground to traverse, covered by cannon the length and breadth of it, with a water-filled trench and stout wall to surmount for those lucky to reach so far. The Regulars, well, they enjoy formidable defenses."

Unlike us, I could not but help thinking, for we possessed neither walls nor heavy guns. And if they should choose to attack our line, the only escape lay in climbing the slopes into Roxbury, under the eyes of their gunners the while. "The Regulars do indeed have the advantage of us," Captain Willes said. "They chose their positions well."

"Clearly they made careful study of the terrain. We lacked their luxury of time." He surveyed us one by one. "If there is nothing more, I have instructed my officers to pull the men from their forward positions at nightfall."

"We will be prepared to take their places then," Captain Willes assured him. With that we shook hands all around; then departed to issue our instructions.

The company transfer took place in darkness, with some confusion though scant noise. Our enemies fired not a single shot though I found I had held my breath for two minutes together, and more than once. Now, we men of Connecticut formed one of the first links in the chain wrapped tight round the city.

Crouching so that my free hand constantly went to the damp ground, I moved along my portion of our line. Seeing the faint, momentary glow of a pipe, I leaned in. "Heman," I whispered. "You seem quite settled in."

"Other than this blasted wet," he replied with grin.

"Come morning you'll wish it were deeper, wet or no," I said.

"If I'm to dig this earth I'll have more need of a bucket than a shovel."

Patting his arm, I moved along. My brother I had placed next. Only the back of his hatless head could be seen. "Azariah," I said. "What are you about?" I peered close and saw that he knelt in a firing position, oblivious to the condition of the ground. The barrel of his weapon perched upon a slight mound. It faced the enemy.

Without turning, he said, "When the moonlight shines between the clouds, I can make out a sentry. Just there, on the rampart above the carriage gate."

I stared in that general direction, and at that moment could, in fact, make out a flat, black outline. To see a man patrolling I required the aid of a glass, and daylight too. Clearly my brother did not. I blurted out, "You are not to fire!"

A ripple of hurried words and sudden movements spread out in both directions along our trench. "What's amiss?" Eli called in a sharp whisper. "Elisha, is that you? Have you spotted something?"

"No, First Corporal," I called back to him. "It is nothing."

"Very well."

Azariah had turned to face me. I whispered to him, though somewhat harshly. "You understand you are not to fire unless expressly ordered."

"Certainly, Brother. After all, even I could not be sure of hitting such a target from this distance."

His teeth did not show but I sensed he was grinning just the same. Imp that he often was, how could he find humor in the thought of targeting another in such a way? I stared at where the wall surely stood, but it had disappeared along with the moon. To shoot an attacker; this must be borne. But to fire upon a sentry keeping to his rounds; why it amounted to little more than execution. I rose, fully intending to take my leave.

"Brother," he said.

"What is it?"

"With a rifle I am certain that I could."

I stared hard at him for just a moment, hopelessly snared between the anger to which an older brother was entitled, and the duty of a corporal. As the former, I cringed that he might desire such a weapon, and for a purpose such as that. As the latter, I should be what, pleased that a lethal combination of a sharp eye and cold conscience was counted among my platoon? My God, how I despised this place to which we had descended. A sigh escaped my lungs, my lips. Saying nothing, I crept off towards where Noah knelt.

The remainder of that night passed without incident. Sunday, April the 23rd, marked our first full day in the trench. In the bright sunshine I felt as helpless as a mouse huddled on a bare floor with a row of watchful cats stationed above. Such was the degree of our exposure beneath those massed guns, each jutting its round, black, gaping maw directly at us.

"They cannot reach us where we lie," Adonijah Fenton said. "Is that not so?"

If my brother had spoken, or Heman, or many others even, I would have known it to be in jest. But since it had been the younger of the two Fenton brothers, they who had joined us in transit, I grasped that his inexperience had prompted his question. That, and perhaps his fear. I advanced on him straightway. Surely he could not have forgotten the ball fired on us just yesterday morning; that whizzing dark blur that had crashed hundreds of yards farther on then where we now crouched. I worked passed Azariah, then Noah. After each I sunk down even into the mud, and scanned the bastion before moving on.

"Otherwise they would certainly fire," Adonijah said to me as I came up. "Would they not?"

His eyes, somewhat overlarge and brown, darted now between the line of guns and me. I removed my canteen, and offered him a drink. He did, though his own dangled against his hip. I smiled and tapped his powder horn. "You recall how precious this stuff is for us." He stared at his horn a moment, as if failing to make any connection. At last he nodded, though vacantly, and returned my canteen. "Well," I told him, "it thankfully is in short supply for them too. Thus they can ill afford to waste shots."

"Oh, yes, of course," he said. "One mustn't waste shots." On this point they had all been admonished, and often.

"Which is why," I relayed to those on either side of us, "why we ought keep low, and move to the rear only when we must, and then only one or two at a time. Offer them no tempting targets, or if there's no help for it, only one backside at a time." This elicited laughter from most, and what passed for that from Amasa Allen. His high-pitched squeal came and went for a full minute or more. For once I was happy to hear it, for before Mister Allen was done Adonijah smiled at our comrade's racket. With that, I worked my way farther along to see how everyone fared, and perhaps, to keep my own fears in check.

We ate at midday in shifts, with Sergeant Carpenter's reserves taking the place of men pulled from the forward position. The carts had been hauled down the road at night; the horses' hooves wrapped to muffle the sound. Our tents had been unloaded and erected at once - in the dubious shelter of the hollows. The fabric would, at least, shield the men from the damp sea air. Some yards back from the tent flaps, cooking kettles too had been set up. They hung now on iron tripods. Beneath each a fire blazed. Thankfully, in the strong daylight neither the flames nor the wispy, whitish smoke could be discerned from afar.

I understood at once that dry, clean-burning wood would be a priority. So, too, would the need for water, which had to be hauled in buckets from Stoney Brook. This stream spilled down the hillside hundreds of yards to our rear. Such thoughts reverberated in my head as my comrades gathered to receive their tins of fish chowder. The soggy earth surrendered moisture with each step they took.

Eli knelt beside me. He held a cup of steaming coffee in each hand, and offered one to me. I gratefully accepted it. From our vantage point we could see the bastion off to our left, the men just below us at the fires, and Roxbury above us to our right. He joined me in scanning the whole of this scene. "What do you make of it?" he asked.

"In truth, we are pickles in a barrel, trapped, lest someone sees fit to pluck us out of this."

His head snapped 'round at my comment. "And wet all the while," he said. "Yes, an apt metaphor indeed." Though I appreciated his candor and agreement, the latter merely reaffirmed my anxiety.

"I received a note from the Colonel, my uncle," he continued. "It arrived with the Captain's dispatches." I waited, for surely he meant to say more. "I am to behave in such a way as to bring honor to the name of Chapman. Whatever may befall us."

Never had Eli spoken in my presence of his family, and certainly not of their expectations of him. I struggled for something meaningful to say by way of reply. I simply, silently sat beside him. Together we surveyed the tight spot in which we found ourselves. A minute later he excused himself - to check on his men, he said.

"Damn," I muttered, after he had gone; for he had sought me out and I had given him nothing.

Chapter 35

The weather warmed as April gave way to May. The rising heat impressed upon us that just across the road stood a host of tanneries. Shuttered they were, but the stink remained. Whenever the breeze carried in from the sea, we rushed handkerchiefs to our noses so that we would not retch. When the wind shifted about, the rot from fish long dead wafted over us from the mudflats. And always, each day and night, the ground oozed into our every garment and pore. How I longed to walk behind the plough; my nostrils drinking of the scent of fresh-turned, rich earth. Here a man could not stand upright without exposing himself fully to our enemy's guns.

If only to occupy my mind, I thought often of the confidence Eli had shared. It had revealed an irony that nagged at me. Despite all that had passed between my family and me in recent months, their sole wish was to see me, and my brother, returned home safely. I even allowed myself to imagine that Father shared in this. The Barrows, I congratulated myself, did likewise. Yet Eli, despite his prominent status and his family's sterling reputation, must court glory if he was to be assured of a Chapman welcome.

What, I wondered, did Eli himself seek? Was a glorious outcome what he longed for? At times I was convinced of it. On other occasions,

I recognized in his face doubts like those that flared within my own breast. Here there existed only boredom, broken by moments of terror.

Why, this very morning, the battery's sudden, explosive roar had near stopped my heart. Like a startled deer, I had practically leapt from the trench and into the open. The second gun to the left of the gate it was, and it directly opposite me. The crash and the smoke shocked both my eyes and my ears at practically the same moment - so close do we lie to the wall. Only the Captain's presence, for he was making his rounds, restored a sense of order. "A wood-gathering party is all," he reassured us; pointing to the far side of the causeway. "No casualties, it appears. A near miss that will teach our Connecticut neighbors to neither gather nor tarry in view of the gunners."

Amasa Allen had put his own stamp on the event by then proclaiming: 'Aye. Near enough to harvest some shitty breeches on the Norwich side of the road.' I stared now at the unkempt fellow as he tore into a chunk of bread. Unsavory he was to be sure, but his contemptuous tongue had given rise to his companions' laughter.

I surveyed my brother, my friends and acquaintances too; all comrades now. Yes, we desperately needed more of the humorous here. I chanced a glance over the lip of the hill. My eye still darted straightway to that second gun. Now that we had come, what was it that I sought? Certainly not glory. Just as certain I longed to see once more those familiar faces that came to me- even in my sleep. Yes, this I wished, but as leaving was out of the question, dwelling on them would not do.

With a sigh I shifted about. My clinging seat provided an uncomfortable reminder that I must find more oilskins. Neither of the Fenton brothers, nor my Mister Allen possessed one…

"May I join you, Brother?" Azariah asked. He plopped down beside me without waiting for a reply.

"You may."

To this he grinned as he slurped his stew. If I had not known so already, these repeated spoonfuls of watery broth would have confirmed this as beef stew day; for whilst the chowder contained actual bits of fish, not a morsel of meat had yet been discovered in any man's stew. "Do you laugh at my manners, Brother?" he asked.

"No, truly." I reached across and touched his arm to prove it.

"May I join you, Corporal?" Heman asked.

His smile warmed me as much as ever it did. "To what do I owe this pleasure?" I asked, determined to rise and procure my own cup of broth.

"Be on your guard, my friend," Heman said. "Azariah here has a favor to ask."

I remained seated. My brother wiped his mouth with his hand. This slight courtesy convinced me that I must prepare myself. "I do, in point of fact," he said. "The other day, our first day here it was, I made mention of a rifle. You may recall it." I winced to think what he must surely mean to ask. Anger followed close behind for my oldest friend had not seen fit to warn me. He might even have encouraged my brother in this folly. "Well, Brother," Azariah continued, "since then, when running a message up to the parsonage it was, I learned that rifles are being made available. By some captains to selected men."

"And with what ends in mind?" I demanded, much too angrily.

"Why, to target the enemy."

There lurked no guile in his expression or his voice. He saw no evil in it. "We have no rifles," I said flatly. "Not for any purpose."

He paused at this. My face he studied. "If we are to get some," he said. "Would you put my name forward?"

I hated him just then, him and Heman both. "I will consider that should the time come."

"I see. Yes." With that, he stood and strode away, pitching his stew at the ground.

I, too, rose to a knee, if only to separate myself from the pair of them. Heman's hand restrained me. "Elisha. A moment..."

"How could you encourage him in this?"

Rather than release me, he drew closer. "He needs no encouragement once he sets his mind to a thing. You know this far better than I, my friend."

"What then? You came to watch; to see if I would bless his becoming a murderer?"

Heman drew back at last. "A what? Elisha. You are his brother; his corporal too. He meant to pester Captain Willes for a rifle. I thought you could intervene somehow. Find some other use for him. He'll not be reined in. Not for long at any rate."

"Heman, I misunderstood..." But if my friend heard me, he turned not as he left my side.

Watching them both walk away, guilt swelled in my chest. I had failed them as I had Eli. I, who had once prided myself on being the one upon whom my family could rely. Here I was of help to no one. Self-pity crept in. I fought it off. Envy came soon after, as my brother and my friend fell in with others of our company. Studying them all, resentfully at first, it finally dawned on me – a purpose. I needed no other rationale than this. These men, they were my responsibility, as my family had been in Tolland. Whether we languished in this fetid salt-marsh or faced a charge from without those gates, I must concentrate on them; on what they might need to see this through. I slid down the slope, and stood upright.

"Corporal's finally got an appetite," Amasa Allen said.

"Do join us, Elisha," the First Corporal added.

I smiled in acknowledgement to them all, and partook of that watery, meatless broth.

The following morning the low clouds and steady drizzle made it difficult to tell when dawn gave way to day. Regardless of the time, the weather determined this to be an ideal chance to replenish our stock of water. I was chosen to lead the party. Both Azariah and

Amasa volunteered but that did not imply that my brother had forgiven me, nor that Mister Allen had surrendered his resentments. It merely proved how dearly each loved an adventure. I selected Heman to round out our foursome, for none was more dependable than he. I glanced at my friend from time to time, determined to renew my apology at the first opportunity.

I chose the shortest route between our camp and the brook. This way ran straight over the base of Meeting House Hill. No path lay more directly before the enemy's guns, but the mist, I decided, would serve as our shield. The choice wrung grins from Azariah and Amasa.

Our group advanced quickly and with little sound. Azariah led off, while Amasa brought up the rear. Being small and quick, they were charged with ensuring we were not surprised. Each carried his own musket, as well as a second. Heman and I needed our arms free to tote small casks. These I had opted for in lieu of buckets. They held more water, and would lose nothing to spillage upon the return. Their lone disadvantage was their bulk and weight once full, but Heman's long, lean arms, and my heft, should prove equal to the task.

We reached the stream in mere minutes, and set about filling the casks. The water cascaded cold and clear down from the hill. Even the air here smelled fresher. If Captain Willes had not selected me so often for assignments such as this, I would have been forced to volunteer quite as much as my brother. I glanced downhill now in search of him, for I had sent him scouting towards the shore. Heman lowered the second barrel into the stream, where he and Amasa kept it submerged. I set the bung in the first one, standing there on the bank.

Azariah dodged between a pair of scrub pines. "Not a soul," he reported, squatting nearby. The lack of enemy, I knew, and not the climb, had cast him down.

With the second cask bunged up, Heman and I each hoisted one. Off we went in the same order as before. We had gone about halfway, at a much slower pace, when Amasa called to me. "Corporal Benton, sir." I stopped our party at once, for rarely did he use my surname, and never had he addressed me as sir.

"I spotted that ball them Redcoats fired the other day," he said. "The big smasher."

"Is that all?" I asked, panting from my exertions. Annoyed I was, but in truth Heman's chest resembled a bellows just as did mine. "We rest here a moment," I told them.

"Them balls is precious, sir," Amasa said. "Ain't they, Azariah? Yer brother, sir. He heard it so from the General himself."

Whereas Mister Allen's eyes had widened with his pleas, Azariah's expression was indifferent. "I ran a message up the hill two days back," he told me. "General Thomas bemoaned our lack of large caliber shot. To a colonel this was. Said he'd give a gallon of rum to the man that could fetch him one of those 24 pounders."

I turned back to Amasa. Tempted, I was, to ask whether the reward of drink had inspired him. He might have sensed this for he dropped his eyes. "How, Mister Allen," I asked, "could you spot anything in this soup?"

"We both saw it, Brother," Azariah replied for him. "Yesterday, when we came hunting firewood with the First Corporal."

"I see. And he refused you permission to recover it."

Azariah shrugged. Amasa though caught at my sleeve. "Too dangerous, First Corporal said. But sir. Yesterday it were bright out and like you said yerself, today it's nothing but soup."

I stared at the pair of them, and then at where Mister Allen had first pointed. In truth, if I could not make out the roadway from here, there wasn't a gunner yet born who could target us in this. And Captain Willes himself had complained of our possessing little but four-pound shot. "Could you find it again?"

"Oh, yes. Yes, sir!" Amasa said. Azariah spoke not but his face brightened.

"Not a quarter hour, do you hear," I instructed. "In less time than that you will rejoin me here on the path. Or there will be hell to pay.

Do the two of you understand?" Their heads wagged like the tails of hunting dogs. "Take your own pieces. Heman and I will stand guard over the water."

Without waiting for me to change my mind, they launched forward into the surrounding brush. Within seconds the thick air had swallowed their sounds. I regretted letting them go almost at once.

"You were right to let them search," Heman said.

"Was I?"

"We all of us need something. The littlest thing to keep our wits. For them, this ball will do."

"If they find it."

"It doesn't matter. You let them try."

"Heman. About what I said..."

He smiled then. "There's no need, my friend. Listen! They return."

Sure enough they did, and if that little rooster didn't have that monstrous ball cradled like a prized pig in both arms. His gap-toothed grin stretched from ear to ear. My brother smiled just as broadly, and pumped both muskets aloft.

We had to burden Azariah with all four weapons so that we could cart our prizes back to camp. All of the company not serving in the trench had gathered for coffee and biscuit by the time we returned. At sight of us they rose up and swarmed about us. Laughter and jests filled the air. Men stuck out hands to pat the black iron ball. Our party had merely plucked spent shot from the hillside, but seeing the men's faces, one would have thought our company had won some great victory. "Huzzah!" they roared. "Huzzah! Huzzah!"

Captain Willes and the Lieutenant emerged from his tent before the last shout. They made no attempt to quiet us - though it's certain our voices carried to the bastion's walls.

Chapter 36

Another morning began with the summons from Captain Willes. As my platoon had already risen and hung out their bedding to dry, with but little encouragement from me, I hastened over at once. The Captain's small writing desk served as a table around which he, the Lieutenant, Eli and I squeezed. The folding camp chairs had been provided by the General, as a sign of favor to our commander I imagined. Though far too small to offer comfort to a man of my height, the one in which I hunched kept me well clear of that awful ground. Eli and I had entered together, and so too had we sat. We exchanged glances as the Captain, head down, finished attending to the sheaf of communiques clutched in his hands.

"I wish, gentlemen," he addressed us at last, "that I had some good news to share. I do not." He shuffled through the pages. "This one first, I believe. Dr. Warren, and he known to some of you, has penned an historic correspondence. A Mister Benjamin Franklin, our representative in London, is to convey its contents to the inhabitants of Great Britain. The letter concerns the events of April 19th, and includes depositions of witnesses to the atrocities committed by the King's troops. It avows undiminished loyalty to King George, yet seeks redress of the wrongs suffered by innocents. Here, for instance, he writes: *'...to the tyranny of his cruel ministry, we will not tamely submit'.* The acts of parliament, to which he refers, do you see?"

'I should perhaps share the final casualty lists from that fateful day." He produced another slim document.

"Of militia units, forty-nine men killed, and some three dozen wounded. The Regulars lost about two hundred and fifty troops all told."

"A bloody day, to be sure," Lieutenant Parker said.

"Indeed," the Captain replied. So many grieving families I thought - both here and in England. "Despite his losses," our leader resumed, "General Gage has in excess of 6,000 soldiers under arms within the city. We have this on good intelligence. What's more, he can and is being reinforced by sea." With my own eyes I had witnessed warships sail into Boston's harbor, unimpeded too, for the only navy afloat in these waters belonged to the King.

"What is our strength, sir?" Eli asked.

"One would expect us to know it to the man but we do not. So many companies coming and going, and each under separate command. I have heard wild estimates, from as few as a thousand, to more than ten thousands."

"As many as that?"

"Big numbers to be sure, but with no organization and in some cases indifferent training, what does it amount to?" He scratched at the stubble coating his jaw. "And the lack of cannon. The pitiful supplies of powder. Not one musket in 10 can boast of a bayonet." He caught himself and focused once more on his audience. "Allow me to be frank, gentlemen. Our position is not one of strength. If the Regulars launch a determined attack, in large numbers and supported by field pieces; well, how our company will respond, and those of our neighbors equally untested, is uncertain. We must, therefore, gather every intelligence concerning the enemy's movements as we are able; whilst denying the same to them. Our defenses must be strengthened. Patrols will be commenced. We will also employ riflemen - to keep their marksmen low, and their skirmishers within their walls."

The Captain stared at me as he said this last. The cause may have been none other than habit, yet I could not help but think he had knowledge of my brother's wishes. Though I may have flinched, I met his gaze. "Particular orders," he concluded, "will be distributed to each of you this afternoon."

Eli and I left as we had entered. Neither one of us, I realized, would be needed in the trenches for another half an hour. "Might we have a private word?" I asked him. He kept to my elbow as I wandered towards the bay. In a protected cove, where the officers were wont to bathe, we stopped. Judging by his solemn silence he appeared intent on speaking with me near as much as I desired his advice.

"My brother Azariah," I said, "he longs to be one of these riflemen the Captain seeks." I had intended a preamble, but the pent up truth of it would not be denied or delayed.

"I know of it," he replied. "I have for some time. The day that he made the request of you. I overheard." This I had not expected, and thus lost the force and direction of what I must ask. He filled in the gap. "If I may be so bold. What do you plan to do?"

"I swear, I do not know. I abhor the role. An executioner of men is what it appears to me. But what the Captain said just now. It makes some sense, as always he does."

"Just so. If we employ such men, we will safeguard our own sentries from the enemy's riflemen. And what's more, as Captain Willes intends sending out patrols, it is a means of providing covering fire should they be discovered. My uncle the Colonel has spoken to me of similar precautions."

"So you think I should let my brother volunteer?"

"What I think matters not. Clearly, he wishes it. Just as plain, our company has the need. The question is, as his corporal, do you think him qualified?"

I wanted to strike him just then, for his cold and calculating manner. "It counts for nothing then, to you, what I feel as a brother?"

He placed his hand on my arm. “I will not pretend to understand the pain you must feel, as his brother. That is why I speak merely as one corporal to another. But trust that as your friend you have all my empathy in this.”

His friendship in the face of my sudden anger shamed me. “I thank you, Eli.” I stared out to the bay, where the creeping tide had overwhelmed all before them. “’Tis true none has a sharper eye than he,” I admitted.

“If that is the extent of your praise, Elisha, you do him an injustice. I have made no secret of the fact I watch you, for the example that you set. Well, in truth, I have also observed him. Much have I learned from both Benton brothers these many weeks. About the two of you, and myself. From Azariah, I know that what I considered in myself to be dependable courage, is no more than a sense of duty. Whether I possess true courage, I am yet to discover.”

“Eli Chapman…” I protested.

“Your brother, I’ve come to believe, is valor itself. Think on it, Elisha. He volunteers without consideration of risk or hope of recognition. Like you he accepts any responsibility and most humbly. Like himself alone, however, he welcomes those tasks utterly lacking in the safety of precedent; just the type of challenge before which most men shy. He is a man fashioned for glory, and I can only wonder at him.”

Hearing in my friend’s words what I had long surmised but little considered about my younger brother, filled me with familial pride… and dread. I took Eli’s hand in my right, and covered it with my left. “May God help him,” I said, “for I fear you are correct.

‘Thank you, my friend, but now I must take my leave. I must speak to our Captain…alone.”

It was only when I stood outside the tent, waiting to be called, that I realized that I let Eli down a second time. In the first instance, he’d gone so far as to confide his family's expectations. Now, in praising Azariah's courage, he'd exposed doubts concerning his own. "Damnation…," I muttered. So focused had I been on my own family that again I'd offered him nary a word of comfort. As First Corporal he shirked nothing. As a friend he bared himself courageously. But had I convinced him of his virtues? No, I had not even tried!

"Enter, Corporal," a voice called from within. Both Captain Willes and Lieutenant Parker remained largely where they'd been seated earlier. "What brings you back to us, Elisha?" the Captain asked.

"Sir, if it pleases. About the call for riflemen. I have the name of a volunteer."

The officers exchanged a brief glance. "So soon?" he said.

I cleared my throat. "Aye, sir. My brother. There is no finer marksman in the company."

"No doubt. And do you speak as highly of his temperament?"

"As I understand the role, sir; his skills as a hunter seem to qualify him."

"Mister Parker. Might you excuse us a minute?" The Lieutenant rose at once. He touched my arm as he eased outside, and loosed the flaps behind him. The Captain beckoned. "I have known of your brother's interest for some time. It matters not how," he quickly added. "Suffice to say that on the occasion, we had no plans in that regard, so it mattered not. Now that it does, and greatly, I am pleased to hear that you endorse him."

"Sir," I said, at risk of interrupting him. "I thought to come to you earlier..."

"Elisha. You possess many qualities upon which Lieutenant Parker and I have come to depend. Chief among these is that the men respect and admire you. They will, we are both of us convinced, follow you, come what may." This praise, from him, from both these men, made me swallow and repeatedly. Yet I knew that something more was to come, and that this would be what he most meant to say. "Another attribute, what in normal times is a quality of the first importance, is your fine feelings. You care for others as if each was, well, kin to you I suppose is the nearest thing to it. As I said, it is a fine quality, and bound up no less, with the reasons men readily do as you ask."

"Sir?" I offered. "I think I understand you. You think I am not, not fit to be a soldier." I had misjudged him. His expression of puzzlement, then frustration, confirmed I had gone too far; said more than I ought.

"Heavens no! I had no such thought in my head." He stood, paced completely around the table, and sat down where he'd begun. "I speak of your rank, and as a consequence, having your brother and friends under your command. This and nothing more. It is a hard thing," he added, in words spoken more softly, and slowly, "to perchance order a beloved sibling, or son, or a cherished friend, into harm's way. It has broken men, I have seen it happen. Or led to partiality that in the heat of battle, has cost others their lives." He leaned forward, planted squarely on his elbows. "I merely want to convey that it is natural and right to hesitate as you have, in advancing Azariah's name. But, but, you have to accept that this must be the way of it in what may, what likely will come. As Corporal you must decide, and on the instant, what needs doing and by whom. In all else you've accomplished here, we find you lack nothing in terms of decisiveness. So too it must be, where your brother, or your friends are concerned."

He was through, and seemed content that he had discovered how to say what he must. So, too, should I. Though my knee quivered, I had to speak. "Captain. I understand you fully. I have delayed. I have denied, even, what my brother wished. Never did I doubt him, or even I suppose, the need that you now view as indispensable. It is the very necessity of this appalling role, however, and his qualifications for it, that have caused me to act as I have.

'There is more to it than even this. I don't know precisely why I marched with you, Captain, or what I thought to do. Maybe I meant to prevent another Lexington perhaps. To keep those Redcoats we both saw from trampling another common. Yet a month and more has passed and they threaten but little, and we, we hunker in the muck whilst our clothes rot upon our backs, doing nothing, protecting no one." He opened his mouth to speak, but this time it was me stopping him with a raised hand. "This nothingness should be quite enough for any body of men to endure, but no, now we must hunt our fellow man as we might turkeys. Nay, it's worse than that for we are to order our kin to pop off their heads."

I sank. Seldom had I felt so drained. I had said all of what had long troubled me, yet in manner of expression I had far outdone my qualms. Where I had felt confusion, I had claimed opposition. Where genuine dismay, I had declared revulsion. I dared to close my eyes a moment so that I might squeeze my temples. What had begun in truth had ended in hyperbole. I looked up expecting to confront a look of disgust in my Captain's face.

Instead he met me with warmth and openness; his own fatigue in evidence. "Elisha. Is it your wish to return home? I beseech you tell me true."

If he had ordered me from his tent, from his sight, I would not have objected. I deserved at least as much. Instead be offered what so much of me desired. His liberality filled me with gratitude…and shame. I knew in that instant that I must accept that which I would likely never grasp. "I will never leave, Captain. Not till you tell me we've done what we must do."

He studied me for such a time, and with so familiar a tilt to his head that I might have sat before my Grandsire. "Very well," he said at last. "I will consider this discussion closed. Quite as if it never happened." His tone, more than his words, put me at peace; and this despite all that I had said to embarrass myself and my family's name. "I will," he said, "send you the particulars for Azariah once the rifles I've requested arrive."

If this mention was a test of my new found resolve, I found myself up to it. I rose on steady legs, for I sensed I had been dismissed. "I will await your orders, Captain."

"One thing more, Corporal. I wish you to go into town at dusk. Make arrangements to select a man of your platoon who can take over in your absence. For no more than a few hours I would judge."

"Do you have need of a runner, sir?" I asked, for I had many choices other than Azariah who would prove far more fleet afoot than I.

"I have need of going myself, and should like you to accompany me."

"Very good, sir." I left him then. For an awful moment I wondered if I was, after all, to be marched up into Roxbury, and there thrown into the guardhouse - for dereliction of duty, or worse, cowardice. The thought chilled me. To be so disgraced; worse, to be the source of my family's disgrace. Was this to be my reward for baring my soul?

I stepped aside as Lieutenant Parker, responding to Captain Willes' hail, nodded to me as he slipped into the tent. I sighed once more, but now in relief. Neither of these officers had ever gone back on their word. They would not now.

A short ways off, Eli's platoon stood in formation. Just beyond I spotted the First Corporal himself, good friend that he was, busily lining up my group. His haste made clear that we must be overdue to relieve those in the trench. I hurried forward with confident steps – confident in both the commanders at my back, and my comrades to my front.

Chapter 37

Once we replaced the Sergeant's platoon in the line I sought out those to whom I must speak. So apart were we spaced, none closer than a half-dozen yards, that I would be assured a degree of privacy. I confirmed that the enemy's dispositions had not changed, then made my way to Heman.

"Well, my friend," he said as we crouched together. "You are looking like yourself once more."

"Am I?" I shrugged, to cover the extent of my relief, for the conference with Captain Willes had proved beneficial.

"Indeed you are."

"You should know, it is right that you do, that Azariah is to have his wish granted after all."

He took my arm. "It will be for the best. You will see."

"Ah, many of the times I have spoken such words. All will be well."

"Elisha..."

"No, truly Heman. Do not trouble yourself. I am resigned to the necessity. The Captain says we need such men; and if we are to have them, none could be a better choice. And I promise to listen with both ears should ever you and Azariah dare seek me out." His smile made him look of an age with Brother Jacob. It warmed me to see that grin of his restored. "Now, Mister Baker. I will have a favor from you."

"Name it."

"You are to lead the platoon this very evening." He protested, but to be singled out this way pleased him immensely. The men liked him, for as had been the case with my brother, they found in him one always disposed to listen. And unlike Azariah, my friend's patience was boundless. Equipped with no more than a pipe full of tobacco he proved equal to even Mister Allen's complaints.

Leaving him, I made my way carefully along the trench, more sodden than normal from the overnight rain. I advised each man in turn of the temporary change in command. Invariably my news evoked a smile, then a tilt of the head, as each sought out Heman to catch his eye.

Azariah responded much the same. "A good choice," he said. "And what of you? Why the absence?" He had apparently decided to ignore the matter of rifles, at least for the sake of politeness. Our conversations consisted of little more than such pleasantries of late. What I had to relate would work a change, and, I hoped, for the better.

"I am to accompany the Captain," I told him. "Up into town." This secured his full attention. "I am not privy to his purpose for going, you understand. But my guess is that he intends to request rifles. A half-dozen or so I should think."

"For heaven's sake, Elisha, tell me! If he secures them; what then?"

"Your intelligence is proven correct, it appears. We are to have marksmen." Unwilling to keep him in suspense any longer, I added, "And you are to be our first."

I had expected to see that cold light that gleamed in his eye when out hunting. Thank God I saw that not. Nor did he gloat as the younger brother in him often did. Instead, he simply sighed. "Thank you, Brother."

I leaned forward till our heads nearly touched. "You will be prudent will you not? With your life and that of others?"

He met my gaze - as one man to another. It set me back. "As my brother and my corporal," he said, "I will obey you. But know this, for I believe it in my soul, some men there are who deserve to be killed. And we have come face to face with them Brother, you and I."

I left him soon after. I did so with the clear and awful knowledge of what his words conveyed and his expression confirmed - the steel of determination. So strong was its forged iron that I felt its heat in me.

At the appointed hour I prepared to slip away from our frontline. I had already shaken hands with Heman and wished him well, when Amasa waved frantically from a good three places distant. In what served as a whisper for that shrill voice of his, he called, "It's an eye out we'll keep fer ya, Corporal."

"Whatever can he be at?" I murmured.

Heman merely grinned. "He had planned to thank you properly, when you made your mid-watch tour along the trench."

"For what?" I asked, knowing that he had thanked me a dozen times already regarding the cannonball. The reward of rum had already been long drunk; though he had surprised me by sharing it roundly.

"The oilskins you arranged for arrived this very day. Sergeant Carpenter distributed them whilst you were with the Captain, and gave you the credit of procuring the coverings."

"I did no more than request them."

"Convince our comrades of that," Heman said. Farther along the line, the Fenton brothers commenced waving. "Now off with you, Corporal Benton, or you shall be in hot water with the Captain."

Captain Willes and I made our way up the hill in silence. Though by no means aged, he had accumulated a good many more years than I. As a result, I had not known what to expect of his ability to scamper about the brush, up a comparatively steep slope, and aided only by the moon's pale light. Additionally, he was burdened by a pistol in one hand and the need to still his sword sheath with the other. He paid these hindrances no never-mind, and kept to the pace I set. Once upon the road he drew alongside. I said nothing for a full minute as his breathing did come rather hard.

"Where to Captain, if I may?" I eventually asked.

"To the parsonage. There is something I would have you see."

So, it was to be the General's quarters after all, though he chose to keep me in the dark as to why. The Captain had been admitted to General Thomas' office practically at once. The speed of it surprised even the grizzled sergeants who occupied the desks in the outer room. I thus was imbued with a degree of reflected importance, which was just as well, for my insides tumbled with doubt as to what my esteemed officer might even now be communicating about me to a personage as great as the General.

Though the room could have accommodated far more people, and likely did throughout the day, only one other shared the space at present: a courier, judging by the straps crisscrossing his chest and the pouches dangling at his hips. Working from a short stack of letters, he read the covers one by one, and slipped them into one pouch or the other about his person. At that moment he turned to me. "I was told your captain might have post for Hartford."

Hefting my musket, I took a step or two closer to him. "Aye, he does. If the General has nothing to add, he means to send them from here."

"I can wait."

"That's good of you," I replied. "Do you ride straight through? To Hartford?"

"That is my usual route. Though the correspondence I carry often travels on to New York."

"I wondered about towns closer in; along your route? Tolland, for instance."

"Tolland, Connecticut you mean? Why yes, your Captain in fact has often charged me with dispatches for a colonel in that town."

"Colonel Chapman that would be," I said while scanning the space for a piece of paper or anything that might accept a jot of ink.

Just then an officer entered, a colonel judging by his blue coat. "Might the General be at his leisure?" he asked.

The nearer sergeant had stood up immediately. With apologies, he explained that the commander was in conference with another officer. The Colonel cast a hard glance at the closed door, then doffed his hat with a gesture as sweeping as the brim was wide. He pulled out a chair at the empty desk opposite where the courier and I stood. With but a single look in our direction he seemed to decide we posed no impediment to whatever he might say or do next. "Sergeant," he said. "Paper and ink, if you would." These were brought to him, along with an explanation that no more than this could be had in the headquarters at present. He then asked the sergeant, in as near a whisper as a man of his self-importance could manage, "Is the General himself this night?"

"Sir?"

"Come, man. Is he over this business of Artemus Ward being selected over him?"

The sergeant, for all his rough and ready appearance, colored at this remark. "General Thomas, if I may be so bold, sir, has given every soldier in Roxbury to understand that your superior officer has been chosen for overall command."

"I am heartily glad to hear it. Though I will amend your speech in one particular. General Ward is made every man's superior. Now, if you would be so kind, perhaps you can acquaint General Thomas of the fact that I am waiting, and carry word from the General himself."

"As you wish, Colonel." The sergeant turned crisply, but not fast enough for me to miss the bitter resentment that flashed in his eyes. With a knock, he disappeared inside the office.

Despite this performance, or rather because of it, I knew that I had but little time. I advanced on the colonel. He drummed on the paper that he had so curtly requested. He did not turn his gaze on me with any kindness. "What is it?"

"I wonder, sir, if I might beg paper and ink. A single sheet would be a godsend."

For a moment I thought he might accuse me of mistaking him for a quartermaster, and heave the requested material at me. His reddish face turned a plum color. "Are you a member of Thomas' staff?" he demanded.

"No, sir. I am of the Connecticut militia. Stationed opposite the enemy's fortification on Boston Neck."

"Ah! All the way from Connecticut are you? And here to join the fight. Good lad!" He set to working my arm like a pump. "Paper is it? Well you've come to the right place, for I'm well-supplied." Into my hands he forced all that he'd been given. He demanded a supply of quills. Not once did he ask what I intended to do with this largesse. A moment more and he was admitted to the General's office. As Captain Willes had not emerged, I hurried over to where the courier still stood.

"I had you marked for the guardhouse!" the courier whispered hot in my ear. "That officer can be fuller of himself than a cow overdue for milking." I laughed, for I might yet end up in that dank cell before the night was done. He continued chatting merrily along as I wrote,

My Dearest Jemima,

I have but a moment. Forgive me this scrawl if it comes out all wrong. Even with time I could not hope to write what I feel, for ledgers are more familiar to me by far than letters. I should ask how you fare. Your parents too. I can only trust that you and they are well.

As I am a selfish fool I must turn straightway to what I would say. Captain Willes compliments my fine feelings as he puts it. What he implies is that I am perhaps not soldierly enough for the business at hand. I find no fault with his critique of me. I am a farmer. That and little else. I live to work the soil, to hold it in my hands, to plant things and help them grow. I lack the notions of soldiering, especially the instinct for killing. Forgive my bluntness, and my weakness both. I should not convey such crass and upsetting particulars to one so tender as you. But who else will hear me? There are those whose counsel I do trust, but I am corporal to them, and should not, will not, take the liberty. Eli Chapman might yet be one such who I may seek out, in time. You must scoff to hear me say so. Trust that he is not the man I knew. Perhaps, though, he is unchanged and only now can I make out his character. Forgive me, there is little time and less blank space.

How I miss you. I long to gaze upon your face. And just as surely I keenly feel the absence of your wisdom. Why did I fail to recognize all that you are to me, Miss Jemima Barrows? How I regret the days we might have had. Will it shame you if I dare mention - and the nights too?

Forgive me. I should put none of this to page. Show no one I beseech you. Tear it up or burn it if you choose. I have nearly crumpled it half a dozen times just in the writing of it. I must fold it now or never will you comprehend how I think and dream of you. This above all is what I strive to tell.

Stay safe, My Jemima.

I scratched my name below all this. I dared not read it over for fear of what I'd be forced by modesty and right behavior to do. The courier, seeing me set down the quill, sprinkled powder on it so as to hasten the drying of the ink. His act committed me to release it.

"To a lady?" he asked with a wink.

"My fiancée."

"Well then, special care will I take to see it safely delivered. For it ranks above mere dispatches for Tolland," he added with a grin. With that he produced a wax rod and warming it over the candle between us, so sealed the folded sheet. I hardly had time to shake his hand when Captain Willes emerged and waved my new acquaintance to his side.

The courier winked again as he hurried past a minute or two later. I kept the door ajar for the Captain but a pair of officers approached from the darkness. I recognized Captain Abraham Tyler for his company defended the far side of the causeway road. He introduced his companion as Colonel Jedidiah Huntington. I had heard of yet never met this regimental commander. My first reaction was near amusement, for in size he more resembled my littlest brother than a full grown man. His confident air, however, and Captain Tyler's respectful silence beside him, spoke well of him. When they continued on into the First Church these gentlemen left a favorable impression in their wake.

No sooner had they departed, when an old woman, clad entirely in black, appeared in the darkness. I stepped back, so that she might enter the headquarters. "Forgive me, Madam." She lowered her eyes in acknowledgement and passed by without a sound. The sergeants' greetings could be heard, coupled with profuse apologies that the General was engaged at present, but would she care to sit. After what I'd witnessed from them, the warm words surprised me no end.

"We may now take our leave, Corporal," Captain Willes said. "What is your impression?"

"Pardon? They seem like fine men, sir."

"No, no, Elisha. The Captain and Colonel Huntington are doubtless fine officers and gentlemen. I mean your impression of her. I thought for a moment I had the wrong night but lo, she came at last."

"The woman, you mean?"

"Of course, the woman. It is she I wished you to see. She petitions the General each week on this same evening. She pleads for a stipend, or a pension, or anything at all he has promised to secure for her. I believe he persists, though he's so far met with no success. For heaven's sake, Mister Benton, her husband was among those killed on the road from Concord to Charlestown."

The woman had to be as old as Mother Sarah; her husband then endowed no doubt with hair as white as Grandsire's. "But she is so, forgive me, of such advanced years."

He scoffed. "The Regulars must have forgotten to inquire as to her husband's age when they shot him. In his house this was, if I have it correctly." He took me by the arm and led me down the empty street. "Come, Elisha, you must forgive my ill humor. I am freshly emerged from a bout with a somewhat vexed commander, and find I carry some of his vexation away with me. Now then. You certainly recall our own conference of late." I satisfied him with a solemn nod. "Yes. Well, at that time it occurred to me that a glimpse of this unfortunate might put your conscience to rights."

A pair of sentries lifted their shielded lanterns so they might see our faces. With apologies to the Captain, they let us pass.

I saw his method at last. If our foes could snuff out the life of a grandfather, leaving an aged widow to beg of strangers, then I must find solace in stopping them; by any means. "Whether your intent was to fan my hatred, Captain, or rather pure disgust, you have succeeded."

We went on for a time before he spoke again. "I have fought alongside such men as these, Elisha. They are not like you and me. Lifetimes of rigid training and ruthless discipline have schooled them to fight. To the death if need be, and to give no quarter if victory demands it. If we are to defeat them, we too, must be hard."

"I do understand," I said, standing beside him there in the near total darkness.

"Enough then. Let us hurry back for I have much to share with you, Mister Parker and the rest. An agreement has been reached with General Gage to allow civilians in and out of the city. We and Colonel Huntington's forces are tasked with questioning the transients at the barricade. At least for the coming days. It will pull men from our line but it cannot be helped. This flow of people will bring us intelligence, and far more coming out to us than will trickle in to Gage."

"And, sir. The rifles?"

"Next week at the latest. Your brother must be ready, as I trust you now are." He patted my back, and then gave way that I might lead us down onto the Neck.

Chapter 38

No sooner had the Captain and I returned from Meeting House Hill, could be heard the faint yet insistent drums. Lieutenant Parker ordered Noah Whipple, who had been required to surrender his fife for a drum, to beat to arms. This brought the camp alive with off-duty men. They clambered forth from their tents, half-dressed and less awake. The Lieutenant and Sergeant Carpenter soon had matters in hand, allowing me to hurry towards my own platoon.

"It's you, thanks be to God," Heman said, as I tumbled down beside him. His musket shifted away from me and back towards the void of the marsh before us.

"My apologies," I said. "I should have called out to you."

"What's amiss?" he asked.

"The general alarm sounded from Roxbury. Keep your eyes peeled." Patting his arm I scampered along the trench. Most of the men exhibited the same or greater degree of agitation as had my friend. I announced myself to each with a hail before approaching. Only my brother's voice sounded like his own.

"At last," he said. "A reason for our coming hither." The scanning movement of his head put me in mind of the studied, confident movement of a prowling coyote.

"We do not know yet why the alarm," I replied.

"It matters not. Let the bastards come."

His utter assurance of an imminent attack sent my heart racing. I stared into the darkness, struggling both to see, and for control. Eli's words played in my mind - Azariah was bred for moments such as this. I glanced right, hoping, then trusting, that the First Corporal had his men prepared for whatever might befall us.

A squat form came grunting along the trench from the direction I had traveled. Noah Grant. "Elisha, is that you?" I pulled him down beside us. "Heman sent me to find you," he said, panting.

"What say he? Has he learned something?"

"Aye. Word comes of a landing. In force it's said; at Dorchester Point."

I whirled to the east, then arrested the foolish movement for the tip of land lay a mile or more off. "How are we to respond?"

"A company marches from Roxbury even now. They are to traverse the hill in our rear."

"And we are to remain entrenched?"

"Yes, Corporal. Lieutenant Parker will bring up the rest of the company directly."

"Very well. Thank you, Noah. Return to your position. I will inform the others."

Azariah took my sleeve. "I could skirmish forward, Brother. See if I can discover how far they've come inland."

"No!" He stiffened. "Your eagerness commends you, Azariah. But on such a night, with enemy troops and our own on the move, it would be far too easy to be shot by the one as the other."

"I do not mind the risk, Elisha. Truly I don't."

His courage did amaze me, for thinking a man possesses such a quality is far different than experiencing it in the moment of one's fear. But prudence can be a virtue too, and in this I felt I was right. "You can do something for us," I said. "Work along the trench till you find Eli. Relate to the First Corporal what Noah has said. Be sure to tell him that should his men hear a good deal of noise behind our position, they are not to fire. It will be the Roxbury Company crossing our rear. He might wish to advise Huntington's people as well. The Colonel himself was up in the town, so word may not yet have reached them."

"If that is your wish, Brother."

"Thank you, Azariah." He turned, but I held him back. "One week, Brother. One week and you shall have your rifle." He grinned and scampered silently away. Though he had gone I whispered, "And remember, announce yourself."

Some hours after the Roxbury militia had marched out; an endless period this was; starting at every sound upon the marsh; we heard them trudging back up the hill. A runner came confirming that the alarm had been false. Even so, when pulled from the trench we were ordered to lie by our arms the night through. Come morning our camp resembled upright corpses. Barely a man spoke as we breakfasted on coffee, bread and a dried white fish.

I had slept for an hour or two at some point, and must have dreamed of Jemima, for I awoke with regret; regret that I had written that sniveling note. I slumped at our cooking fire in no more mood to speak than were any of my companions able to do so. What man of real substance would complain as had I to his own wife. Only a pitiful creature indeed would behave so, and I had done him one better. I had whined of my fate and my failings to my fiancée. What a horrid start to make.

Azariah plopped down beside me. Coffee overflowed his tin, as did crumbs from his chewing mouth. "What do you want?"

He laughed, sparking the fire with a spray of whatever he had shoveled inside his grinning face. "Did we sleep ill?" he asked.

We might have been camping in Father's woods, so brotherly a look did he bestow upon me. "My God, Azariah," I blurted in a whisper. "How I have used Jemima ill."

"What?"

"This letter I wrote. I'm ashamed of it."

"Come now, Brother," he said and sidled next to me. He held the coffee to my lips. I first stared at it; then accepting the offering; drank. "I am quite sure it's not as bad as that," he insisted. "You wrote after all, and that's a start."

"The content would shame a convict. One pleading for his life. At least such a one would have just cause to scrape and whimper."

He stifled another outburst with the back of his hand. His arm about my shoulder surprised me - that he had done so, and with the comfort that it conveyed. "Little Brother," he whispered, "must I remind you that I am charged by her with the care of you?" Though sorely tempted, I did not push him off. "If your only crime was to bare your heart to her," he continued, "you've done no wrong. Being whom she is, Jemima will only love you the more for it."

"It shames me to admit it," I confessed. "Though I journeyed here of my own free will, I bemoaned my fate to her."

He nodded and peered into the embers. "There is not a one who likes this place," he said.

"Perhaps not, but there are some who thrive herein."

"That may be so, but leaderless we are nothing; and you, Brother, are born to the role. You mustn't surrender it." He stood. "When you write to her once more," he said, "send my sister her brother's love. And yours, too, for I sense you need reminding."

May in Tolland, when the fields sprouted green was my favorite time of year. May, here on the Neck, witnessed little change from the doldrums of winter. Surely the clumps of grass surrendered their pale, lifeless hue, but the landscape's swath of spikes stood as unappealing as ever it had. What's more, rain fell almost daily, turning the soil even more slippery.

Some days ago we had established a barricade on the road. It principally consisted of carts that could be rolled back at the approach of travelers from, or less often into, Boston. Sentries stood guard day and night. Our company provided men for one watch, whilst Captain Tyler's company manned the other. Some days I pulled this duty. Most others I spent in the forward trench, which now boasted what the Captain termed chevaux de frise. Prepared from the sharpened branches of felled apple trees, they defended likely places of assault with rows of wooden spikes.

On this particular morning I had been ordered to lead those who had volunteered as riflemen up into Roxbury. Typically any change was welcome but I knew in this case the Captain meant to test my resolve with the assignment.

The upshot of his earlier request was that we were to receive only four rifles. These much sought after weapons would arrive, we were assured, early in June. This left us but a few days to practice with the single demonstration rifle we had been awarded. Twelve of our company had volunteered for the coveted places. I led this dozen up the open hillside in loose formation, for while the Regulars had kept their promise of not firing upon the barricade, none believed the road itself enjoyed this same protection.

A number of targets had already been erected on the town green. Hay had been mounded behind them to the height of a man. The size of the open space was not dissimilar to that of Tolland's, and I had it on good intelligence that coincidentally the towns' populations were of a like, 1,000 or so inhabitants.

Azariah waited patiently while others clamored to show what they might do with such a fine shooting instrument; lent for the purpose by a New Hampshire colonel. The elder Fenton brother accepted it from me, and admired it prior to loading. In length it resembled our muskets, though it boasted a more comfortable weight. The wood stock was finely tooled but this had more to do with the owner's wealth than the gun's purpose. What set it apart in this regard was the thin barrel, or more specifically the grooves that spiraled down inside of it. It was these that would impart a spin to the ball, thus enhancing its accuracy twofold at least.

Observing Asa Fenton's struggle to ram the ball and wad home I was reminded of the snug fit that was said to contribute to the velocity when fired. "I could load and fire twice afore he's seated the one," Amasa jested. We laughed, but Mister Allen had certainly hit upon a distinct disadvantage should one face a charging enemy.

"You will fire on the far righthand target," I instructed Asa. "It is two hundred yards distant." A few whistled at this, for the muskets we held could not be relied on at half that distance.

Leveling the barrel carefully, he aimed. The report and smoke flashed as one. At the targets, a spotter signaled a hit. A cheer went up.

"Nice shot, Asa," I said. "You have assured us of a fine beginning. Amasa went next. Despite his earlier ribbing, it took him even longer to load the piece. He, too, scored a hit, and even closer to the center where a square of red cloth served as a mark. After the cheers for Mister Allen died away, we endured three more attempts without even the indication of a scratch upon yonder bed sheet. We then had a string of hits, though none bettered Amasa's mark.

After a pair of misses, Azariah suggested that the barrel be cleaned. I followed this suggestion without hesitation or inquiry. We celebrated one further hit. The red cloth, had however, not even been stirred by our efforts. To Azariah, I handed the rifle. He peered down the bore, and loaded it with a practiced hand. He studied for a moment the leaves of a downrange tree as they waved to and fro. The piece he snugged to his shoulder. The barrel rose up, then sank down, down... The shot came unexpectedly. Up went the signal flag. And down fluttered the red cloth.

We had our marksman, and three others besides.

Chapter 39

June arrived at about the same time that our allotment of rifles did. A runner brought the news just as I was preparing to lead a change of sentries to the barricade. Azariah had been among my party, but one glance at his face convinced me to release him. Somewhat surprisingly, Amasa offered to take his place. Much as he had anticipated the arrival of the guns, Mister Allen evidently found barricading the road more to his liking. I had an inkling as to why, but at the moment my brother occupied more of my thinking. "Do not be squandering the company's share of powder," I playfully admonished him.

"I am quite sure I'll be denied practice with these precious weapons," he replied, his impish grin restored.

A smiling Corporal Chapman confidently led Azariah and two others up the hill, this side of which was drenched by the rising sun. I headed off towards the road with Heman, Noah Grant, the young Cook boy and Amasa. Despite the jovial mood of the men, I harbored a feeling that this would be a long and eventful day.

A stream of foot traffic dotted the long stretch of road leading to what we now termed the Fortification. So many downtrodden refugees, in fact, that the men grumbled good-naturedly when I insisted the carts be rolled back into place following each group. Captain Tyler had impressed upon me the formidable strength of the King's cavalry and the utmost necessity of preventing a sudden charge catching us unprepared. "What better have you to do with your time, Mister Allen?" I gently mocked, for he was a target that all relished seeing teased, and he could be counted on for a salty retort.

"Drinkin' rum, fer starters," he muttered, at which our fellows guffawed.

I laughed too, at his splendid predictability. The opening of the bastion's carriage gate caught my eye. While the door allowing foot travelers stood ajar throughout the day, this larger pair rarely opened. Horses emerged. At once I trained the glass that the Captain insisted be carried by the commander of this post. It was a team, fine chestnuts by the look, and they pulled an equally smart carriage. I lowered the glass. "Roll back the carts," I said. "It appears we'll be entertaining a gentleman and his lady." Ever so smartly the men leapt to the task, none quicker than Mister Allen.

Heman could not resist sharing a wink. "Amasa's bride to be she is," he said. "See how he puts his shoulder to the wheel." The others enjoyed Mister Allen's muttered denials quite as much as the jest.

The driver was dressed every inch the gentleman; from his beaver-hair hat to the silver buckles on his leather shoes. If his clothes left any possible doubt, his manner of expression vanquished it. In a single sentence he provided me his name, his place of residence in the city and the reason for his present removal - that English officers had seized his home for their quarters. A minute more and I understood that his political affiliations may have played a part. It was then implied but not spoken that whilst his Beacon Street home could accommodate numerous visitors, even a single King's officer under the same roof with his daughter was unsupportable.

Sensing her gaze upon me I doffed my hat. Her eyes fell immediately. Even in that instant, however, their lustrous green had shone brightly. The blond curls peeking from beneath her hat surely complimented them. "And may I inquire as to your name, sir?" her father asked.

"Mister Elisha Benton. Corporal of the Tolland militia. Down Connecticut way."

"Pleasure, Mister Benton," he replied.

I had not meant to stare so boldly, yet the beauty of her high cheekbones was not easily denied, nor the coquettish look she'd cast my way. How long it had been since... A sudden movement at the rear of the carriage drew my attention. Amasa had elbowed the Cook lad. Seeing his leer I felt instant heat flood my cheeks. "Mister Allen! Please finish your search of the luggage. With dispatch!"

"Aye, Corporal. With dispatch it is." Even so, he grinned as he jammed what could only be the young woman's undergarments back into the trunk.

"My apologies, sir," I begged the father, and thankfully just before he turned to see what was keeping the sentries. "We are required to search everything, and everyone."

"None needed, to be sure. Though I do regret having been made to surrender a brace of pistols to the Regulars."

His daughter wrapped his sleeve in her gloved hands. "But you'll have no need of them now, Father. Now that we're among friends once more." Another sly glance did she risk, and this one made my heart catch. The loud clearing of her father's throat brought a blush to her fair cheek and restored me to my duty.

"Heman," I called out.

"Nothing to report, Corporal," he replied. Reacting to my earlier check of Mister Allen, he had fallen in with him and hastened the proceedings to a conclusion.

I was about to let them pass when the gentleman beckoned me. For certain he meant to have a word regarding the uncouth behavior of some of my companions, or perchance my boldness. Instead, in a whisper, he said, "Mister Benton, you might wish to report to your superiors that whilst detained at the Fortification, I overheard a lieutenant give instructions for strengthening the enemy's outer works."

I stiffened at once. "Did he elaborate, sir? Was defense the intent, or do they mean to extend their lines?"

"A valuable question, Corporal, but I heard no more."

"Very well. And sir. Would you object if I give your name to my Captain?"

"Not at all. I shall be staying at the family's country house in Quincy. Anyone can direct a caller to my residence."

I bowed to them both. It was with a mixture of reluctance and relief that I saw them move on.

The heat built steadily throughout the day. Occasionally the echo of a sharp report reached us from Roxbury. I could only assume that Azariah had convinced the First Corporal of the necessity of practice shots. As for Mister Allen, that he had been deprived of this opportunity did little for his humor.

Once I sent word to Captain Willes of Gage's preparations, there was little of a military aspect to occupy my thoughts. The refugees trickled past, weighed down by anxiety and whatever they could carry. Unable to offer more than water and the assurance that they were now safe, my thoughts wandered to the sparkle in the eyes of the lovely miss. The intense green had been rivaled only by the equally rich hue of her elegant gown. Nor could I forget the gentle heave of her bosom above that ruffled bodice - when she had leaned far forward to take her father's arm.

"There's a rare sight," Heman said.

I turned where he pointed, towards Roxbury, though my thoughts trailed somewhat further behind. I must cease this lusting after a woman who was nothing more than a stranger to me. Lovely she was to gaze on; seated high on her fine carriage. But what cause had I for looking? Why ever would I, when such a one as Jemima saw fit to favor me.

"Elisha!"

A cart maneuvered opposite the natural flow, traveling down the hill, bent on the city. It was drawn by a single horse, and upon the seat sat a middle-aged couple with a boy of 10 or so scrunched between them. The problem lay not with them, but our own Mister Allen. With his voice ascending to its familiar screech, he ordered "Climb down! Down, I say!"

"What is amiss, Mister Allen?" I asked. He handed over the reins.

"A Loyalist, Corporal, that's what! I found him out, I did."

I handed the reins to the man, and instructed that he set the brake. "Now, Mister Allen. What have you discovered?"

"Silver! A horde of it! God's truth. Here, sir, under the hay." Feverishly he knocked aside bundles of the family's clothing and tossed out handfuls of hay. "There! Silver!" He snatched out a goblet in one hand and a plate in the other. A jumble of forks, knives and spoons lay on the cart bed. "Like as not he meant to trade with the enemy."

"These are family heirlooms," the man pleaded. "I swear it."

"Bah!" Amasa exhorted. "We should confiscate the lot."

The woman gasped and the boy began to cry. "Why do you journey into the city?" I asked the man.

"Why? Because you people stole our home!" He checked himself, though his outburst had proven sufficient to make Heman and Noah, who had looked sheepish till now, glare up at him. Amasa took up his musket.

"Tell me again," I said to the man. "Why do you come this way?"

"We have no choice. Your soldiers. They came to our door the evening last. Already they had seized our livestock. This night, they demanded our home."

"I see. And do you have family with whom you might stay?"

"On Fish Street, yes. My wife's brother. A small home he has, but we have always been welcome at his door..." His voice trailed off.

I wanted to apologize to him; to his entire family. But doing so would be unjust to my comrades, and make mockery of our presence here. We all suffered with what had come to pass. Pitiable as their situation was, they had clearly amassed wealth in the preceding years. Their treasures would not be stripped away by me. "You may pass," I said. "Noah. Release the mare."

"But Corporal..." Amasa said. I silenced him with a glance.

"Thank you," the woman whispered, turning her pale face towards me. "Bless you."

I watched them go, feeling anything but blessed.

Chapter 40

The interlude with the Loyalist family had depressed the spirit of our party. Amasa felt wronged, or deprived of his due or some other such grievance about which I cared not. The general air of discontent he and I thus exuded seemed to cast a pall over the rest. It was my duty to address this, yet a lingering distaste for the episode, combined with the sweat-inducing heat, left me ill-disposed to make the attempt. And so we carried on, rolling the carts back, harassing the beleaguered with our probing questions, and shouldering the barricade into position once more.

A sharp report caused me to twist about. We had heard such sounds off and on the day through. This too had been a rifle shot, but not from Roxbury. "Where from?" I demanded.

"I've no idea," Heman said.

The reverberating boom of a cannon rocked us. "Down!" I hollered. Right there on the road the five of us dropped to hands and knees. "Into the trench," I ordered, and on all fours we scampered to our left. The road ahead and behind was clear of refugees. Thank God. "Which gun fired?"

"The farthest floating battery," Noah replied. I followed the direction of his arm. A smudge of smoke drifted lazily over the mudflats, its placid progress a stark contrast to the earlier roar.

"And their target?"

"Down there!" Amasa cried out. "The clammers. Them bastards fired on 'em." I caught sight of a knot of men carrying a prostrate form whilst others scattered. The vast stretch of mud reduced their progress to an ungainly plod, despite the need for utmost haste.

"How exposed they are," I whispered. Another rifle shot cracked. One of those bearing the fallen soldier now slumped down, nearly toppling the group.

"They're firing from the bastion," Noah yelled.

"Damn the bastards!" Amasa shouted.

What I would have given for a rifle at that moment. "Fire!" I ordered. "Fire on the Fortification!"

"Elisha!" Heman exclaimed. "We can't reach them from here."

"Will their marksman know as much," I snapped. "Like as not no. A revolving fire," I ordered. "Amasa, you first. Then Heman. Noah last."

"What of me?" the Cook boy asked. Never had I seen him hit a target; not even within the peaceful confines of our village green. "You and I will keep our weapons in reserve," I promised him.

As the shots commenced I studied the rampart through the glass. A marksman I did discern, halfway along its length and close on to the bay. The distance had to exceed 300 yards. Even so, to my relief and satisfaction, his head dropped from sight with each report. By the time of Heman's second discharge it stayed down. The party of clammers had by then fled the flats. "Cease firing," I said. "Our comrades have escaped. Well done."

Though we served out the long watch, I was to find no rest. The First Corporal led the replacement party up to the road under cover of dusk and drew me aside.

"The Captain asks for you," he said. It was typical to report the day's activity at the barricade but Eli's tone conveyed that something else entirely lay behind the request.

"Can you tell me what's afoot?" I whispered.

"I think he means to send a marksman out."

I inhaled sharply. "On account of the shots fired today?"

"Yes. He intends sending a message. If our men are to be targeted this way, so too will Gage's troops. General Thomas has given his authorization."

"Like a flock of geese those fellows were," I said with some heat, for my brother would likely be the means of retribution. "Waddling about on the flats. At midday no less. It's small wonder the Regulars fired."

"A passel of muttonheads to be sure. Their company arrived just this week. The General is furious that his standing order regarding gathering in sight of the enemy was ignored."

"Were any killed? I saw two fall with my own eyes."

"I was still up in the town, with Azariah, when they staggered up the hill lugging two casualties. The doctor thinks both will live."

"God's mercy, then. I best report."

"Elisha, the entire company is aware that your party's return fire forced that rifleman to quit what he was at. A brilliant stratagem. My uncle will be proud when he learns of it in my next post."

I hustled my small band of sentries back to camp. Proud of them I was, yet it had not occurred to me how our actions would be viewed. At the time I had only thought to save those clammers, muttonheads or no; whilst praying that our potshots did not incur, in turn, the cannon's wrath.

Captain Willes and Lieutenant Parker listened to my report without interruption. A few particulars they asked about both the gentleman in the carriage and the episode with the Loyalists. Throughout these discussions, intent as both officers were, clearly another topic impatiently waited. The Captain cleared his throat, and advanced it resolutely. "I mean to send Azariah out this evening," he said. I replied not. "You seem unsurprised, Corporal."

"I imagine you intend to respond in kind. The enemy threatens our men, and so you mean to..."

"What we intend, Corporal," Lieutenant Parker interrupted, "is to shoot them as they've shot us." Never had he interrupted me, nor anyone; or spoken with what must for him be fury. I clamped shut my mouth.

Captain Willes leaned forward planting both fists on the table. It quivered. "Thank you, Lieutenant, for clarifying my intentions."

"Beg pardon," the Lieutenant said.

Discord between them marked another first. Might they be suffering, too, from the pain of doing little, whilst our comrades were daily subject to targeting? And had today's blood-letting proved a straw of sorts?

The Captain exhaled and spoke. "Gentlemen. It is necessary that we send out this night a marksman. If possible, come daylight I would charge him with negating the threat posed by the enemy rifleman. Am I clear?"

"And my brother, sir, represents our best likelihood of doing so."

"Aye, Elisha. He does."

"Then I have but one request, sir. That I be allowed to accompany him on this patrol."

Captain Willes allowed himself the hint of a grin. "Allowed? Bloody hell, Mister Benton, there will be no patrolling otherwise. Come now, cease your gaping. Our entire company can be rightfully proud of your brother's marksmanship, but Lieutenant Parker and I quite depend upon your soldiering. Were it not for your quick thinking at the road, our forces would likely have suffered more grievous losses this day. Now, be off with you."

I left them then, and filled my head with the varied and numerous details that needed tending. Heman, for instance, would need to be told the platoon was his once more. Extra water and powder would be required - for two. From Sergeant Carpenter a bit of smoked meat or dried fish might be obtained…

Word had reached Azariah before me. "When do we head out?" he asked.

"At full dark. Wait here in camp. First, I want to ensure that every man in the trenches is aware that we'll be out there, in the marshland." What I didn't volunteer was that if we were to be shot at this night, I preferred that it be done by our foes, and not our friends.

⁂

Captain Willes loaned me his spyglass and for this I owed him much. Having alerted the frontline sentinels, and with the route we would take etched in my mind, I made my way to Azariah in twilight.

"Now?" he asked, fully prepared to lead off.

"Aye, and you will follow me."

Shock showed in his face for he was incapable of concealing a thing. A sullenness came next. "As you wish," he said at last.

Up out of the trench I rose and scurried off towards the first clump of marsh grass. I bothered not to check that my brother followed, or to listen for his footstep. He would be there. I crouched at our first destination, and paused till my breathing slowed. Not since he was 10 or so, I realized, had I preceded him on a hunt. Yes, a hunt; that's what this was. At once I set off for the next checkpoint.

Three more series of scrambles, awful balancing acts of making haste and fearing discovery, led us to the intended place. Attempting to still my every breath left me near exhausted. Sinking onto one knee, which itself sank inches into the weedy muck, I surrendered myself to the deep rise and fall of my chest.

Azariah poised beside me. "You chose an indirect route, Brother. This is good. We are now far enough downwind that should they have dogs, our scent is unlikely to be picked up." Of dogs, I had thought not one whit. My heart jumped at the notion. "Now," he went on, "might I suggest we make straight for the wall."

"We go no farther," I ordered. My flat statement met silence. "I reckon the Fortification to be 150 yards, more or less. At break of day we should be afforded a clear line of sight to the ramparts. You should, that is. Azariah, I am convinced you can make the shot from this distance, or trust me, I would have moved closer in." I did not bother to explain that from this place, the ground fell slightly away towards the bay, liberally dotted with depressions that might offer concealment and aid escape.

"Very well, Brother."

"Shall I take first watch then?" I asked. At this he busied himself with shielding his weapon from the wet. Satisfied, he lied down. In mere minutes, he was asleep. A breeze came up soon after. Recalling Azariah's earlier observation, I was relieved to think it more effectively carried off any scent we exuded, for I had sweated clean though my shirt. The wind also stirred and rustled the stiff, waist-high grass surrounding us. Insects added harsh notes that started, stopped, and began again. When I roused my brother, I needed rest most desperately.

I awoke with such a start that Azariah clamped one hand on my mouth, and pressed me back down with the other. Seeing that I recognized him, and the place in which we found ourselves, he let go. Instantly though, he put a finger to his lips. Then with that same lone forefinger he pointed.

Dawn threatened. Silently I cursed that he had let me dream so long. I rolled to my stomach and rose up to my elbows. My musket I unwrapped and inched forward. The Fortification traced the horizon as an unbroken line of black, backlit by the fast-approaching day. There, right where my brother had indicated, I could make out the pumpkin-shaped silhouette of a man's head. Suddenly my heart leapt to my throat. The moment the sun sprung clear of the sea, we would be blinded. How had I not thought of this? Azariah's tight jaw convinced me he grasped full well time was of the essence.

"I must fire at once," he whispered.

"My God," I muttered. I re-checked the path along which we would withdraw. "Yes, at your choosing." Hurrying the spyglass out of my coat, I scanned the wall. Other soldiers there were, but sentries only, passing to and fro; exhausted from a tedious watch I hoped.

Azariah had loaded his rifle and was settling in. Through the glass, I could make out the shape of the soldier's hat, or cap rather, for it was not the tricorne typically worn. Also visible was an upraised barrel. This was the rifleman who plagued us yesterday. He had conveniently taken the same position. I made a fine adjustment of the brass barrel. The fellow's features came into focus...

At that moment an explosion echoed in my right ear. The glass jammed against my eye.

"Got him!" Azariah said quite loudly.

In mere seconds, I had snapped the glass shut, slipped it into my clothes and scrambled up. "Come!" I called to him. "Come on!" Azariah popped up at once and we fled.

When we reached the shelter of a stand of reeds and grass, I threw myself into the thick of it. Azariah slid in beside me. His sucking breaths rivaled my own. I twisted about so that I faced the bastion. The sentries had converged on the place where the rifleman had stood. One or two stared out over the marsh. Shouting could be heard. As yet, we had not been discovered.

"I hit him," Azariah mumbled.

Again I saw the last image framed in the circular glass field – the cap and head of the marksman at the moment of impact.

Chapter 41

Before we reached the safety of our own lines, shots rang out. I ducked into a stand of reeds and yanked Azariah down beside me. Men shouted in the distance. I trained the glass. Redcoats swarmed like enraged hornets onto the ramparts. They hollered, they pointed and they fired, but at everything at once and nothing in particular. "They've not seen us," I whispered, despite being well out of earshot. "Azariah. I believe we are quite safe." He did not speak. Not even did he nod. We started off for the final leg of our return.

As fate would have it, the last bit of cover stood nearly opposite where Heman hunched low; Eli beside him. Their heads bobbed. Clearly they sought us out in that waving sea of grass. It startled me to think how close one could approach without being seen. "First Corporal!" I called. "Heman Baker."

Their shouts of recognition and welcome swept along the line. "Huzzahs!" welcomed our leaps into the trench. The First Corporal had to rise more than once to restore order - lest we invite the big guns to play upon us. To me he said, "What news?" So, they knew not of our success. In the dawn's faint light they would not have seen the consequence of Azariah's shot. And judging by my brother's blank countenance, none might guess at the perfection of his aim. "Elisha?" Eli repeated.

I squeezed his arm. "Our mission is accomplished, but pray ask no more just yet. I must report," I said to all. "Come, Brother, our work is not yet done." With some difficulty I led him along the trench, and back towards camp. I determined to lead Azariah to our tent, thus giving him some moments to collect himself. His silence baffled me. It scared me, too. I was not to have my way, nor he his needed solitude.

"We heard the ruckus," Lieutenant Parker called out. "I'm with the Captain. Come!"

I made my report to our seated officers. Throughout, Azariah stared at the fabric wall billowing above their heads. My words brought grim smiles to both men's faces. As I went on, they looked more towards my brother. When I had finished, the Captain asked him, "And you, Azariah, you concur with what the Corporal has conveyed? That you believe the marksman to be the same who brought down our comrades yesterday, based on his position along the wall, and that he was felled by your shot? Azariah Benton?"

At the mention of his name, my brother seemed to focus. "His head came off," he said, in a low voice. "It was there. Then it was gone."

Captain Willes cleared his throat. "I see. Yes. Then, that will be all. Corporal, you may escort the private to his tent. You might ask Mister West to pay him a visit. Then rejoin us, if you would."

"Sir," I replied, and led my brother by the arm.

I did as they had bid me, and more. I lingered in our tent whilst Jeremiah plucked instrument after instrument from his bag. His gentle, melodic voice kept up a steady stream of pleasing sound while he performed one test after another. Through it all, my brother neither assisted nor inhibited the doctor's manipulations of his limbs or re-arrangements of his clothing. At the conclusion, Mister West put his head near mine. "With his body, there is absolutely nothing amiss. He is, in fact, one of the fittest physical specimens I've yet to study." With a smile for his patient he added, "It is best we let him rest now. Azariah. Close your eyes." My brother did, and we stepped outside.

His vacant stare scared me. "What is it?" I asked. "What's happened to him?"

"Shock, if I had to guess. Do you remember the Miller family? In Willington this was." I shook my head no. "No reason you would. My services were requested, as their doctor was called away by a complicated birth. The town elders requested me because there had been a fire. A bad one. Nothing left of the family's home but the chimney. Both parents died trying to save the children. They did pull three of them out. The oldest it was who behaved afterwards, well, like Azariah now does."

"And what became of him?"

"In truth, I know not. I was still completing my training under Doctor Cobb you understand, and beginning to acquire patients of my own, in Tolland. I journeyed to Willington on a few occasions, to see how the boy got on. He did ultimately manage to function on his own. But, I do not recall that they ever awarded him responsibility for his younger siblings. I am sorry, Elisha, perhaps this was not what you wish to hear."

"No, no. I must know the way of it."

"I will follow your brother's condition most closely. Of that I can assure you."

I thanked him then, and with another glance inside the tent flaps, returned to the Captain.

No sooner had I been admitted to our commander's tent than the orderly was dispatched for the First Corporal. I was left standing whilst the Captain and Lieutenant Parker pored over a map. Even upside down, I discerned it was not of the Neck. It appeared to be of Charlestown, and the entire peninsula just north of Boston. Captain Willes glanced up. "How is he? Your brother?" The Lieutenant looked up at this, recognized my discomfort, and immediately resumed studying the map.

"I have never seen him like this, sir. The doctor, though, finds him fit, and believes that time will restore him."

"I see. Unfortunately, time is a precious commodity at the moment." Before he could say more, the orderly announced the First Corporal. Eli entered and stood at attention beside me. "There you are," the Captain said. "Very good. Gentleman — dire news, yet it may hold an opportunity for us all." Eli and I exchanged glances. "Word comes from the city that Gage plans to launch an assault. Only two days hence, we believe." And herein lies an opportunity, I wondered? Good God.

"Apparently he intends putting those reinforcements who arrived last month to use; and us to the test. His troops are to land by sea, both just to our south in Dorchester, and also on the Charlestown Peninsula to the north. He intends to occupy and fortify the heights at both locations. Think, gentlemen, should the enemy manage to haul cannons up to the crest of those hills..."

"They could fire down on top of us," Eli said.

"Precisely so. And upon Cambridge just as easily from Charlestown, and this is where the leadership of the Committee of Safety currently resides. So, you can see that such an eventuality is not to be allowed. The Committee intends to seize the initiative from Gage. Colonel William Prescott will lead a force of over 1,000 strong onto Charlestown Peninsula."

"When, sir?" Eli asked.

"This very night. Among their number will be a Connecticut contingent of approximately two hundred. A certain Captain Thomas

Knowlton is to be placed in command. Though he was appointed by General Israel Putnam, and not our own regimental commander General Spencer, we need not hold that against the good Captain. He proves by happy coincidence a neighbor - hailing from the town of Ashford.

"Now, to stop your wondering, I asked General Thomas whether an open offer for volunteers can be extended to our companions. The General's answer was no. Our company is to hold the line here, in case the Charlestown action fails, and thus undeterred, Gage moves on Dorchester Heights."

"We're meant to sit here?" Eli asked. I'm sure it occurred to him, as it did to me, that Captain Willes had asked about marching to Charlestown for his own sake as well as the company's at large.

"First Corporal," the Captain said, "a few, a very few volunteers are sought. It is likely the Regulars will attempt to contest any occupation of this, what is the name of the hill, Jonathan?"

"Bunker Hill, sir. Elevation of something over one-hundred feet."

"Bunker Hill, yes. As our enemy will most assuredly contest possession of these heights, for they overlook Boston itself, marksmen will be needed - for harassing fire to hamper enemy skirmishers, for disrupting runners and so on."

My thoughts flew to Azariah. He would have leaped at such a chance. He would hate me if I volunteered him not for such a mission. And now what was to be done? Both officers waited. Their looks were probing; patience barely maintained. Eli's expression seemed utterly perplexed. Why, he must wonder, did I not advance my brother's name? "Amasa Allen is our most expert shot at present," I said. "The elder Fenton brother is a close second..."

"Very well, Mister Benton. Two will prove sufficient. After all, we cannot strip this command of our limited supply of riflemen." He glanced at the First Corporal. "There is one thing more. As this is a night action, with numerous independent commands present, there cannot possibly be enough non-commissioned officers present to maintain order. Therefore..."

"Then please, sir," Eli said, "accept my offer to volunteer."

How quickly had my friend done so. Marching off at night to this distant peninsula, fortifying heights within range of the enemy's cannon, on shore and at sea, all of this whirled in my mind, yet he had already committed himself. And he thought my brother heroic. Captain Willes' eyes found me. Thus was his intent made clear – that we both should volunteer.

The calmness of my voice surprised me. "I, too, sir, should like to offer my services." I don't know why I said as much. Perhaps it had to do with Azariah, lying still, unable to do what he had been born for. And maybe it only had to do with me.

The officers stood. Lieutenant Parker extended his hand. "I dearly wish I could accompany you. Godspeed."

"I will not be stripped of all my gallant commanders," the Captain said with a smile that softened the web of wrinkles at his eyes. In my palm he slipped a folded, sealed note. "This found its way into the express messenger's pouch," he whispered. "No telling how."

I recognized the hand at once. Jemima. Into my blouse it went.

I had touched my brother's shoulder. He woke, and smiled wanly. I said nothing for fear of drawing him full awake. I left his side with an image of him lying quiet, as he might have done in the loft at home whilst I began a day of chores. But labors of a different sort awaited me this night. The next stop was no easier, for Heman suffered at remaining behind, as much as for seeing me go. I found I had no more wish to leave his side, then he for parting from me.

"I can rightly lay claim to this platoon," my friend said, "if you persist in leaving it in my care." We both began to laugh, then stopped abruptly. I wonder if it had occurred to him, as it did me, that before dawn his jest might prove prophetic.

"Watch out over Azariah, will you?" I asked.

He squeezed my hand. "Be safe, my friend." With that, he faced the marsh.

"And you." I did not dare look back as I hurried off into the dusk.

Chapter 42

As ordered, we fell in with a large detachment marching out from Roxbury. Many other units were already said to be on the road, and they stationed closer to the peninsula. As a consequence, Captain Knowlton, upon whom we had not laid eyes, hurried us along at the quick march. Eli, Amasa, Asa and I formed one rank of four abreast, with the First Corporal and me anchoring the outsides. Both of our marksmen had conveniently volunteered so none other had been asked. In the scant moonlight I could not make out my companions' faces, but judging by their confident, steady strides, they were eager for what might lay in store. I wondered what the hours ahead would hold, but felt more anticipation about Jemima's unread letter, which now rested warmly over my heart.

We occupied the rear of the column, along with a few other ranks of auxiliary troops. I could taste the unseen, swirling dust of our passage. The thud of our feet upon the packed earth kept the cadence for both drums and fifes had been silenced for this night march. We left Roxbury behind us, and little more than an hour later came upon the Great Bridge. The wooden span, its decking replaced since the earlier foray by the Regulars, creaked with our hurried passage over the Charles River.

Here in the Towne of Cambridge the company halted. Soldiers and civilians milled about as though it were a frenzied kind of market day. Shielded lanterns swung from many a hand. Goodwives were about, offering hard cider or water, sometimes bread, and always a kind word. Some of the women were dressed all in black. One, of an age with Jemima, served me, but if ever she had enjoyed the bloom of youthful beauty, it had quite abandoned her now. "Thank you, Madam," I said, in deference to her widowed state. She curtsied, then moved to the next man without ever lifting her eyes. The order to resume came with a restrained shout. I felt for Jemima's note in my blouse as we marched away.

Another hour saw us approach a narrow, inky isthmus of land, surrounded by gleaming water on both sides. "Charlestown Neck," explained a passing sergeant. "No talking from here in. The guns of the enemy's warships can reach this place."

"Boston Neck. Charlestown Neck." Amasa mumbled. "Too many bloody necks if yer ta ask me." For the first time this night I laughed, as did my companions.

A harsh "Sssh!" followed. From the Sergeant no doubt.

We trudged, stumbling often, up the broken slope of what someone in the ranks ahead called Bunker Hill. On the road we had merely followed the man ahead. Here, the ground fractured our formation, scattering men. "Keep each other in sight," I whispered, hoping my three companions heard.

No sooner had we reached the mob of soldiers at the summit, when we began to descend the far side. "Where are we off to?" Eli's voice demanded.

"We Connecticut men are to move forward," someone replied. "To the shoulder of Breed's Hill." On the Captain's map this lesser rise had appeared just inland from Charlestown and the warships that guarded Boston.

At last, we reached level ground once more. Here, however, my boots squelched in unseen wet. "More bleeding marsh!" Glad I was to recognize Mister Allen still to my left, but I had not the wind for laughing. My parched throat wished for another such lass as had come to me in Cambridge. At least her offering had preserved the contents of my canteen.

In the dark, up we went; a ragged mass of bobbing shapes. We were directed to traverse the hill. Thus we did, slipping on knee-high grass slick to the touch; it so blanketed the earth that one's footfalls were never certain. Up above, the blows of picks, the scrape of shovels, and the grunts of men tumbled down on us.

"A redoubt is being thrown up." I recognized the voice as Eli's. "Come on," he said. "We are just down here."

"What? Down again?" For once I understood Amasa's grumbling nature.

From my left, another voice issued a series of commands. Men were positioned forward as sentinels. Others designated as messengers. Sergeants and corporals were assigned sectors of a line I could not yet see. And everyone was commanded to dig. Throughout, the tone conveyed urgency without panic, expected obedience without stirring resentment.

"Do we entrench, then, Corporal?" Amasa asked.

"We do indeed." Though only one shovel and one pick were assigned to the four of us, we took turns. Those not digging used bare hands to shift and pack earth forward of what we hoped would become a defensible ditch. At some point in the night, a pair of fence rails were brought up. These we incorporated into the mound growing to our front. Coats had been removed early on, but Eli and I eventually discarded our waistcoats as well. Side by side our foursome worked in shirtsleeves. Our new companions on either side did likewise. So often did we reach for our canteens that I counseled mere sipping when gulps were much sought after.

The sudden roar of cannon fire sent us scrambling for our weapons and the relative safety of the depression we had thus far secured.

"How close were they?" someone asked. "Are we in range, do ya suppose?"

It was Eli who answered. "From the far side of the hill came that last. The harbor I would guess. A warship most like."

Thus encouraged, Amasa added, "Not yer right big smashers neither. We know, ya see. Down at Boston Neck they've fired the twenty-four pound balls at us. I found me one. Didn't I Corporal? Me and Azariah."

"That you did, Mister Allen." I replied, as those on our flanks marveled at this bit of news.

"Right then, men," came the reassuring words of the officer. "The enemy seems to have entertained us to their satisfaction. What say we resume digging in?" Suddenly a tall figure loomed above me. "From where do you men hail?" asked that now familiar officer's voice.

Something in his tone led me to stand. His posture had an erect, refined quality. "We, the four of us here, sir, are stationed on Boston Neck – before the Fortification. We are men of Tolland, Connecticut ... and Stafford too."

"Neighbors, then. I am Captain Thomas Knowlton. From Ashford." I introduced my comrades and then myself. "Pleased to make your acquaintance, gentlemen," he replied. We could have been standing on his common or our own so calm was his demeanor. I bowed before realizing that the effort was likely wasted in this poor light. One of his lieutenants came up just then but he still thought to thank us most handsomely before he went away.

"The Captain approves," Amasa said, admiring the scratched out hollow. "Thankin' us like he done."

I allowed myself to comprehend that Captain Knowlton, good officer that he was, appreciated that we followed him here far more than he contemplated our digging prowess. Such thoughts I need not share with Mister Allen, however.

I peered hard to the east as though I might hurry the sun's disk from the sea. Just downhill, our entire left flank consisted of water. I thought it, too, was the sea until someone identified it as the Mystic River, and this practically its mouth where it emptied into Boston Harbor. River or sea its proximity proved shocking, for warships sailing up it could blast us from this hill at point-blank range, or land marines in our laps.

Directly forward the ground pitched downward in the direction of a protruding knob perhaps half a mile distant. A narrow strip of sand bordered the left hand side, running from just below us out to that elevated point. From there the coast turned south towards Charlestown. The town itself was blocked from view by Breed's Hill upon which we squatted. The man who knew about the Mystic announced his family came originally from Gloucester, and were fishermen all. He was happy to inform me that my knob was commonly known as Moulton's Point.

"What do you make of the redoubt?" Eli asked.

The earthworks had made of it a flat line. It ran more than a hundred feet to a side, and each protected by a ditch. The walls rose taller than a full grown man in height. Dozens of heads poked above the one facing north, which overlooked our position. They must stand upon a rampart within. "An impressive achievement," I said. "And in just one night..."

"Indeed. Even Mister Allen terms it a proper fort. Though without cannon..." A crash of guns, the truly big smashers this time, silenced him.

"Down!" I cried. And draw down our heads we did. The thunder rolled on and on but we soon discovered that whatever the intended target might be, we were not it. Though the air shook with repeated concussions, this dawning realization returned men to their feet. Just as suddenly the firing stopped. Day had come.

Captain Knowlton strode immediately along the trench. His upright form revealed how pitifully shallow were our defenses. With one hand upon his sword hilt and the other gesturing as he exchanged greetings, he came steadily on. "Welcome news, lads," he said. "Our enemies may have a harbor full of ships, and countless guns upon them. But we now know they lack the trajectory to reach the redoubt, or us along this crest I would hazard. Therefore men," and here he paused to glance left and right, "if they want us off this hill, they'll have to damn well march up here and try to take it from us." A spontaneous cheer erupted. "Do we intend to let them?"

"No!" we chorused.

"Well do we?"

"NO! Huzzah! Huzzah! HUZZAH!" We smiled back at him as he moved on. As the cheers died away, the reality of our exposed position sank in. The sea, or river along our left, which the Regulars could exploit at any moment, and open, gently sloping terrain to our front. A few discharges from field artillery, followed by a determined bayonet charge, and we would be swept off this Breed's Hill.

"We will need an officer of his mettle, I fear," Eli whispered.

"Aye," I replied. "If Captain Willes cannot be with us, I am relieved that we have him." Eli gave my thigh a pat, though the gesture may have been to reassure himself as much as me. "If they do come on," I said, "we shall have a long, hard slough."

Nodding, he studied the line of men draped along the slope. "We must have two companies worth of Connecticut militia," he said.

"A good two hundred, I would agree. And easily twice as many comrades up there judging by the activity on the ramparts." Contemplating our numbers restored a bit of my confidence. "It's a strong force we've mustered, and with commanders like Captain Knowlton..."

"Stoutly defended to be sure," he murmured, thus interrupting me which was not his way. "But why do so many hang back," he went on. "That's what I wonder at." I followed his gaze to the significantly higher Bunker Hill in our rear. The crest crawled with Provincial troops. "Our lines here are thin," he said, "what with so much ground to cover." My heart sank for his ability to assess the terrain far outweighed my own. If it came down to a contest of volleys, ours would be a paltry, ragged thing, compared to the dense, rolling fire of two or three massed lines of Regulars.

"Perhaps they are being held in reserve," I suggested.

"If so, they are at too great a distance. Why we would be overrun sure, before they could come up." I tugged his sleeve at this comment, for Asa Fenton had cocked his ear. "Forgive me, Elisha," Eli whispered. "I forget my own earlier advice to you. Perhaps I should leave such matters to our superiors."

"We could use more water," I offered. "And maybe word as to how powder will be re-supplied."

"Indeed. I am off then to speak to one of the lieutenants. See what can be rustled up."

I explained the First Corporal's mission to our marksmen. The news brought them a degree of relief. I then sat facing the river, as this was the only direction that did not threaten to pitch me downhill. The climbing sun lit the right side of my face. Though I had touched neither pick nor shovel for a full hour, sweat trickled beneath my hat, and along my stubbly jaw.

Finally alone, I slipped my hand inside my shirt and grabbed Jemima's letter. I clutched it with anticipation. Snapping the wax seal, I smoothed the page flat upon my knee.

Dear, Dear Elisha,

How happy you make me. Am I truly 'Your Jemima'? How my cheeks glow at that. Yet what am I to think of your impertinence concerning nights, as well as days? Need I say more, Mister Elisha Benton? I think not.

Oh, I find it gives me no pleasure to tease you when you are not here, with me, that I might find such humility in one who stands as straight and true, as you.

Forgive me, but as you wrote in haste, so must I. A dozen letters have I written since receiving yours. Each I discarded. They either said what I did not feel, or my feelings changed when next I wrote. Do not doubt my constancy regarding you, Dear Elisha. My contrariness concerns only what to put down, when these few words must stand for all - of me. How easy it is I find, to take down the speech of others, than to write one's own.

This effort I must relinquish to the courier, however. The Colonel is away in Hartford and now's my chance. Unlike the Captain, he frowns on me serving as scribe. Would that he might be more like you, Mister Benton, you who seem quite unaware that you never once questioned why I, a woman, was granted such a role. The poor Colonel, how he would fuss and fume if he learned I meant to enclose this note in the pouch reserved for dispatches. You will forgive me I know, as I hope Captain Willes will. If he is disappointed in me, please tell him I know no other way to get word to you. Perhaps he can solve this dilemma, for many here other than I wonder at what our fathers, brothers, sons and our lovers too, must face in Roxbury.

Do write to me once more. Tell me how you fare. And of Azariah you simply must; and our other acquaintances too. I am shocked what you write of Mister Eli Chapman, but so happy you have found in him a confidante. So long, that is, he does not usurp my place as she who upon whom you most rely to think nothing but good of you.

Stay safe, Your Jemima.

PS. Through my father, who has it from Daniel, your family is well, and send their love. Your brother did want you to know that your grandfather is unchanged. I pray this is not ill news.

I read the note twice more through, but by then the blurring of my vision made another attempt impossible. That Daniel and Mother and the rest were well offered a bittersweet blend of relief, and longing. That Grandsire had not recovered pained me. "My God," I muttered aloud. How I missed them all.

Yet, I had her. On the strength of this note I held her in my hand. Slowly, carefully, I traced the place where her fingers had written her name. I glanced up, blinking, only to find Amasa Allen staring. At once my entire body coiled, prepared to repel with violence any sarcasm that might usher from his lips.

Instead, I watched his eyes slowly brim with tears. "Helps ta hear from family, don't it, Corporal. Glad tidings?"

I exhaled. Gently, I squeezed his shoulder. "News from home is always welcome, Mister Allen."

"Amen to that, sir." With that we both gazed out over the windswept grasses that cloaked the slope, all the way to Moulton's Point and the sea.

Chapter 43

Though the enemy had unleashed an ineffectual barrage upon us at daybreak, hours passed without them stirring further. Captain Knowlton had returned with a pair of buckets brimming with water, and a ladle clamped in his teeth. We had cheered him then, but the noon sun now beat down, scorching the pates of those lacking head coverings of even the meanest sort. My own cap I doffed repeatedly so that I might pass my sleeve across my brow. Above us barely a puff of white floated in the blue sky offering respite.

This time Eli stayed behind and I pestered the nearest lieutenant for provisions - anything that might slack our hunger or thirst. Returned to the First Corporal's side, I merely shook my head. In this way, the men did not hear that I had scampered about in vain. Nevertheless, they knew full well why I had gone off, and that my hands were empty on my return. To their credit, neither Amasa nor Asa cast looks of reproach in my direction. "Bloody Redcoats," I hissed. "Why don't they come on?"

Eli shot me a warning glance. Amasa reacted too, but in a completely different manner. First he tried to spit, found he lacked the saliva to do so, and so croaked, "That's the spirit, Corporal. Give them bastards hell."

"Perhaps they dare not attack," the elder Fenton said. "Might that be so?"

He rarely spoke, so I did not know whether to think he trusted in our strength, or rather prayed that we possessed it. Either way, I was a fool to have let my own fear show through with my burst of impatience. "Perhaps not, Mister Fenton," I said. "Until they make up their minds, however, why don't you wear this?" I settled my cap on his head. "Not a bad fit."

"Sir, I could not. You'll have no covering."

"I insist. Share it with Mister Allen there. Take turns. As for me, this waistcoat of mine will do the trick." With that, I sat down and draped my discarded vestment coat over my head. They both laughed and traded my hat back and forth, trying it at various rakish angles. Eli nudged my boot and smiled.

Suddenly his lips tightened. "What is it?" I asked.

"The tide. It's stolen the river clean away." Sure enough, the thin strip of sand had now widened to a good 40 or 50 feet or more of exposed bank. Ranks of a dozen abreast could march through the gap, flanking us. So slow had it shrunken away I'd not noticed till now. "Go tell the Captain, at once."

I did as instructed. So hurriedly did I approach that I stilled an animated discussion amongst the Captain and a pair of his lieutenants. Curtly, he informed me that he was well aware of the gap and had been for some time. "Of course, sir," I replied, taken aback by this change in his demeanor. I was about to leave when he bid me to stay.

"Corporal Benton," said the Captain. "I thank you for coming to us with this observation. We are even now discussing what must be done. Reinforcements, you see, were promised. Some time ago."

"And if they do not arrive, sir? Before the Regulars I mean." At once, I wished I had not asked. Eli had already observed how thin were our lines. This officer certainly needed no mention from me of the dangers of stretching them wider still.

"Well," the Captain replied with a grin, "we can certainly set about erecting a barricade. We've nothing else afoot this day, have we?" His ready confidence could not be denied. At that very moment a swarm of provincials rushed through the swampy gap between the two hills. The echoing fire of ships' guns pursued them, but without obvious effect. The Captain's smile spread wider still and he turned to his officers. "If I am not mistaken, that will be the 1st New Hampshire Regiment requested by Colonel William Prescott. And that stout fellow in the lead must be Colonel John Stark. There, Corporal, our flank is secured."

I returned to my post where my comrades greeted me as though I had somehow summoned the timely reinforcements. Together we watched Stark's companies erect a barrier of stones that extended quite into the Mystic's lapping waves.

To my amazement, sweat continued to bead at my brow and dampen my shirt, long after my throat felt like I'd taken a bite of the beach below. Such idle thoughts as these careened about inside my baking skull. Perhaps, as Mister Fenton had dared give voice, Gage had accepted our presence on this patch of sloping earth.

An elbow prodded me from my reveries. I turned to Eli. Even his normally squared shoulders had slumped. He gestured towards the rear, using no more than his head. A body of men moved slowly, awkwardly down from the redoubt. Those in their midst carted a door at waist height and upon it lie a man. His limbs appeared to writhe. I sat up. "Poor fellow must have been injured," I said. "In the cannonade."

"No doubt. But, consider Elisha, are eight soldiers required to convey but one?"

I sat straighter, as if the act of doing so might clear my muddled mind. "Do you imply," I whispered, "that they intend leaving the fight?"

"I imply nothing. Those men are deserting."

The band had already reached the marshy area between the pair of hills. In truth the hands of those not attending the casualty were burdened with muskets, coats and whatever kit they possessed. Their return was highly doubtful. "Can nothing be done? Can no one stop them?"

"There is so much confusion, what with numerous militia companies scattered about, and so many mixed commands."

Eli and I silently watched the departing group shrink as it climbed Bunker Hill. Before much more time had passed, others took the same route, wandering away singly, or in pairs.

"I could pick off one or two," Amasa muttered. "Might discourage the rest." When I tilted his rifle barrel up towards the clear blue sky, he did not resist.

"Quite right not to fire," Captain Knowlton said. None of us had heard him climb up to our position. He shared a tight lipped grin. "The powder is far more precious, than men cut of such cloth as that." Amasa guffawed at this, and nearly choked. "We can at least thank God they are not Connecticut men," the Captain said, and moved along the line. When he had gone, the First Corporal and I refocused our attention on the ground to our front.

A sandy-haired boy, precious older than Brother Jacob and stationed just uphill of us, cried out. His arm pointed seaward. Like blinking lights they were, dotting the sea off Moulton's Point. Shading my eyes, I saw them for what they were - white longboats. Like a broken strand of pearls, they stretched for near a half-mile over open water. The line began as specks, some as far off as the ferry landing in Boston, and reached nearly to the beach, our beach.

"Make yourselves ready, lads," Captain Knowlton called out as he came slowly down among us. "We won't have long to wait now." He made it sound like an assurance.

The warships partially screened the boats, but not so much that we could fail to note that each was densely packed with red-suited figures.

"We will be first to face them," Eli said, as though thinking aloud. Just as he spoke the lead boats touched at the point. Red forms swarmed over the sides and up onto dry land. Sure enough, if they made a frontal assault, we would receive the brunt of it. I tried to swallow but lacked the saliva to do so.

More boats ground ashore. Each discharged another mass of men, and all clad in crimson. Pushed back into the surf, the oarsmen reversed course - intent no doubt on fetching another identical cargo as that just disgorged.

Their coming rendered the massacre in Lexington but a tale we had once been told. One that kindled horror, yes, but to folk other than us. Silent we crouched, the mouths of my comrades' agape, as these invaders leapt forth, splashed forward and formed up. Barely more than the range of our rifles separated the two charged bodies - ours motionless, the other a hive of activity.

The enemy's lines grew at both ends along the high tide mark. After a brief pause, and in a single movement, the entire force faced right. Only then did the shouted commands that had caused this act reach our ears. The stomp of hundreds of booted feet followed. So did they cross our front.

"What do you make of it?" Eli asked.

"Is it the river's shore after all?" I said. "They must mean to flank us." That must be it. Sweep through us and the New Hampshire regiment, and they would be able to cut off the redoubt - trapping all within. Though not blessed with Captain Willes' tactical expertise, nor the First Corporal's, the criticality of our defense seemed obvious, even to me. Therefore we must hold, to the last. And a man such as Captain Knowlton would see to it that we did so. I checked the supply of powder in my horn, though I had done so twice already this day. Seeing me thus engaged, Eli checked his as well.

"Corporals, sirs," Amasa said. "Lookee here."

Our enemy had stopped. After having marched no more than a few hundred yards the column had abruptly halted. Before our eyes, it now disintegrated into a milling mob. More echoing commands. The Regulars shed their packs. In small groups they settled in.

"Bloody hell!" Amasa cursed. "They're eatin'." Our enemy dug deep into their rucksacks and began to picnic below us. "Can we fire on 'em?" he begged.

Never had my hunger and thirst felt so keen, nor my frustration. "They are out of range, Mister Allen."

The discharge of a cannon snapped our heads 'round. Was that ours?

No sooner had it fired from up in the redoubt, that a slow, rending crash reverberated. Screams came after. Eli and I exchanged glances. Both downhill and uphill of us, men begged to learn what had befallen their comrades. Officers stepped among them, encouraging men to sit down, to settle down. Word soon came that our lone cannon, and that a mere four pounder, had fired only to have the rampart give way beneath it. The carriage was a complete loss. The news cascaded down the slope, dragging morale lower as it went.

Now I figured was as good time as any to share out what remained in my canteen. My companions protested, saying they had drunk theirs up and fair was fair, but I would have none of that. I told them they must drink, for they were to do the fighting whilst I, their Corporal, lounged in the shade. As shade was as precious as water, and just as hard to find, they laughed twice as hard. To others we must have sounded like cackling geese, but our lips we did wet, and together we faced what must surely come.

As another wave of longboats drove their bows into the distant, stony beach, I suffered the indignity of a growling stomach. How odd that my body would give voice to hunger at such a time as this. Odder still that the noises would yield embarrassment. My appetites and sensibilities be damned, the enemy's reinforcements came on.

Captain Knowlton positioned himself nearer the left flank of our line. Here the gradual slope fell away to the beach, crowded now by Stark's regiment. The Captain hollered up to us. Like our own Captain Willes, he had mastered a shout without sacrificing calm. "We are not to fire, boys," he encouraged us, "till we see the whites of their eyes."

Amasa slapped the barrel of his rifle. "Then what's the point a havin' this?" he demanded.

I stepped behind our marksmen. "We must mass our fire to have the utmost effect," I assured them.

"I'll have an effect on 'em, alright," Amasa retorted. "Why, I already picked me out a spot. Down there at them brick kilns. Soon as they reach..." At the touch of my hand on his shoulder he stopped. "Aye, Corporal," he said. "Whites a their eyes it is."

The fair-haired lad who'd sighted the boats struggled with the strap of his horn. "Might I help?" I asked.

He covertly glanced at his nearer companions, a pair of leather-faced fellows, and likely veterans of the last war. He nodded. The strap had snagged beneath his cartridge box, positioned more across his back then at his hip. I untangled the one, and repositioned the other. "There, that arrangement should make reloading a tad easier."

"Thank you, sir," he said. His eyes, as wide as they were blue, darted from his gear to the ruddy swarm at the point. He hardly met my gaze at all. I told him my name. I inquired as to his. "William, sir."

"That was my uncle's name. How bravely he fought against the French. Our family remains proud of him to this day." I shook his hand. "A pleasure to meet you William. You have got yourself a good name."

All smiles he was. "Thank you, sir."

"Elisha! Quick!"

Never had I heard such a note of alarm in Eli's voice. Casting a hurried glance at Moulton's Point I understood why. "Listen for the Captain's commands," I whispered to the lad, then rejoined my comrades.

"They come," Eli said. "They come at last."

With their martial music rolling like breakers up the slope before them, a line literally a hundred men across and four ranks deep, advanced. Shoulder to red shoulder they came. The cruel steel of their bayonets sliced the air with their passage. If ever they got close enough to use those...

"I marvel that they can move at all," Eli said. "See how tight is the cut of their sleeves; how high their collars." For my part I could not fathom how they did not faint with the heat. Yet I prayed some would. "Their cadence!" he exclaimed. "How quick they come on." The incessant pulse of the Regulars' drums warned of the harnessed power of these silent, scarlet lines. They parted at an abandoned kiln, then instantly reformed; the works appeared swallowed by their passage. "Broken ground poses no obstacle," the First Corporal said.

Oh, must he go on so. Quivers played up and down my friend's tight jaw. Just then Amasa unleashed a string of oaths that made no sense. Could this be fear having its way with them? Was it fear that tightened its grip on me?

"Lock and load, men of Connecticut," Captain Knowlton said. "Hold your fire until I give the order.

"Ready, now!"

I lifted my uncle's musket. My thumb trembled as I drew the hammer full back. A shimmering, oncoming wave of red swept along the beach, spilled up onto the lower slope of Breed's Hill. The probing bayonets shimmered in the heat.

"Aim!"

Never before had I sighted upon another man. Is this trembling what Azariah had felt? Tall dark caps topped their heads. White straps crisscrossed their chests. How odd; the overlap created a perfect mark. I sought one out amongst the cascading line. Choose.

The stomp of hundreds of boots rivaled the pounding of the drums.

The wood of the stock felt smooth to the touch. The barrel hot from the sun. At the man's throat, an officer he was, a small, shimmering metal plate bounced. It bounced with each step he took. Strange regalia with a name equally so. What was it? Someone had told me once. Uncle William, perhaps. "Oh yes. Gorget."

"Fire!"

The roar of our discharge was deafening. An erupting cloud of smoke obliterated sight of the massed red, the breeze drove it right back into our faces. Great holes had been torn in that crimson wave. Of the officer and his gorget I saw nothing.

"Reload!"

Frantically our hands snatched cartridges from the open boxes at our hips. I bit off the end of one, nearly gagging on the sulfurous grains. Poured the charge down the barrel. Rammed home the ball; the wad. Powder spilled from my horn. Most missed the pan. A bit more. Already, the New Hampshire men loosed another volley. The King's soldiers had plugged the gaps. Ever nearer came the packed lines.

"Ready," the Captain called. "Aim." I settled on another crossed set of white straps. I avoided seeing the face. "Fire!" More screams split the air.

The enemy lines had broken. Shattered were those magnificent ranks of marching men. Mere crimson clumps remained, and these fled - leaving writhing forms, and still ones too, on the ground. Amasa leapt up shouting, even as the order to "cease fire" echoed up and down the hillside. "Huzzahs!" rang out.

I sank down on my hunches. My hands began to shake.

"They will come once more," Eli whispered. "Men such as these will surely come again."

"I got me one, Corporal!" Amasa insisted that I pay him heed. "Dropped him in his tracks I did."

There was no questioning his courage, however I might loathe his present joy. "You've done well," I croaked to both him and Asa - whose hands tightly clasped his rifle. "Be sure to reload. We expect they'll have another go at us." I glanced uphill at young William. His face had gone white, but he managed a brief wave. I smiled and returned his salute.

Over his shoulder I saw a dark, billowing column of smoke. Charlestown had been set ablaze.

"They come!" Eli said. "Columns this time. Ten deep."

Again we defenders waited. Again the precise lines advanced. Closer and closer they came. At the "ready, aim" command, the stock tucked tight against my shoulder. The oncoming men swelled above my barrel. A wig I saw; white with dark hair protruding beneath it. "For heaven's sake, how long were we to wait..."

"Fire!" The wig fell away. The man collapsed. Another took his place. "Reload." "Aim." "Fire!" The discharges stung my nostrils. Smoke blurred my vision. Jets of flame pierced the rolling haze. A return volley by the Regulars. Whizzing sounds nearby; screams from above and below. Another ball tumbled down the hot mouth of my musket. The rod jamming it home. My God! They were almost upon us.

"Fire!"

"We've turned them back!" Eli shouted and pumped his weapon aloft. Huzzahs drowned the irregular crack of muskets.

"Cease fire! Spare your powder. They retreat."

Another scream, this one from mere yards away. On the matted grass above, a slender form writhed on the ground. "William!"

I scrambled up to him. With little effort I lifted him up and placed him behind a protective mound of earth. Just as easily, I pried his thin, bloodied hands from his abdomen. So torn it was, that his intestines could be seen to glisten. Gut shot, and there was no denying what that meant. He did no more than whimper, as tears forged channels along his dirt-caked cheeks. I resisted the urge to hug him to my chest.

"Lie quiet now," I said. "That's a good lad. You'll be fine," I lied. With my knife, I cut his blouse away and tore it into strips. "This will hurt, but I know how brave you are." Lifting him once more, I wrapped him 'round and knotted the pieces tight. He groaned, but that was all. His waist was no thicker than a girl's. My own tears came then. I could not seem to stop them.

"Elisha!" It was Eli again, and I knew what his shout signified.

"I will return, William," I said. "I promise you." It required all my strength to lay his pale hand in the dirt.

"See, there they advance," the First Corporal instructed. "And there. They are reinforced, and mean to attack on all fronts..." His voice faded away. Never had he sounded so helpless. Grasses bent under the onslaught of hundreds of black gaiters and heavy boots driving ever upwards. Packs had been discarded. Walking wounded had joined the ranks. The enemy meant to press their attack; and at all costs.

Amasa muttered something unintelligible. It was not an oath. It might have been a prayer. From the redoubt, stragglers slipped over the wall and made for Bunker Hill. I cursed them even as my feet longed to fall in with them. I cursed, too, the hundreds upon that summit who refused to come to our aid. For one moment, one long, horrid moment, Eli's eyes met mine. He, too, thought to run. I extended my hand to him. He snatched it. At each other's touch, we turned back to our men.

Suddenly the oncoming lines of armed men shifted. They pounded up the slope, but now away from us. "The redoubt!" Captain Knowlton shouted. "They mean to attack the redoubt." And so they did. A crimson surge flowed into the trench ringing the fort. Ragged fire rang out from the defenses but not near enough.

"Ammunition," Eli muttered. "They've no more ammunition..."

The tide swept up, cresting the wall and spilling inside. Hundreds of bayonets slashed in the pitiless sun. Militiamen turned empty weapons about and swung them madly to and fro. No match were these for the plunging bayonets. Screams, horrid screams split the air as steel pinned men's bodies to the earth. Others tossed their useless muskets aside. A trickle, then a torrent of unarmed men poured forth from the rear of the redoubt; hotly pursued by Regulars mad for vengeance.

"Rally to me!" Captain Knowlton cried. "Rally boys!"

Eli, Asa, Amasa and I raced to his side in a surge of Connecticut troops. Hastily, he formed us into something like a defensive line, strung along the rear slope of the hill. Pivoting, the New Hampshire regiment formed on our flank. At the commands of Colonel Stark and our Captain, a front rank knelt whilst those of us in the rear stood. Across our combined front the fort's defenders fled. Close behind and even among them raced the Regulars; firing, thrusting, roaring.

"Wait!" the Colonel ordered. "Wait!" A brief gap opened between pursuers and those pursued. "Front rank. Fire!"

Our volley disintegrated the lead elements of red-coated infantry. Staggered, they fell back. Those few British officers who had not fallen along the beach struggled to re-form firing lines.

"Rear rank. On my command! Fire!" Fresh holes were torn in the fledgling enemy lines. "Withdraw men of Connecticut!" Colonel Stark ordered. "Men of New Hampshire, form up around me. Orderly does it, men. Well done!"

We raced to the base of Breed's. Here Captain Knowlton did his best to position our scattered companies. Once the New Hampshire line volleyed they leap-frogged us and established a new defense upon Bunker Hill's lower slope. And so we went, taking turns providing covering fire. Confronted by our fighting withdrawal, pursuit waned. Reaching the summit of Bunker Hill at last, we gazed down upon a mad exodus of provincial troops. They fairly carpeted the isthmus linking the peninsula to Cambridge. Cannon fire from the enemy warships erupted amongst them. We too must endure this gauntlet.

"Corporal," Amasa said. "I've no more cartridges." I pressed two of my dwindling supply into his sweat-stained, blackened palm.

The First Corporal patted our backs, one after the other. "We'll get out of this yet," he said.

I was about to voice agreement when a jolt of panic seized me. I cried out as might a wounded animal.

"Elisha!" Eli shouted. "Are you hit?"

"William! I've left him!"

Chapter 44

The sun had dipped low in the sky but the day's heat hung heavy upon us. Only by concentrating could I place the date. The 17th of June it was. My comrades sat on all sides, as if to prevent me from attempting a return to that awful peninsula. Only Eli, however, kept up a vigilant watch. I turned from him for he had been the prime architect in hauling me away. The heads of the others hung low, almost between their knees. Our muskets and rifles, as useless and empty as our cartridge boxes and powder horns, lay in the grass of this nameless Cambridge field. Hundreds of our fellow militia sprawled about. Despite our numbers we produced but murmurings. Here and there a man cried out, though most casualties had been helped to tents set up nearer the road.

We had retreated along that dusty lane until we reached the safety of the fort atop Winter Hill. All the way from the slopes overlooking Charlestown had we come. That town still burned, a pall of smoke blowing inland to our left. And on Breed's flank, a boy lied where I had left him. Did he draw breath, I wondered, alone there in the dirt?

A tug there was at my sleeve. Eli's haggard face leaned near mine. "You do understand why we couldn't let you go? Tell me you don't resent me doing so."

"No. Never again, though, will I leave someone dear on a field of battle." In time his hand fell away.

⁂

We slept that night in the field. Not a blanket did we have to warm us as our sweat cooled, nor to keep off the dew come morning. No food was offered when we rose.

Others moved about as we stirred. Women, many dressed in the colors of mourning, moved in pairs. There would be far more so attired this day. Carrying buckets between them, they offered water. I lifted a hand. They came at once. One wore black, the other the plain frock of a goodwife. "The four of us here are parched," I said. "If you would be so kind..."

With the briefest curtsies they dipped a ladle. Amasa drank from it and passed it to Asa. When it was refilled, Eli insisted I take precedence. How blessedly cold it was. I could almost picture the well from which it was drawn. I endowed it with a lining of stone. It was Father's well that I imagined. With rushed thanks for the ladies, I passed the ladle to my friend.

"Were you perchance among those at the redoubt?" asked the simply clad woman. She brushed dark hair back beneath her white cap as she spoke. Pain showed in her eyes.

"On the slope just below it," the First Corporal said.

"Oh," she replied, with a hint of hope. "A neighbor friend says he saw my man there. In the fort, this was." Again, I relived the crimson tide topping the earthen wall; the thrusting steel of the bayonets. "Ezekiel," she said, peering into each of our faces. "That is my husband's name." I could not hold her gaze.

"They do not know him, I think," said her widowed friend. "Come, Beth. There are so many here that have need of drink. And we may yet find him among them."

"Yes, of course," the goodwife said. She curtsied once more, and they left. I watched them for a long while - tending to those of us scattered about the field; and asking, always asking.

Later that day, they marched us back through Cambridge. Over the bridge spanning the Charles River we went, and thus on to Roxbury. There we Connecticut forces were returned to our pre-battle duties. Captain Willes had come into town and asked that we postpone our return to camp until he had met with the headquarters staff. He invited us to await him in George's Tavern along the causeway road, with the proviso that our drinks be on him, and that we be able to stand upon his return.

These conditions buoyed Misters Allen and Fenton, but I found even a cool tavern and a pint of beer failed to fill the hollow inside me.

"They know not what to make of us," Eli said. As our pair of marksmen had stepped outside to piss, I glanced around to comprehend of whom he spoke. Only a few older men were seated about. "They seem to eye us as did the soldiers garrisoning the town above," he went on. "Are the likes of us to be cheered for having fought, they wonder; or shunned for having been defeated?" I could not deny he seemed to be on to something, for each man's gaze fell as I returned it. "There is a truth none can deny," Eli concluded. "And that's the price we made the King's Regulars pay." He raised his tankard. "To us, then Elisha, and all defenders of Breed's Hill." He paused, then added, "And to those brave bastards who swept us off it." I clinked his cup with mine, and swallowed the last of my pint.

The Captain joined us in due course. He paid for our rounds, and hoisted another with us. Hurried it was, however, for he seemed anxious to return to camp. Back with our comrades there was no holding back. "Huzzahs" rang out before we reached the cooking fires. The unseen front line picked up the cheer, for the entire company had been told to expect our return. Troubled though I remained, there was no denying the warmth engendered by this reception. This glow spread at the sight of Azariah standing amongst the boisterous throng. Far too quickly Captain Willes ushered Eli and I inside his tent. Lieutenant Parker and Sergeant Carpenter awaited us.

"I will be frank, gentlemen," the Captain began. "This was a costly engagement to be sure. The butcher's bill is expected to top four hundred killed and wounded on our side." The Sergeant's sharp inhalation earned a sharper glare from the Captain. "However, the enemy has been bled much whiter. His losses are estimated to be twice ours. Perhaps topping one thousand casualties."

"If this be a victory for Gage, sir," the Lieutenant said, "he can ill afford another."

"Precisely the Generals' view, Mister Parker. We will maintain a doubling of our sentries, but the fear of an attack on Dorchester is now much diminished. The King's forces have been too seriously depleted to make such an attempt; leastways, until further reinforcements arrive from England."

I cleared my throat. "So then, sir, our sacrifices, they were not in vain?"

"Certainly not," he said, taking my hand. He next grasped the First Corporal's. "Perish the thought, gentlemen. We are all of us in your debt."

It was William's lifeless body that occupied my thoughts, and for him I bowed to accept these thanks.

The briefing resumed. My attention wandered a bit as recollections came and went of faces I had seen yesterday along that slope; men whose names I had never learned. Did they live today as did I? The Captain's mention of Doctor Warren snapped me back to the present. As a newly appointed general yet without a command, the humble Doctor had taken his place as a private within the redoubt. There, at the battle's climax, reports suggested he had been slain. What greater massacre might there have been, and how many more women widowed, if not for Stark and Knowlton?

The Captain spoke just then of Knowlton. "I had the pleasure of an introduction this very day," he informed us. "My surname was unknown to him, however, and this despite his having commanded some of my troops. Apparently these men acquainted him with the name of our town, but not that of their Captain. What a dreadful oversight this might have been," and here he paused to smile at us, his corporals, "if not for the fact that those guilty of the omission covered themselves, this entire command, and Tolland herself I daresay, with glory on the field of battle."

There could be no reply to such a speech. Even Eli shifted his weight. Thankfully it was the First Corporal who was next called upon to speak. As he related the prior day's events from our direct experience, my thoughts drifted away. So, the horror of yesterday had won a measure of safety for our comrades here in Roxbury, and by extension every soul in Tolland. Jemima it was who I thought of first, even before members of my family. My surprise gave way to shock – for I'd pictured her in the garb of the Cambridge widows.

"Mister Benton? Are you well?" Captain Willes asked.

"Aye, sir."

He dismissed us soon after, though bid me remain. "Your brother," he confided, "seems quite himself. I have restored him to his prior duties. As his Corporal, you may reserve the right to elect otherwise. Only advise me if this be your intent." I nodded. "Will there be anything more, Elisha?" he asked. "I have the leisure of time should you wish a word in private."

"Thank you, no sir," I replied. "All is well."

Eli sat a polite distance from the tent; facing the opposite way. In the background off duty soldiers swarmed our marksmen; the pair of whom held sway as if selectmen at a town gathering. Some in the crowd called to the First Corporal. He returned their waves but clearly had waited on me. "There you are," he said, rising. I joined him. Together we listened to the joyful babble. "As you see, Elisha, and just as Captain Willes said, we have done the company proud."

"Does pride not mask a sin," I replied, "when the killing of men is the source of it?" Even to my ears the words sounded like sermonizing. If I had once needed convincing of the need for such a heinous act, I now resented how effectively I had managed to commit it. My friend seemed to sense the hollowness of my argument.

"Better pride than shame," he said. "You heard how the generals are to prosecute certain officers." I turned to him for I had not attended these comments by our Captain. "Yes, Elisha. More than one officer, and they gentlemen, will likely be charged with cowardice. For failing to reinforce those of us on Breed's."

My gaze drifted to our companions once more. "There is a thing worse than dying it appears," I muttered.

"Quite right," he agreed.

Never had my back endured such a joyous thumping, and I had years of playful warring with a multitude of siblings to my credit. The one brother here with me hovered nearby. Through our comrades' gleeful attentions he wore a smile, yet it could not disguise the pain he carried. Far better I reckoned to glimpse his private agonies than that vacant look that had stolen him clean away. I finally managed to separate Azariah from the throng. We said little, but soon found our way to the edge of the bay. I intended drawing him out, but there proved no need.

"I should have been at your side," he said.

"And I'm glad you were not," I replied. "There was far too much horror and bloodshed." I had meant this to counter the talk of glory around the campfires, but he took it as an insult; that was plain in his stiffness. Azariah of old would have flared at once. Now he merely sat, in an awful silence. How to assure him that my intent had not been to remind him of the sentry and his shocking reaction? How to convince him that I was not his judge?

"Brother," he said in a voice so low I had to ignore the cries of the gulls to make out his words. "I freely admit I let you down, and under fire no less."

"You did no such thing. The mission was accomplished. Only you could have done as much."

"And promptly fell apart. Me, who has only the ability to hunt to recommend me."

"Nonsense! You have more fine attributes than..." He stopped me.

"You must allow me to own it," he declared. "I did let you down. And I swear to you now. Never will I do so again."

How could I refuse his desperate urgency? I could not. Freeing one hand, I tucked it 'round the back of his head and drew him to my chest.

Chapter 45

The passage of a largely quiet and increasing sticky fortnight brought us into the month of July. I prayed that the crops ripened in the fields at home, for I witnessed little change to the tidal flats and salt marsh that comprised our constant prospect. As foretold by the Captain, our enemy seemed resigned to remain within its walls. Thus with each passing day, the company became more and more preoccupied with the rapidly approaching end of our enlistments.

Eli had persuaded the officers that he be allowed to share in the secluded bathing cove they had claimed early on. With but a simple request, so he said, the invitation had been extended to me. I cared little for the privilege and had declined joining him there since our return from the peninsula. On this particular day, however, I felt inclined to visit the spot, and convinced Heman to accompany me. We had enjoyed few private moments since the battle, and I longed for his steady and reserved companionship.

We had already stripped away our sodden clothing that had worn to an increasingly threadbare state these past few months. Rinsing, then wringing them out in the sea, we repeated the process in a small tub of fresh water - with the aid of a cake of lye. Our skin came next, though for this the salt water alone had to suffice. The stream was too far off to carry a quantity sufficient for bathing; and not even the officers were allowed to immerse themselves in its cooling waters for fear of fouling our collective drinking supply. With our clothes spread upon a convenient tree trunk that had washed up upon the shore; and our bodies cleansed; we sat. For a few moments at least we were grateful for the warming sun.

Around the next finger of land a few of the others could be heard shouting and splashing. They knew well enough by now not to tempt the gunners by gathering in full view. Even so, Amasa, for I heard his shrill cries among them, loved nothing more than waggling his bare bottom in the direction of the enemy ramparts.

"I am glad of this chance to be apart," Heman said. Typically that would have been quite enough for he who could be relied upon to go a quarter hour in pleasing, silent company. I was mildly startled then, when he continued. "Elisha. I have often wondered. Can you tell me what it was like on Breed's Hill?" This I had neither expected, nor desired to discuss. Rarely had he made me uncomfortable, yet here he had chosen a most painful subject. He must have sensed my reluctance for he immediately added, "You will forgive my prying. We need not if you prefer it."

Something broke free inside me; a thing that had remained bottled up despite the many kindly exchanges with Captain Willes, the soul-searching with my brother, and the commiserating with Eli. "I nearly ran," I blurted. "I saw other men running, Heman, and I swear to God, I set my feet under me."

My confession hung there in the summer air. It seemed suspended on the wafting breeze from off the bay. I flinched, as if my hand might reach for my still damp clothes.

"Yet you did not, Elisha. You stayed, and you fought. Bravely, the Captain himself says."

"There was no choice in that. We fought or we died."

He smiled. It traveled no farther than the width of his closed lips, but he produced more warmth from it than the widest grin I knew.

"Strange that you say that," he said. "No choice had you, is that it? Well, my father once told me that a man without fear is a fool. That to know fear, and overcome it; to choose thus, is the true mark of a courageous man."

"Did he?" I asked, remembering clearly the face that so resembled my dear friend, only grown older and wise.

Heman did not answer me. He sat in that blanket of silence that fit him so well. Then, still gazing seaward he said to me, "I hope that, should the time come, I am such a one."

Without hesitating I replied, "I would give my right arm as proof of it."

The news of the great man arrived before ever he did. A Commander-in-Chief he was said to be, and we to serve under him. All of our separate companies were to be folded into his Continental Army, and this George Washington of Virginia was to be made general over all other generals. Upon hearing that he had arrived in Cambridge, and would soon be touring our lines on Boston Neck, we set about tidying things as best we could. As we had little enough to claim as our own, this took but scant time. Even so, General Joseph Spencer sent word reminding Captain Willes that all in the camps must be put to rights, and so we and Captain Tyler's men began anew to pound down our tent stakes and stow our bedrolls. We even cut our trench walls more sharply, but the sandy soil nearest the flats soon rounded their edges once more.

Finally he came. The second week of July this was and he rode a fine chestnut charger which stood a good sixteen hands high. A group of high-ranking officers accompanied him but none sat as tall and elegant in the saddle. I do not know that I had pictured what this man might look like, but I was prepared to admit pleasant surprise that we should be led by such an impressive gentleman. Their stay was so brief as to afford no other observations of him. Given the danger posed to a mounted party in such proximity to the fortifications, their rapidity in leaving only spoke to the General's common sense.

Despite this favorable impression created not only in me, but in my fellows too, we soon came to harbor a bit of resentment regarding his visit. Word filtered down to us from Roxbury that our defenses had been found sorely lacking, that our hygiene appeared grossly inadequate, and as one rumor had it, we more closely resembled common rabble than a fighting force.

"Rabble is it?" Amasa said and quickly spat. "And where might this dandy have got hisself to when we faced them Regulars on Breed's Hill?" He had read the mood well, for a grumbling rolled along our line in both directions.

"Now then, Amasa," I said. "How can we, rightly commended for coming here from distant Connecticut, belittle a man who volunteered like us, then rode all the way from Virginia?" This quieted the grumbles somewhat. "We all know how rumors spread; and distort. Consider. The good General might have observed a man or two squatting along the mudflats, tending to the necessaries. Say he commented on this to a colonel beside him. Well, a dozen pairs of ears and 12 tongues later none of us know how to wipe our bottoms." The men wore smiles by now. "Or perhaps he merely caught sight of Mister Allen waggling his white rump at the Regulars, and thought our entire company content to shake ourselves clean."

So loudly did the men roar that the number of sentries doubled at once on the distant wall.

Not long afterwards our company was finally relieved. To be withdrawn from the front line was a happenstance for which we had all come to wish. Many were the compliments bestowed on us by General Thomas and our own General Spencer. While we delighted in this, the opportunity of sleeping on dry ground within the protective ring of Roxbury's defenses brought us far more in terms of restorative repose.

Sheep had been slaughtered in celebration. This and a seemingly endless supply of rum was our reward one late July evening. Many were the happy, greasy faces surrounding our camp fires as a result. The Fenton brothers toasted our good fortune, whilst Noah Grant explained some aspect or other of keeping a plough blade running straight and true to young Cook – who as a townsman had no notion of the tool's usage and so proved an attentive audience. On one side of me Heman drew on his pipe, and lent an ear to Azariah. On the other, Eli squatted though quietly. Bawdy tales soon needed telling, and Mister Allen surprised no one by carrying on as was his way. When he decried the arrogance of so-called gentlemen, however, my ears pricked. Up here in the town, the pairing of certain names with such a complaint could land him in the guardhouse. It was not Amasa though who pursued this dangerous vein.

"Unfortunate, indeed," said the First Corporal, "that the General criticizes some of the very men who defended their town common on the 19th of April last."

"Rumors, Eli," I said to him. "No more than that. Besides, the way I heard it no mention was made of Lexington..."

"To mock any one of us is to insult the whole," he continued, quite as though I had not spoken. "Has the man forgotten that we mere militia caged thousands of Regulars in Boston for months? Good enough we were to bleed the King's troops nearly dry on Breed's Hill. Did these truths escape him?"

Though he had not spoken overloud, his words would not bear the scrutiny of any passing officer. "Eli," I said, taking his arm. "You must take care."

I thought he might flare at my cautioning him so, but he instead, smiled. "Friend Elisha," he said, struggling against the unaccustomed effects of the drink to keep me in focus. "We must learn from this.

Men in authority must take great care, mustn't they, in what they voice about other men?"

"They must indeed," I replied. Still smiling he clinked his cup against my own, sloshing a good deal of the contents upon us both. We drank to each other's health. And then once more. Wearing a pleased expression he leaned back until he was prone.

I gazed out over the flames. Soon our enlistments would expire. Each day thoughts of ripening crops and a harvest yet to come crammed my skull. Other soldiers had taken our places in the line. And though the enemy remained formidable, we had drawn his fangs. It was high time we headed home. I scanned my fellows once more. Aye, we all longed for home and hearth. At Azariah I stopped. My breath caught. Of him alone I could not be certain. Would he return home with me? That I must discover.

That night I slept little, despite the comparative luxury of our new accommodations. If Azariah insisted on staying, many a Continental captain would be happy to add a marksmen to his ranks. New units were being organized what with the casualties we'd suffered and the efforts of Washington. John Lewis, a well-liked veteran, had said that he planned to join Huntington's Regiment once the 5th Company set off for home. Such a transfer might prove attractive to Azariah. I could bring the authority of a first-born son to bear, but in this armed camp that counted as little. The heartbreak in Mother's eyes, the disgust in Father's face, these would greet me should I return home without my little brother. No, to leave him behind I could not live with. If he stayed, then so would I.

At Captain Willes' briefing the following morning my likelihood of succeeding with Azariah fell to nil. A regiment was due any day from Pennsylvania, comprised entirely of riflemen. I had never heard of such a force, but the Captain swore it was so. Frontiersmen they were said to be, and outfitted all in fringed hunting shirts. To them my brother would surely be drawn. On learning of their existence, he might even petition to join them immediately upon their arrival.

"Are you aware, Corporal," the Captain asked, "whether any of your men intend staying on?"

"Pardon, sir. With the riflemen?"

"Here in Roxbury is my meaning."

"Not to my knowledge, sir, no. Though there is one who might. I, um, I intend to ask him the moment we are dismissed."

Understanding dawned at once in his face. His brow smoothed, though traversed by fine lines it remained. "I see. In that case, do inform me of his intentions." I bowed. "Dismissed, gentlemen."

Outside, Eli could barely contain his eagerness to be of assistance. I had come to cherish this attribute near as much as Heman's subtler counsel.

"It is Azariah is it not?" he asked. "Over him you fret." I nodded. "Allow me to accompany you, Elisha. I can make the argument that we men of Connecticut should serve together."

"Thank you, Eli. If I fail to convince him as one brother to another, I shall rely on your appeal to his sense of duty."

"Very well. I understand."

I went in quest of Azariah, borne along by the support of my friend.

Chapter 46

My brother was sitting cross-legged as I approached him from behind. He hunched over something that lie on his lap, a weapon. And he was cleaning it with utmost care. His head cocked at my footstep. I came on quickly and was dealt another surprise. The gun was his musket of old, and not the prized rifle.

"I trust that was not your attempt at a stealthy advance," he mocked.

I laughed. "You heard me then?"

"You ought to join the cavalry, Elisha, what with how you pound the ground." I gave his back a pat, and sat beside him. He fixed that gaze of his at me. "Well?" he inquired.

"You are aware, of course," I began, "that the company is soon to return to Connecticut." He shrugged. Oh, how he could make things so difficult. "So, what I have come to ask, what I beseech you..."

"You wonder whether I plan to accompany you, Brother. Let me put your mind at ease. I fully intend to," he said with a grin. At that he resumed wiping the smooth barrel.

"Before you commit yourself," I hastily cautioned, "you should know that a detachment soon comes from Pennsylvania. Every man of whom carries a rifle. As you can surely appreciate, the skills of these specialists are much prized."

His movements ceased. "My dear, elder brother, whether an army of said marksmen comes hither it is as nothing to me." I sat in confused silence. "Where you serve, I serve," he said. "And so will I until I've proven to us both that you can rely on me."

He had nothing to prove to me or anyone, but there would be no convincing him. Besides, we would be marching home together.

By August a handful of our number had been allowed to shift their enlistments to other companies. The only one who seemed unwilling to end our stay in Roxbury turned out to be the Captain himself. Even so, the day set for departure arrived at long last. He had ordered camp struck at a leisurely 10 o'clock in the morning. As punctual as he was, this in itself was unnatural enough. Then, having formed us into column, we remained standing for a good hour more.

"He regrets departing," the First Corporal whispered. "Best report to him about the state of our water," he advised.

Captain Willes had left the column behind him and wandered to the crest of the hill. When I reached him his spyglass was trained on the Fortification below us, and the city visible in the background. It was the very vantage point we had chosen for observations on the day of our arrival for the siege.

After a decent interval I cleared my throat. "Sir, every canteen in the company is full. In addition there is a securely bunged cask in the first cart." There was no reply. Not even an acknowledgement that he had heard me.

Finally the glass lowered, though he continued staring at the besieged city. "If I learned anything in the war against the French," he said, "it is that one should never leave a potent enemy to one's rear. Unfinished business this is. Leaving at such a time."

"Captain. There is an army here now, to take our place. And the men's enlistments are nearly up. You have often said that they are entitled to..." He turned to me. Never had I seen such sadness.

"Of course, Elisha. The men have done their part. They must be allowed to return. Farmers, especially, men such as yourself, must get back to the fields. If not, where will any of us be, come winter? Let us not keep them waiting."

To the tunes of our fifers, Noah Whipple and Stephen Steel, we took our leave from Roxbury. Many were the friends we'd made, especially in Colonel Huntington's 8th Regiment, and these lined the road and sent us off with a proper round of cheers. The company began to sing, and I joined my voice with theirs. Full-throated though we were, the sound could not drown out the image of our Captain's face, nor the recurring thought that we had abandoned the fight.

With each mile we marched westward I had expected that images of home would multiply in my mind. But my head was crammed by too much else. I could not seem to rid myself of William, bled pale upon that slope, nor of Boston herself, silent and suffering in our wake.

The inhabitants of the towns along the turnpike offered us what little they could. Women, and so many there were, afforded us empathy of a sort normally reserved for kin. If our stays had been of any duration, I'm convinced they would have offered to stitch our threadbare clothes and nurse the sores that plagued our feet and legs. Yes, their small and many kindnesses had begun to work upon us. For me it provided, at last, a glimmer of Tolland.

Then, outside of Medway, we came upon another company of provincial troops. Untested militia they were, and unlike us not yet absorbed into the new army. By their flag they appeared to be out of New

York. They had halted at a stream, and so Captain Willes saw fit to take advantage of the open road. Even as he passed word to accord them a 'huzzah', one among their number shouted out the first remark. 'Short-term enlistees' I believed it was. Then came a shout that every one of us heard.

"You're heading the wrong way! The Regulars are to the east!"

"That's why they march west so fast!" responded another. Raucous laughter followed.

"Cowards!" was the cry that split the air.

At once our company whirled en masse to the right. Shouldered arms now leveled. A scattering of hammers cocked. "Belay that!" Captain Willes demanded, shoving his way rearward. I too pushed through until I stood between our men and the now silent body of New York militia. Their arms had been stacked; they stood with hands empty and eyes wide. "Company, to attention!" the Captain ordered. Lieutenant Parker had reached his side; the steel of his sword glinted in the harsh sunlight. After a horrible moment the long, iron barrels angled skyward. Despite sullen, set faces, my companions did as he had asked. At the command to face left, a stomp of 200 feet gave proof that they obeyed. "Men of Connecticut. March!" And so we left our tormenters behind. Not a single oath pursued us.

As we continued along Middle Post Road, I knew then that if this command, if these same men ever had cause to encounter an enemy again, of any strength and in any place, then I would be among them.

In the days and nights that followed, Captain Willes never referred to this nearly mutinous event. For his forbearance, I admired him more. Whether he felt obliged to include it in a dispatch to Colonel Chapman was not a matter of conjecture for a mere corporal. And if Eli ever learned of any communication to his uncle, he did not mention it.

At sunset of the fourth day, for our pace had been oddly less than brisk, we made camp on Connecticut soil once more. The better part of four months had passed since we had left our homes. Success or failure of the planting and growing seasons on Benton lands had fallen squarely upon Daniel's shoulders. If the former, Father would doubtless have thanked Providence; if the latter, blame would have been laid at my brother's feet. Arriving in time for a portion of the harvest, I might yet offer a buffer of sorts. If Daniel desired my aid, that is. And if not, what then would be my role on the farm, if any?

As if by its own accord, my hand found Jemima's note. How worn were its folds. Though each word had long ago been committed to memory, I smoothed the page and read it through. Again I saw her racing from the Meeting House, her long hair flying free; her feet bare. And how her eyes had blazed as I sought to hire men for that harvest - nearly a year gone by. Then, suddenly it was the face of the Cambridge widow I saw, and not Jemima at all. Refolding the note I stashed it quickly.

"Anxious to see her I trust," Heman said.

"That might not be the most accurate word to describe my brother's feelings," Azariah joked.

For once I welcomed the order to resume the march.

As he had the prior year, the Captain wished our party to make a united return to Tolland. And again the men prevailed upon him that they be released as we reached their respective homes. Outside of Stafford Mister Allen left us. His departure was as raucous as the man himself, and so quite fitting. He had managed to exchange the water in his canteen for rum. With this, we toasted him. As he saw value in my well-worn greatcoat, I gave it to him. With less fanfare but as much disappointment, it was to both Fenton brothers that we next bid farewell.

With a shrunken company, and my platoon likewise diminished, we finally reached Coventry. There Lieutenant Parker and our neighbors from that town left us. We proceeded due north to Tolland at something under two thirds of our original strength. Neighbors like Noah Grant soon fell away. At the Benton lands, it was time for Azariah and me. With Heman and Eli we ignored farewells in favor of promises to meet soon - to erect one friend's home, and to rent the other's oxen.

The Captain said nothing as he shook my hand. His eyes, however, conveyed that which he had expressed on that hill above Boston. My brother and I watched them march away until we could neither see nor hear them.

"I thought you might go on into town," Azariah said.

"Soon," I replied.

"She will worry, you realize. When the company returns and you are not among them."

"Aye." A puff of wind stirred the otherwise damp air.

"Will you join me then, Elisha? I am off to Father's."

"You go on ahead," I said. "Tell Mother I will come by and by." He nodded once, then moved soundlessly along the track, his musket cradled effortlessly in one hand.

BOOK III

Long Island, New York – 1776
Battle of Long Island

Chapter 47

Many were the places to which I should direct my steps as I stood upon the crossroads. And doubtless many people, loved ones all, would feel pain at my inexplicable absence. I cursed my selfishness, yet pursued a path of my own.

Up into the orchard I wandered. A fine crop of glossy red Baldwins peeked from beneath leaves so green. It took but a little time to reach the spot. Grandsire had chosen well. Even in the heat of late summer the shadowed, shallow stream spilled sparkling waters over a stone-strewn channel. I removed my half-rotted boots and slipped my feet into its cool embrace. A stand of oak and maple co-existed on the higher ground behind me. Clumps of birch straddled the cascading brook. Openings afforded views of a gentle slope falling away to the south and east. How I should love to build upon such a spot. How pleased Jemima would be. And it was to be mine; it would be ours. Grandsire's promise made it so.

Though surrounded by beauty, Breed's Hill haunted me, as did those months of siege. But I owed my despair in the midst of so much promise to more than each of these alone, or even allied together. As foretold by the Captain's bleak expression, we faced so much more than a single battle, or a lone city under occupation. On the return journey he had spoken of an expedition being planned for the north, perhaps as far as Quebec, and that he might play a part. We were an entire people at war, and with our king. There was no going back. But how were we to move forward? How was I to start a life in the midst of a revolt?

After an hour or more, I emerged at the parcel's edge, within sight of the road into town. I had settled upon a course. God help me but I knew what must be done. In one hand I held my musket, in the other my boots. The long, stiff grasses irritated my bare feet, but the air so played upon them that I balked at encasing them. Perhaps the packed earth of the roadway would offer freedom without such discomfort.

That's when I saw her. Jemima. Her slight figure moved forward at a brisk pace. Clearly she had not seen me for soon she would pass me by, sheltered among the trees as I was. I touched the note within my blouse, and strove to calm my heart all with a single motion. A straw hat she wore upon her head; secured by a ribbon 'round her throat. Her dress I did not recognize. A pale blue it was; surely such a hue would enhance the color of her eyes. The fabric clung to her waist and thighs with each hurried step.

I emerged.

"Elisha!" My name exploded from her lips; died as a stifled cry. For a second, I feared she might collapse there upon the road. She leapt the ditch and rushed up the slight rise. She had done all this and I had barely managed to set my weapon against a nearby trunk.

She threw herself against me. Words would not come; from either of us. Tearful exclamations broke the silence. Some time had elapsed before I realized that I held her clear of the ground. Our cheeks burned, pressed hard together. Never did I want this moment to end. Never.

"Why did you not come?" she scolded. "The company marched in, yet you were not there..."

I set her down. "I asked Heman, and Eli too, to look out for you."

"They did, and thank goodness! They told me you were well, that they had left you at your family's lands. Elisha. How I fretted when I did not see you among your friends. I feared the worst, for we had heard so little." Tears flooded her eyes.

"Forgive me," I said, wrapping her thin shoulders within my arms. "I did not think."

She dabbed at her eyes with a handkerchief. "It counts for nothing. You are here. And safe." Her eyes darted about my person. In that one, pained glance my loss of weight, and the general state of my clothes and body was borne in upon me. She flashed a quizzical smile. "Why what has become of your boots, Mister Benton? Is this any way to greet a lady?" I began fishing about in the knee-deep grasses. "Did you forget your manners in this Roxbury of yours?"

"They are here," I explained whilst her laughter overspread us. "Somewhere."

After I pulled on my boots I stood. She wrapped her arms 'round my waist. Her head came to rest upon my chest. "I know of Breed's Hill," she whispered. "I read aloud General Spencer's report on the casualties to Colonel Chapman. He cited that Connecticut men had fought. That some had died."

"Why did you not give up your position," I asked.

"If something were to happen to you, Elisha, in this role I would know of it at once."

"Oh, Jem. You are so dear to me."

We clung together for a minute more. Her thin arms squeezed tight. "Captain Willes' letter came after," she said. "From him I learned you were safe. It was he who told us how bravely you fought. You and Mister Chapman."

"We were soldiers. We did only as we must." I lifted her face as gently as I knew how. "Jemima. I am still a soldier."

Her hands dropped. "No," she ordered. "Your enlistments are nearly up. You are home now, with your family ... and with me."

"All true. But we are at war. You of all people comprehend this. You who have heard the reports. Surely you know..."

"I comprehend nothing of the kind! For you, the fighting is finished!" Her eyes blazed. "Dear Elisha, you have done your share. Far more than that even, and so much more than most men."

A part of me relished her appeal. I longed to be convinced that I had played my part. But this conflict was not done. Our enemy would not quit. Here to Tolland they still could come. And if not here, then to some other town with people just like us two.

Pain flooded her face. "You still intend to marry me?" she asked. "Do you not?" She smiled. "If only to make of me an honest woman."

Or a widow I thought, but would not say. "Perhaps," I stammered. "Perhaps we might wait, for a time."

"Elisha, what are you saying? Are we not to be man and wife? Have your feelings towards me changed?"

"No. My feelings have not changed, I swear it..."

"Then what do you mean by this?" She took one quick step back; followed by another. I reached for her. "No!" she said. "What is it this time, Elisha? Your father cannot be blamed, for you've already used him as an excuse." By this point she'd backed halfway down the hill. "Mister Elisha Benton returns a war hero. Is that it? The great man made greater still, and will not have the likes of me. The daughter of Jon Barrows is not fit for one as grand as you." She reached the edge of the trench that traced the roadway. "Perhaps I never was. But I'll be no man's fool. No, not even for you!" At that she hopped across, stumbled, caught her balance and raced away towards town.

I called her name more than once, but my heart was not in it. I could not give her what she wanted. Would not. I would not curse her with my hand; the hand of a soldier in the middle of a war. I would not make her a widow. Gathering up my musket I left Grandsire's parcel. Not once did I turn around.

The welcome of my family was everything I had envisioned, and now counted upon. I tried not to dwell on Jemima, for doing so would render me insensitive to their embraces. Mother had held back in the kitchen, so that the children might come to me first. Hannah sobbed. Jacob clutched her and me together with arms that I swore had lengthened in my absence. In the background, Father kept to his place at the head of the table, fully aware of my presence yet content to simply stare. Just then Azariah climbed down from the loft with Daniel. Azariah playfully pulled the young ones away. Tears flowed from Daniel's eyes. I yanked him into my embrace. Happy I was to note that he had seemed unaffected by Father's stony figure. "Brother," he whispered. "Welcome home."

By way of reply I could merely thump his back, and repeatedly too. Daniel gave way to Mother. "My son," she whispered. "How we have missed you. How I have." She held me tight.

Father finally stood. I slowly stepped towards him. "Father," I said, extending my hand. He said nothing, yet he did shake hands with me. Content I was with that. He then surprised me, holding me in his grip a heartbeat longer than I expected. I searched his face for the meaning of this but his eyes had turned away. I left him then as he had greeted me, without a word.

A short time later, after yielding to Mother's insistence that Azariah and I eat, we left to visit Grandsire and Mother Sarah before nightfall. The children's inquiries increased in rapidity and urgency with our imminent departure. Mother shushed them, though she and Daniel seemed to likewise hang on our every reply. Some inquiries we could not answer; some we would not. When they probed for details of the attack upon Bunker Hill, it was an easy matter to dwell in detail about the redoubt erected in a single night upon Breed's, its neighbor. Asked if we had struck down many Regulars, Azariah's face paled; I hastened to explain that we had both fired on the enemy, and how volley fire, with hundreds of pieces discharging in an instant, deafens every ear and blinds every eye. So it went until we pulled the door closed behind us, promising to soon return. Not once had I lied to them, but hardly ever had I told the whole truth.

"Thank you for that, Brother," Azariah said, the moment we were out of doors.

I said nothing for his feelings towards me would certainly alter the moment he learned how Jemima and I had parted. For now, however, we both were content. Side by side we hastened along the path; he eased to the front. So had we hunted, with Azariah finding the way and setting the pace, me following in his silent wake.

Chapter 48

While Mother prepared dinner, Daniel had run up to Grandsire's, so they would know Azariah and I had returned and soon would visit. I had been grateful for his innately considerate nature. Now, as Mother Sarah insisted on feeding us a second time, Daniel's praises were repeatedly sung. Among his many new responsibilities was assisting our grandparents. At this he had by every account been especially diligent. Relief that they had been well cared for warred with resentment at learning how easily and effectively my services had been replaced. The feelings were petty; sprung of vanity, yet they were real enough. Thankfully, Azariah kept up a ready flow of conversation that masked my annoyance.

"A fine compliment you pay me, Azariah," Mother Sarah said, ladling more food onto his plate. "Now if only your eldest brother would display his manners." At this, she gave a wink.

"Thank you, truly," I said. "I believe I ate more than my fill of Mother's cooking."

"Fie!" she retorted. "Why, look at you. Half-starved you are, and such a fine figure of a young man you were when you left us. Has he not shrunken by a stone, husband?"

Grandsire had found his chair back long ago. He sucked on his pipe, and released a small cloud of smoke. "Indeed, a change has come over him." At once, I knew he spoke not of my weight.

"I find I must eat and run," my brother told them. "I promised Daniel an account of our exploits in Massachusetts." I found myself wondering whether it would be a full accounting. "Will you join us, Brother?" he asked. "Or do our grandparents have a prior claim on you?"

"I will stay here tonight," I said. "If they will have me."

"Do not be silly," Mother Sarah said. "We have counted on you living with us."

"Then I'm off," Azariah declared. He hugged our grandparents and smacked my shoulder in passing. His going sucked vitality from the room, and I was in a poor way to replenish it. Mother Sarah busied herself with the clearing of plates, leaving me alone with Grandsire. Much as I desired to speak with him, now was not the time. How could I seek wise counsel when I behaved so small?

"The parlor, I believe," he said. With that he used his cane to stand. Over our repast I had learned that though he had carved it himself, the sturdy, forked branch of cherry had been selected and cut for him by Daniel.

Grandfather settled in his favorite chair, the rocker crafted by Jemima's father. I replenished the fire and took the seat opposite. His eyes had followed me the while. "Well, My Boy," he began. "I dare say your mind is as care-worn as your body is ill-used." Azariah had spoken already of the miseries of the water-logged trenches, so there was little point in repetition. As to the cares that plagued my mind; where to begin? "My dear Sarah has her work before her," Grandsire said. "Why, if you are ever to regain the robustness of your brother Daniel, she must fatten you and your little brother up."

I stiffened at mention of his name. Suddenly a sly smile appeared in one corner of his mouth. It spread. "What, Grandsire?" I asked, my peevishness betrayed by my tone.

"I do declare." He laughed, then coughed, then laughed again. "You are returned to us a veteran. In fact I have it from the Colonel himself that you and his nephew are the talk of the selectmen. No two young men have done our families and this town of ours so proud. Yet here you sit before me, quite as jealous as a jilted girl. And over your brother Daniel no less. Tell me I'm wrong!"

I had not experienced such embarrassment in his presence since he had caught me sneaking a jar of preserves from the root cellar when a mere lad of 10. Having no defense, I sat in silence. Never could I unburden myself now.

"Come closer," he said. "Come. Drag that chair over here so that we might talk." I did as he asked but kept my gaze elsewhere. "Look me in the eyes," he insisted. "You must realize, My Boy, that love your brothers I do, but never will another take your place in this old heart of mine."

A wave of emotion washed over me. I began speaking of Boston and Charlestown. Of Azariah's shot that fateful morning I said nothing. Of the officer's gorget I did. I confessed leaving the boy William on Breed's Hill. Widows in Roxbury and Cambridge, I mentioned seeing, but not how they had cost me Jemima. We sat, staring at the fire.

Mother Sarah brought hot tea. Sensing the mood she rubbed her husband's back, and touched mine before leaving us be. Grandsire watched her depart. "Men die in war, My Boy. As the death of our own dear William taught us both. This you will come to accept, as you perhaps now do. And women, some will be widowed. That is the way of things."

"But a man should not needlessly expose a woman to such loss. A young woman with prospects, I mean."

He took up his pipe. Knocking out the cold ash he took his time refilling it. "We speak now of that lass of yours, I take it." I did not deny it. "I see," he said. "Unfortunate though they be, these are the times in which we find ourselves. We must live in them."

"If you had but seen the widows' faces, Grandsire. How empty were their eyes..."

"Of what use is fighting for liberty, Elisha, if you deny yourself the joys of life?"

"I cannot, Grandsire. I will not see done to Jemima that which has crushed hundreds outside of Boston. What I suspect will destroy thousands more…"

His hand squeezed mine. "That is your choice, My Boy. I respect you for it; though we see the matter quite differently." I had not expected he would disagree. Nor had it occurred to me that my decision might be wrong. I knew not what to say. With a pat of my hand he leaned back. "Have you plans to clear the parcel?" he asked. I shook my head no. "Of course. At present you would not. Well, yours it is and always will be. And as it is but land, it will wait for you."

The failure to win Grandsire to my way of thinking unsettled me profoundly. I carried on as if circling in a dense fog. Never before had he and I had a meaningful disagreement. And to have left it, with no hope of resolution, cost me my footing entirely. Days passed. I found myself increasingly wary of private conversations with those most likely to draw me out. Mother, Daniel and Azariah I avoided as though one or the other of us carried the plague.

At Father's table, however, I rested with reasonable assurance. Mother and Sister Hannah accompanied me and they did cast many a furtive glance my way whilst they prepared the season's preserves. Such attentions worried me not, for my peace of mind tended to be their sole object.

"I thought surely, Elisha," Mother said, "that you would accompany Daniel this morn. Especially since his errand took him into town." Daniel's name proved unsettling in and of itself; for I neither wished to crowd him whilst he hired men for the harvest nor stand off to one side whilst he did so. What's more, I had not ventured into Tolland since our return... "Perhaps your brother does not hear me," Mother confided to Hannah.

Sister replied, "Perhaps not, Mother. See how mindfully he pushes the stitch through the leather."

In times past I would have been the instigator of such teasing. Now I struggled to play along with them. "I did not wish to hang upon his shoulder, Mother. Daniel knows what he's about."

"Well, my son, does that not yet leave another reason for going?" Jemima. I knew it. She intended grilling me about my intentions.

"Perhaps my brother dislikes pie," Hannah said. She and Mother exchanged coy looks, quite as school girls might. Like Jacob, my baby sister had matured in my absence, for she had developed a cleverness that left me quite confused.

"How sad," Mother replied, clearly playing along. "My Elisha was always so fond of my pies."

"Especially your apple recipe," Hannah burst out.

This apparent witticism launched a round of laughter, and entirely at my expense. But their delighted squeals, their swaying forms, finally won me over. "What is this about then?" I demanded.

"To town you must go if you're to discover that," Mother said.

"He'd better hurry or his pie will be cold," Hannah blurted out, prompting another round of giggles. Again my mood swung. My tolerance for being the butt of jokes had grown as short as my patience of late. Mother sensed this.

"Forgive us our sport, Elisha," she said. "It stems from happy tidings. It so happens that upon learning from Captain Willes that the company was to return, a certain Miss Jemima Barrows paid us a visit." My breath caught. "Calm yourself, my son. Your father was quite civil to Miss Barrows on this occasion."

"For what reason did she come?" I asked.

"That's the best part!" Hannah said.

"She begged my apple pie recipe," Mother interrupted. "She knew it to be your favorite, I know not how..."

"Daniel told her," Hannah blurted out. "She asked him in town which kind Elisha liked best? Well she did, Mother."

"Thank you, Hannah. So that is all, Elisha. She promised to bake a pie for your return. Though in telling you we may have spoiled her surprise."

Jemima had returned to Father's door. She had risked his wrath; over a pie, my favorite pie. Though I loved her the more for doing so, was not the depth of her affections all the more reason to spare her pain? Why could she not comprehend my motives in this? Yet I had failed to convince her. Or Grandsire. The unrepaired reins slid to the floor.

Mother ushered Hannah into the adjoining room. Mother returned alone. Why could they not let me be? She knelt down and took my arm, though I resisted. "My son," she whispered. "What has happened? Did you have words with Jemima?"

"I set her free," I whispered back. My voice broke. I told her then what I'd done, and why.

"One thing alone I would say to you," she said when I had finished. "I do understand your choice. Proud I am, too, of the fine feelings that led you to seek to protect her in this way. But consider, my son, is Jemima not entitled to choose for herself?"

Hollow had I been rendered. So alone was I when she left my side. But I would not undo what I had done. Never could I, whilst those black-clad widows roamed my skull.

Chapter 49

Harvest season kept nearly all of us Bentons engaged from sunrise to sunset, and often beyond. Azariah had once again taken up residence with a family in town, but his place in the fields was ably filled by Jacob. What our youngest brother lacked in strength and experience, he more than made up for in eagerness. Daniel oversaw not only our efforts, but that of the contract laborers. When necessity brought them and me together in his presence, strangely his awkwardness persisted, whilst my sense of relief blossomed. Not in a decade had I been relieved of the constant making of decisions for others, and of the responsibility for the outcomes of collective efforts.

Now that I had, pleasure in the work itself began to blossom anew. It flourished despite the sweat that daily overspread my back, or the protests of my muscles come the increasingly cool mornings. How I did love the heavy smell of the hay, field-dried and packed so high and safe in the barn that it crowded the rafters. Fresh-turned earth likewise worked its magic.

Mother and Hannah saw to the yield of the fields, orchards and kitchen garden. Along with Mother Sarah, they performed identical tasks for the two households. At other than meal time the tables in both homes were crowded with tubs and baskets, pans and knives, and, of late, apples in various states. Bunches of sliced, dried and strung fruit hung from the rafters. Peeled and pared apples boiled into sauce in large kettles hung within the hearths. Whatever was not being fermented into hard cider or vinegar became their province. The three women worked hours every bit as long as that of us men, and still found time to bring us food at midday.

On one particular afternoon, I had been preparing a field of Father's for the winter to come. Upon seeing Mother's approach, I stopped Eli's oxen beneath the thinning shade of a maple growing directly against the stone wall.

"You have had a busy morning of it," she said, scanning the furrows.

"The earth is neither too damp nor too dry," I replied, wiping my brow with the kerchief secured at my neck. "Readily it yields to the plough's touch." She smiled and set out a chunk of bread and slices of pork, for yesterday had provided an early cool day - ideal for slaughtering. Her expression turned serious. "What is it?" I asked.

"I spoke with your father last night."

"Did you?"

"He will not speak against your return to our home. Should you desire it."

There was a time, I supposed, when such a concession on Father's part, half-hearted though it seemed, would have deflated my worries; perhaps even filled me with joy. Such a time had passed.

Though it pained me to disappoint her, my mind was quite made up. "I intend to stay on for a time with Grandsire. He and Mother Sarah assure me I am of service. And I've convinced myself that my efforts lessen Daniel's load a tad."

"And what of your grandfather's gift? Have you no plans for it?"

"Please, Mother, do not try to make me speak of Jemima."

"I said nothing of Miss Barrows..."

"To me Jemima is the land. Surely you understand this. Without her I care nothing for it."

"But my son, both are equally yours. Why Daniel tells me that each time he journeys to town Miss Barrows inquires..."

"Mother. No more, I pray you."

"I am sorry, Elisha. I only wished to help you see..."

"I know," I interrupted, and took her hand. "And I thank you."

Mother fiddled with her hair, if only to mask a quick brush of her eye. "The pork is quite tender," she said. "Let me pair a piece with this bread. Fresh today it is." I ate while she busied herself for my sake. "You mentioned your brother earlier," she said. "I take it you no longer object to his changed role?"

"How well you understand me, Mother."

She smiled. "Of that I am guilty, I must admit. But Daniel may not grasp near so well that you have forgiven him."

"Forgiven?"

"Of course. For having learned so well the lessons that you taught him."

"Ah, thank you, Mother. I will speak to my brother." For this I received another smile, and a second helping of food.

As it turned out there was no need to seek out Daniel. That very evening he visited Grandsire's, bringing salt from town. "A beneficial trade you made of it," I casually told him when we stepped outside.

"Sheer coincidence it was," he muttered in absolute humility. "Mister Goodrich needed to re-stock vinegar at his trading store, and we will soon have a surplus on hand."

He passed it off as nothing but I recognized the makings of a shrewd yet fair trade. "You are far too humble, Brother," I told him. "I am pleased we have this time together," I added. Still he kept quiet. "I have wanted to thank you, Daniel. For managing Father's farm, and Grandsire's too, whilst I was away."

"You wish the role back?" he asked. "Of course, I have oft wondered this since your return. I've no objection. The role is yours by rights, Elisha."

All this he blurted out and at once. "Brother!" I protested. "You misunderstand me. Completely so. Your efforts have done our family a great service. By continuing to do so, you put me in your debt."

"In my debt? But how?"

I wished we had a place to go; some spot where we could sit and see each other's faces. How much I wanted him to know the sincerity of what I had to say. As we did not, I endeavored to let my words and expression convey the gratitude I felt; how since Roxbury and Breed's Hill I had lost my way, and by taking my former burden upon his shoulders he kept me from losing my will as well. Not once before had I revealed so much to my younger brother. Never before had he seemed less a youth.

When I had finished, he said, "I will tend to these duties until the day you wish them back again."

"I will not ask for what you have earned, Daniel." After a moment longer, I suggested we go back inside.

"Thank you, but I should return to Father's. I need to make an early start tomorrow." I took his hand. "Elisha. There is one thing I would ask of you."

"It is yours. Name it."

"Should the fighting resume, I wish to go with you."

"Daniel. Have I not just described how much the family needs..."

"Is that your only objection?"

"Is it not enough?"

"Then you'll be pleased to discover I have planned for our joint absence. Truly, Elisha. Regardless of the season or the chores needing tending, I have a plan. I worked it out whilst you and Azariah were away."

How earnest he was. And I had committed myself...

"I intend to accompany you, Brother," he said. "I have already told Azariah so."

The events of April last had shaped a change within every one of us. Gone it seemed, forever, were the boys that we had been.

I awoke early the next day, intent on speaking to Daniel, though doubtless to little avail. The attempt must be made, for his sake and that of the family. Events in Boston or Quebec or elsewhere may yet induce my brother, or brothers and I, to again leave Tolland behind. If I could not dissuade him, I should at least learn the particulars of his plan. And so I rose before both the sun and my grandparents. Pausing only to draw water from the well, and to restore the kitchen fire, I hustled along the path to Father's house. The sun peeked through the increasingly bare branches to the east as I reached the clearing. Movement within the open barn drew me.

"Good morrow, Jacob," I said. "Is Daniel about?"

"Elisha!" In the crook of one arm he cradled a basket full of eggs. Just behind him the hens clucked noisily. "I am sorry, no. He just left. For the mill. Should I run after him?"

"That won't be needed," I said, mussing up his hair. He had grown inches this year. "You look as though you've come straight from bed."

"Truly I did. Mother rose when Brother Daniel did. She tried to get him to eat more than bread and apples but he hurried off just the same. As you were wont to do." He blushed should I take this as impertinent.

"I remember all too well," I said, to put him at his ease. "So is everyone up then?"

Just then, I heard a sound from behind us. It was Father. The rising light framed him in the entry. He addressed Jacob. "Best you hurry those inside," he instructed. "Now that the family is awaken; every one of us." My youngest brother darted off, slowing only to squeeze around Father.

I approached him then. Respect demanded it, plus I wanted to position myself that I might better read his expression. Since my return, not once had we been alone. I had not avoided him, nor had I sought him out.

"I have learned that your plans have changed to an extraordinary degree of late," he said. "Not a word of these alterations did I hear from you! That girl, for instance. I understand you have now abandoned her." My pulse hammered at this. "And," he continued, "you are also said to have determined to make no improvements to a parcel that my father seems intent on granting you."

"Why is it you relate these speculations to me, Father? You cared little enough of what I intended when you demanded that I quit your roof." His expression morphed at once from wary attentiveness to a cold, closed off mask that revealed nothing. The change back happened just as quick. He did want something, and badly too.

"I come to you on a matter of joint interest, that's why. Assuming at least that you've no notions regarding the parcel."

"I have none. Not at this time."

Planting the stick, he moved a half step closer. "You have matured, Elisha. Since your enlistment. Perhaps now you can appreciate the value of a decision made today that can reap fruits for many a tomorrow." I stiffened, for I had no idea of his intent.

"There is a parcel, a truly significant piece of land," he said, managing to slight Grandsire's gift. "Long have I had my eye on it, and only now might it be available for purchase. What I propose is simple. Wonderfully simple, yet grand! I make an offer, of sufficient cash to garner interest but with the balance to be paid in production from the land. Once cleared, of course."

I understood him instantly. For a moment, I had allowed myself to believe he was reaching out to me. Might in fact be struggling to resurrect the relationship we had enjoyed as father and son - when I was his first and only boy. But I was disappointed again. His purpose here was ambition and greed, and I was to once more be his means of satisfying it. "So that I understand you," I said. "My labors are to accomplish the clearing, and the production."

"Exactly. Why, you don't think me capable of such grueling work any longer?"

"No, Father. I do not."

"Do not use that tone with me! And do not sneer at what I offer you."

I laughed. Too loudly and far too crudely, but it could not be helped. "Offer me?"

"Precisely so! Why, in time the fruits of this piece of property will far outstrip whatever yield you might enjoy from your grandfather's gift. This would comprise my legacy to you."

"Once I have paid off the loan that is. And how many harvests under your eye might that entail?"

"And what of it. A young man such as yourself. What is five or even ten years of labor to you? At the end of it, you will enjoy outright ownership of acreage that matches what I now possess, and what I suspect is far more fertile. What you call greed and ambition, I term the safeguarding of our family. Land is the lifeblood of the Benton clan, as it is for any family that farms for a livelihood. It is high time you learn this lesson."

"How do you manage it, Father?" I asked.

"What? Manage what?"

"To declare so often how much you care for this family, whilst feeling so little for any member of it?" I stepped 'round him without waiting for an answer.

"Someday you will thank me, Elisha Benton!" he shouted. "Thank me, I say, for the actions I must take for your sake. For all your sakes!"

Chapter 50

September brought a shifting of the winds from out of the northwest. Soon they would howl from the north, bringing frigid temperatures, deep snow and impassable roads. Long had I comprehended that I could not be content to bury myself in daily chores on Benton lands. I was overdue for a promised visit to Aunt Sara's. The path to her door lay across town. I also longed to visit Heman, who twice via Daniel had asked if I would come to lend him a hand. To reach his new homestead I would likewise need to pass through Tolland. And living therein, of course, was Jemima. How she must despise me.

As I planned to remain with Heman for a few days, I had packed the night before. Rising early, I saw to my grandparent's fires and filled the large kettle that I hung on its hook, taking care to swing it wide of the hearth's flames. With my partially filled rucksack I wandered down to Father's barn. April whinnied at my approach. On hearing of my intended journey, Daniel insisted I take her; thus preventing me from having to ask. I saddled without causing any undue alarm amongst the beasts.

The mare danced sideways upon the open road. Eager she was to be out so early; inhaling air so crisp. We traveled east, facing a lightening sky that promised fair weather. On a whim I urged her up a knoll and carried on across the promised parcel. Satisfied, I guided her to the roadway once more.

I had not set eyes on the town green since the alarm so many months earlier. With a tug on the reins, I bid the mare stand so that I might view it clearly. Knee-high grasses waved in islands where it had not yet been grazed. Its long, narrow shape remained as unchanged as its purpose. And framing both the left and right sides stood the buildings, as familiar to me as the inhabitants - many of whom now had begun to venture out of doors. How often had I walked those paths, greeting neighbors and conducting the business of my family. Proud, I was then, the first-born son of Daniel Benton. Stuffed full of arrogance and conceit, Jemima might have said of me. Would say so still no doubt.

At her father's door I glimpsed no sign of life. No welcome could I expect to receive there. Had she ridiculed me as "the great man" to her parents? In her pain, she might have paired my name with oaths. As I was the cause, I could hardly begrudge any persecution I suffered at her hands.

The merest flick of my heels sufficed to advance the mare. I stopped her when only yards from the Barrows' residence. Before I could dismount, the door swung open. Jemima's father filled the opening. Completely closed remained his face.

"Good morrow, Mister Barrows."

"My daughter is not at home," he barked. "What is your purpose here? Have you not done quite enough harm already?" This last was more a declaration than a question. His broad chest rose and fell as might a bull's - preparing to charge its tormentor.

I slipped the hat from my head. Once in my hand I saw it for what it was; the shabby, felt tricorne suitable only for the fields, yet the sole one I now possessed. "Perhaps you are correct, sir," I replied. With that I backed the mare, and left their home. Behind me I heard the sounds of a woman, his wife, voicing her dissent. Then the door slammed shut.

I nearly turned full about – prepared to abandon my journey. Other stops I had promised, however, and so I pushed on, farther into town. Many acquaintances now hurried to and fro. I kept one hand free so that I might doff my poor hat should any seek to recognize me.

Young Cook's father was first to take note. "Why, Corporal Benton!" he hailed. "So good to see you." In a moment he was beside my mount. "How Mrs. Cook and I have longed to thank you for looking after our boy. He speaks so highly of you."

From my opposite side, Jeremiah West, now a doctor, appeared. "Elisha! Where on this earth have you been!"

More inhabitants gathered 'round; the lot of us visible no doubt from the Barrows' home. I dismounted. A dozen and more friendly faces, each mouth moving, crowded round me. Before I could do more than greet one, another extended a hand or patted me on the back. Whether I felt more gratitude for their reception, or embarrassment at being singled out so, I could scarcely tell. Half an hour or more had passed before I disengaged fully, and reclaimed the mare from the tranquil spot to which she'd removed.

Though I had intended to visit the smithy and the trading shop, I now resolved to tackle those errands on my return.

Captain Willes emerged just then from the Meeting House. He strode down the steps towards me. "You have been missed, Elisha."

"And you, sir."

"Well, let's have a look at you." He stepped back and swept me from head to toe with that appraising eye and air. "As fit a soldier as a captain might hope to see! You are quite recovered, that's certain."

I could not conceal my pleasure from his compliments. "And what of Boston, sir? Any news?"

"None to speak of. The odd skirmish here or there, but no, by all accounts our enemy remains trapped in the bottle into which we stuffed them." Then his expression grew serious. "This happy state of quiet cannot last forever, Elisha. This we both know. Either General

Washington must discover how to drive his way in, or Howe must attempt to break his way out."

"Howe, sir?" I asked.

"Forgive me. Gage was replaced following the fighting above Charlestown. Cashiered I suspect, which conveys the King's notion of who won that battle. It's General William Howe who commands the Regulars now. He'll wish to make his mark one could guess."

"So, then," I muttered. "More men must become casualties. And more women widowed..."

"Any chance for peace, Elisha, died I fear, with your companions upon Breed's Hill. Some of those in Congress later penned an olive branch of sorts to the King, but he dismissed their petition out of hand. No, it is war we face. Make no mistake of that." Nothing he said surprised me. To hear my fears confirmed, however, and by him... "I am soon off on a mission," he continued. "Tut tut, no questions, if you will. There is some secrecy involved so this is for your ears alone. Rest assured, however," and here he took my hand, "I have arranged to have word reach you. Should the time come, and whether I am here or no."

"I understand. I will be ready when needed. And sir, Godspeed." He left me then. As in Roxbury I marveled that he covered ground so quickly without ever appearing to hurry.

A soft footfall on the stair behind me drew my head slowly round. Jemima - caught in mid-step. She had seen me first, that much was clear. It staggered me to realize too that she had meant to pass me by.

"Will you not even greet me Jemima?"

She stopped at this, but would not look my way. "And if I did not, Mister Benton, what difference could that possibly make to you?"

"Jemima, please! I cannot bear it if we are not able to exchange a civil word."

She began to speak but her voice cracked. Her head she tossed back, as if she might confound the tears that had come to her eyes. "How ironic, Mister Elisha Benton. You can stand to not hold me in your arms. That you can do. You insist upon it. But should you be prevented from shaking my hand, why...."

I stepped close. I reached for her, intent on drawing her to my chest.

"No! Do not!" Her command struck me dumb in the street; one arm extended. She slipped her cool, soft hand into mine. "If civility is all you would have of me," she said, "then I give it freely."

"Jem..."

She hurried away from me. So quickly did she flee that her hat slid onto her shoulder. A wave of auburn hair cascaded down. Only now did I discern the numerous inhabitants watching. I mounted, though I had no sense of my boot in the stirrup. To the east I rode.

Aunt Sara greeted me as warmly as ever. In her liquid, brown eyes I saw not a hint of recrimination for my long absence. Her three children shouted my name. The boy manfully took my hand whilst the older girl leapt into my arms. The youngest insisted I haul her from her feet, and swing her about in full circles. Never had they thought of me as a cousin, and so I reveled in the role of a sort of youthful uncle. A few carefree moments with them helped to push back for a time the scene on the common. Minutes were all, unfortunately, that my aunt could spare, and she eventually steered her brood back to their many chores.

"And do you have a list for me, Aunt?" I asked.

She retrieved it straightway. "Daniel visited last week," she said. "He conveyed your instructions; that I was to prepare this for you."

I scanned the items. Much more, I imagined, than these alone required doing. Even so, addressing these few would be of some value for her, and do me a world of good.

"Is it too long?" she asked, peering over the edge of the sheet. "There are one or two that need not be seen to just yet."

I stuffed the page into my blouse and kissed her on the cheek. "I shall have them set to rights before sundown. Next time make it longer so that I have an excuse to dine with you and the children."

"Oh, you are sitting down with us this evening, Elisha Benton. Either that or I shall see that word of your discourtesy reaches your good mother."

Like all the Benton women she was not to be argued with. "Are the tools still in the barn, Aunt?"

"Right where you left them last. Oh, and Elisha, you are staying the night, for I will not see you ride off come dark." I kept my smiling mouth closed.

My uncle's tools were bearing up well. The sharpening and oiling had kept them in a state for ready use despite months of storage. I began by repairing the gate where the animals grazed. My aunt could ill afford to lose even one of the goats or sheep. Not since my uncle's passing had they been blessed with a horse or cow.

Next, I replaced boards that had sagged dangerously in the loft. In the course of eliminating this chore, I discovered another. The latch to the main door of the barn would not hold. I chiseled a new location and made it secure. Now an ill wind could not blow the door ajar, inviting a coyote or fox in at the chickens. I had worked up a fine sweat by this time, and though Jemima's face came to my mind, toiling hands required constant attention.

That night, as I settled down on a bed of quilts before the fire, my aunt looked in on me just as she had earlier with her own children. Did I need anything, she wanted to know. At her kindly offer I suddenly wished to speak to her of widowhood, and of my Jem. One glance at those soft, sad eyes sufficed. I assured her I had need of nothing.

Chapter 51

The following morning, after having first promised on my honor to return within a fortnight, I took leave of my aunt and gleeful cousins. The boy William, with his persistence and mischievous grin had, during the course of our breakfast managed to pry from me some tales of Roxbury. Queries concerning Breed's Hill I had successfully parried, much to my aunt's relief.

I left them with the first sense of well-being I had enjoyed in many a month. There was no accounting for it. I had accomplished little enough for my uncle's family, and thoughts of war and widows had certainly granted me no rest. Even so, I rode along the narrow, country lane whilst a smile came and went upon my face. Leaves tumbled from trees on either side in the surging breeze. The mare sensed the season and my mood, for she set about dancing sideways near as much as forward. Normally I would have checked such silliness. On this morn I gave her whatever rein she wished. With a carrying whinny she tossed her head and played the filly.

This buoyant spirit lifted us up the rise to the crest where the town common stretched away to our left. My object was to continue westward till I reached Heman Baker's homestead, but something made me tend to my errands. Once these were completed, I began a loop of the green.

Despite scanning near and far, and twisting awkwardly in the saddle, I saw no evidence of Jemima. I greeted passersby with little more than a touch of my brim for I had no wish to wear out the warm welcome of the day before. That's when I saw her. The familiar straw hat sent my heart leaping, but it was secured to the mother's and not the daughter's head. I slid down so that I would not startle her.

"Good morrow, Mrs. Barrows," I said, my hat already off my head, and the mare trailing me.

Her look of alarm gave way to a closed expression that compressed her lips into a brief, flat line. "Mister Benton," she replied with an absence of emotion. I feared she would break away without another word.

Embarrassment swelled within my chest, but if I were to drop my gaze, she would without a doubt abandon me. Jon Barrows would not admit me to their home. Jemima would do no more than shake my hand, and even that in spite. Her mother was my only hope.

"I tried to explain to Jemima," I began. "Perhaps she failed to understand. Perhaps she did, yet disagreed with my reasoning." The mother's lips might as well have been of stone. I was only making matters worse. "Mrs. Barrows. Never would I abandon your daughter. I only meant to spare her pain. I mean to still. I love Jemima. That's why I suggested we wait. Till the fighting is done. For that reason alone..."

I was rendered mute by the warmth dawning upon her features. In the natural openness of her expression and posture I recognized what drew me to the daughter, and what now in the mother might denote forgiveness. She unfolded her arms and I received a hug of which any of the Benton women would have been proud.

"I will speak with her, Elisha," she promised. "Leave Jemima to me."

A few moments later the mare and me were heading west. We had frolicked before, now we galloped, my face pressed far forward alongside her flying mane.

Before we reached Lake Shenipsit I had slowed our pace. My mind raced, however, with endless possibilities, most of them favorable. I couldn't fathom the change in my behavior. Perhaps the gaiety of my young cousins had turned my head. I had reached the junction. Surely it was more than that. Chapman land lay on three sides. I vowed to visit Eli upon my return. For now, however, I must keep my long overdue promise to Heman.

Taking the right hand turn, we followed the road north for not more than half a mile. The route traced the lake's eastern shore. Heman's parcel occupied a rise that offered a view of the expansive waters.

The echoing bite of an ax drew me through a copse of birch and towards the clearing. A small cabin had sprung up within 50 feet of a spring-fed stream. Complete it was, with four walls of notched logs, a chimney of brick on the near end and a planked roof. A simple structure to be sure, but Heman and his family had done much since I had last been here. He had himself a proper home. How fortunate he was.

"I see you put those logs we downed to good use," I shouted.

"Elisha, my friend! Come up, come up!" Our embrace was brief, for he was in an instant lather to show me 'round the place. Scarcely had he ever talked so fast or said so much. With the barest encouragement from me, a nod or a smile sufficed, he continued on as if I had begged him for more.

Finally I took hold of his arm. "There is no need for haste," I assured him. "I am yours for as long as you have need of me." This settled him at once. We stabled the mare beside his own in the barn, a stout structure of posts and beams.

"No doubt you wonder why more care was taken here than with the cabin," he said. "Let me explain." He led us back outside. "The barn is permanent you see. The cabin need but see me through the first winter or two. By then I'll have sufficient acres cleared. The yield from those fields will provide the wherewithal to erect a proper home."

"One fit to house a proper wife?" That I had joked about the female sex surprised me. He too looked taken aback. "Clearly we have much to discuss," I said. "What say we catch one another up over that coffee you promised?"

Heman soon confided that on various trips into town for supplies, both of my brothers, on different occasions, had seen fit to inform him of my troubles with Jemima. He had long intended to visit me to learn the way of it, but my repeated avowals to visit him had kept him at bay. I now confided all, including the conversation with her mother that very morning. At the conclusion, I leaned back in one of his two chairs. I cared little if he said not a word; preferred it in fact. So many of those who loved me desired to advise me. Tucked within the advice, judgments lurked, even if unintended. With Heman my ears and heart had little to fear. The sharing had lifted a weight from off my chest, and his silent companionship did the rest. I even closed my eyes for a time.

"More coffee?" he asked after a bit. "To warm your cup at least." I held it up. From the way he perched on the edge of his seat I realized I was to be disappointed in my dear friend. Advice was coming, and soon. "Elisha. Surely, my friend, as concerns Jemima Barrows, none but you are fit to judge what is to be done. Even so are you perhaps making too much of these widows? 'Tis certain there were some. I spied one or two myself. But Elisha, can you really know what they thought, how they feel?"

"You sound like my mother now, Heman."

"And I assume that's a compliment, my friend." He said this to make me smile. After a moment I obliged him. "It occurs to me, Elisha.

That if you'll not take your mother's advice, then what of your aunt's? Who better to ask than your Uncle William's widow?"

"I almost did ask her. Last night."

"You should have done."

"I trust I found the answer in her eyes. So sad they were. Even after all these years." We sat silent then, brought low by a shared inability to hit upon a solution. My earlier excitement dissolved. Mrs. Barrows would speak with Jemima, but to what end? Even if she would converse with me once more, a resumption of courtship would only subject her to my eventual departure, to Boston or in the Captain's company on some secret mission - perhaps to never return. "Ah, what's the use," I muttered.

Heman apologized, evidently taking blame for the rapid deterioration in my mood. This would not do.

"Tell me how you came to meet with so much progress," I demanded. "And I insist that you do so whilst tools fill our hands." A smile leapt to his face, his long arm wrapped my shoulders, and to the cutting of firewood we turned our attention.

By the end of two days we had increased his modest supply to four full cords. With but the one fireplace, this quantity should suffice to warm his hearth and home whatever winter had in store. The logical next step was creation of a lean-to. Using milled boards left over from construction of the roof, we extended the overhang from a sheltered wall of the house. Snow would be unlikely to drift as badly here, keeping most of the firewood dry, even while remaining convenient to the door. A day more witnessed the completion of this task. By the following noon we had stacked the wood itself.

"What now, Heman?" I asked. "You mentioned wishing to excavate that cave mouth for a root cellar."

"I couldn't possibly ask that. The Bentons will think I've taken you captive."

We both avoided any talk of wages. He was content that I no longer refused them, and I had grown suddenly more interested in earning them. "They will hardly miss me," I replied. "Daniel has done remarkably well. And he enjoys the considerable assistance of young Jacob. You would be amazed how the boy has grown. Already he rivals Azariah in height. With none of his vaunted independent streak," I laughed.

"How does he match up as regards ill temper?"

"What?" I asked, turning to see what had drawn his gaze. Azariah it was, coming on fast despite the incline, and it studded with stumps. My brother's movements were typically effortless, yet he wore a strained expression. I raised my hand in greeting.

"How could you, Elisha?" he demanded, clearly in no mood for pleasantries. Nor was he disposed to let me answer. "I have seen Jemima," he went on, sticking his jaw forward, the top of his head nearly beneath my chin. "And to think I had been on your side, what with all you suffered on Breed's Hill. To postpone the marriage is one thing. Clumsy though that was. But then to expect her to be content with bare civilities?" He stared at Heman as if expecting agreement as to my cruel nature. "Of the kind you extend to the merest acquaintance no less."

"Azariah..."

"Do not Azariah me. I'm not finished with you. Hear this Heman, for the worst is yet to come. Your comrade here, my wise and brave first-born brother; he will not content himself with first abandoning and then insulting his fiancée. No!" He forcefully poked my chest. "How does he proceed you might ask? By an abject and public apology? By falling to his knees before the girl's father? No! Not our Elisha. He attempts to ingratiate himself with her mother." The contact had frayed my patience but it seemed best to allow him to talk himself out. If he was apt to. Of Heman, he asked, "Where is the honor in his intent?" Of me, "Where is there courage in your method?"

How could I respond to such charges? I had no method and never had with Jemima. All was the best of intentions and the sorriest of execution. A muddled mess I'd made of it and had no defense to make.

"Look at him, Heman. Your friend. My brother. It is unnatural and unjust that one who acts as he has done, somehow finds success. By duping innocents he succeeds."

"In what way?" I asked. "How have I?"

Azariah backed off. "If you do not know of it, I'll not be the one to tell you."

"Tell him, Azariah," Heman said. "If our bumbling friend and brother has stumbled back into love, for God's sake let us hear of it!"

My brother's brow furrowed. "Mrs. Barrows swallowed whatever bait you fished with, Brother. She's convinced of your goodwill, and makes your case daily to her daughter. And my friend, Jemima, she is this day swayed..."

"Is she?"

"Despite my objections, she seems inclined to give you the benefit of sincerity. That's not to say she forgives you."

My hand went to my face. "She's not lost her trust in me then." A deep sigh escaped, heating my palm as it left me.

"Can it be that you love her again?" Azariah asked from directly before me.

I met his probing gaze. "I cannot stop loving her."

"What will you do now, my friend?" Heman asked, coming to stand with us.

"Whatever I must." The three of us stood side by side for a time. An unspoken accord was reached - all that needed saying had been said. Directly behind my brother and my friend stood the rock shelf that shielded a shallow cave. "Is anyone of a mind to begin digging that root cellar?" I asked.

Azariah twisted half-way round. "But Heman has no crops." To Heman himself he said, "Why you've not even a single field that's been properly cleared."

"I have a family with baskets of preserved fruits and vegetables they're eager to bestow upon me." The freckles shined on his smiling cheeks. "And picks and shovels I have aplenty."

Chapter 52

Azariah left us after a few days but not before we had dug a root cellar that would keep Heman's stored goods well below the reach of ruinous frosts. The pit floor consisted of nothing more than dirt, but this served our purpose. Exposed rock formed the ceiling and the better part of the sides. The remaining wall Heman and I lined with shale. All in all the structure would keep the air moist, yet water out.

"I cannot thank you enough, my friend. Without your help, and Azariah's..."

"I am mere hired help," I interrupted with a grin.

"That you are, and so you'll accept your wages without argument." I bowed low. "Good man. Now as for your brother, do tell him how grateful I am."

"If I can find him," I jokingly replied. "A full four families of the town he hunts for now."

"So he told me. Room and board and payment in services besides. He makes a right comfortable living with that musket of his." Heman cast a glance my way.

His sudden wariness convinced me that my brother had confided in him about shooting the sentry. If so, this opening up must be a sign of Azariah's recovery. "So he does," I agreed. "And as he hunts near the lake on occasion, you might even lay eyes on him before I do."

"Perhaps I shall at that."

"Do you still plan on visiting your family today, Heman?"

"Aye. They are desperate to fill that new cellar. Besides, I made a promise to your brother."

"What's this?"

"He convinced me that if I persist in letting you help me, we will never return you to his friend Miss Barrows. So you see, I've no choice but to leave. And to release you."

We parted soon after, but not before I too had promised - to return before the first snow fell. As I rode April back towards the junction, I pulled my collar tight against the stiff breeze. It had shifted from out of the northwest during the night, and some of that region's cold bore down upon me. I would have to see if Mother had stored my old great-coat. Hopefully it still had some wear in it.

Though the mare made the turn towards town, longing for home and her stable mates perhaps, I recalled my earlier wish to visit Eli. At the Chapman's I stopped. I regretted it almost at once. Eli had been visiting his uncle, at the big house that dominated the rising ground. Only a handful of times had I come before, and each time on business. As a consequence I had always been attired in my best clothes, and so felt only somewhat conscious of my station in life versus their own. Now, surrounded by Chapman splendor and a host of Chapmans, I stood in their parlor like some storm-felled tree in a sparkling stream. In my hand I concealed my worn cap of felt. There was no hiding, nor no excuse that could be made for my wrinkled coat, the complete absence of a waistcoat, and certainly not the dirt-streaked trousers that might shame a transient.

A dark face appeared amongst the august gathering, capped by a white wig. "Newport!" I said, much too loudly.

The company turned towards their slave, who bowed to me, saying in a voice equally polite, "Mista Benton, sir." His manners and his dress both outshined me.

"Elisha met Newport when we journeyed to Boston," Eli quickly explained. "When we brought sheep to the populace." This clarification received universal acknowledgement. "Now as my friend says, he can only spare a few hours from his charitable works, I insist on having him to myself. You will forgive us." With that, he led me towards a second parlor. Entreaties to stay, or to join them at least for tea before leaving pursued us back across the foyer.

"Thank you for that," I told Eli soon as we were safely within these other walls and alone. "Though assisting Heman hardly qualifies as charity."

"A slight exaggeration that everyone happily accepted. There's no harm done."

I gestured at my clothes as if there might be some excuse for appearing at their door in this fashion. "If not for missing you, I would not have come. I was contracted to our friend if truth be told."

Eli coughed at this admission. "Speaking of such matters," he said, "it puts me in mind of a few names I have for you. Neighbors and farmers these men are, who have needs that might appeal to you. I'll jot down their names." His sudden laugh covered the awkward silence. "As to your attire, think not on that, my friend. Trust that my uncle, the Colonel, comprehends not a single article of what you wear. You are a hero under this roof. We both of us are, and so can commit no faux pas." He poured out a glass of wine, then hesitated. "Something stronger perhaps. You look positively ashen."

I finally laughed myself. "Wine will be just the thing. Thank you." I took a sip. The fruity red calmed my throat. Eli insisted that I sit, and so I did. We caught each other up on affairs of the town. Attentive he was to the pouring of the wine. When business was dispensed with, and Daniel's acumen in this regard roundly hailed, he made an oblique reference to Jemima, saying he'd seen her at service one week earlier. I smiled at his cautious opening, and proceeded to inform him that I meant to court her anew.

He leaned forward to clink his glass with mine. "Then congratulations are in order. To your joint health!" After we had swallowed the last, he refilled our glasses once more. "So, then, Elisha, if I may ask. Have you put Charlestown and her widows behind you?"

"I confess I do not know. Widowhood it was that led me to postpone talk of marriage with Jemima."

He shook his head. "Here you've not even set a date with the girl, yet you fill your mind, and hers too, with that? For shame. May the saints preserve us! Your courting needs study, Elisha."

He meant to ease my mind with his gentle ridicule but he better than any of my acquaintance knew full well the source of my turmoil. Too many hundreds we'd seen fall on the slopes of Breed's Hill to think our own lives charmed. "I thought to spare her pain, Eli. If her attachment to me was not over strong, I reckoned she might forget me, in time. And if it was, well, as deep as mine for her, then she could bear the waiting."

"Yet you now abandon that plan. Your courtship is renewed..."

"If she'll have me. You see, she put it in her head that my aim was to abandon her. I freely admit I made a shambles of it. Now I must start anew. Should she reject me, the loss will be mine. And should she accept me back again, the risk to her remains. I've solved nothing, you see. What I have done is cause all manner of pain and confusion."

"You are too morbid by half, my friend. Of course she'll want you back. And yes, the war will rage on, and just as likely we'll be caught up in it. But we returned safely once. So we shall again. Come! A toast to our long and happy lives."

The feeling that had gnawed somewhere inside me hunched there still. It had since Charlestown. For all that, Eli's smiling eyes and raised glass demanded and deserved a gesture. "Ah well," I replied. "I am too poor at any rate to marry soon, so I shall need to live a long life if ever an offer is to be made. Long and happy it is!"

We drank. Decency then required me to return the compliment. "And to equally long, and endlessly delightful courting then! With only the loveliest of lasses. You must find such a one as my Jem!"

"To courting success and your Jem!" he cried, loud enough to be heard in the neighboring rooms.

I realized then that the wine had made a distinct impression on us both. I had worked hard these many days, and eaten but little. This lovely red had gone straight to my head. Why else would I broadcast my poverty and innermost thoughts to not only my inebriated comrade, but likely his entire family, and they Chapmans all!

He smiled so good-naturedly at me that I could not resist returning it in full measure. "I seldom raise a glass at this time of day," he admitted. I snorted at this, which launched a spasm of grunts and giggles from us both.

One of the maids appeared at the entry with a tray piled with cold meats, cheeses, bread, and fruits. "Begging your pardon, Mister Chapman," she said, and curtsied. "Your uncle wonders if you and your guest might be in want of something to eat."

Eli and I turned to each other and broke out laughing. It required a minute or more before we could assure her that indeed we would.

For the next quarter of an hour we greedily ate. Practically the only sounds within the room consisted of the working of our jaws, and sighs of contentment. Finally we sat back in our chairs. A somber look stole over my companion's face. "What troubles you?" I asked.

"My uncle. Last week he mentioned that Howe is reinforced."

"There will come another battle I suppose. Has he any sense of when?"

"Sooner, perchance, than any of us thought. You heard we captured Fort Ticonderoga?" I nodded, for news of this victory along Lake Champlain up New York way was old by months. "Well," he whispered, "if I swear you to secrecy I can tell you that cannon might be soon on their way to Boston."

"Big guns? Not those puny four pounders we had in the redoubt."

"Big brass ones, yes, and enough of them to tip the scales of that stalemate. A Mister Knox from here in Connecticut is to lead the party."

"So, the city is to be bombarded?"

"I imagine so," he replied.

In the pause that followed we both contemplated the deaths of untold numbers of civilian inhabitants, and soldiers too. It eased my mind little that most of the former still within the walls were Tories. "An attack would follow?" I asked.

"I aim to be there if it does," he said. "Will you come with me?" This time I pressed my glass to his.

Chapter 53

I had hoped to pass through town unnoticed. My return to Grandsire's was overdue, shifting more work onto the backs of my brothers no doubt. Much as I longed to see a certain someone in Tolland, further delay would not do. Besides, after a week of hard labor, both my clothing and I had reached a state not fit for female companionship. The Chapman visit had certainly convinced me of that, if I had needed any convincing. As it was, I found I must refuse their invitation to stay the night, with Eli's oft repeated. And so as dusk fell I welcomed this ally of stealth. To the mare I gave rein, in order that she might pick her way along the deserted road.

We arrived at nightfall. Outside the Meeting House a lamp had been lit. The now whip-like wind threatened to put it out on the instant. After passing the row of huddled houses, we neared the end of the common. My breath caught in my throat. The door to the Barrows' home stood ajar. And in the light pouring forth stood a slight figure - my Jem.

She advanced at once, oblivious to the cold and intent it appeared on intercepting us. Her hurried steps slowed as she reached the roadside.

"Whoa," I whispered to April.

"Will you dismount?" she asked. "And speak with me."

"I am not fit for the company of a lady." My embarrassment had led me to admit this, and foolishly to, for surely she could not discern my appearance in this light.

"Am I a lady then, in your eyes, Mister Benton?"

Her voice was soft, her tone gentle. I had heard it not when last we spoke. I swallowed, fighting the lump born thus in my throat. "You are my lady, Jemima Barrows."

She stepped forward; her hands sought mine. "Elisha..." I released her, but only to slip down from the saddle. "Forgive me," she whispered as I wrapped her within my arms, my soiled garb forgotten. "Forgive my vile temper..." she managed to stammer. "Mother convinced me I had misunderstood your intent." A brief gasp of a laugh escaped. "Azariah was far blunter. He called me more sullen than a mule. Oh, why didn't I listen to what you tried to say?"

"Jemima stop. There is no cause for this. If either of us has been foolish it has been me."

Her fingers pressed soft against my lips. "I do ask your forgiveness, Elisha. I must have it. All you ever did was try to spare me pain. And I, not once did I attempt to soothe yours. How you must have suffered on that hill. Must suffer still."

I pulled her close. If I held her long enough, the black-clad figures might even grant me rest. "I love you, Jem," I said.

"Then I am truly forgiven."

Despite the best protection that my encircling arms could provide, her shivering only increased. These tremors caused me to release her at last, despite her protests. As her father needed more time, she said, I did not ask to accompany her back inside. His motive was no darker than wishing to protect his daughter, and I did not begrudge him that. I was not to worry regardless, for Jemima promised she would see to his convincing, as her mother had done with her.

Away from Tolland I rode, alone and shivering myself by this hour. Somehow I minded neither state. For I carried the certainty of Jem's love. And it had been tested. Though doing so had never been my intent. I felt a grin upon my face, exposed high upon the saddle, in the cold and dark. "Come, girl," I muttered. "Get this fool upon your back safely home." She whinnied and quickened her walking pace - the night be damned.

For the next fortnight I labored like a man possessed. Having seen at once to every need of my grandparents, and then having lent Daniel a hand with a few outstanding chores from the harvest, I turned my attention to my land, nay our land. I walked it from end to end and during every minute of daylight. Again and again I traversed its length and breadth until its secrets were tucked safely within my mind. The stream and orchard were already familiar to me. Now I also knew in what places the one ran fast; and where its waters were still and deep. Likewise I could go at once to where the trees hunkered low from the prevailing wind, and where the branches bent most bountifully come fall. Every rise and each fold of ground became imprinted. From the current low arc of the sun across its surface I calculated where the spring and summer sun might shine. Where rock-strewn and where fertile was the soil I understood. And each square foot brought me joy - in the contemplation of what was, and what could be.

One evening at table with Grandsire and Mother Sarah, after a particularly long day that began with the chopping of their firewood and ended with the felling of marked trees upon my acreage - various hatchets having occupied my hands from before sunup till post sundown - I drifted off, awakened by my grandmother's touch upon my forearm. "Shall I warm this for you, Elisha?"

I focused on the plate, still laden with food. "Please, yes," I mumbled. Smiling, she lifted it clear. I noticed then that my right hand still clutched a tankard full of hard cider.

"Might you be burning the candle at both ends, My Boy?" Grandsire asked. A shawl had been wrapped close about his shoulders, this despite the fact that Mother Sarah had insisted he relinquish his seat at the head of the table so that he might sit where the fire warmed his back.

I took a slug of the cool liquid if only to awaken my voice. "Perhaps," I replied. "But I've never known a pleasanter exhaustion. It's all for Jem you see." They both turned their gazes full upon me. I do not know why I had spoken thus. Perhaps my waking state had lowered my guard. And perhaps the reserve I had once taken pride in had deserted me completely. Whatever the cause, my grandparents could not have bestowed kinder smiles upon me.

"It does me a world of good," Grandsire said, "to see you take such pleasure in the land."

"Oh, fiddlesticks, Husband," she interrupted. "You men and your talk of soil and so on. When are we to have Miss Barrows to dine with us is what I want to know?"

I laughed. "Soon. I promise you." Raising my tankard, I offered a mute toast to Grandsire, for we both knew that his gift was what made my dream possible. If, like Heman, I shaped a homestead from its contours, come spring I could, I would, ask for Jemima's hand.

Comprehending my gesture, he winked. To me, he lifted his pipe.

Winter's impatience plagued Daniel at every turn. An October storm caused us to liberate the pumpkins from near a foot of snow. I joined my brothers in this tiresome effort that left us soaked to our thighs. Wet again were our feet, when some days afterwards we gathered the last of the apple crop and carted them to Mister Stimson's mill. More days passed, yet the ground retained its blanket of white. We shifted our efforts to the shucking of the late corn so that the cattle would have feed for the coming months. We moved within Father's barn. Here we were dry and safe from nature's timetable. So many dawns to dusks had I committed to my brothers that the opportunity must now be taken to break with them. Countless more trees and stumps awaited my return. Spotting Daniel coming my way I resolved to tell him so, in gentle terms.

"Elisha," he called. "How can I thank you, Brother?"

At once I regretted my resolve to quit his side. "There is no need."

"Without you we would have fallen so far behind that Father would have granted me not a minute of peace." How strange to hear him speak so of Father's wrath. "Now, however," he continued, "I fear I trespass on your goodwill. And this cold weather that hindered the final harvest days, shall prove providential for the tasks you have in mind."

His evident pleasure eased my conscience. I glanced out of the partially open door. "'Tis true the sledge will glide easily over this ground," I agreed. My mind began at once to calculate how many loads of timber Eli might accept in exchange for the use of his oxen; leaving the entirety of the remainder, if need be, to construct a house.

Daniel's shoulder bumped mine. "Today, in fact, seems ideal for hauling," he mused. "Should you not be off?"

He spoke true as regards the weather; though it would be week's end at least before I could ride to Chapman land, come to terms, put in some days of labor out that way, and return with beasts of burden - assuming a team was not already bespoke. "Yes, all right," I said. "If you are sure you won't need me."

"What do you think, Jacob?" he called. "Have we need of our elder brother?"

From the loft, our youngest hollered that they had no need of me whatsoever. I took a step back so that I might see his face. He wore a grin that stretched from ear to ear. "What are you about?" I demanded. "You are both of you up to something." Silly grins I got and nothing more. "Might I saddle April?" I asked, eager to be away from them and their intended mischief.

Daniel laughed in my face. His guffaw was eclipsed by a cackling from Jacob. "He desires to ride!" Daniel said, tears coming to his eyes.

I was transfixed by what in times gone by would have been, by his own description, an act of unspeakable impertinence on his part. "You shall walk!" he roared. "Shan't he, Jacob!"

"Walk!" came the shrill cry. "Walk! Walk!" they chanted in unison. It was quite as if they had both gone mad. A smile came unbidden to my face. Clearly they were in raptures, and at my expense, but I had absolutely no idea as to...

"Hello the barn!" a voice called. I stared out at Eli Chapman, mounted on his gelding. "Unless my ears deceive me," he said, "the surprise is complete."

Jacob descended from the loft. "Never in life has our brother been so confounded," Daniel hollered in reply. To me he said, "Behold your reward, Brother!" The pair shoved open the door.

Directly behind Eli stood Newport. And beside him were a yoked team. "What is this?" I asked.

Daniel prodded me forward. "I should think you of all people would recognize a pair of oxen. The good Lord knows you work quite as hard as these hairy creatures. And always for this family, Brother. Go on. They are yours for as long as you require."

My younger brothers had rendered me speechless with their compassion. I embraced them each in turn. I could not help wondering whether Daniel risked Father's wrath with his generosity - for surely Father would not have approved of an expense incurred for me alone. Or perhaps Eli had chanced his own family's displeasure by offering terms that none deserved. My friend bent forward when I reached for his hand. "And you," I chastised. "Not a hint did you give me when I came for a visit."

"I am innocent of being either clever or thoughtful. Daniel only outlined this plan when we spoke in town last week."

"Then you, at least, are forgiven. And you as well, Newport," I added, for his grin outshined the day. "But as for you two..."

Newport's assistance had, I soon discovered, been part of the arrangement. He was to stay by my side, and manage the team for as long as I might need them. These terms were, of course, outrageously generous. I intended to clear the land the winter through, or at least as long as the snow depth enabled passage. No purse could support engaging Newport and his team for such a time. Thus the true length of the engagement was wholly dependent on my common sense and decency. And I intended to put an early end to the arrangement. I was not, however, inclined to squander their gift. I worked, therefore, for days together, like the devil himself. Newport and his beasts were equally game. Together we loaded and hauled to the mill by sledge every log that I had felled thus far. Once milled, I would have sufficient beams and boards for a proper house.

I must not forget the needs of Eli's neighbors. Like as not these would yield an equal harvest. With it I could secure brick to build a chimney sporting double hearths, and procure all the nails and ironwork that might be required. There might even be a surplus in the form of ready coin. With this I could purchase seed for a first planting, and perhaps even a cow.

At Grandsire's barn on the last morn, I parted with my ever-smiling companion. "Again, Newport, many thanks. Please do tell Eli that I am eternally grateful for what you have done for me." He stared at my extended arm. We shook hands. "Yes, sir, Mista Benton," he said.

As I watched him lead the oxen away, I was disappointed only in that even now he refused to address me as Elisha. I had at least discovered that he had a wife, named Martha. Before a roaring fire one night he had also spoken proudly of a brood of six children. With his youthful face, I never would have thought he would have half as many. For the first time in my life, I wondered what kind of a father I would make.

Chapter 54

During October and November, my labors were divided, though not equally, amongst five different properties. My first responsibility remained addressing every need of Grandsire and Mother Sarah. This called upon all of my powers of observation, for they only sought help on half of what the season required. Whenever I managed to get ahead of these tasks, I next would offer my services to Daniel, who dealt directly with Father for any chores pertaining to the collective Benton lands. With these well in hand, for never could they be satisfied, I hastened to my own particular parcel. Somehow I also found time to keep my promises to both Heman and Aunt Sara - returning to help them on two separate occasions over the span of six weeks. Whilst in the western part of town I fulfilled my contracts with Eli's neighbors.

Each evening I collapsed in the closet-sized space off my grandparents' kitchen. With the curtain tied back, the warmth of the hearth reached me where I lay. So deeply did I sleep that the flashing steel and leaking blood of Breed's Hill gradually faded from my dreams. When, from time to time, I did awake in the night, seldom did I see the pale faces of women clad in black.

More often Jemima visited my dreams. Sometimes these would wake me, but with an agitation of a far different sort. My longing for her grew - of the spirit and the flesh. I woke in just such a state one December morn. In this case the reason was clear, and near at hand. She was to join the assembled family for dinner late that afternoon. It would take place in the very room barely visible from my bed in the pre-dawn light. Somehow or other Mother had prevailed upon Father to come. I had expected him to refuse. His doing so would have angered me, for it would constitute an insult to Jemima, and Grandsire too for she would be his guest. That Father would be present caused me perhaps more turmoil. If he should choose to insult her, before the entire family...

By noon I had accomplished all that I had hoped. Surprisingly I found time to bathe, as much as one could using well water heated in the big cooking pot. Even this hurried sponging elicited a warning from Mother Sarah that I would catch my death. For once, I ignored her advice. Far more important it was to me to smell and dress my best this day. And so I then donned the clothes purchased with the wages earned since my return, including some that Grandsire had insisted upon paying me. The boots fit my overlarge feet perfectly, and the new tricorne cap of beaver sat snugly on my head. I emerged to the approving nods of my grandparents.

"Perhaps it was worth all that splashing about," Grandsire said. "What say you, Dear Wife?"

Mother Sarah hustled over and kissed my cheek. "A pleasing effect indeed. The handsomest man under this roof to be sure." Grandsire burst into laughter which I could not resist.

Mother, Hannah and Jacob joined us soon after. All three had come loaded down with provisions suitable for a fortnight, though but the one repast was planned. Now the preparations for the meal entered full swing. Though I had lugged in water and wood sufficient for every task now at hand, I soon learned that my presence amongst the frenzied foursome merely blocked the industry of their far nimbler hands. Making excuses that went unheeded by everyone but Grandsire, I eased my way into the parlor. There I stretched myself before his fire, and opposite his empty rocking chair. For a second my heart stopped, imagining my life without him. His low, contented voice from the adjoining room set it beating normally once more.

The spiraling winds had deposited a swirl of crystals upon the lowest row of window panes. Somewhere out there, Daniel would be on his return leg. Within the cart would be bundled Aunt Sara and my cousins, and last to board, Jemima. Though I regretted these moments not spent at her side, I was grateful to Daniel for his insistence that he alone go forth. With care I adjusted my breeches about my wool stockings. If I had gone off as I intended, either the cooking would have been delayed, or I would have arrived looking as unpresentable as I had that night in town.

"There you are, my son," Mother said. "Might I interest you in some coffee?"

"Yes, of course. Thank you." I took the cup and held it level whilst she poured. "So at the last Father elected not to come," I said. "At least he and I are spared a scene." She straightened immediately. Fixed me with a stare, she did. My words had acted as windblown across embers, and how they burned towards me. "What is it, Mother? What have I said?"

"Your father is to come. And you are to fetch him."

"Me? And what does he need with fetching?"

"If you had visited us in the last few months you would know the answer to that yourself."

I set the cup down and stood. "Forgive me, Mother. I had no wish to upset you. Is Father unwell?" Her free hand went to her mouth. So unsteady did she appear that I maneuvered the pot from her grasp.

"I thought it best to stay away," I murmured into her ear. "We seem to agree on nothing anymore, him and me."

She clasped one of my hands. "I know he is difficult, towards you especially. But in his own way, my Daniel still wants what he has always wanted - the best for you and all of us."

"I know Mother but his way is..."

"He is still your father. And you his eldest son."

I nodded. "I will go to him. And see him safely here."

A fresh inch had fallen overnight along the path connecting the homes of our family's patriarchs. The knowledge that Father's condition had worsened of late explained why Mother Sarah had insisted, for she rarely did, that at daybreak I clear even this accumulation away.

I had begun the short trip with my normal strides, gobbling ground in chunks despite the slippery surface. Now as I neared his house I slowed. How had we come to this state? Though I had been very young at the time, there had been many years when there were only the two of us, who wandered the land. The breadth and beauty of it had amazed me. And all of it described by father to son as a treasure belonging to our family. How he had loved it; and feeling his joy, I too had become entranced.

Even when Daniel had come along, followed by Azariah, it had changed nothing between Father and me. By then I possessed sufficient knowledge, and even strength of limb, that I contributed as much in labor as what I required by way of additional instruction. What changed then? Had he alone brought us to this impasse, or had I too played a part?

It felt strange to raise my hand to knock upon the door behind which I had been raised, but I did so.

"Enter!" his voice ordered from within. I did, and closed the door behind me. A scuffling about from the parlor alerted me as to his location. Taking a deep breath, I entered. "There you are," he said, with barely a glance at me. "And here your mother had said you would be along directly."

There was no retort that would not indict Mother for this imagined slight, so I said nothing. I waited whilst he busied himself by gathering to him the small necessaries he intended to bring. His hair had surrendered brown to gray. More rounded too had his shoulders become. With a sudden rocking back and forth he heaved himself up from his chair. I stepped forward but he waved me away. Even with the cane clutched in his good hand he did not come fully upright. The slump of his shoulders seemed of a piece with the bend in his back. That his physique now more resembled Grandsire than himself saddened me, but I would say what must be said. Better to have it out now than before the entire family. "I would speak with you of Jemima, Father."

His eyes glared. "There is no need. Your mother warned me the Barrows girl would be at my father's house."

'Warned you, is it!' I wished to hurl back at him; but I checked myself. "She is not the Barrows girl, Father. She is the woman whom I intend to make my wife."

I prepared myself for oaths hurled in my face; accompanied perhaps by flecks of spittle. I was subject to nothing of the sort. Anguish vanquished his features. "Why must you fight me at every turn?" he asked. "You had abandoned her. You yourself told me as much."

"That you believed it I have no doubt. But know now that I never abandoned Jemima. Nor ever will I."

His expression morphed into fury. "A maddening child is what you've become Elisha Benton. You know not your own mind yet willfully discard my advice. A perfect match I arranged that would have assured your station in life and enriched our family in the bargain. Yet this you refused, and why? To waste your promise on this, this..."

"Say no more, Father! I warn you!"

He stomped his cane once, twice upon the floor, but his thrusts made but modest noise and no mark upon the wood. At the stick he stared, undone it seemed by the loss of the power once at his command. When he met my gaze once more, his anger appeared largely spent. "What of the parcel?" he asked. "You had no plans for it."

I breathed out long and slow. "I changed my mind. As she will have me, I have need of it."

He interpreted my sigh as an opening, and came forward half a step. "We can still swing that tract of land northeast of the town. It is as attractive as ever it was, and what's more - the location puts you near your aunt. Think how easily you could assist her and your cousins, my nephew and nieces, if you were neighbors to them."

There had been a note of something akin to pleading in his voice. Vulnerable it made him appear, almost. "Be assured I will help them wherever I live. Aunt Sara has my promise in this. The journeys to and fro are nothing." I reached out, nearly touching his hand, though it clutched that stick. "Father. You must understand. Grandsire's parcel gives me the chance to build a life of my own. A life with she whom I love."

His eyes hardened before ever he drew back from me. In the end I did take his arm to assist him along the lane; yet for all that he leaned upon me, never did our skin make contact.

Chapter 55

Everyone arrived in a boisterous mood. Azariah had come after all, and so the cart fairly bulged with happy humanity. Borne along they were upon a wave of greetings. I had not even the chance to speak with him or Jemima, for my cousins swarmed me. By the time they had done with me the party had swept indoors. I broke away then, insisting that Daniel get inside to warm his bones. Jacob and I led April to the barn. That done, I released my youngest brother to his cousins and proceeded to cover the mare with a blanket and pitch hay into her stall.

I returned to the house and encountered a wall of sound from the hall. Family filled the space. Food covered the table from end to end. Not a serving vessel of any description had failed to be pressed into service. Once more my young cousins latched onto me. I shivered despite the embraces of their thin arms for I'd gone outside in little more than my shirt and breeches. Sensing my state, they tugged me towards the fire and its warmth.

Azariah stood across the room; Jemima beside him. He winked and pointed at her. She swatted at his finger and blushed my way. I fought back tears.

Daniel crossed in front of me; shaking my hand as he went. "Thank you, Brother," I whispered. His knowing smile meant the world to me.

Only the patriarchs had been seated. Father had chosen the head of the table, and there he sat – his, the only face that lacked a smile. Grandsire had vacated the place of honor so that he may rest nearest the hearth. I leaned over him. "May I fetch you anything?"

"I need nothing more, My Boy." He took my hand and kissed it. "Greater love hath no man." I noticed Father look away. Never had it occurred to me that he might harbor jealousy, and of Grandsire and me no less.

A light touch upon my arm caused me to turn. "Your mother says you are to don this," Jemima said. She held out my waistcoat, so that I might slip it on.

"Thank you, Jem," I said, facing her once more. Smiling, she assisted me with the last button. "For coming, I mean to say." The color rose once more, suffusing her cheeks.

"You are to sit here," she said, gesturing towards a short bench suitable for two.

"Are you certain? Mother Sarah can be quite specific about..."

"It has been arranged, Elisha. You here, with me beside you."

Quite happily I took my place. Happier still was I when she eased down, with me on her right and Grandsire her left. Only then did I notice the smiles conferred upon us by Mother and Mother Sarah. On Jemima's lap, I located her fingers. Without hesitation they curled 'round mine. I fought the instinct to clasp tight, for my heart hammered so I would surely do her harm.

When everyone had been seated, Grandsire said grace. For this I relinquished hold of Jemima, as we were to hold hands the table 'round. After a brief prayer, he expressed his deep gratitude that we had been blessed to be gathered together this day, in health and in happiness.

When he added, "As one family," Jemima's fingers squeezed mine. Her eyes watered at once. Mine did too.

Grandsire had a surprise in store. "I now invite anyone else to profess his or her thanks," he said. Though my vision had blurred, I thought I detected him turn, ever so slightly, towards the head of the table.

Father cleared his throat. "I would, thank you," he said. Mother's expression confirmed that if any arrangement had been made, it did not include her. Father took a quick gulp of his hard cider. "I wish to express my thanks," he began, "towards my son Daniel." My brother's face registered shock; a shock that was shared by one and all. Mine quickly ran to disbelief - would Father resort to praising one son, in a bid to belittle the efforts of the rest. No! Not if Grandsire had a part in this. "He served this family, and faithfully," Father concluded. Jemima flinched. My grandfather's white-haired head now faced fully towards the table's end. Father took another swig. "In this year now ending, all of my sons served either this family, or our colony. And thus for each I am grateful." His tankard landed heavily; quite as if his speech of thanks had near exhausted him.

"To our sons," Grandsire said, breaking the stunned silence. And so grace segued into a type of toasting.

"To sons!" Azariah cried. With a wink he added, "And to daughters too." I lifted my glass, first to him for a toast I envied, then to each of the ladies present, ending with the dear one beside me.

Dinner and conversation commenced. Though we exhausted more topics than courses, the latter of which there were plenty, no more surprises occurred. The one had proven quite enough for me, for I found it shocking, and pleasantly so, that Father would have said what he did, and before everyone. The effect resonated with my brothers too, for when Daniel had occasion to pass behind me, he whispered, "To sons..."

Whenever the flow of talk took up residence at one end of the table or the other, my hand sought out Jemima's. Always had she arranged to have one at rest, there in her lap. At my touch it sprang from the folds of her dress, enveloping me with its soft warmth. No one saw, nor I think suspected, what we were at.

Not, that is, until Hannah found us out. She had risen to help Mother hand around the slices of pie. I had not heard her light step come up between us. Her eyes widened at our entwined forearms, pressing upon Jemima's thigh. I straightened, hoping my sister would not react in any way that would draw attention. After a moment's pause, she simply set down a pair of plates, each adorned with a wedge of pie. "Thank you, Sister," I said. Her reply was no more and no less than a kiss planted upon my cheek. Jemima received one next. And then Hannah flitted away.

Contented sounds emanated from the head of the table. Father held up a laden fork. It disappeared into his mouth. "Hmmm! Delicious, Wife," he said, whilst still chewing.

"I am so glad you like it, Husband," Mother replied. "The recipe is mine, but we have Jemima to thank for the baking."

For a second I thought bits of crust and apples might spill from Father's mouth. "Indeed," he said. After a moment of reflection, he briefly nodded in Jemima's direction, and resumed eating.

I doubted whether he had made eye contact with her, but my chest swelled just the same. Jemima's reaction mirrored my own, for this time her fingers squeezed mine. I leaned into the wisps of hair that cascaded along her ear. "I too love your pie," I whispered.

Jemima only left my side once it was time to clear. My aunt chose this moment to pause beside me. She had been glancing at us often, especially towards the end of the meal. While she did retrieve my plate, it was my hand beside it that she sought. "There is something I would ask you, Nephew."

"Yes, Aunt. Anything."

"Is it true what I am told, Elisha? That you hesitate to marry Miss Barrows because of this war?" Instinctively I turned towards Mother. She and my aunt had always been close. I could scarce begrudge them being in each other's' confidence. "I see that it is so," she said. "Then let me tell you about your Uncle William. Throughout each of these many years I have missed my dear husband. Doubtless this comes as no surprise to you. What you may not know, however, is this. The memories he left me, and the children he gave me, they have ensured that never was I alone."

A moment more and she rushed from my side to relieve Hannah of an armful of dishes that threatened to overwhelm her. Nonetheless my aunt's wisdom and touch lingered. I caught her eye at the sideboard and mouthed 'Thank you'.

Jemima took the long way 'round the table that she might have a word. "Should I be envious, Elisha Benton? That I catch you flirting with your aunt."

I had half a mind to snatch her 'bout the waist and plunk her on my lap. But if gentlemanly behavior alone did not forbid doing so, then the load she carried surely did. I contented myself with a touch of her sleeve. "You should give her thanks," I murmured, "for she pleads your case."

"And do I need such a worthy advocate?" she replied, sauntering away. The exaggerated sway of her hips sent the hem of her frock to dancing. She fell in with the older women. Their exaggerated whispers soon led to cries of 'What impudence!', and the like; all directed my way. I hung my head in mock shame.

"Perhaps you might take refuge with me, My Boy," Grandsire said. "Within my parlor." He held out his arm and I helped him from one warm seat to another. We spoke of this and that, yet before long he drifted into sleep. I tucked a quilt about him, and watched over him till Mother Sarah came and took my place.

Too soon the shortened daylight forced the festivities to an end, and the company to part. This time Daniel assisted Father whilst Azariah and I saw Jemima, Aunt Sara and our cousins off to town in the cart. Everyone had seen to it that Miss Barrows shared the seat beside me whilst I guided April along. As it turned out, however, so often was she drawn into the conversation amongst my passengers that I was left alone with my thoughts. This I did not regret. Not that I wanted time to myself. Rather because I enjoyed the banter that flowed back and forth like the small seas swirling and overlapping in a cove. To see and hear her so accepted by my family produced a blockage in my throat that I did not fight.

After the lane joined the road, and we had turned east with the dimming light at our backs, a notion entered my head. I would do it; and now! At the spot that would result in the shortest walk, I urged the mare to the roadside.

"Does the cold bring on nature's call?" Azariah joked.

"For shame, Azariah Benton," Aunt Sara cried in jesting reproach. "Children! Cover your ears and hear your cousin not." They giggled in unison.

Jemima fixed me with an odd, quizzical expression. I turned to them. "Will everyone forgive me a brief stop; of the shortest duration? If Jemima would accompany me..."

My cousins began at once to ask what for, but my aunt hushed them. "Of course we will wait, Nephew."

A smile overspread Azariah's face. Stepping down, I offered Jemima my hand. Blushing, she took it.

I led her up the slope and into the tree line. Where the snow had drifted higher than her ankles we paused. "You've not the footgear for this," I said. She must have thought I meant to turn us back, for she gasped when I swept her from her feet. I surprised myself with my boldness, and at how any person of such fortitude could weigh so little. "It'll not overtop my shoes," I lamely offered, "as it surely would yours."

"I do not mind it," she replied. So close were our faces that her breath warmed my neck. What with the disparity in our heights I had seldom gazed upon her features from so near.

Setting her down in the clearing, I did not release her. She looked down, but only for a moment. When next our eyes met I knew she wanted what I longed for. I kissed her. It was only a little kiss; our lips just touching at the center. How warm and soft they were. I tasted them again and fully.

I paused then, but only to explain where we were and why we'd come.

"This is for you," I whispered. She followed my outstretched arm. Together we took in the rise of ground that marked the clearing. Tracing the far edge of it, peeks of the stream were afforded where it spilled, gurgling, over shiny rocks. I had declined to remove the stand of birch, bending now beneath the snow. Farther down the slope the orchard's bare arms poked upwards against a field of white.

"Elisha. It is so tranquil here..."

"Grandsire gifted this piece to me. By spring I hope to raise a house. For us, if you will have me."

"Not a house; a home. Our home. And yes. Yes I will!"

Chapter 56

I who had once prided myself on possessing reserve had, since Roxbury, exposed my every innermost feeling to nearly all who shared a kinship with me. To friends and family alike I had divulged each successive joy and disappointment. Some aspects of this openness I treasured. But too facile a practice of this sort could, I feared, render me a feeble object, devoid of constitution or resolve. As it was, I had, in the span of a few months, taken every one of our acquaintance on a needlessly agonizing ride. And so I determined to tell no one of my offer of marriage. I secured Jemima's reluctant agreement in this. Only when I had secured the means necessary to care for her, would I share our secret with those who loved us.

Thus the new year of 1776 arrived and still none other than she and I knew of our intentions. As fate would have it, my wariness proved well-founded. The heavy snows, coupled with persistent frigid temperatures, had armored the ground with a formidable shield. Despite my best efforts progress on the parcel slowed. It resumed in spasms of labor lasting no more than a day or two together. Then nature forced me to retreat to my familial duties once more.

By the end of February I had somehow succeeded in clearing the home site completely, including removal of the stumps that Newport and I had dislodged before the ground froze. The felled timber, however, could not be milled until the spring melt swelled the river, forcing round the water wheel and its belts. Till that was accomplished there would be no raising of walls or nailing of boards.

Nearly an entire field had been cleared of trees before winter blanketed the land. A start had even been made on removal of stones. Drifts of white now adorned the open expanse. The boundary walls begun in November would, however, rise no higher till spring. I laughed to think that my first crop would be of fieldstone.

This particularly stunning early March day I had felled a handful of trees within what would become a second field. On the return, I wandered along a rutted path I had tramped across the first. Shielding my eyes I surveyed its contours. Until a cash crop could be won from the soil, I could not set a date. It would not be right.

Jemima disagreed with me in this. Willing she was, to make any sacrifice that might bring us the sooner together. I, however, would not be the cause of us starving; nor reduced to begging from Father so that famine be kept from our door. Her own father seemed well aware of the dangers faced by couples starting out, for more than once during my infrequent visits he seemed as intent on my progress as my intentions. Though a man far too polite to put the question to me directly, his eyes revealed that he worried whether I could provide for his only daughter - be my surname Benton or not.

If her mother learned of my springtime promise, she would certainly rejoice. Jon Barrows, however, would be shocked by the prospect. He knew as did I, for I had shared particulars of some of the work before me, that even the coming of fall and a successful first harvest may yet prove too ambitious. "So glad am I that I told none but her," I confided to the snow-covered field. As I plodded off I even tried to muster regret at having promised Jemima herself a date. I could not. Too joyous had been her face that day to ever wish it otherwise.

While I headed towards Grandsire's home the sun had already begun its descent. As I carried a brace of buckets from the well, I entered from the rear. Mother Sarah was tidying their bedroom so I left her be. Setting the water in the kitchen, where it would be convenient for her, I removed my greatcoat. Men's voices carried from Grandsire's parlor - him and Father. Their debate was sharp. I tensed, for I was the cause of their dispute.

"There is no point, Daniel," Grandsire insisted, "in wishing the match undone. It is as fixed a thing as the sun rising in the east. I believe, in fact, that my grandson will propose marriage the very day he harvests his first crop."

"He deserves far more than a townsman's daughter."

"What he wants is this girl, and if you troubled yourself, my son, you might understand her worth. As he does. And as do I." Grandsire's warm defense of Jemima stilled my urge to contest Father's insults.

"You forget I have met her," Father said. "More than once at that. She would be a fine catch, I'm sure, for many a youth, but our Elisha, he deserves more, as do we Bentons. You and I must hold to that."

"What he deserves is his inheritance from you, Daniel. Especially now, at this pivotal time in his young life. Far too long have you laid claim to him. It is unseemly to withhold what is his by birthright alone; and what his labors have since earned twice over. The lad has given over his life to this family, and to you. Yet you treat his choice of future wife with disdain. Do not deny it for I have witnessed as much with my own eyes. Assure me that it is not within you, my son, to couple the sin of ambition with neglect of your own issue. I refuse to believe that you would reward his unquestioning sacrifice by disinheriting one such as he."

I strained forward that I might hear how my father would answer this...

"Elisha!" I whirled to see Mother Sarah. "I did not hear you come in."

"I left water…," I said, pointing.

"Who's there?" Father demanded.

"Elisha has returned," Mother Sarah called.

"It is I, Father," Moving to the doorway I nodded to both of my elders. Grandsire had a broad smile reserved for me. Father's gaze was set and hard, yet it fell almost at once. Having eavesdropped I had no right to look down upon him. I committed to re-stock the hearth with wood and left them at once. I avoided eye contact with my grandmother as I hastened outside.

The repeated thwack of the hatchet kept me from hearing what, if anything, passed between those left indoors. I tossed the split kindling into a growing pile. Tired as I was, this task helped dispel the tide of resentment threatening to dam up within me. Had I always expected, despite everything contrary that had passed between Father and me, that he would make a gift of land, or at least confer upon us a share of the coming season's harvest? I must have, for now that all hope had been extinguished, I did resent him. Hated him, more like.

So hard and recklessly did I deliver the next blow that the hatchet bounded off a knot and buried its shiny blade in the wall of the house. An inch to the right and it would have been my knee. "Dammit!" I wrenched it free and then sat on the upright chunk of log I used for splitting. Without help of some sort there would be no wedding. Not this spring at any rate. Damn Father and damn me for being a trusting fool!

The whinny of a horse carried from somewhere downslope. I recognized April's cry of alarm. My steps had already turned towards the house and my musket there above the hearth when I heard the beat of hoofs, coming on fast despite the state of the ground. A moment more and Eli broke into the open, astride his gelding.

"Eli! What news?"

So fast did he dismount that he nearly hung his foot in the stirrup. I steadied him. "Elisha! The cannon reached Boston. The heavy guns we spoke of. For weeks now they've been there." I checked myself, that he might tell me more. "A few nights ago," he said, "two or three perhaps, General Washington had them dragged to the heights of Dorchester. You'll never guess by whom; our dear friends and comrades – Huntington's men. And Elisha, they've fired upon the city!"

"What?"

"You'll not believe what I tell you. Howe is to evacuate Boston!"

"Evacuate? Without a fight? How can this be?"

"Oh, he tried, that's certain. Yet his guns cannot reach ours. This despite all those great ships of his in the harbor, bristling with their rows of iron brutes. We can hit him, you see, and he cannot hit back!"

"Are you certain? Truly certain?"

"It is over, Elisha! The British are to leave on the 17th of this month. It is all arranged between the generals. If Howe does not put the city to the torch, then Washington grants him safe passage."

"Thanks be to God! Come! Come inside and tell my grandparents. Wait! Did you stop at Father's house?"

"I sought you there. Your mother knows of it. And all the rest as well."

I hugged him, and then pushed him towards the house. "You go! Tell my grandparents. I will see to your horse. Oh and Eli, my father is with them."

With one hand alongside his mouth he said, "Even he should welcome news of this sort."

Despite the lateness of the hour and the near pandemonium that followed in the wake of Eli's tidings, he, Daniel and I had saddled and rode back to town before the light had entirely deserted the sky. Behind us we left a celebration that we promised to soon rejoin.

Our ride was marked by outbursts of nonsensical fellowship, for again and again we congratulated each other. A passerby if there had been one would have thought us responsible for some great deed, though we had done nothing other than learn of a long-sought victory. In this happy mindset we rode into town.

Swaying lanterns and even flaming torches lit a spectacle of citizenry crowding the roadway and even onto the steps of the Meeting House. The turnout was to be expected, but not the mood. Our mounts slowed in unison; before our voices died away. The glad tidings that brought us hither had somehow been eclipsed. An awful silence gripped Tolland.

My companions and I dismounted at once. People doffed their caps as Eli, Daniel and I advanced. Not one of the town leaders did I glimpse outside. My jaw tightened at this. With muted greetings for those whom I knew best I led my comrades up the steps.

The crowd parted. There stood Jemima - directly in my path. She rushed forward and placed her hands against my chest as she would stop me. I did stop. "Do not go," she said. "Please, Elisha. I beg you."

"What has happened?" I asked, staring over her head in an attempt to make out the proceedings within.

"You must not. Stay here. With me." Tears crowded her eyes. "Please, Elisha. Please..."

Eli and Daniel strained forward; barely resisting the urge to desert me. "Jemima," I whispered, laying my fingers against her cheek. "You know I must."

Her hands covered her mouth. Without once looking away she stepped aside. I kissed her. We three then passed in a single file.

Captain Willes stood at the lectern. How thin and drawn he appeared since the disaster at Quebec. He noted our presence, but did not pause to greet us. "Let me restate, gentlemen," he said instead, "that General Washington has ordered new regiments to be formed. Of those in Boston he has dispatched many if not most. Already are they on the road. Their destination? The city of New York. It is there that he expects Howe to strike."

"But Captain," someone yelled. "We understood that when the British fled the port, that they were beaten. That they would return to England."

"A fervent wish of every man here, no doubt," the Captain replied. "Alas, it is naught more than a dashed hope now. Per the message I hold, the General is quite confident of his intelligence. New York it is to be, and we must get there first."

Even as those in attendance absorbed this announcement, he burdened us with more. "I am to be commissioned Lieutenant Colonel and will report to my superiors now en route to Manhattan. On my person I have a list of regiments in want of recruits. Colonel Huntington, who defended our company's flank in Roxbury, is to lead the 17th Continental. His need is acute. He has forwarded me the names of a few men in particular whom he and his officers wish might join him. I plan to march to New York in the company of these, in fact all those who enlist. I leave the moment preparations are complete."

The Captain continued speaking for many minutes more. My ears heard his words, but I reeled at the impact of his declaration. Nothing had changed in these many months. Now once again men would die, just in another place. And women, they would be widowed.

"What is to be done, Elisha?"

I gazed into the eyes of my brother Daniel. Wide with amazement they were, but not fear. Perhaps he knew too little of war to be afraid. And in this ignorance his natural acceptance of responsibility came to the fore. He would need all this trait that he could muster, for I remembered his vow should another alarm come. He meant to accompany me, or he had at any rate. I took hold of his upper arms; squeezed them. "What we once spoke of," I said. "Are your feelings unchanged?"

"I am ready. Just tell me what to do."

Long had I known how I would respond to the eventuality confronting us. Now saying as much meant three brothers would march out together. I inhaled. "We must prepare ourselves, Brother." I patted his cheek. "The first thing is also the hardest. We must let our loved ones know that we are soon to depart." A few yards off, though separated by dozens of men, I caught sight of Azariah. He had been bearing down on us. He now stopped. At my nod he turned and made straightway for the double doors. "How will they bear it...?" I muttered.

"Mother and Father?" Daniel asked.

"All of them. All."

Eli had broken away for a moment. Returning, he extended the enlistment scroll. *17th Continental Regiment, Colonel Jedediah Huntington commanding* was inscribed at the top. "Just think, Elisha. The man who can rightly claim he drove the British from Boston. And he asks for you and me."

Just below Eli's signature, Azariah's proud scrawl appeared. To their names I added my own. Daniel took up the quill.

While he signed, Eli leaned close so that he might the better be heard. "My uncle will communicate these new developments to my family. Should you need to ride to yours, Elisha, I can remain here. For us both I'll learn the details of the intended march from the Captain, or Lt. Colonel rather. If that is to your liking."

"Thank you most kindly, Eli. I will return soon as ever I'm able." Taking Daniel by the elbow I forged a path out for the pair of us. Just this side of the entry I pulled him close. "Azariah will arrange for our powder and ball."

"He will?"

"Trust me in this. He is tending to it as we speak. Now, as to our family. Is it too much to ask you to convey such troubling news to them?"

"Alone, you mean..." He swallowed, thinking no doubt of the myriad reactions. "I will do it," he said without equivocation. "They will learn of Howe's intentions. And their sons' as well."

"Thank you, Brother," I replied, for I was more grateful for his strength, than surprised that he possessed so much of it. "As for me," I said. "I will be along directly." He left me, easing his way forward with one sincere apology after another. Coming alongside Jemima, he took her hand. After glancing back towards where I stood, he parted. Like an island in a tumultuous flood she stood alone. I made my way to her side. "Jem, I..." Around my neck her thin arms stretched. We stood silent in each other's embrace. Commotion engulfed us yet seemed of a time and place apart. I do not recall when it was that I began swaying with her, to and fro.

I felt her words before hearing them. Against my chest they tumbled, still bearing her warmth. The same refrain oft repeated; almost like a prayer. "Come back to me, Elisha. This is all I ask."

The precious few days and nights that followed flowed faster than the grains of sand from an hourglass. Like the year previous, the alarm had come just as our backs had begun bending to the demands of the soil. Not once did I now have opportunity to set foot on my parcel. To the pressing requirements of our family did we direct our every effort, just as the womenfolk sought to provision us. Little enough could be done as regards to food, for the larders had dwindled through the months of dark and cold. Whatever could be darned or laundered, however, was, and thence into our knapsacks it went. Azariah had seen to powder, ball and flint, so here at least our needs had been met. Despite the striving of one and all, we never really finished what we ought. One morning our frantic labors simply ceased, for the company was to march that day to Hartford. There they were to fall in with an entire regiment of soldiers - the 6th Connecticut State Levies, newly formed for this campaign. Others, like my brothers and I, would accompany them, though we were destined for the 17th Continental Regiment, now said to be setting sail from New London, and also bound for New York.

My brothers waited on me at Father's house. Only the wish to address a few outstanding promises to Mother Sarah saw me gathering my belongings beyond the appointed hour. Burdened by my overstuffed pack, I entered Grandsire's parlor. I had expected to see both of my grandparents within. I found neither. Once again the sight of his empty rocker chilled me. I moved to the window, then exited via the front door. "There you are," I whispered, so as not to startle them.

They turned, Grandsire supported by his cane on one side and Mother Sarah's arm on the other. I took care when hugging them, overloaded and somewhat unbalanced as I was. My words tumbled out as awkwardly. The kindness in their eyes, that I saw and clung to, made up for the fact that I caught little more than the warmth of their gushing words.

On an impulse I paused some little ways along the lane. Grandsire's flowing white mane could not be missed. His head and upraised palm faced my way. My hand shot up high though I suspected I had passed beyond his sight. I lowered it at last, for the wet must be swiped from my cheek.

Azariah practically bounced in place between Father's barn and house. "Elisha! What has kept you? We must leave at once! The company will march without us."

"Hush now!" Mother insisted. "No more rushing!" Even as she spoke thus she hustled forward, hands joined with Hannah's. I did my best to embrace them together. Tears spilled down over the smiles they wore. Beyond them, Father stood. How pale he appeared in the harsh angled light of morning.

He too took a few halting steps forward. He seemed about to speak. Mother's head nodded, as if encouraging him. Yet if he held something there that he would share with us, with me, I heard it not; for words did not escape his lips. I smiled for Mother, to ease her disappointment. She had tried, I knew, and if any could read the thanks I conveyed in a single glance, it was she.

"Elisha!" Daniel had joined Azariah in this plea.

I dared not put them off longer. To Father, I gave my hand. He grabbed it and held me tight, even as my brothers dragged me away. My head snapped 'round to make out Father's expression, but for the pack's bulk I saw him not.

Jacob had insisted on coming as far as the road to town. There we made our farewells. "Is it true Elisha," he asked, "that you are made sergeant?"

"As is my friend Heman. At Captain, pardon, the Colonel's insistence it would appear. But enough of soldiers. Let us speak of farmers, and of you. We quite depend upon you now, Jacob."

His head nodded up and down, up and down. A solemn handshake he offered to each of his older brothers. He extended his hand, which I shook. When he squeezed with all his grip, I could have wept. He must have sensed this for just then he broke free and ran up the lane; tossing a wave to us as he disappeared.

One moment on the road I broke into a trot. The next I fell back to a hurried walk. The cycle repeated. Each time I slowed, Daniel looked back at me. Less subtle by far, Azariah chastised my pace for that of a snail. He had already opened a gap approaching 50 yards.

"They will have left the green by now," Daniel urged.

I feared he was right but could not help myself. The sooner we joined our comrades, the sooner I must face leaving her. And to what? The agony of waiting, and wondering, for word of our fate. The very pain I had meant to spare her.

Azariah hollered. I could not make out his words. It is true I had tarried. What if I should fail to see her as a consequence? I jumped forward in near panic. Starting small in my guts, it swelled; overtaking my chest and near choking off my breath. I was supposed to be the calm one. On this I prided myself…

I had drawn even with Daniel. Azariah, however, had slipped around the bend ahead of us; his lead doubled. In an instant he reappeared - arm and musket pumping above his head. "They come! The column comes!"

"Oh, God, no..."

Lieutenant Colonel Willes, only just assigned to the 6th, strode along at the front of a phalanx of men. He was flanked by Eli and Captain Ichabod Hinckley, appointed to supplant the Colonel as company commander. At the quick march they closed the distance. I studied the Colonel's face; anxious to discover if he would grant me leave so that I might race into town.

Azariah folded into their midst. The notes of the fifes and the deadened thump of feet upon muddy ground enveloped Daniel and me off to one side of the road. "Colonel," I called out. "Sir, I beg a word…"

"She follows just behind the company," he replied in clipped tones. "And Sergeant. We've no time for stopping."

Abandoning Daniel, I sprinted backwards along the ranks. Comrades of old shouted my name as I passed them by. Our neighbor Noah Grant was there, of course. Amasa Allen had come from as far away as Stafford, and the Fenton brothers marched alongside him.

I had no trouble finding her, trailing the supply cart as she did by a mere few rods. She clutched her mother's hat. A wave of sun-kissed auburn hair spilled down and along one shoulder. The hem of her dress was caked in muck near as high as her knees. Her bosom heaved with the effort to keep up. Her eyes had been locked on the mass of soldiers. They alit now on me. Never had she looked so radiant. "Jem. My Jem..."

We folded together there in the road, partway between Tolland and Benton lands. The martial sounds diminished. "Elisha. You must go to them," she whispered, through tears. Already I could see little more than the fast-dwindling cart.

"I will wait for your return," she said. Into my hand she pressed something. "Pussy willows. They signify life on the verge of blooming."

Soft and folded up each bud was, there upon the twig. Waiting, each seemed, for the coming of spring. I tucked them inside my blouse. I met her gaze. How steady it was despite her tears. "I will come back to you, Jemima Barrows. I promise you this."

At that, I broke away, racing from the one whom I loathed to leave. I looked back, just the once, before the bend stole her away from me. Her face shined like a beacon that one day, I prayed, might draw me home.

Chapter 57

Eli had been commissioned a lieutenant. To him I ran, after catching up with the column. And he it was who told me which of the men comprised my platoon; subject of course to the approval of the senior officers of the 17th. With a sudden remembrance of Captain Tyler, I allowed myself to hope that we would be made a part of his company. At this moment, however, my chief concern was in dropping back to, and falling in with ranks of those who took great pleasure in guiding me to them.

"This way, Sergeant!" Mister Allen called as I raced painfully alongside the fast-moving column. His neck twisted this way and that as he made his sport. "Here we are, sir. Yer little chicks!" He cackled a string of high-pitched peeps, which drew a roar from the men ahead and behind. His comic relief, even at my expense, would do us a bit of good, I thought. And so I raised a hand in surrender as much as greeting to one and all.

Nearly breathless, my pack fighting me at every step, I fell into the space left for me at the end of the first rank. Azariah leaned over from my left. With one deft movement, he tightened a strap. "Better?" he asked. I nodded my thanks. "And Jemima? Did you see her?" I smiled, and reaching across, gave his right arm a squeeze.

To his left Daniel had taken his place. He seemed focused on keeping his steps aligned with the rest of the rank. Nearly a year had passed, I remembered, since he had turned out for drill. Azariah noted our brother's struggle and winked. The two of us would easily make a parade soldier out of him. Onward we three brothers went, side by side.

The platoon and I had been honored by being placed first in the column. The company commanders strode just to our front, with our fifers, Noah and Stephen, a few paces ahead. Lt. Colonel Willes and Captain Hinckley moved with deliberate strides. The Captain hailed from Tolland but from the far northeast corner. His lands, or so I believed, bordered the Willimantic River. I could discern but little from his profile. Stern he was, perhaps, if the set of his shoulders and head were evidence. So, a new Captain the company would have. A new regimental commander as well, for we were to join a Colonel John Chester with the balance of the 6th in Hartford. Eli's uncle, Colonel Chapman, was also meant to take a separate command south to Manhattan. And once on that island Eli and I would have our own entirely different set of officers. Perhaps he might be able to make sense of these new formations. I discovered Azariah grinning – likely at the furrows in my brow. I smiled right back for he was quite right that neither sergeants nor privates had the right to worry about more than putting one foot before the other.

Eli, just to the right of the superior officers, seemed quite at home at the head of the column. It must be said that the green cockade in his hat, the mark of his new lieutenancy, fit him splendidly. He must have felt my eyes upon him for he glanced my way. Letting loose his sword hilt, he waved.

The 20 miles flowed fast beneath our feet. An incessant chatter had filled the air from the outset and though Captain Hinckley cast disapproving looks rearward, the Lt. Colonel seemed content to condone the venting of nervous anticipation that gripped us all. From White's Tavern in the Bolton settlement a watchful eye could catch glimpses of the Connecticut River Valley to our front. As we descended, each mile marker inched ever closer, then disappeared beyond our right flank. The string of them drew us towards the banks of that mighty stream. The melting of the snowfields had swollen her broad waters. Ever southward the river wound; emptying at last into Long Island Sound. Like as not we would trace its route as far as we were able, till our path took us southwesterly, and on to Manhattan. New ground this would be for me. I surveyed my companions. Unknown territory for the entire company would be my guess.

In East Hartford, the column divided into platoons. The ferry would take us piecemeal from east to west. Never had I reached this landing without some beasts or harvest piled high for the thriving market on the opposite shore. Heman came to my side with his hand outstretched. "Thought you might have given yourself over to your land," he joked. "And given up soldiering."

"And trust the fighting to novice sergeants?" I replied.

"Like yourself, you mean?" At this retort I could only laugh.

Eli marched up to us. "What's this?" he demanded; a mock glare furrowing his brow. "Do I hear dissension between my subordinates?"

I gave his cockade a flick, as though it needed dusting. "It suits you, Eli. Truly." He was proud of the green feather there, and I for him.

"Can mere privates speak with the likes of you august gentlemen?" Azariah asked. Daniel, Noah and Amasa accompanied him.

I turned to the Sergeant on my left, then the Lieutenant on my right. "In honor of this fine day," I said, my nose tilted towards the heavens, "we shall make an exception." I dropped my chin just in time to avoid my brother's friendly swat.

The wind had picked up as the day wore on. Being ever the landsman, I clasped the ferry's slender rail as we made our way across the great river. The snow melt would propel it over its banks for weeks to come. Chunks of ice spun slowly, carried inexorably downriver. My knuckles whitened at the approach of those jagged obstructions, bent on a collision course. The impacts reverberated throughout the hull.

"Not a man of the sea, I take it?" said a voice behind me.

"No, Captain," I replied. "A farmer, sir, born and bred."

Captain Hinckley's face softened a tad. "Yes. I've heard of your skills upon the land, Sergeant. Charlestown comes to mind. Well, take heart. We'll be ashore in a thrice." With that he sauntered along the rail. I could not deny a measure of pride, for his knowledge of me could only have reached his ears from Lt. Colonel Willes. Had I known he would share command of this 6th Regiment with Colonel Chester, and thus retain the Tolland trainband, never would I have enlisted with Huntington; and this despite the man's sterling reputation.

On the Hartford side we plunged into a milling mass of armed men. Other companies and other regiments attempted to assemble there on the dock. Up along the length of King Street they spilled. The senior officers had chosen this spot by design. So had too many others and for the same reason no doubt as many roads converged here. Hasty introductions commenced. Finding it impossible to form in rank and file where we stood, they led us towards Meeting House Square. Once the combined force of nearly 600 had been positioned along the road yet somewhat out of the traffic of men and beast, an informal conference commenced.

As a fledgling lieutenant of the 17th, Eli had been excluded from the impromptu gathering of captains and pair of colonels of the 6th. I moved next to him. "Never have I seen so many shops set up," I practically shouted despite our proximity.

"No! Nor customers crowding them. War, it seems, is good for business."

I nodded, despite the note of sarcasm from my friend – rare when military matters were invoked. The scene about us bordered on riotous. Whereas we had been ordered to parade rest, swarms of soldiers from other units elbowed their way up to and nearly overtop the stalls. They sought all manner of wares, which some men stuffed into packs already filled to bursting. "If, like us, their destination is New York," I suggested, "they are apt as not to toss out half of what they buy today."

"Aye. It is a long road ahead."

Daniel had come up to us. Patiently he waited at my elbow. When I turned to him, he asked, "Whose flag is that? It seems the Union Jack, but with stripes." He pointed it out. There were a number of them flapping in the breeze, but I knew the ensign not. To me it appeared too close a cousin to the one that had waved in our faces whilst we hunkered below the bastion.

"The Grand Union Flag," Eli explained. "They say General Washington himself designed it."

"So that is what we are meant to fight under," Heman said. The words of a warrior, from out of his freckled face, brought a smile to my own.

At the order to form in companies, I moved along the ranks. My former greatcoat hung loose about Amasa Allen's lean frame, though he did his best to square up as I passed. Upon each other, we both knew we could rely. The Fenton brothers, Asa and Adonijah, stood together, each wearing the confident expressions of veterans. The youth anchoring the next row was quite as beardless as Adonijah had been last spring. Slender as a reed, he was, of average height and shy. His intense gray eyes, though, seemed to take in all about him. My approach he had watched as might a wary cat an oncoming dog. "My name is Sergeant Benton," I said. "And you are?"

"Jacob Brown," he replied.

"His name is all we've had from 'im, Sergeant."

"Thank you for that, Mister Allen." To the lad I added, "Welcome to the 17th, Jacob, and of course the 6th."The youth merely nodded. The gray eyes blinked. And the corners of his mouth may have twitched. With a simple nod, I moved on.

It occurred to me then, that the day might soon come when my baby brother Jacob would enlist in this army of ours. Who would be his sergeant? And who then would work the Benton lands?

Chapter 58

As had been true when we marched in relief of Boston, the company numbered near 100. The 6th Connecticut Regiment was comprised of fully a handful of such units, bringing the fighting strength to over 600. Never had I found myself part of such a formidable martial force. The citizenry turned out to cheer our departure. Our pace quickened, feeding on their enthusiastic send-off. The vibration of 1200 feet throbbed like drumbeats beneath the shrill notes of the fifes. Soon we swept into the countryside, heading south beneath the snapping of the Grand Union Flag.

Somewhere back, a fine tenor voice began to sing. A few others joined in. When the officers made no attempt to quell them, the refrain was picked up by a hundred throats or more. Though I had long behaved indifferently to public singing, and dancing too, chills now did race along my arms.

Within a few miles the urgent pace kept up by the officers put an end to song. Men needed their wind to keep in step, for we were sorely loaded and the day had turned hot. I minded it not, because with the growing discomfort my sense of sobriety returned. The younger, and aye, the merely less experienced men like Daniel, would need all the schooling I and others could provide.

"Sergeant," a voice called.

I turned to John Crandall. That black hair of his, contrasted with his fair complexion, gave him the appearance of being perpetually unshaven, haggard almost. Now he seemed especially earnest. "Yes, John."

"Is it true, Sergeant, that the British sailed away without firing a shot?"

Others eagerly awaited my reply, Jacob Brown among them. How these youngsters longed to hear that our enemy was no match for us - in courage, numbers or fighting prowess. My God, how I had learned otherwise. "From Boston, I take it you mean?" I began. "Well, I had returned home before ever that great day dawned, but I am told their fleet unleashed many salvos. Unfortunately for them, not one of their massive naval guns could be elevated to reach our positions."

"But Sergeant," the younger Fenton added, "did they not run the very day we brought up guns as big as their own?"

"I'll not dispute the coincidence, Adonijah. But our men, you see, they enjoyed the supreme advantage of the heights of Dorchester. From there they could rain shot and shell upon the heads of our enemies at will, and without the risk of return fire."

I might very well have won the argument on technical points, but scanning the ranks I knew that I had made little impression on the boundless enthusiasm of the raw recruits. Perhaps it was just as well that they be allowed their confidence for as long as possible. At any rate, we would learn the God's honest truth from our friends of the 17th upon our arrival.

When I faced front once more Daniel looked quickly away. Of war, I was reminded, he too knew nothing.

That first night we made camp in Wallingford. By early afternoon of the second day we had reached New Haven. Here we abandoned the Upper Post Road in favor of the Lower. This turnpike hugged the

Connecticut shoreline. It would guide us onto the island of Manhattan and at its southern tip, the city of New York. I tried turning my mind from fears that Howe's navy, with his army crowded aboard, might even now lie there in wait.

To foster this distraction, I attended to the land about us. It helped that every step presented virgin territory. Just prior to dusk the visual treasures of the coastal community of Milford were revealed to us. Here we broke ranks.

Many of the labors of non-commissioned officers such as Heman and I began only once our packs had been discarded. First we saw to the posting of sentries as decreed by the officers, and then to the erecting of tents and the arranging of provisions for the men. With Eli as both experienced lieutenant and boon companion, we could anticipate his sage placement of the watch. Likewise were we blessed that the veterans of Roxbury needed scant reminding as to the stacking of arms for ready use, or the timely gathering of wood for cooking fires.

Before full dark we thus had settled down at the edge of one group that included my brothers. Supper of cod and bread had been greedily consumed. Men lounged as near to the flames as they dared. Heman drew upon his pipe, and released a cloud of smoke into the cool night air. The tilt of his head reminded me of Grandsire.

"What must it be like," I wondered aloud. "To make one's living from the sea?"

"Nothing I know of the life, 'tis sure," he replied. "But judging by the open ways of these folk, there's much to recommend it."

"Indeed," I replied, rubbing my contented stomach and thinking of the kind, weathered faces with whom we had traded upon the dock. I laid straight out then. Countless stars twinkled in the vault of the sky. The same light that shined on me in this seaside village would be shining on Tolland. I felt for the slim branch within my blouse. Would Jemima have come outside this night? Did her pale skin glow beneath heaven's touch?

During the evening the prevailing winds from the southwest had warmed us as we lie packed tight within our tents. They also pushed in wave after wave of clouds. By the time we set out the following morning, so leaden and full had the sky become that fat drops pattered down. It grew to a pelting din that drowned the sound of our pounding feet.

I had re-positioned my brothers. Daniel was now sandwiched so that Azariah and I could offer him timely and subtle advice. Steadily the particulars of drill returned to him. No longer did he watch his step for fear that he might trod upon the heel of another. So too had his palm learned to cradle the butt of his musket to best relieve the strain. His progress freed me to move alongside the column, seeing to the needs of those less able than he. Alternately forward I surged, or backwards I dropped, offering encouragement to the one, or a suggestion to another. The adverse conditions exposed our weaknesses, and so presented an opportunity for improvement. Onward we went, burdened further by the weight of water drenching each garment, and the mud sucking at each footfall. Though we worked much harder for each rod of advance, we made but horrid time.

A few paces ahead the faces of our officers appeared uniformly strained. Of the men I knew, like Eli and Lt. Colonel Willes, physical hardship alone would not be the cause. That minutes passed far faster than miles logged, yes this could haunt such men as these. How many leagues, I began to wonder, could a King's warship sail in a day? And how many separated Boston from New York? With a start I realized the simple truth that whilst we slept each night, ships sailed the nighttime through. So quickly did I lunge ahead that I nearly confused the cadence of two ranks or more.

Our passage ground the road into what might pass for a cattle pen, if such an enclosure could be stretched out, mile after mile. Any among us who had begun the day fickle as regards the elements, had long since abandoned any effort to keep dry or clean a single stitch of cloth upon their person. Like a slimy, suffering serpent our body of men wriggled along until, mercifully, Colonel Chester signaled a halt. By this time we were informed we had crossed William's Bridge, and the Bronx River below it. Now before us stood another bridge, spanning yet another swift current.

"There lies the East River," Lieutenant Chapman relayed to one and all. "And on the opposite shore, Manhattan!" The regiment roused itself for three huzzahs, though the calls hung in the air as damp as the clothes upon our backs.

With no more than the chance to fill our canteens, and catch our breaths, we set off once more. At last the sun broke through. The Colonel seemed intent on marching us dry, for we continued without pause. Muck dried to mud upon our weary limbs. Young Jacob seemed entranced by a long streak of it dangling from the knee of his breeches. "Knock it free, Mister Brown," I suggested. "You'll find your load lightened if you do."

With a swat, he sent it flying, earning, as I had hoped, the cheers of his comrades. And when the men began offering to clear away other such baggage encumbering their fellows, then doing so without being asked, I said not a word. The thwacks and the laughter were the pleasantest sounds I'd heard in many an hour.

People did emerge from their homes but seldom as they had on Connecticut soil. Accustomed we were to entire families coming to the roadside, encouraging us with waves and shouts. Some had offered ladles of cool well water. Most here held back in their doorways. Silently they watched as our column trudged passed.

"A glum parcel of folk that last," Noah Grant offered. His observation opened the gates on what chafed a number of the men.

"Call a halt, Sergeant," Amasa said, louder than the rest. "I'll give 'em something to frown about I will."

"No more of that now, Mister Allen."

"But Sergeant, don't ya agree, sir? Look at 'em. Look at that bunch there." As he pointed a pair of heads drew back from either side of a glass-paned, front window.

Such furtive behavior hardly endeared these people to me, but agreeing with Amasa was out of the question. Sodden and footsore as we all were, the slightest spark could fuel a rampage. "Have you considered, Mister Allen," I said, "that for us to halt may be what concerns these people most?"

"Sir?"

"Why you alone would lay their cupboards bare. And we've 600 mouths here to feed." The men's roars carried us quite around the bend. Amasa reveled in the attention despite his being the butt of the joke. And from the head of the column many were the heads that gave a nod my way. Even Captain Hinckley touched his cap.

By the time we reached the triangular-shaped Common in the heart of New York I strained forward quite as anxiously as my superiors. Though I could not make out the answers to Colonel Chester's questions, the relaxation of his shoulders made the import clear enough - there had been no sighting of enemy sail within the harbor. While the news disappointed the rawest of our recruits, it filled me with relief. Eli and Heman, too, judging by their glances. Azariah seemed of two minds at the tidings, whilst Daniel merely stood and chewed upon his lower lip.

Before I could speak with him we were set to marching. The entire complex of buildings serving as barracks already overflowed. The 6th must press on. Swinging left we poured down Broadway. The citizens took to the shade of the trees lining either side of the wide thoroughfare. A few men doffed their hats but far too many merely followed our progress with wary eyes.

"They seem scarcely more than indifferent to our coming," Daniel whispered.

"So it would appear," I replied.

"The people of Massachusetts," he continued. "How did they greet you, Brother?"

"Warmly, by and large." Only then did it occur to me. "But we came to liberate them - from an army of occupation. Here we are, perhaps, the occupiers."

Chapter 59

Immediately upon entering the city, the 6th took up quarters within a warehouse on Stone Street. Like many such structures along the wharves, this building had previously been occupied by British troops. Despite this regrettable history, the building provided certain shelter from the elements. We congratulated our friends and neighbors, then with an exchange of huzzahs, we parted. The act of releasing Lt. Colonel Willes' hand occupied my thoughts as Lieutenant Chapman led us in search of the 17th.

We discovered them in a tent encampment whose population in fighting men surpassed that of Tolland herself. Ours was but one of the regiments quartered here, in this level expanse bordered by the East River on one side, and New York harbor to the south. A common parade ground served this city of soldiers.

Eli was a bit disappointed that Colonel Huntington was not available to greet us, for our arrival coincided with a gathering of the brigade generals and their staff officers. Captain Tyler, however, assured us of their joint pleasure at our timely transit. After a brief inspection of our comrades, he ushered us back inside his tent. After reclaiming his folding chair, and glancing at the papers Eli had presented him, he looked up at us with a welcoming smile. "You are to be congratulated, gentlemen. Not only did you make good time, but you managed to safeguard the condition of your men." Eli nodded whilst I stood still, for after all, Colonel Chester had set our pace. "Yes," the Captain continued, "trust that I appreciate the effort required, for it was the selfsame poor state of the roads from Boston that convinced the Colonel to sail the regiment from New London. He thereby preserved both time and the men's strength. By God's grace we reached New York before our enemy." Without waiting for a reply he returned to his study of our papers, which consisted for the most part of letters from Lt. Colonel Willes and a written copy of our enlistments.

I had seen the Captain often during our time at Roxbury. In manner he reminded me of Captain Hinckley, and he a man to whom discipline and appearance mattered greatly. Like Hinckley, however, both seemed to possess a measure of compassion for those under their command, though they did not wear this upon their sleeves.

He set the correspondence aside. "If I may speak for my, pardon, our Colonel, I believe he will have no objections to the stipulations, well, let us say the requests, of Lieutenant Colonel Willes." He stood. "Welcome to the 17th Continental Regiment, Lieutenant Chapman. Sergeant Benton." We shook hands. "You will hear us referred to as the 'black facings', gentlemen. On account of our uniforms that is. And so one of your first responsibilities will be to see that the platoon is properly outfitted. The quartermaster will provide you the necessaries. Do not be tardy in this regard, as the Colonel believes, as do I, that the men's appearance is directly tied to unit discipline. Need I say more?"

None of us had ever worn clothing that matched in any way. Thus the new uniforms instilled an immediate sense of belonging. While bonds already existed within our small band, it sped up the sense of comradery felt between us and our hundreds of new comrades within the 17th. And some of us like Mister Allen had never been so dashingly attired as when adorned with the butternut coat with black linings that once turned out yielded contrasting lapels and cuffs. So overjoyed was he that he voiced no objection even to the withholding of shillings from his monthly wages to pay for the clothing.

The stuff of mustering was utterly lacking in dash, however, and this was how we began each morning. Following roll call and drill, we were separated into small working parties. Before many days had passed we had raised a breastworks atop nearby Jones' Hill, and it dubbed Spencer's Redoubt in honor of our General Joseph Spencer.

On some occasions we were ordered to parade down the streets in formation. I pitied the poor citizens that had a morning appointment to keep when this flood engulfed them. Having learned the way of our drill, however, most inhabitants cleared the road at our approach. Occasionally, though, our noisome arrival frightened a horse near out of its traces, or drove a bystander, of the Tory persuasion more like, to speed us on our way with an oath.

So numerous were the disturbances between these Tories and the Whigs, that the Colonel had issued orders to not attempt to intercede. As sergeants, Heman and I were thus ever on the alert for situations that might result in direct altercations between the citizenry and our soldiers. That some of the former muttered 'Rebels' as we passed by, and that some of the latter despised them in turn as 'Yorkers', more than warranted our diligence.

Despite these earnest efforts, on a humid morning in May, a lone man, a barrister by the cut of his clothes and the wig upon his head, was knocked to the cobbles not three paces from me. He had had the ill judgment to think he might dart between Heman's platoon and mine, at the worst possible moment.

"Blasted rebels!" slipped from his lips. This would have proved sufficient provocation but he compounded his problems by pairing it with a string of oaths.

His wig had been dislodged. It now received a kick that catapulted it a yard farther from his grasp. On hands and knees, he pursued it. The gray stubble that lined his skull glistened as his head bobbed this way and that. He swore once more as he reached for it. Away again it went, borne upon another shoe.

"Enough of that, Mister Allen," I ordered. Fearing that another man might do as Amasa had done, I reached down and retrieved the now shapeless, dirt-streaked thing.

The bare-headed gentlemen regained his feet. His scarlet cheeks worked like a bellows. "I trust, sir," I said to him, "that you will not report the untimely journey of your covering. For my part, I shall say nothing of a decidedly dangerous reference to rebels. 'Tis certain the civil as well as military officials would frown upon such talk."

His eyes bulged further still. For a long moment I thought he might dare to strike me. But in the end he exhaled quite as loudly as another might pass gas. I deposited the remnants of his wig in his hand. "Good day to you, sir."

As he strutted away, I saw dozens of barely contained grins adorning rank upon rank of my comrades.

"Might I be of assistance, Elisha?" Eli asked, hastening to my side.

"None needed, Lieutenant," I replied, grinning now myself. "All present and accounted for, sir."

Later that day, Eli and I walked the short distance to The Fort. This route we often followed, arranging for company provisions or carrying orders to and fro. The edifice was massive, with walls in places that jutted straight out of the bay. With our message delivered, and receiving no reply, we chose to wander along the water.

Busy were the quays, despite the threat of invasion. We yielded to the horse-drawn carts of more prosperous merchants. The crush of handcarts pushed this way and that, and so too sidestepped laborers bent low under bulging sacks. In every corner cordage was piled. Upright barrels stood like soldiers on parade. Perhaps soon Boston, like this port city, would resume a prosperous trade. From our chosen vantage point we could make out Long Island to our left, Staten Island far across the shimmering harbor to our front and if one followed the opposite bank of the Hudson River – New Jersey. I was about to comment when Eli's somber expression stopped my tongue.

"How is he to do it, do you think?" he asked. "How are we?"

"Do what, Eli?"

He turned. "The Colonel told us last night. Told the assembled officers of the regiment. General Washington is charged with defending not only the city, but also all that we now see before us." The sweep of his arm encompassed the fortress' bulk as well as the coastline. "How is this to be accomplished I ask you?"

"We have more than ten thousand men under arms..."

"Indeed we do. From New York, Massachusetts and Pennsylvania. From Delaware and Maryland too. Did I fail to mention Connecticut?"

"Eli, what is it? We both know all this..."

"Yes, Elisha, but think. Some are state levies like the 6th. Others, like us, are Continental regiments. So many commands, and each with its own commanders."

"Yet they all report to Washington."

"Aye," he said. His gaze traced the distant shores.

Always had I prided myself on a reasonable grasp of terrain and tactics. I was raised a farmer, however, and thus readily subordinated my judgment to those of a military background. Eli, I had always held high in this regard. To see him now so unsettled, threatened to unman me. "What else troubles you, my friend?" I asked. "Beyond this matter of disjointed command?"

His arm stretched forth. "Out there, Elisha; surrounding us. Blue waters. And we have no navy. Not a single ship."

As the weather warmed and the weeks passed, again and again we drilled the men until the least among them could keep to a formation of company or even regimental strength. The more able the man, the more he chafed at the sameness, the dullness of it. And still the expected enemy did not show itself. Like a pernicious wound that never quite proves fatal but which daily weakens, the heat and routine sapped our morale. A spreading camp fever further eroded our numerical strength and aggravated all.

On a particularly humid afternoon Heman and I were ordered to appear in the cramped first floor room of a house reserved for the regiment's junior officers. We stood before Eli, not as friends but as sergeants summoned to their lieutenant.

"I'll have the men's names," Eli demanded. "Sergeant Baker. You begin."

Just beyond the open door the orderly's head turned at the unexpected bite in the Lieutenant's tone. "Nathan Root, sir. A private soldier. He bears no other mark against his name." Heman cast a furtive glance my way after this last. It had probably occurred to him too late that I could not make a similar boast regarding my brother.

"Root. Nathan," Eli murmured, scratching the name into the record. "And you, Sergeant."

My blood and temper both rose at the unaccustomed hardness in his eyes. "Azariah Benton. Private."

Lieutenant Chapman sighed. The quill he dabbed with a cloth and set down. "Elisha. Close the door, would you." He stood then and gazed out the narrow, many-paned window before turning back to us. "What was it this time?"

I swallowed. "Both of our men insist they discovered a jug of rum in the cellar of an empty home. The civilian swears it was taken from him. By force."

"And this civilian. He is a Loyalist of course."

Impulsively I leaned onto the edge of my chair. "Eli. You know as well as I that my brother has no want of drink."

"I do, I do. That is what I find more disturbing." He sat. "A city of 20,000, with half of them Loyalists and the other Whigs, of one shade or another. 10,000 Tories who even when they aren't fighting patriots are crammed into the same streets as an equal number of Continentals. And summer coming on. This cannot end well, my friends. First boredom, then bouts of drunkenness, now fisticuffs - and over naught. Soon the men will trade blows amongst themselves. If we're not careful, we might find we lead a pack of jackals; not a company of soldiers."

At this dire forecast I nearly yearned for Howe and his fleet to appear over the distant horizon.

"What of the forts?" Heman asked of a sudden. "You told us yourself, Eli. Captain Tyler you said. 'Tis he made mention that more are to be built on Long Island."

"Near Fort Stirling, yes! General Washington himself wishes it so."

"And the construction will require strong backs," I added, grasping now what my friend was on to.

Eli swatted at his report, stirring papers all about. "Yes, indeed! Far better that we put shovels in the men's hands than they pummel others or each other like drunken louts. No offense meant towards Azariah, of course."

"And none taken."

"Excellent!" Eli announced. "I'll see to it at once. I trust that both Nathan and your brother will be among the names forwarded. As volunteers." We all grinned. "Let me have any others you recommend by say, dusk today."

"And if the men are chosen," I added. "I should like to accompany them. To get a lay of the land across the East River, if nothing more."

"If it's within my power, consider it done."

My hopes had risen for a time following the prospect of changes for at least some of the platoon. A new setting and new duties, even if no more than swinging a pick, would prove a welcome distraction. As days stretched into weeks, however, most lost interest in the very act of eating.

"Not bread and salted pork again..." John Crandall lamented. "And not the meanest seasoning to mask the salt."

Though his lips dribbled with cider and his jaws worked a mouthful of food, Amasa Allen shook his head in dispute. "Grateful is what ya should be," he insisted. "Why, ya should 'ave been with us in Roxbury. Right Sergeant?"

I glanced up from Jemima's letter, received that very morn. Carried it the day through I had. So long in fact that upon sitting beneath the shade of this sweeping chestnut tree I'd resorted to peeling it off my chest. Meantime, Mister Allen swiped at his stubbly chin and proceeded quite as though I had backed his every word.

'Why the Sergeant will tell ya. Half a mile we had to walk to dip a bucket for water, and not a safe step owing to the Regulars' big guns." Our trials at the siege had worsened with each telling and Amasa dearly loved the tale. His high-pitched voice rose and rose still more when the details demanded. "Why," he exclaimed, "as John Lewis and I were sayin'..."

"John Lewis?" I interrupted. "You've seen him?"

"Aye, Sergeant. In Captain Brewster's Company he is. Him and me been acquainting the youngsters with the way of things on Breed's Hill, and up on Dorchester Heights..."

"Tell him would you that I will ask for him at Brewster's headquarters." Soon I heard Mister Allen no more, for Jem's letter beckoned. I did not get far. Backwards I went and re-read the line. "What!"

"What's that, Sergeant?" Amasa asked.

"Nothing." I spotted Daniel approaching with a platter of food. "Brother!" I called. "Come! Join me!"

Sensing the urgency in my voice, he hurried over. "What is..."

I shook the letter. "Is this true?" I demanded. "What Jemima tells me!" Daniel colored at once. My declaration had also drawn the attention of a score of our comrades. For our family's sake, and his besides, I did my best to lower my voice. "This is your plan for the farm? That if we've not returned come harvest time, my betrothed is to pick apples. And in Father's orchard no less!"

"She would be but a small part of it, Brother..."

"What of it? Am I to be appeased that she picks drops and not the fruit from his trees! Does it comfort me, you think, that my love's labors are to be valued no greater than a child's?"

"The idea was her own, Elisha, though the fault rests with me. A year earlier this was. When you'd gone off to Roxbury. I'd walked to town to shoe the mare. I asked Jemima if she had any word of you. She showed me Captain Willes' report, for he was still a Captain then. He had written that the company was like as not to maintain the siege beyond the autumn. At that news I fretted aloud about the harvest – how it was to be managed without you and Azariah. I should not have done so, and knew as much almost at once, but before I could say another word she volunteered to help. She begged it of me, Brother. I swear it."

"All right. So now you merely took her up on her prior offer."

"She renewed it. Almost the moment she learned of our coming to New York. I've meant to tell you. This and the entire plan of the planting. For the harvest too. But you've had no time."

I thought of how often I'd sought our younger brother out. How repeatedly I'd fashioned ways to keep Azariah's energies directed towards pursuits that would safeguard him from harm. On Daniel's knee I laid my hand. "I've had no time for you alone, is what you mean." He moved to deny it. "No," I insisted, "this must be said. Always do I find occasion to be a Sergeant, and brother to Azariah. But you who ask so little, I offer far less." I placed my hand 'round his neck and drew our foreheads together. "Forgive me. I shall strive to make amends."

Chapter 60

In the anteroom just outside the junior officer's domain, in a building nearby the tent city, scarce space existed for two desks, each with a chair. Shoved against the opposite wall stood a pair of cabinets, and two straight-backed chairs for visitors. During mess, only one orderly was on duty. He now occupied the desk nearer the door. Eli had offered the other to me. For a full quarter hour I had attempted to compose a letter. An attempt I had made, but it had been in vain. Nearly a page had I covered in precious ink before realizing that Jemima needed no words of approval from me. Rather, my task was to thank her for the kindness of her offer. This I began to do, before again belatedly reasoning that her casual mention of apple picking proved that she had assumed I knew of it from Daniel long before. Groaning, I crumpled another sheet.

The orderly's eyes darted to my small yet growing pile of discarded paper. Letters, especially to a woman, were so much more difficult than making ledger entries in books of account. I dipped the quill. Of apples, I resolved, I would say nothing.

Dear Jem. Might I call you thus, Jemima. For you are a gem to me...

Ten minutes later I sat back, quite amazed. Not another word could I squeeze in. My fingers bore evidence of my pace, and black splatters spread here and there upon the parchment, but somehow the words conveyed my feelings. Powdering the effort, I carefully folded and addressed it.

"There'll be a courier at the stroke of the hour, Sergeant," the orderly offered. "I can see to that if you like."

He was probably anxious to put an end to my squandering of his supplies, but I thanked him regardless. Handing him Jemima's note, I stepped into the baking sunlight.

"There you are, Elisha!" Eli proclaimed. "Walk with me. I have news of the building of forts."

The mood of those whom we'd taken to calling the volunteers mirrored the surprisingly fine weather. Chatter filled the air as we swarmed the dock along the East River. So many of us there were, that in addition to the ferry, boats of varying descriptions had been pressed into duty. All would be employed in carrying us across to Long Island. I led my allotment of a score of men over to a likely craft. Prime seamen, by the looks of their weathered faces, gripped oars along both gunwales. Crudely yet good-naturedly they mocked our clumsy efforts at boarding.

"Bleedin' landlubbers," one laughed, even as he helped Amasa over a seat shaped like a backless bench.

"Are you Boston men?" I asked the round-faced fellow who gripped the stout tiller in his meaty hand.

"Do ya know Boston, then?" he replied, with that curious flat "a" sound in many of his words.

"We are Connecticut men, though some among us served in Roxbury. And Charlestown too."

"Why then welcome aboard, mateys, for glad we are ta 'ave ya. We hail from Beverly, we do. The 'andsome lads like me, leastways. Others we 'ave from Marblehead an' Salem. Colonel John Glover's men, the lot a us." By now each soldier had secured a place. The boat I feared could not have accommodated another soul, yet the tillerman glanced expectantly 'round the dock. Startled I was by his cry. "Cast off! Now bend yer backs, lads!"

The bow swung out, nosing slowly at first into the stillness of the river at slack tide. How close the waters lapped along the lip of one gunwale. Within half a dozen synchronized strokes, the murky liquid carved up and away much as well-turned soil yielded to the slice of a plough blade.

"Am I to thank you, Brother?" Azariah asked. "For putting a pick in my hands."

He had learned from Heman that the alternative had very nearly been a few days in the guardhouse. This sarcasm was merely his way of offering thanks. "Shovels and picks are indeed in your future, little man," I replied. "But not this day at any rate."

He leaned in close. "Do not toy with me, Elisha. Have you arranged something?"

"We both have Lieutenant Chapman to thank. He has assigned me a patrol. Of two days duration. Or certainly not more than three."

"Where? And what are we to do?"

"You will learn more when I assemble the squad on the opposite shore. Suffice for now to know that it involves something at which you excel. We are to hunt."

"Game? For the company?" I shook my head. "What then? There have been no sightings of the enemy."

"Not ones wearing scarlet coats at any rate." So tormented he looked that I described in some length how sentries on the island had disappeared from remote outposts; in numbers that desertion would not fully explain. My patrol and others were charged with seeking out a particularly virulent strain of Tory skulking about these lands.

"You make an odd choice for this work, Brother," he said when I had finished. "You who proved yourself tolerant of Loyalists outside Boston."

"I've no tolerance for those who smile to one's face, only to wield the knife when one's back is turned. Rest assured, Azariah, we will hunt these men. And you will serve as our scout." At these tidings he smiled and cast an appraising eye along the length of his meticulously cared for weapon.

Having marched up a long incline from the Fulton ferry landing, we came upon a plain, and there a hamlet, Brooklyn, by name. The Captain in overall command of the party provided us sergeants with a lay of the land. To our far left the ground fell away to Wallabout Bay. A string of forts in various stages of construction ran from there across our front. Fort Putnam secured one side of Flatbush Road upon which we stood. Forts Greene and Box guarded the right-hand side. From Box to a cove by the same name ran Gowanus Creek. "Tidal in nature and not to be scoffed at," warned the Captain.

Soon after, my squad made its parting. We stood aside whilst the others veered off to the right. Their destination was Fort Greene, or at least the prominent ground in the process of being transformed. At this very hour a good 200 men already labored there - stripped to the waist and wielding shovel and pick.

I scanned the faces about me. Daniel had stayed behind, more willing he'd been to assist Heman in some of the platoon book-keeping in my absence. Azariah on the other hand had welcomed the opportunity of escaping Manhattan. He now seemed eager to press on into the open countryside. Standing beside him, Jacob Brown, like my brother, moved faster and for longer periods than any other pair in our company. Noah Grant and Amasa Allen neither behaved nor looked anything alike, yet on each I could fully rely. "Beware that expression of smugness Mister Allen," I warned. "You'll be sweating on yonder mound of earth soon enough."

"Not today I won't, Sergeant," he replied with a confident leer that made us laugh.

Having studied the Lieutenant's map, I had intended to ford Gowanus Creek, and sweep the farms dead south, before turning left and returning along the line of distant hills until we fetched Flatbush Road. A few minutes of field observation revealed that what last night had been but an innocuous, squiggly line, was every bit as treacherous looking a waterway as the Captain had suggested. Now, with the tide rising fast over the saltmarsh and mud lining both banks, I was obliged to reverse course.

"We will take the bridge," I ordered. Once over it and beyond the sentries stationed there, I called a halt. Behind us lay the line of forts linked by trenches. Perhaps one mile ahead a steep, wooded ridge spanned our entire front. "Azariah," I said. "Jacob. We will patrol as far as the hills. I want you to scout ahead. Keep to each side of the turnpike. If any man flees at sight of you, detain him until we come up." Azariah began at once to move. Jacob hurried after. "And Brother," I called. "Do keep me in your sight." He pumped his musket aloft in acknowledgement. To the others I said, "We will stop at farmhouses along the way and question the inhabitants. Civilly," I emphasized.

After more than an hour we had succeeded in nothing more than exercising our legs and lips. Inquiries as to the number and whereabouts of residents aged 16 to 60 had found most within the homes or working the fields. In more than a few households, doors might have been slammed in our faces had we not carried arms. At only one did we identify two men eligible to serve whose absence could not be accounted for. Of the location I made mental note. Eli or the Captain would most surely make further inquiries as to these fellows' political leanings and location.

The Bedford Pass lay along the Flatbush Road. It was one of three or four breaks in the steep, densely wooded ridge-line that separated Brooklyn from the interior. No sign was there of my brother or Jacob.

"Somethin's amiss, Sergeant," Amasa said. He spat.

The reception at the homes to our rear had worked up Mister Allen. Ready he was for trouble. Beyond his state of mind, however, I too, was concerned with our comrades' tardiness. Staring round the compass headings I realized I had neither made nor communicated a plan for this eventuality. Thankfully we had not long to wait. Across a field to our right a pair of soldiers moved swiftly.

"It's them!" Noah announced.

A minute more and Azariah and Jacob came alongside. "Whenever you care to report," I said, whilst they recovered their breath. "Take your time."

Jacob signaled his intention to defer with a glance at Azariah. My brother felt no such hesitation. "We sighted a fellow shadowing our movements," he said. "Jacob spotted him. We chased him down with little effort."

"Was he armed?"

"A hatchet. Nothing more. A youth he was, of sixteen. Family name of Fox."

"Not one of those we turned up," I said. "Yet he is of an age. What excuse did he give for observing your movements?"

"The boy lied, Brother. He said he took us for enemy spies. And this despite our uniforms. He is a Tory and himself the spy. We forced him to lead us to his home. Down along the banks of the creek this was. There to the southwest. Only a woman and some girls did we find there. His sisters. A father and brother he has, too, but no sign could we find of them."

"You have both done well. Come, men. We must get word of this to Manhattan. Tomorrow we patrol that area along Gowanus Road."

Chapter 61

By the latter part of June, a defensive line dominated by three forts secured the western tip of the great island. The intimidating positions bristled with nearly three dozen 18-pounders. What's more, the natural barrier of Gowanus Creek extended the defenses from the waters of Wallabout Bay in the northeast to Gowanus Bay in the southwest.

Despite these manmade achievements, Azariah and hundreds more continued laboring in the connecting trenches. Breastworks rose higher still. Driven into the earth before them were countless sharpened stakes. I had been ferried across the East River that divided Manhattan and Long Island on three separate occasions. Each time I had led a patrol. Arrests had followed but the problem remained. Our army's every movement was observed, and no doubt recorded. Sentries and couriers alike continued to disappear. The land hereabouts simply crawled with those more loyal to an English king than their American countrymen. This reality could seemingly neither be denied nor altered.

How I had come to detest the business of attempting to root them out. With my whole heart I disliked the glares and furtive glances directed at me and my men. Nonetheless, I could not manufacture hatred towards those whose homes we forced ourselves within at the hammer-knock of a musket's stock. How I feared that one day a certain look or word might prove the tipping point; and a man like Amasa might respond with the brutal thrust of his bayonet. And I, how would I make report if he should?

With a sharp inhalation, followed by a long exhale, I pushed back from the barrel head that served as my writing surface. The report of the last patrol was, at last, complete. While the ink dried I tabulated in my aching head what came next. Doctor West had advised me of those too ill to report for duty. A new rotation of sentries must be created, with the names of those on sick call deleted.

I massaged my temples. Would that my name could appear among them. "Ah, nonsense!" Shifting my position so that I might push such defeatist thoughts away, I set aside the patrol report. "Let me see," I muttered. "By day's end the Lieutenant must be advised of the count of cartridges on hand. Per man." I inhaled deeply once more. Air, it seemed, could not be had in this musty closet of a room.

A head stuck in at the open door. "Daniel!" I exclaimed. "How good to see you."

"I've come to tear you from your pile of papers, Brother."

"I would love to," I replied, knowing it to be impossible.

"Come. I refuse to take no for an answer." With a single step he reached my side. "They aim to sink a ship in the East River. We must witness it together." I shook my head but he tugged at me. "I promise to help you with all this the moment we return," he insisted. "Come you must! We've little time!"

I found I could not resist - neither his enthusiasm nor his offer to help. Besides, I had heard of the plan to block the passage of enemy warships in this manner, and longed to see it done with my own eyes.

"I have meant to tell you," I said as we hastened along, arm in arm. "How much I value your assistance. Heman tells me what a boon you've proven. Without you these missions to Long Island would have seen me sunk - in parchment."

"As it happens, Brother, I like the work."

"It's true that it suits you. So much so, in fact, I have recommended you for corporal. Eli supports the notion."

His face lit up. "If you and the good Lieutenant insist on paying me more, I shall not argue the point." His tone made light of it, but the recognition pleased him. Besides, he seemed quitc at home with the rigors of administration.

'Just there!" he said, yanking us to a stop. Dozens of people, both soldiers and civilians, had gathered along the docks. A few rods off-shore sailors swarmed over a vessel at anchor in the stream. Farther out two more boats strained at their chains, their bows facing the current.

A pity, it seemed, to sink them, but I remembered one of the Beverly seamen describing the intended obstacles in unsavory terms. 'Well past their prime,' he had said. 'Mere hulks is all, what with their masts and rigging removed.'

"See how they strip anything of value," a gentleman pointed out to his wife. Like monkeys the mariners scampered about, with seemingly no regard for where they placed either hand or foot. "Soon they will open the seacocks," he promised, "and perhaps even wield axes at the water line."

"Will that not sink them, Husband?" his wife asked in alarm.

"Why that is the point, my dear. To block the channel. The hulls will slip beneath the surface, yet not so far down that they cannot act to rip out the guts of any ship passing overhead."

Her fingers rose to her lips. "How gruesome a fate for those onboard..."

"But only those aboard an enemy warship, my love. For only the King possesses craft of such deep draught. Come, my love, it must be so if we're to be made safe." At last, I thought, a patriot. Despite the man's many and earnest explanations, however, the couple wandered away before the climactic act.

A quarter hour on, the nearest vessel began settling low in the tide. A final pair of seamen scampered into a dingy and shoved off. "Now's the moment," Daniel said. The dark silhouette lingered like a carcass heaving dead upon the sea. It listed, revealing mutilated stumps and gaping holes where seated masts had once soared heavenward. Vast globules of air belched from these wounds and from without the hatches. The groans reached near human pitch, the volume far exceeding even battlefield cries. And then the ship that had been, disappeared. Bits of debris swirled on the surface marking its final resting place. "What smells rise from it," Daniel said with his sleeve to his nose. The stench of rot and the sight of swimming rats drove many to other pastimes.

On to the next rowed the sailors. How, I wondered, did they endure lives lived not unlike the struggling vermin, trapped within dank, dark hulls. Death might be preferable. "Come, Brother," I said, and we left them to their unenviable task.

Reluctant to return to the paperwork that awaited us, I suggested we strike out towards the triangle-shaped Common. Situated at the opposite end of Broadway from our camp, this place afforded shade from the relentless sunlight. It also offered sights that could distract the most feverish mind.

We had not yet completed a circuit when we spotted Heman. He sat propped against a tree trunk, cradling his white clay pipe. Lounging about him were the Fenton Brothers and a handful of men from his platoon. We needed not even the invitation of their spontaneous hails to fall in with them.

Whilst I acquainted Heman with the goings on at the East River, the younger men resumed their assessment of each lady who passed by. The prettier the face the faster they spoke. Soon a striking creature bedecked in flowing golden folds struck the lot of them dumb. The v-shaped waist of her dress accentuated her slender figure. Her wide-brimmed hat revealed just a hint of her dark eyes. When she did glance our way, our group exploded with shouts and exclamations. Her escort, a gray-haired gentlemen who I presumed to be her father or uncle, cast us a look, and hurried her off.

"'Twas me who turned her head," proclaimed one of Heman's soldiers. His boast was met with hoots of derision.

"You're mistaken," Asa Fenton retorted. "It was the sergeants who caught her fancy."

Their concentrated gaze made me break off with Heman. "If either party took notice of us old men," I managed to say, "it was the gent at her elbow. And his look was none other than that of any irate father."

"Father?" the boastful one said, rallying. "Gentleman friend more like. The little strumpet." This description seemed to put the indifferent female neatly in her place, gold gown or no. The matter thus settled, the soldiers turned their attention to the next lovely creature coming along the walk.

"Have you lost any men to prostitutes?" Heman asked.

"Disease?" I asked. "No, thank God. Some do frequent the most ungodly whores imaginable, however."

"'Tis true," Heman agreed. "I've warned the lads time and again, but like mongrels to a bone, some just cannot keep away."

Daniel had taken to gesturing and whispering along with the others. "It seems a good lot you have here, Heman," I said.

"That they are."

On an impulse I asked, "Have you set your cap at anyone? Back home, I mean." The question was awkward at best, given our talk of whores. But if I expected any candid reply it would be a quick denial. My friend, after all, had always proven to be of a shy nature where the fair sex was concerned. Instead of answering he took great care in knocking the ash from his pipe. "Heman?"

"There might be a one." He furtively glanced at the others. "Perhaps," he whispered, "when my house and land are ready, I may find the courage to ask her."

"Excellent news! Her name? Who is this fortunate girl?"

"Anne. Her name is Anne. Her family lives west of the lake so I doubt you know of them."

As he seemed intent on divulging little more, I gave him a pat. "I am so happy for you, my friend. I will await the glad tidings of your engagement. When we are home again."

"Aye. When we are home."

I had wished to spend the afternoon in the company of my comrades. Yet I knew I must desert them in favor of reams of reports. Neither was to be my fate. It began with but one bell.

The stem of Heman's pipe slipped from between his teeth. "This is not a Sunday..."

"There begins another," Daniel said, straightening. "And a third..."

"All the bells are set to ringing," I added. Soldiers, sprinkled everywhere across the green, snapped their heads this way and that. Civilians clutched one another. I stood. "There can only be one cause. Come, brothers! Rally 'round. To the waterfront we go, but first we must collect our arms."

"Look at 'em," Amasa exclaimed. "Will ya just look..."

We did, staring with wide eyes and mouths agape. The vastness of New York Bay spread before us as we stood upon the city's southernmost tip. Opposite the coastline of Staten Island could be made out overtop the shimmering waters of the Lower Bay. Billowing clouds of white appeared upon the sea, and they so close-packed that they choked The Narrows.

"How many sail do you make out?" Lieutenant Chapman asked.

A dozen I could distinguish. I turned to Azariah who had returned this very day with one of the construction battalions. Peering beneath his upraised hand, he softly counted. How I wished he would hurry. "Twenty-six," he answered. "No, one more. Make it twenty-seven." None questioned his sight or his count at such a distance.

"Frigates in the van," called out one of Heman's platoon, and he a man originally from Haddam and no stranger to the sea. "The smaller ones just there, nosing along the shore."

"Smaller?" Daniel breathed at my elbow. "Never have I seen the like. They are veritable forts. Forts that float upon the sea." Remembering he had never seen the fleet at Boston, I laid my hand upon his shoulder.

"How fast they come on," Young Fenton said.

Fast indeed, for they curved now in a seemingly endless line that swelled in length and proportion with each passing second. To take one's eye away for but a moment risked horrific, unchecked growth. In Charlestown we'd stood upon the heights, and thus in relative safety. Here, near level with the waves lapping at the dock, the cloud-like spreads of canvas dwarfed us despite the distance. What was to be our defense when they closed to within range of their guns? My musket seemed as but a stick in my left hand.

"Forty now I see," Azariah declared. So intently had I observed the ships in front, I'd ignored those coming up behind.

"Two-deckers," the man from Haddam declared. Joseph Arnold I believe Heman had said. "Sixty, seventy guns apiece I'd reckon. Mebbie more."

"Why, anyone of them holds more cannon than our forts combined!" exclaimed a man behind me.

"God save us," another muttered.

"Calm yourselves, men," Eli ordered. "Stay calm!" His voice was not equal to his words. I honored his attempt, however, for I did not trust myself to utter a sound.

"Do they intend coming straight on?" Daniel whispered. His body shook.

At that moment, the vessels that had advanced farthest now hauled in their sails so bright. The massive hulls swung about as anchors pinned them to the seafloor. Broad bands of white appeared as the warships presented the entirety of their otherwise black lengths. Every few yards the painted stripes running from bows to sterns were broken by dark rectangles. From each a cannon's snout protruded.

"You see!" Eli announced. "They mean to anchor." A cheer rose up, but it was thin, and did not last. Between where we stood and Staten Island, the enemy fleet had chosen its mooring place. And we, we could do naught to drive them from it.

"Forty-five I make it," Azariah declared. "And that's an end of it."

Like the rest I stood silent and watched for a long time. Flanked by my brothers I was, the three of us side by side.

For three days running the 17th was urgently assembled with the cry of 'enemy making sail'. To the docks we hastened only to discover that whilst the armada had not stirred, more ships entered The Narrows. These soon joined those that had come before. The vast anchorage now swarmed with dark hulls whose bare masts split the sky like a forest stripped of leaves. Not even Azariah could effect a count, so densely packed were they. In excess of a hundred, Colonel Huntington informed us - if warships and transports were tallied together.

"Far more than they had up Boston way," Noah Grant explained to Jacob, who numbly nodded by way of reply.

"More than I knew existed in the wide world," John Crandall said. He had but murmured yet his words rippled like a wave of shock through rank and file, silencing one and all. I thought better of censuring him for such talk. The enemy host had proved humbling enough this day.

For once I welcomed the mundane demands of drafting reports and the giving and taking of orders. Content I was to do no more than this for a week of days. The entirety of July could pass with me thus engaged. It was not to be.

Barely had the month begun than the frenzied ringing of the church's bells sent us scrambling into regimental formations. For hours the men stood beneath a blazing sun. Meanwhile, we sergeants ferried messages back and forth between The Fort and our officers. How my breath caught in my throat each time Colonel Huntington broke a seal. His expression I studied for any sign. None did I see. Our commander must be a phenomenal card player, I thought, standing before him. Either that or...

"The Regulars have landed all right," he advised Lt. Colonel Clark beside him. "But upon Staten Island. Out there, across the bay."

"What of the garrison, sir? Are they putting up the good fight?"

"This says only that the Continentals are in retreat."

"Damn!" Lt. Colonel Clark removed his hat. With his handkerchief he mopped his brow. Suddenly he asked. "Sir! What of the militia?"

Colonel Huntington glanced quickly at me. Then, crumpling the note, he turned to his assembled officers. "Regrettably, gentlemen, the New York militia has gone over to our enemy. En masse it is believed." A gasp escaped this typically stalwart band. Their reaction shocked me near as much as the ill news.

"I trust, Sergeant," the Lieutenant Colonel added, "that you will keep this last in confidence."

"I vouch for Sergeant Benton's discretion, sir," Captain Tyler was quick to reply. Though Colonel Huntington himself seemed not at all concerned by my presence, it was nonetheless satisfying to hear my Captain rise to my defense.

Doing no more than noting the exchange between his officers, the Colonel offered me a courteous nod and resumed his briefing.

Though the official announcement that followed made no reference to the militia's heinous act, their treachery soon became common knowledge among the troops. Relations between occupiers and occupied ebbed further. July's heat and the fear of imminent invasion rose in awful tandem. Though we all suffered under the same twin evils, the suffering served to build not bonds, but hate.

I convinced myself that the state of things could not worsen. Near month's end I was proved wrong. A letter arrived for me in the post. From Tolland it came, and addressed to me in Father's hand. Despite months spent here and in Roxbury too, not once had he written me. Upon receipt of this, his first correspondence, I knew not what to think. With a vague foreboding I withdrew. To a dock I directed my steps. So marked was its disrepair that it seldom saw use, and thus made a fitting spot.

To my eldest son, Elisha,

These sad tidings I address to you, though they bear on all my sons. As first born, I look to you to convey the truth of it to your brothers.

Somehow, having read these few words alone, I knew. Before me the swift current poured darkly passed. The tide was out - unstoppable and relentless; racing for the sea.

My father Daniel, and he Grandsire to my sons, has passed from this world.

I could no more stifle the sob than I could staunch the tears that sprang into my eyes. Oh, that I had crumpled this note before ever reading what ill tidings it contained.

> *In God's care he now rests. Join our family in prayer for his departed soul.*

"Grandsire. Grandsire..." Some minutes more passed before I could husband the strength to endure more such words. Father had pivoted, however, and effortlessly too.

> *All that my father possessed in life, now is rendered mine by his passing. He has willed it so.*

Shaking my head I willed myself to continue.

> *His house only is excepted from this, and is henceforth Mother Sarah's to dwell within as long as she wishes, or has need of it. What is perchance of more specific interest to you, Elisha, is that my father's will made no reference to a certain gift to you. I trust you know of what I speak. In any event, my wife, your mother, and your grandmother too I might add, vouch for my father's wishes in this. In brief, I mean to honor his bequest to you.*

How could Father manage it? Even when seeming to act justly he infuriated me. Mother must have labored mightily to win this concession from him. I crushed the letter. Up I stood, intent on tossing it far into the stream. Yet I could not. The tidings here were not for me alone. Seated once more, I flattened the sheet upon my thigh. How could I convey such loss to my brothers? How might I comfort them? In time lengthening shadows bathed me. Their cool embrace served as a reminder of what must be done.

Azariah had left us the instant he learned of Grandsire's passing. Still seated, Daniel and I followed his rapidly departing form.

"So like him to run away," Daniel said.

The reactions of both of my brothers surprised me - the one's resentment perchance more than the other's flight. I must strive to judge neither, for my emotions still swung wildly, too, and I had the luxury of far more time to weather this blow.

'Always has Azariah fled responsibility..." Daniel added, with perhaps even more heat.

"Calm yourself, Brother. Consider that in caring for our grandfather as you did, you witnessed firsthand our elder's gradual decline."

"That proves my point, Elisha! If Azariah had behaved as a grandson should, he would have tended to him as did you or I, and not be so shocked at his passing."

It would serve no purpose to point out that Daniel had only assumed this role of caretaker whilst Azariah and I were stationed in Roxbury. "Let us set aside why he did not attend," I counseled, "and focus instead upon this possibility. Our younger brother likely remembers Grandsire as the one adult, more than any other in his life, who never found him lacking. As the only man who accepted him for what he is."

"And what is he, exactly, Elisha?"

Daniel's grief poured out in spite; that suited him not at all. Swallowing down my rising anger I tried to fashion an answer for him. In doing so I discovered one that suited me as well. "Our brother is a sort of spirit I should think. One destined always to seek his freedom. And content to die in quest of it."

Chapter 62

For weeks rumors had circulated almost daily of additional landings by the British. A good many were deemed sufficiently serious that the officers hastily assembled the regiments. On occasion we were even marched to one point or another along Manhattan's coastline, or down to the ferry dock across the East River from Long Island. Always we returned within a matter of hours.

"How fare the men?" Captain Tyler asked as Eli, Heman and I gathered after one such pointless foray.

Always I had responded with truth, leavened with some encouraging words. "They are exhausted," I replied. "In body and in mind."

His back stiffened at once. But this posture did not last. "I see," he said. "And you, Lieutenant, do you share the Sergeant's view?"

"I do, sir. It wracks the men's nerves; these endless alarms."

"Yet we must be ever vigilant. Our numbers shrink daily whist the enemy's strength of arms grows. They are now thought to count upwards of 30,000 troops; together with a navy comprised of 400 sail ready to deposit said force upon our threshold at their whim." Admitting as much drained his face of color - almost as if his very strength seeped from him.

"In Boston," I offered. "Time was their enemy; and our ally."

"How do you mean, Sergeant?"

"Each passing day spelled greater want for the occupiers. From those who fled the city we learned when their hay ran out, and later still when they began to eat their horses."

"Ah, now I follow you. How true you speak. Here in New York, daily it is Tories who go over to them, adding to their manpower, and their warehouse of information. About us."

"That's it," Eli said. "In this way they discover where we are strong. And in which ways weak."

"Like our will," the Captain said. He clasped us each by an upper arm. "So we must stay strong, if we are to survive. Leaders like yourselves must believe so fervently in this that the men are convinced of it just by speaking with you." To me he said, "Can you do this, Sergeant?"

"Aye, sir. I will do my best."

The next rumor that reached us turned out to be true. Generals Howe and Washington had engaged in negotiations. The very mention of the word 'peace' unleashed a torrent of hope. Though I tamped down such speculation so as not to set the men up for dashed dreams, I found ample excuses to linger outside the headquarters. If a truce was to be declared, my first act would be to rush home and walk my land, Grandsire's blessed gift to me - to us, for at my side would be Jemima.

On seeing Heman returning from The Fort, I hurried to him. "What tidings?" I asked.

He took me by the arm, and in hushed tones said, "I saw it with my own eyes, Elisha."

"What? Tell me!"

"Howe's letter. To the General. Addressed to George Washington, Esquire, it was. Not to our Commander-in-Chief. Nor even General Washington. They say he refused it. Sent it packing to Howe without so much as opening it."

I sagged against the building's kiln-hot brick. "Thus ends the negotiations," I murmured.

"It would appear so, my friend."

I stepped clear of the wall. Passersby went about their business as usual. If the day of reckoning had come at last, how would these folk of New York respond? Did they pray at night for an American victory? Or was it news of a British triumph for which they longed?

'There is an announcement that will be shared," Heman confided. "The entire regiment, all regiments in fact, are to be formed up. The Congress, our new Congress, has signed a declaration it appears. Dating from the fourth of this month we are independent from the mother country."

"What?"

"'Tis true enough. This Declaration of Independence will be read to the assembled brigades upon the Common. By order of General Washington himself."

"So war it is to be."

That evening, surrounded by comrades, with my brothers near to hand, an undeniable charge raced through me upon hearing the speaker's words.

> *"We hold these truths to be self-evident, that all men are created equal, that they are endowed by their Creator with certain unalienable Rights that among these are Life, Liberty, and the pursuit of Happiness...*

I clung to these last words. The land, my own bit of land, I felt beneath my feet though I stood at attention upon the soil of New York. And Jem's face I conjured with but little effort. Who did my brothers glimpse, I wondered, as the words lifted us up? Azariah smiled. Nodding, I returned it in full measure, for so rare a gift was that of late. Daniel, thinking it meant for him, touched my sleeve. And so, too, it was.

> *'That whenever any Form of Government becomes destructive of these ends, it is the Right of the People to alter or to abolish it, and to institute new Government..."*

When the declaration had been read in full, the people, we soldiers and hundreds of citizens together in a single body, surged down Broadway, borne on a current of patriotic fervor. At Bowling Green, some in the crowd swarmed over the iron fence. Ropes from the nearby docks were fetched. Cast up, these were, ensnaring the statue of King George III - seated high upon a majestic steed. With shouts and cries, the leaden monarch was toppled. Dismembered, his shattered limbs were carted away, melted down I later learned into the round projectiles that would be fired at the tyrant's soldiers. During the whole of this near riot not one order did we receive to quell the frenzied celebration of independence. Behind locked doors thousands of Tories must have quaked the long night through.

Such a watershed of jubilation could not last. It did not. Within days the report of a British ship sailing up the Hudson River fueled a stampede for the city's lower west side. The towering masts and massive hulls of not one, but a pair of warships, proved the rumor.

"Can nothing be done to stop them?" Daniel asked after our company had been drawn up facing our foe.

As if in answer the roar of cannon erupted from Governor's Island. The elevated shot sent up thin columns of white water, well short of the mark. Cheers died in men's throats.

Though undeterred by the ineffectual fire, the men-of-war unleashed answering blasts from their stern-mounted guns. Civilians scattered, for we and not the out of range fortress were targeted. Even some of the ranks broke, though no shell exploded near us.

"Steady, Brother," I whispered to Daniel, for well I remembered the horror of being under cannon fire for the first time. He reclaimed his position in the line and shouldered his piece with his eyes cast down.

Near as I could make out, the only damage was to a fish drying rack that had been reduced to splinters. "Azariah," I said. "Can you make out the name on the transom? The nearer one."

"HMS *Phoenix*. She boasts twenty ports on her starboard side." He turned to me. "Of forty guns at least that makes her. The other is the *Rose*. Of thirty I'd say."

"Seventy in all..." Daniel muttered.

Others surely detected the trembling in his voice. That would not do. I moved briskly among them, busying the lot with the squaring of their shoulders and the dressing of our lines. The attentions served to distract them and occupy myself. When we were marched off we had at least the look of soldiers.

July succumbed in time to August. Humidity joined forces with the relentless heat. When the men were not at drill, or digging, digging, digging, or struggling to sleep, they resorted far too often to drinking, or fighting, or whoring. Disease claimed an increasing number.

I at least had Jemima to cling to. She had written some weeks after Father. While her mention of Grandsire re-opened an unhealed wound, her words soothed whereas Father's had rubbed salt. So often had I read her lines that I knew them by heart. This was just as well, for the paper, like the pussy willows before them, had begun to disintegrate within my shirt.

How the summer crawled by in this place. Back in Tolland the picking of blueberries must be nearing an end. Already a second crop of strawberries would be reddening. Soon enough apples would be harvested. And she would be among those picking them.

"Guess what I have here?" Azariah said, plunking down on an overturned crate just opposite. Happy I was to see him, of course, and even more so that a smile overspread his handsome face. On recognizing the hand flowing across the upheld letter, however, a tinge of envy sprouted in my breast. "From Jemima it comes!" he boasted.

"And what does she have to say?"

He flipped his prize open. "To begin. She and her parents are well."

"Glad I am to hear it."

"This part will shock you, though, Brother. She says our father is aged, no sadly diminished is her description. Altered, Mother tells her," he added more somberly, "since Grandsire's passing. Are you not amazed, Elisha, to learn that Father has gentle feelings?"

"Jemima would do better to bestow her empathy on a more deserving Benton. Mother Sarah to name one, or Mother herself."

Azariah's smile disappeared so fast he appeared to have swallowed it. "We all can list countless faults of Father, Elisha, but failing to honor Grandsire's bequest to you is not among them. Is this not rather proof of the change in him that Jemima cites?"

"She confided as much, did she?" My tone bit, for I had chosen to withhold Father's grudging promise from my brothers.

He folded the letter. "Always have my dear friend and I confided in each other, Brother. And it is just as well for you, for many were the times I sung your praises when she questioned your manner."

"My manner was it?"

"She wondered at your haughtiness. In times gone by."

I exhaled forcefully that I might expel the heat that rivaled this brutish day. Resent it though I might, I could not argue a charge of behavior that had once bordered on arrogance. "I cannot help but wonder, Brother," I replied instead. "Whether you or Jemima Barrows comprehend in what ways Father will exact a price for this single act of supposed compassion."

"How do you mean?"

"Oh, trust that there will be conditions affixed to this gift. Ones that Grandsire never intended. Mark me. Father will so entangle the parcel that its weight will drag me down by the throat."

Chapter 63

I had lain awake for a good while in the predawn hour that rendered all gray. My covering had been kicked clear but still a blanket of heat oppressed me. Azariah was beside me. I owed him an apology. A strange thought occurred to me. What if he and Jemima were right? Was Father capable of change? Might Grandsire, in passing, have bestowed some of his gift of kind and learned counsel upon his son?

A bell tolled slowly as though he who pulled upon the thick rope did so with a conflicted mind.

"Not again," Amasa groaned. "Damn an' blast."

In the center of six I had the clearest path to the tent's flaps. "To arms," I spoke in the twilight. Forms rose up as if from the slabs of a crypt. "We will line up outside."

Before we finished calling the roll we learned that sickness had claimed Colonel Huntington overnight. An out of breath courier thus raced up to Lt. Colonel Clark. A minute later he drew the captains aside. Even from where I stood, anchoring the end of the first rank, I could not make out their words. The first probing rays of light revealed their taut expressions, however. How ill it bode to have lost our Colonel at such a moment.

Azariah leaned around Daniel. "What do you make of it?"

Many were the ears that hungered for whatever reply I might make. I said nothing. My brothers, however, realized that our months of waiting were at an end.

Not a minute more and Lt. Colonel Clark stepped before the regiment. He cleared his throat. "Men of Connecticut. Soldiers of the 17th Continental Regiment. My comrades, and my friends. Word has come. Our enemy. At long last they move."

Other bells had begun to toll. Fiercely now they pealed. The Colonel bespoke the captains. The captains in turn summoned the lieutenants and sergeants. And so it was that we learned the Regulars had landed in Gravesend Bay on Long Island; in force.

"They came ashore across The Narrows from Staten Island," Captain Tyler responded to Eli's question. "Two understrength rifle companies have withdrawn before them. They put the enemy's numbers at two thousand. What's more, they are said to advance under the guns of a warship."

Heads swiveled at this news. "It seems too few for an invasion," I risked stating. "Have we not far more than that on garrison duty within our forts?"

"Good point, Sergeant. The senior officers believe this may be no more than a feint."

"Then where do they intend to land next? If I may inquire, sir," Eli asked.

"I'm certain a case of brandy would belong to the man who could answer that," the Captain replied with an uncharacteristic wink. He seemed anxious to get on with it, whatever it turned out to be. By the time we left, I had come around to his way of thinking.

For the days that followed we stayed within hailing distance of our quarters. The waiting, somehow, was easier to bear, for this time it was bound to end.

"How fare the men?" Eli inquired, for what must have been the third time that afternoon alone.

"They might worry more, but they argue less," I replied. Heman grinned and nodded his assent. "Have the British moved again?"

"The Regulars now hold Flatbush, or so we believe. It's the town opposite the pass you reconnoitered."

"What of their strength?" Heman asked.

Eli stepped closer, so as not to be overheard. "It is as Elisha has said. Unlike Boston, here we are the blind men. More have landed, perhaps in the thousands. We simply do not know."

"What of this report of green-coated troops?" I asked.

"Hessians, yes. Unfortunately true, I fear. German mercenaries I'm told. And merciless when they prevail upon the field. Best we not speak of them. The men have enough on their minds."

By noon on the 22nd of August, we sergeants were again called before the Lieutenant. Inside his office we crowded. A note fluttered in his hand. "You once asked, Heman, of the enemy' strength. I now have a number for you. 10,000." We fell back as one. "Steady on. One report says far more. It gets worse. Field pieces have been off-loaded too." He set the paper down. "That is what we know of their preparations. Now, as to our own. We are to deploy almost at once to the East River ferry landing."

He produced a map of Long Island, which we peered over. Soon each hurried forth so that the company might ready itself. Many veterans of Boston scratched out wills. Others jammed their packs and even their pockets with whatever foodstuffs they could lay their hands on. I devoted my time to the newest of our recruits. For them the months of drill would not prevent them from neglecting cartridges, flints or even the state of their canteens at such a time. Daniel, I discovered, had shoved handfuls of spare cartridges into his food pouch, but carried no flint other than that fixed in his musket. Having righted this confusion, and seen to the pressing needs of others, I had a minute at my own disposal. On an impulse I took up the half dozen larger silver coins that I possessed. Hurriedly I sewed them into the lining of my coat. When finished I rushed outside with absolutely no sense of why I had resorted to such a caution.

Rain began falling as we marched out. At the landing place a thin mist drifted over the river. Stone-faced sailors hunched sodden in their boats. They had taken the precaution of muffling their oarlocks. The tillerman held his thick finger to his lips. "Make not a sound," I urged the men as we boarded. "There's no telling if a warship lurks in these waters."

Only the occasional slap of a wooden blade against the chop betrayed our progress. Within a dozen strokes the docks lost their fixed angles and mass. A swirling veil soon cloaked all. I tried picturing the terrain covered during our patrols. In this gray air it was easy to shape the steep, forested slopes - gashed in places where narrow paths crept through.

Somehow the helmsmen guided the boats true. On the Long Island side we bid our farewells to the men of Massachusetts. Disembarking, we assembled along the shore. A row of casks, upright and with their heads removed, stood close at hand. Into the nearest I shoved my hand. "Sea bread," I announced. "A staler toast you have likely never bit into, but when hunger comes, you'll wish you had more of it. Load your pockets," I told the men. "And quickly does it."

The climb up onto the plain outside Brooklyn was familiar for some but hardly all. Now safely beyond the danger of enemy ships I figured a bit of chatter might do the men no harm. "Mister Allen," I called out.

"Sergeant?"

"It's a powerful lot of buffing you must do on the morrow, Amasa."

"Sir? What..."

"If you're to restore the shine to my buckles."

For the first time since we'd left our barracks behind, men's laughter broke out. Amasa took his vengeance on another, and then that man took his turn. And so we went, slogging along through the mud. We halted just inside the ring of forts. As we waited, and darkness settled over the land, the twinkling of a light here and there marked the hamlet of Brooklyn. A candle in the window of a small house set back from the road kindled memories of another such dwelling. I held to it as we were ordered to load our weapons, and suddenly marched off into the night.

It did our spirits precious little good to leave in our wake these stout defenses upon which many of our column had long labored. Yet onward we went, nearly blind, towards an enemy of unknown strength somewhere to our front.

Less than a mile on, we swung left onto Jamaica Road. Not two more after that brought us into Bedford, and a second junction. There the column stumbled to a halt. Just ahead I could discern our officers, a knot of huddled forms. Fragments of a sharp exchange reached me. Eli left them and trotted to my side.

"Sergeant. Come forward."

"What is it, Eli?"

"None of us know the terrain hereabouts. And Elisha, I suggested that you might."

"You are Sergeant Benton?" Colonel Clark asked, though he knew it to be so. I snapped to attention despite the wind and wet that forced my eyes closed for a moment. "Captain Tyler and the junior officer present suggest you know the shortest route to Bedford Pass."

"I do, sir. If we turn right here at the fork, we will reach the pass not a mile farther on. It is the third of four passages through the ridge, counting from where our enemy landed in the southwest."

"You seem to know it well. You shall lead us then, for I intend to encamp the regiment on the higher ground west of the pass. Appoint another to lead your platoon on the march. Gentlemen, we shall turn here off Jamaica Road. Now if only word can reach us as to which of our forces protect our flanks, and whom leads them."

"Sir?" I asked. The Colonel seemed perturbed that I remained with them. "If I may, sir. My brother is more familiar with this terrain than I, and a natural tracker. Might I ask him to..."

"Of course. Take what men you deem necessary but act quickly man. This downpour has put us behind our time as it is."

I took my leave at once. "Azariah Benton," I commanded. "Fall out. Amasa Allen, you are placed in command of the platoon for the remainder of the march."

"Me, Sergeant?" He came forward, though his eyes bulged with surprise.

I took hold of his arm as I addressed them. "I expect every man of you to obey Mister Allen's orders."

"Aye," rose from the ranks, though many a man smiled at their temporary Sergeant's obvious discomfort.

With that I gave a nod to Daniel, and hurried forward with Azariah at my hip. Into the void we went, the regiment swinging into quickstep behind us.

Chapter 64

By the time Bedford Pass had been reached, and Colonel Clark had found a position to his liking, full dark blanketed the forest. With a degree of stumbling about on the slick, sloped ground, we sergeants posted pickets. Another Connecticut regiment came up soon after and they provided a welcome flanking force. Thus strengthened, those of our men not on duty were allowed to lie down, though each man was ordered to keep his musket by him. With the whereabouts of our enemy unknown, and lacking tents or coverings of any sort, 'tis precious wonder if any man slept.

Some hours on, and dawn not far off, I sat with my back against a standing tree. Down below, unseen, the narrow pass snaked its way through the ridge-line. This we must defend, for it offered a direct link between Bedford and Flatbush. Eli had shared that the town of Flatbush was now held by the Hessians - recognizable in the field by their green coats, and known for their lack of mercy. With a tilt of my head the accumulated water drained away from my tricorne hat. I should sleep, for soon my brothers and I might face these foes.

Could such fearsome troops move forward in elements such as these, I wondered? We had, though it cost us mightily. My stomach growled. I felt but did not hear it. Hearing anything other than the pattering of drops on countless leaves and the clack of branches swayed by the wind was near impossible. What if even now the Germans crept close? The left pocket of my sodden coat bulged with sea bread. Yet how my bones ached. I would rest, then eat. I closed my eyes. For just a moment. The tree's bark, softened by a coat of moss, cushioned my head.

I awoke with a start. Faint light probed the upper parts of the forest. The rain had eased to a mist. So fine was it that I had to wipe it from my lashes to see. Bodies were strewn all about the slope. Nearest me Daniel lay motionless. On his back he was, with his mouth open to the wet. Bolt upright I came. "Daniel!"

His head snapped up.

"Thank God," I whispered. Neither he nor any of my comrades had been murdered whilst they slept. "Time to wake, Brother." I moved among the men, gently shaking my companions awake. Their eyes struggled to focus from within dark hollows. "Awake, Noah. Jacob..."

The sopped pine needles rendered the footing treacherous. Especially so were the shiny, black roots. Amasa sprawled facedown with his head downhill. At my touch he spun 'round and grabbed at my ankle. "It's me, Mister Allen. Sergeant Benton."

"Beg pardon, Sergeant." He rubbed my shin as if to make it right. "Did I hurt ya, sir?"

"I'm quite myself, thank you. And, Mister Allen, thank you for taking over the platoon during the march."

"A pleasure, sir."

The Fenton brothers had already roused themselves. I instructed the men to fetch something to eat from their packs. There would be no campfires this morn and they needed something in their bellies.

Lieutenant Chapman appeared within minutes. The night march showed in his features. "How do they get on, Elisha?"

"As you see them, Eli. Tired, sure, and hungry, but game I'd warrant."

He motioned me to walk with him. "We'll have need of that last before this day is out, I fear."

"What news?"

"Precious little of the movements of the enemy. Two regiments of Pennsylvania riflemen are, however, advancing along the road from Bedford. Once they arrive, we are to climb up over the ridgeline."

"Towards the Hessians…"

"So it appears. Though no one seems to know where we might find them, how many there might be, nor whether they possess artillery."

"Are we not to have the luxury of Breed's Hill, when we had an unspoilt view of the invading host?" Eli ignored my attempt at a grim sort of humor. He stepped close.

"There exists a state of confusion that we witnessed in that place," he said, having lowered his voice. "The Lt. Colonel does not even appear convinced as to who has overall command. I swear it. None doubt that Sullivan replaced General Greene when he fell ill a few days back. Now it seems Putnam may have the command in his stead. The chain of command below these generals is utter turmoil."

I was about to ask what bearing such changes had for lowly soldiers such as us, when I detected a strange twist in my friend's mouth. It was a smile, yet it wasn't. "Eli?"

Lieutenant Chapman gave a choked laugh. "You'd never guess what a private foot soldier asked of me this morn."

"What was that?"

"Could he and his mates light a fire? Appears they fancied a cup of tea or some such." The odd laugh sounded again. "With untold thousands of enemy troops at our door, and not a dry twig for miles, he longs for teatime. I must check my kit. Perhaps I've got some of Mother's china in there for him."

"My friend…" was all I could think to say.

A moment more and he exhaled. He touched my sleeve, then donned his cap, adorned with its green cockade. "Now, then. I am charged to tell you that we are to rouse the company. We advance in a skirmish line."

Not even Azariah had set foot previously on the opposite side of the long ridge that ran for miles across the front of the ring of forts. Thus it was that we advanced through the trees with cautious step and straining eyes. Time and again I sought out my brother's form moving silently some 30 or 40 yards in front of me. Downward, too, I repeatedly glanced, for the ground fell away much more sharply on this south side of the line of hills.

Of a sudden Azariah's body went stiff. "Halt," I cried, harsh and low. The platoon froze in place whilst I hurried forward. "Azariah. What do you see…"

"Movement in the fields below. They wear green. Green with red facing, Brother."

"Damn." I waved Jacob Brown forward. "Take word at once to Lieutenant Chapman," I ordered him. "Hessians spotted 200 yards to our front. Go now!"

I had just signaled the platoon to draw even with us when we heard the first report. Within minutes, shots rang out here and there along our line. The order soon came forward to resume our advance. Even now a Continental regiment marched through the pass. We were to descend from the slope on their right flank and drive the enemy before us.

With the enemy in sight, we pulled back our scouts. En masse the 17th filtered through the forest edge and into farmed fields. Only glimpses did I catch of fleeing forms, clad in green. Off they scampered before ever the distance warranted me sending a shot their way.

I marveled that Azariah had discerned the red facings of their uniform lapels. Of course he spied them facing us, whereas to our massed strength they turned tail.

Laughter I heard, as some of the men put a stack of grain to the torch. At that very moment Lieutenant Chapman approached. “What do you make of it, Elisha? This driving back of their pickets?”

“It gives the men confidence. Too much perhaps.” More haystacks flared as we surveyed the countryside swarming with our buff-coated companions. Shots were fired at impossible ranges, especially by our youngest.

“Quite right, I think,” he said. “Instruct your men to save their powder. I will speak of this with Captain Tyler.” He paused before turning to go. “Where are they?” he asked. “This enemy 30,000 strong.”

By day’s end we had succeeded in driving our elusive foe to, through and beyond the town of Flatbush. There the Hessian advance units fell back upon their entrenched lines. With cannon and heavier fire they checked us. Our senior officers ordered us to relinquish the nearly mile of ground won so that we might encamp within the tree line once more – and there await, or so we feared, the appearance of the main thrust of the British landing force. Never had the fighting ever been more than sporadic.

Once off sentry duty, I retired to a shelter of tree boughs fashioned by my companions. Weary were the faces I scanned on either side. “Not a round did I fire,” I admitted.

“Nor I,” Heman said. “Too few of them to stand and fight I suppose.”

Daniel also shook his head no. My gaze fell next on Azariah. He neither spoke nor shook his head. He did not look away. So, he had come to grips with that which had tormented him since Roxbury.

On the morning of the 24th we were relieved of duty. Back we marched to Brooklyn, through the very pass we had defended. We drove before us a small herd of cattle we had seized. This beef at least would fill Continental and not Hessian bellies.

Our good fortune was to continue once we were within the safety of the forts: We were allowed to draw provisions. The cooling pulp of fresh watermelons dispelled somewhat the misery roused by miles afoot in the late August heat. Grateful we were when a barn was seized to accommodate us, for it threatened to be a wet evening. The only impediment to sleep that night was the occasional boom of a cannon from over Flatbush way.

That night the rain came. It persisted the following day, as did cannon fire from a few miles off. Casualties began arriving. In numbers they were few. The screams of the wounded, however, jangled the nerves of veterans and raw recruits alike. Was this what it had been like, I wondered, for those men atop Bunker Hill who pondered coming to our aid upon Breed's?

I was not to ponder long. Orders were soon given that we were to march south once more. On this occasion we turned not left towards Bedford but right, heading southwest on Gowanus Road. Our course took us steadily away from the echoing boom of the cannons. Daniel was hardly the only one in our ranks to wear a nervous grin at this development.

Two hours of marching saw us encamped overlooking Gowanus Bay, with the road we'd traveled on our left. Sunday ended as it had begun – with drenching rain. I slowly made my way to those on picket duty. Intermittent shots caused me to break into a trot. "Amasa? What are you firing at?"

"Pardon, Sergeant. Noah thought he spotted an intruder."

"Which direction?"

"Earlier this was, Elisha," Noah said. "I swear I saw someone. But my piece misfired. It's this infernal wet. Anyway, if he was there he crept off in the dark. That's when Amasa here suggested we test fire our pieces now and then. So we can count on our powder should they come on."

"The Lieutenant encouraged us, Sergeant," Amasa hastened to explain.

"I'm certain that he did so. Well done, Mister Allen. I will be sure to share the practice with your relief. Now let us remind the newer men to keep their muskets at hand, and snug."

Given the conditions, I spent the remainder of my watch walking the perimeter with our duty men. By the following afternoon the entire regiment was grateful to be told to again march back to Brooklyn. Less grateful were we to learn that whilst the officers would be accorded a roof, the larger share of us must sleep in the open – so numerous were the reinforcements General Washington had ferried over from New York. The 17th, our numbers reduced to a mere 250, thus lied side by side in the rain on the night of August 26th, 1776.

Chapter 65

Neither officer nor soldier was to sleep for long. Sometime after midnight we were hurriedly awakened. Into Eli's face I stared. "Hurry, Elisha. We must march to Gowanus Road."

"What, again? Are you overdue for another fine meal with Lord Stirling?" This barb I had been ready to deliver the prior evening, after my friend along with all officers of the 17th had been invited to the quarters of General Alexander, or Lord Stirling. I amazed and pleased myself to have risen with this jest at the ready.

"The British are attacking, Elisha! Lord Stirling is already marching south to reinforce our own General Parsons. You must rise at once!"

Bolting upright I struggled into my coat.

"Have the men carry their arms and little else," he ordered. "The ammunition cart will follow. Hurry now, I must rouse the others."

We marched at the quick-step for two and a half miles. My brothers came alongside side of me in the rank, near the front of the column. How wide had been the eyes that stared up at me when I hauled them from their slumbers – Daniel and Jacob, Amasa and Azariah too. Steady firing ahead lent a surge to our harried pace. How awful the sound was, at such an hour.

Minutes more witnessed our arrival upon a field of battle. Lord Stirling himself I saw with what appeared to be the better part of two regiments worth of his Maryland and Delaware troops – strung out in battle formation across our front. General Samuel Parsons was with him and so, too, Lt. Colonel Clark. So hasty was their conference that they held it there in the road before us. How strange they appeared, with arms gesturing here and there whilst musket fire peppered the night not a hundred yards farther south.

Suddenly, both General Parsons and Lt. Colonel Clark broke away. "Follow me!" they shouted.

Off the road to the left we went at a trot. The road sloped away, so down we went. On our right I witnessed Lord Stirling's line re-form. Like a spear point they faced downhill towards an enemy I could not see. The contours of the land soon swallowed them.

"Hold formation!" I yelled, for the undergrowth threatened to scatter us. Dawn could not be far away now, as more and more of my comrades could I make out around me. Keeping out of the clutches of a swampy area to our right, we immediately began assembling. Only then did we discover that a colonel unknown to me, along with his small detachment of Pennsylvania troops, had also been attached to General Parson's command. Together we must number some 300, but who opposed us, and how many were they?

"Eli…"

He fell back a few paces to join me. "We are to cover Lord Stirling's left flank," he whispered, as if anticipating my question. "I know no more than this." Just as quickly, he rejoined Captain Tyler.

With the improving light it was clear that we had formed in a hollow. The ground rose up in nearly every direction other than the swamp. From an elevated position just to our rear, a group of riflemen began a steady fire. The fact that none among us fell proved them to be either Continentals or impossibly poor shots.

"Wheel to the right," came the command. I repeated it and our column did as ordered. This movement made our immediate objective clear. We were to mount the hill directly before us. In height it surpassed its neighbors and should offer up a position from which we could see an attack coming, and better defend ourselves. Or so I prayed this is what the General had in mind. "Forward, march!"

Leaving a rearguard detachment behind, we climbed. Daniel, his lips tight, looked my way. Azariah held his rifle across his chest at the ready. Not once did his head veer from the hilltop. Suddenly, he fired, just off to my left. A second later a volley ripped from an enemy that had popped up from the crest above.

We halted without being told to do so. Some men fell back. "Return fire!" an officer yelled. This much I managed to do. As I then snapped open my cartridge box I saw Daniel raising his musket. Amasa's piece discharged; smoke billowing about him. Azariah had already finished reloading. Again he aimed and fired. Around me came a smattering of reports; then more and more as the 17th regained its composure.

"Advance! Advance!" the General ordered. Lt. Colonel Clark moved forward at once and we could do no other than follow his lead.

"Advance, Daniel," I yelled. "Amasa, Noah, Jacob, come on!" Uphill we surged, side by side. We paused only to fire and reload. Firing and striding forward we quickly covered the 40 yards that separated us from the top. Azariah reached it first and aimed down the opposite slope. I came up on his right just as his shot dropped a fleeing Regular. Dozens more fled; already too far off for me to do them ill.

The ground we had won was littered with the bodies of a dozen British soldiers. Muskets and gear of various sorts were scattered amongst them. And blood. It stained cravats and straps; it spilled out, soaking darkly into the earth. We accepted the surrender of a half dozen more, each wounded to varying degrees. The General ordered a tally of our own casualties. Miraculously we had lost only one, an officer of the Pennsylvania detachment. Some others had received wounds. These were helped back to Stirling's position; along with our prisoners.

Hurried from our sleep out in a field, we had rushed miles to this place only to find an enemy encamped on a high place; from which we had driven him in a single attack. After his dead were piled, I wanted nothing other than to sit. I saw the same wish in the eyes of most of my comrades. It was not to be.

"Sentinels, Elisha," Lieutenant Chapman reminded. "Position them where you will but be sure they have a regard for the stone fence some 60 yards down. And Sergeant, we are ordered to distribute the captured arms to those having but indifferent weapons." I set about the first order on the instant, positioning twice might suffice for a normal encampment. As to the muskets Eli's observation was telling, for the British Brown Bess was far superior to those carried by many of our comrades. We then went him one better, stripping the cartridges from the boxes of our fallen foes.

Dawn came all at once to the hilltop. Within minutes a battery of cannon opened up perhaps a mile to our right, and slightly forward. I had taken the liberty of sitting after all, and Heman soon joined me. To him I turned. "Lord Stirling must be the unhappy recipients of this barrage," I said. "He and his Delaware and Maryland troops."

First one, then a second gun answered from our side. Thin were their barks compared to the roars of the British field artillery. "Be glad it is not us, my friend."

Heavy and instantaneous musket fire hurried us to the overlook. "From the stone fence," I said. With a nod Heman ran, crouching, to his platoon just to my left.

Scarlet coats leapt from behind the piled stones and simultaneously advanced from wooded, high ground farther off. Into them we poured volley fire. Onward they came, pausing to unleash volleys of their own. Rounds whizzed past my head and shoulders but the contours of the hill provided natural cover. Into a bowl-shaped hollow I squeezed. Taking careful aim I squeezed the trigger.

Though the enemy came on smartly, our fire soon stopped the surge. One moment they came steadfastly on; the next they broke and ran. "Cease firing!" Captain Tyler demanded. "Save your powder." He ordered a party forward. Sensing Azariah's eagerness to go I volunteered to lead them. Within minutes we were herding a few wounded prisoners back uphill. Half of my men toted three to four captured muskets each. We scurried back inside our lines even as our regiment's casualties were being carried away.

Eli soon was excused from a meeting of the officers on the lee of our position. He gathered Heman and other sergeants en route. "Gentlemen," he began. "General Parsons congratulates the men under his command for their behavior this day. As do I." Hearing my friend speak so, I was as humbled as any of his audience. "However," he continued, "the General fears we have much bloody work ahead of us. This is how it stands. Lord Stirling is confronted by at least two full brigades. The enemy counts four men to his one. He has thus recalled to him the detachment of riflemen who had been sent to reinforce us. Furthermore, with the enemy's superiority in numbers, we can expect that he will continue to probe our defenses. Among our prisoners we have already discovered soldiers from two different regiments." Eli did not say nor did he need to impress upon us that the 17th was at half-strength. "We simply must not let him turn our flank. Should he do so, he will gain Stirling's rear, and the battle will be at an end. Do you understand me?"

Breed's Hill again, I could not help but think. Except there was no way off of it. Eli's eyes had fixed upon me. As I did not trust my voice

I extended my hand. He took it. Heman's layered over the top of ours, and thence the other men covered his.

Thankfully, our ammunition cart arrived soon after. For in the assault and defense of this spot, we had nearly exhausted our supply of cartridges. I saw to it that our platoon's share was distributed as it ought. Daniel received his allotment with a steady hand.

From our right a battle raged with ebbs and flows of small arms fire. And throughout came the echoing boom of cannon. Though elevated above the surrounding countryside, the forest kept us from seeing what transpired some 300 yards distant. Reports reached us throughout the morning of a hot and bloody action that saw Stirling yield no ground.

Though our own skulls ached with the oppressive heat, and us lacking cover from its onslaught, I took to pitying our nearby comrades. I had not gone far with these imaginings when our sentinels raised another alarm. The Regulars came on as diligently as before, and so it was we received them. In waves they swept up towards us. With salvos we turned them back. Not a quarter hour had passed, yet we had held, with a dozen or more dead or dying men strewn about the slope. We might have had the strength to pursue them, or at least cheer their flight if their retreat had not been within the protective reach of a new regiment upon the field – identified by the kilts they wore.

"Bloody hell," Amasa said. "A third regiment this is..."

A third it was, but they did not attack. Perhaps the rout of their comrades had blunted their ambitions. Perhaps they had other plans than simply another frontal assault. Whatever they had in store for us, our commanders soon dispatched another runner with requests for reinforcements. A half hour passed by but no reply was forthcoming. The officers checked the direction from whence one would come as often as they scanned the enemy encircling our front.

"Elisha?" Daniel asked. "Why has there been no word?"

"Crawl there an' back on my belly I could 'ave by now, Sergeant," Amasa added.

Unless my ears deceived me the battle still raged, but from our rear and not our right flank. I could not conceal my alarm when Azariah sought me out. "Shall I go, Brother?"

"Wait but a moment. I shall get Eli's approval. We'll then go together." Lieutenant Chapman felt the Captain must first approve, and so he hastened to secure this officer's blessing. While we knelt there, looking first to the smudges of scarlet dotting the slopes below us, then listening for the battle sounds over our right shoulders, the report of cannon reached us, from behind and to the left. "Bedford Pass..."

Eli dropped down beside me. "The General is sending scouts now."

"Where?" I said, turning to watch two pair of men race headlong down the hill we had climbed hours earlier.

"Stirling's position. On Gowanus Road. And there," he said, pointing almost directly to our rear.

We waited, and sweated, and tried to not look into one another's faces. Fierce fighting spread in an arc that threatened to encircle us. "Sergeant..." I held up my hand. The scouts burst through the brush below. Only one from each pair, each bolting uphill, and returned far too soon to be carrying a message.

A minute more and the voices of the senior officers reached us where we crouched. Eli was ordered to report at once. The conference ended abruptly. By the time he reached us the Pennsylvania Colonel had pulled his troops from the line. "Eli? What's happening?"

"Stirling is gone."

"What?"

"Gone I said. I don't know where. No one does. Regulars hold Gowanus Road."

"Where are they off to?" I demanded, pointing at the Pennsylvania men.

"He hopes to break through to Stirling. From the firing, the General must have retreated up the road."

"And left us!" Azariah declared.

"We've no time for that," the Lieutenant said. "There are Hessians to our rear. They must have forced Bedford Pass. The General plans to attack them."

"Attack!" Amasa nearly shrieked. "We're cut off an' he aims to attack."

I put my hand on my comrade's arm. No more gently could I restrain him for he'd spoken for every man. As had Azariah. A panic rose inside that had nearly caused me to flee Breed's Hill. Here flight was impossible, it seemed.

"Sergeant Benton," Lieutenant Chapman said, his voice near to breaking. "Please see to it that your platoon is prepared, and at once, to attack towards our rear."

"Aye, Lieutenant," I said.

I had already turned to my disbelieving companions when Eli's hand clasped tight to mine. "In case we," he stammered, "we…"

"May the good Lord watch over you," I said. And with that he was off.

"You heard the Lieutenant," I shouted. "Gather your gear. Prepare to withdraw. To attack…" With a final glance at the enemy to our front, I led my men down the opposite side.

For every 50 yards of forest and swamp we sunk further into an arc of gunfire. Skirmishes broke out to our left, front and right. We pushed through these small swarms of attackers, yet each encounter tore sections of men from the 17th. And on every occasion the size of the assault grew. In coats of red and green our enemy closed upon my comrades.

At some point, and I never heard the order, we reversed course. This abrupt change did nothing to lessen the constant whine of bullets. More men fell. "Are we retreating, Sergeant?" Jacob called out.

"Just stay together. Do not let yourself get separated. Not now." Frantically, I checked to locate my brothers, Heman, all of them. It shocked me each time another face disappeared from our dwindling band.

It shocked me further to realize that I had lost sight of the knot of senior officers. Where they had been fighting, a wedge of scarlet now drove in upon us. Rejoining our commanders was impossible.

"This way!" I cried and the remnant of our platoons veered into standing water. Perhaps across it we might yet find escape. It shocked me to the edge of reason when Heman and Azariah cried out, then fell together.

Chapter 66

The barrels of Amasa, Noah and Adonijah sprouted flame at the same instant. The nearest pursuer reeled backwards into his comrades. Jacob clubbed another Regular who fell at my feet. Discarding my empty musket, I snatched up the enemy's Brown Bess. I brought it up and impaled an onrushing scarlet-coat. With my foot, I dislodged the dying man. Thus did we blunt their charge.

Without pause, screams and shots surged somewhere off to our right. I looked down. Heman, shot in the arm, held Azariah's head above water with the other. "Help me," I yelled to the others and together we dragged both to the edge of the swampy pond. As we dropped upon this scraggly patch of ground, it became apparent that a stand of alders along the bank concealed us somewhat. "Sssh," I whispered to the eight, 10, 12 of us huddled there – Azariah and Daniel among them. "Keep your heads down. No talking." Twelve, I thought, out of so many...

"Brother..."

"Azariah, where are you hit?" He clutched at his waist. Every one of us were bloodied from our frantic flight through brush and bramble. Here so much of it spread beyond the reach of his clenched fingers. "Let me," I said, and gently pried his hands from his hip. He grimaced as I probed the torn flesh. "The ball, thanks be to God, passed clean through. Though it may have nicked the bone." With strips of cloth cut from the blouses of our attackers we staunched the bleeding of our comrades. Jacob, too, for he had fallen in that final clash. He lay prostrate but his chest still rose and fell.

I risked raising my head. A running battle swept through the forest from left to right, some hundred yards to our rear. More firing, cannons too, reverberated farther off on the opposite side.

"No sign a Redcoats just now, Sergeant," Mister Allen reported.

"Thank you, Amasa. Keep a good watch." I sank back down. No Colonel. No Captain. And no Eli. Surrounded we were, and I had lost track of which way led north; which south.

Azariah studied my face; despite his pain. "The Regiment went off to the east, Brother," he said.

"The east. Yes." I patted his bloody, pointing hand. "So the General, he means to break through to Flatbush. Get behind them as they did us; and strive to escape." A spasm of fire forced our heads low. For a minute or more it roared; besting the crashing of heavy bodies breaking through undergrowth. I had to remind myself to breathe. Then, mercifully, there came a type of quiet again. "Can you walk, Brother?" I asked. Azariah lifted himself to one elbow, shuddered violently and fell back.

Daniel clambered over another to catch hold of Azariah's sweat-soaked head. "What's to be done, Elisha?"

Somehow it seemed so clear. So horrid yet so clear. "Mister Allen. Men."

"Sergeant."

"We are to work our way around the edge of this pond. The ground rises beyond it. Whilst we have holed up here, no soldiers have come that way. Beyond it, perhaps a few miles on, lies Flatbush. We all know the terrain thereabouts. Once there, head north and east, keeping always to the ridge and its trees. You must keep out of sight. Use the night to try to reach the coast. Wallabout Bay this will be. With luck you'll find a boat. Take it by force if you must, and cross over to Manhattan." I stared at them each in turn. No reaction did I see.

"Why are you telling us this, Elisha?" It was Daniel who had spoken. "Elisha…"

"One of us must make it, Brother," I replied. "Our family must have the one."

"No! I will not leave you." So forcefully did he brush the hair from Azariah's brow that I thought he must do our brother a hurt. I stopped his hand. "Please. Elisha. Do not make me go…"

"Daniel, you must. Think of Mother, the children, even Father. They need you most of all. And I, forgive me, but I've not the strength to leave our brother."

Azariah's pale fingers rose up and came to rest atop ours. "I thank you for that, Brother," he said. "Though I'd rather you not throw your life away."

"Lie back," I told him, cradling his head. "Daniel," I whispered. "It must be now. Go!"

Tears flooded his eyes. He nodded quickly. "You have my oath," he murmured, and turned away.

"Mister Allen," I said. "You will lead all who can walk. Men, you are to follow his every command. Now go. Godspeed." They did then, with each taking us by the hand as they crept passed. Heman declined to leave our side. Daniel lingered till the last, then he too moved away. "Daniel," I whispered, almost too late. "Let them know what happened here. Tell them we love them. Tell her." Unable to reply, he held his arm aloft and vanished into the dense brush.

"Will they make it, do you think?" Heman asked.

"I wish you had accompanied them," I replied. I allowed myself to wonder whether we might escape. Midafternoon it must be and with the thickening clouds dark would fall fast this day. Perhaps under cover of night… "Heman. What of young Jacob?"

"He is not conscious, Elisha, but he lives. I would venture the same can be said of that groaning lad there. From Brewster's company would be my guess."

"I think you're right. The other I do not recognize at all. And what of you?" I asked, for Heman's skin seemed exceedingly pale, even for him. He shrugged, then winced. The odds, then, did not favor...

"Listen," Azariah said, without opening his eyes.

The snapping of fallen branches came again. Louder this time. I felt about in my cartridge box. Empty. Slowly I lifted the Brown Bess with its bloodied tip of steel. With it I tracked the increasing rustle of leaves. The flashes of color were scarlet.

I rose up onto one knee. First one then another broke through the thickets lining the pond's edge. Coats of red they wore with brilliant white waistcoats and breeches. Half a dozen became a dozen – light infantry every one of them. In their center a British lieutenant emerged, and he with his drawn sword held at the ready. Just feet away, they were.

The bayonet I pointed at his chest. "Elisha!" Heman said. "We've no choice. Ask for mercy."

"They'll kill us regardless, Brother," Azariah whispered. "We might as well die fighting." He got hold of a musket by the stock, but could not lift it.

The British officer smiled without parting his lips. His soldiers followed his slow advance upon our island. Step by step into the water they waded; ankle deep then to their shins. "Your companions speak true, rebel," he said. "Your options are poor and few." The smile vanished. The long blade began to rise. At its movement the score of grim-faced men forged closer, their bayonets probing like steel fangs.

"For God's sake, Elisha," Heman said. "Beg quarter. What chance have we?"

My friend's voice drew the head of the British officer. He stared at the prone, bloodied Sergeant, and the Continentals strewn about. He stared at me, the lone opponent still upon his feet. "I am sorely tempted to serve you rebels out," he said. "Were you not half-dead already. Let the choice fall to you. Death, or surrender?"

At this I let the barrel sink, until the deadly point buried itself in the muck. "We surrender."

"You must address me as sir! Please accept our surrender, sir!" Letting the musket fall, I pleaded precisely as he had demanded.

Our captors had at first ordered us to our feet. Even the most hateful amongst them soon realized that only by carrying our wounded might this bloodied remnant of the 17th ever reach any destination. An hour or more passed before our staggering mass emerged onto Gowanus Road. Our captors prodded us against an outside wall of a stone house set mere rods beyond the reach of the creek's flood stage. Here bodies lay like ruined crops about the absent family's fields. The coats of both armies draped the fallen.

All those held prisoner wore Continental colors - chiefly shades of blue or brown for those fortunate enough to retain their coats. Seated between my friend and my brother, I surveyed those surrounding us. Devastated the whole appeared. "Alive we are," I murmured, "but no longer free."

Heman's head hung low. Azariah, on his back and motionless, stared blankly up at a leaden sky that had once more begun to leak rain. If our torment held a virtue, it rested in the relentless wet that masked men's tears.

One of the soldiers who had joined us during our flight, gut-shot and bled dry, died late in the afternoon. Sergeant Baker kept hold of the lad's hand long after his soul had departed. Eventually I reached over and gently separated the living from the dead.

"What was the boy's name?" I asked.

"Timothy. Turning eighteen on the morrow. He kept telling me so."

His cries at the end had been horrible to hear. I could not deny a certain gratitude that they had ceased. For his sake, certainly, but also for our own. "He is at peace now, my friend."

From the slight rise in ground I could make out the nearest of the American entrenchments. Though it did me no good my eyes kept drifting to the outline of Fort Box, fashioned in part by the work of my brother's hands. I turned to him and wiped his brow with a bit of rag. He forced a smile for me.

Suddenly, a wave of red crested the higher ground to the rear. Rank after rank of Regulars tromped by, heading northeast. Their battle flags and the markings on the soldiers' headgear gave testament to two distinct regiments – each different from the three we had fought earlier. Drums beat them ever forward.

"It's more company you rebels will soon have," one British soldier mocked. Encouraged by his mates he added, "By nightfall we'll lay claim to yonder works!"

"Damn their black hearts..." Heman murmured.

I watched the column as it passed. Black their hearts may be, but their discipline could hardly be equaled. "None can deny that they are well led," I said.

"What's that?"

"In Charlestown, remember how they charged straight uphill at us. Brave yet foolish. Today they swept right 'round. Though how I know not..."

"They were everywhere. And all at once." Heman clutched his injured arm. "May Stirling be damned for deserting us."

"He did not desert us, Heman. His command is here." I gestured to the captive and the slain. "Come," I said. "Its high-time we fixed you up properly. The pair of you." Over Heman's objections, I removed the shirt from Timothy's corpse. With teeth alone, for they'd confiscated our knives, I tore it into strips. These I used to bind their wounds. From my coat pocket I produced a handful of sea-biscuits. Heman accepted a couple. Azariah ignored my offer. "You must eat, Brother. If you are to live you must eat."

Finally, he accepted the offering pressed to his lips.

For two days and two nights following the battle, the wind and the rain drove hard from the northeast. Whenever both let up, fog closed in. Hour after hour we prayed that our comrades would avenge us, or failing that, escape our fate. Despite nature's onslaught, our enemy toiled. Employing picks and shovels they extended their trenches closer to the imposing line of forts.

"How right you're proven, Elisha," Heman said. "There'll be no frontal assault this time. They dare not."

Suddenly aware of the warfare to come, and seething that we would lie here whilst it unfolded, Azariah tried to rise. "Save your strength, Brother," I commanded. "You show signs of mending. Besides, there is nothing we might do to alter the outcome."

A stench permeated the air. Bodies, bloating in the dank heat, were strewn about the burned barn into which a hundred men or more had been herded. I resolved to volunteer on the morrow to join the prisoners pressed into a burial detail.

"Tomorrow," Heman whispered. "'Tis sure. By then the Regulars will reach our lines. We'll see fighting sure enough. Washington and the lads will serve them out good and proper."

I shared my friend's confidence regarding the resumption of the battle. With what I had seen of the respective armies, however, I concluded we were outnumbered a good three to one.

The next day brought breaks in the clouds. It also saw breaches forced in the Continental defenses. From where we sat, we waited for the crash of cannon and the volley of gunfire. Instead we heard silence. It was not long before our guards could be heard feverishly murmuring.

"What's that they say?" I asked Heman, who occupied a spot at the building's corner.

"Gone! Washington's army; vanished in the night..."

"How can that be?"

"'Tis so. It's what they all whisper to each other."

"The Massachusetts sailors. They must have rowed them clean away."

"Yes, Elisha! Under cover of the fog."

"How extraordinary!"

"Then it's true..." Azariah said without lifting even his head.

"What is, Brother?"

"That we here are abandoned. Our fates are sealed."

Each day brought accumulating pangs of deprivation and ceaseless humiliations dished out to those who had lost nearly everything. With the arrival of additional captives, we were forced inside the ruined building. The crowding of soiled and bloodied bodies fomented a pestilent air. Our wounded endured unrelenting pain. No medical care did they receive beyond our pitiful ministrations. The more recent captives shared news of further battlefield reverses. Each defeat drove Washington and the army farther away from where we languished on this desolate tip of Long Island. Men, even those generally regarded as being of substance, began to speak of death as a welcome state. And more did die, one or two hauled away with each morn.

In the light of a late September dawn so chilly we could see our breath in thin strands, I discovered Jacob Brown peering up. Gone was the twisted agony that had masked his face for weeks. In his peaceful features I recognized the boy with whom we had served. The lad was gone.

I closed his sightless eyes. How cool his skin felt. "He spoke during the night," I said. "To whom I know not. His parents perchance.

But more words at one time than he ever shared before." A laugh suddenly escaped my lips. Before I could determine what had caused it, I laughed again.

"Elisha?" Heman asked. "What ails?"

"All this time and I never really made note of his voice. A true baritone he possessed, Heman. And he so slight." Laughter came again, in broken bursts; though I could as easily have wept. My friend's hand upon my arm gradually stilled me.

Azariah, Heman and I occupied a corner of the stone foundation. The cramped quarters possessed a single virtue. A wayward shell had blasted a hole somewhat larger than a man's head a few feet up from the dirt floor. Through it the morning light shined each day. This provided an opportunity to study the construction of the wall. On occasion, when the breeze blew onshore, air wafted in carrying scents that disguised the rot and decay. At such times we would haul Azariah to a seating position. Though it pained him, we did this. His indifference in fact led me to insist on it. "Breathe it in, Brother. Can you not smell the sea?"

"What is that to me? Lay me down will you."

After a bit I did as he had asked. In the shaft of light I examined his wound. It had closed better than I had hoped, but still my brother was weak as a lamb. Without fresh air and more to eat, he...

"I recognize the scent," Heman said, his nostrils pressed tight to the opening. "It's the salt I smell. A farmer I may be but nothing finer did I..."

"Hey you! Aye, farmer. I mean you. How's about giving some others a chance." The heavy-set corporal from another regiment had spoken. He emphasized his interest in the opening with a yank on Heman's sleeve. My friend winced and cradled his wounded arm.

"Leave off," I warned.

"What's that ya say, friend?"

"You gave up that very place to claim the one you now possess. What right have you to demand it back again?"

"It's mighty observant you are, friend."

"Enough so to note that in the three days that you've perched there by the entry, you've enjoyed first dibs on the rations."

"Do ya dispute my turn at the portions?"

"If pressed, I might indeed dispute how you came upon possession of those rights. For I've not forgotten how you pushed another from that very spot."

The corporal's face reddened. "And do ya now think ta push me from it," he said very low.

"If I intend anything, friend, it is for you to leave my true friends be. That, and for you to content yourself with your current place. You chose it after all."

The color darkened to purple, yet the corporal said nothing more. Still rubbing his upper arm, Heman winked to Azariah. My brother had actually raised his head on his own. "Does the chance of a row lift your spirits, Brother?" I asked.

He let his head drop back to the dirt. "It matters little to me. However it might end, we remain as before - prisoners."

"Then what would you say to attempting an escape?"

"Escape?"

"Sssh! If you're to hear the plan, you'll have to join us when we are let out for our daily airing."

Chapter 67

To add insult to our injuries, they put Tories in charge of us. Two of them herded everyone out that afternoon. Heman and I hauled Azariah between us. His left leg could support some weight; his injured right side none whatsoever.

"We mustn't fall behind," I said.

"Not unless you want a steel tip in your buttocks," Heman replied.

Three sets of local men took shifts guarding us. These fellow Americans treated us far worse than any of the British Regulars. And of the six, this pair took the most pleasure in prodding prisoners with their bayonets. "How queer a thing..." I muttered.

"What is?" Heman asked.

"Never mind that," Azariah interrupted. "Speak of this escape. What is your plan?"

Checking the placement of the guards I whispered, "Why, through the shot hole, Brother."

"Not the one in the foundation," Heman replied.

"Our sister could not fit through that," Azariah agreed.

"Not as it stands, no. But have you not wondered why I stand watch over the spot so possessively? Or why I choose to shove my face inside the opening, and holler to our Tory friends about the weather or the date?"

"Glad I am for one," Heman said, "to learn you have cause. I'd begun to wonder if you'd grown mad with the confinement."

Azariah smiled at this jest; the first I'd seen upon his face in many a week. "Tell us, Brother!"

"Well. First off. From my perch I've spied the coastline. Gowanus Bay. Of that I've no doubt. Not half a mile distant it is, and downhill the entire way from that side of our prison."

"Can it be so?"

"Indeed. With but one sentinel upon each of the building's corners. And what's more, only onc to watch the entirety of our side when nature calls the other away."

"What of the opening?" Heman demanded. "If a girl cannot..."

"Give me a moment, my friend. The ball fractured the masonry. For two nights running I've broken small chunks away with my bare hands. I'm convinced enough can be pulled free, in time, to enable us to squeeze through some night."

"What of the noise?"

"Neither of you heard me thus far, but 'tis true. Pulling clear larger pieces could make a racket. It must be the right night. When the hole is grown large enough, we'll depart under the cover of a storm."

The weeks piled up much more quickly than did the wall come down. After the first shattered pieces had been pried loose, the going became much harder. Heman and I took turns, each ripping our fingertips raw as wc gouged away with stone fragments. Sharp and hard enough they were, but we had no leverage. And we could not afford to strike one with another for fear of alerting the guards.

September became October. With a shard, I scratched each passing day of our confinement on the wall. Other than the lengthening rows of marks, little differentiated one day from the next. The sky grew grayer and the nights colder. Men still died each night; more now from disease than from wounds suffered in battle. We survivors had come to accept our current plight, though some of us resisted the thought that this would be our fate. Azariah continued to heal, though far too slowly. Without the hope of eventual escape, I feared for him.

Each day the Tories strove to break our will, but we were familiar with nearly all of their cruel tricks. Most of our number had been mocked or knocked to the ground for sins no greater than lingering at the pit with loose bowels. Many bore nicks, as did I, from the tips of their bayonets. Neither their barbs nor their stabs hurt overmuch anymore. The worst of their lot we named 'Prod' for his liberality with the bayonet.

A few treasures had been discovered, and these men shared. Sufficient spoons we had such that each grouping of six could share one to slurp up the tasteless gruel they served out. As a group leader, I was entrusted with one such valuable possession. I also had within my care a penknife. Amos, the most recent addition to my half dozen, had secreted this rarity past the vigilant Tories, though not even me would he tell how. After a moment's reflection I determined to not ask where he might have concealed it. Though we tore the stale bread they fed us into chunks, on occasion they provided horsemeat or nearly rancid salt pork. When the slim blade was pried from its carved handle, it proved suitable for carving - of a sorts. This service I performed on any and all meat left at the entry.

In personal treasures I had been less fortunate. The trek through the swamp had destroyed Jemima's letter. Her earlier notes, tucked safely I had thought within my field pouch, had been taken at my capture. Thus did I lose most of what I possessed. The coins I still fingered now and then, concealed within the lining of my coat. These I envisioned might yet see us home, should other attempts fail. It would not do to chance a bribe with these Yorkers, however. They preferred our deaths to sterling.

"What are you figuring, Elisha?" Heman asked.

I stopped toying with our spoon. I had made up my mind. “A moment, my friend.” I looked around at the others. At the entry Amos carefully balanced the wood platter as our group’s portion was ladled onto it. He rejoined us and set his paltry yet precious cargo in our midst. I held out the spoon. I began, speaking in hushed tones. “What do you say to our using this, to dig?” They stared at our prized utensil.

“Will it get us out sooner?” Azariah asked.

“It will give us leverage, whereas now we have none. It is more stout than the knife, which dare not be risked.”

“Will the digging not spoil it?” asked one of the men whose injuries required us to feed him.

“To hell with our lips and tongues,” Amos said. “Let us put it to work this very night.”

He had begun helping Heman and me from the first. The gleam in his dark eyes now made me smile. I extended the spoon to him. He had been afforded the right to eat first in thanks for his sharing of the knife. We all now watched him eagerly sup, winking at one and all.

November brought winds howling from the northwest. If we did not make the break soon, winter would render doing so impossible. Yet we were close. Amos, with his narrow shoulders, had fit within the slowly yielding opening since the week before. I had even offered that he try on his own, but he refused - insisting that we leave or stay together. His honor in this relieved me immensely, for like him I feared that even should he get away clean, our captors would discover how he managed it and seal the opening. As it was, Heman could also now wedge his upper body inside. The injuries to the other two of our band prevented them from coming with us, but they had sworn to secrecy. Azariah and I were the remaining handicap, with too-wide shoulders. It was agreed that until we could each pass through the opening, none would.

During that evening I could smell the approaching storm. Feverishly I dug at the mortar underlying a critical stone. Our escape could be, finally, at hand. Frigid the air was, but many were the hours of darkness granted us. If this last could be dislodged, we might slither free during the coming tempest.

Raised voices and moving lights forced me back down.

"Elisha," Heman said. "What is it?"

Before I could speak a re-doubled guard of Royalists stomped in among us. At any moment I expected them to haul me forth. Into Amos' hand I slipped the knife. "On your feet, you rebel scum!" shouted the nearest. He stepped right over me so that he might rip blankets from those few who had them. "Walk or be dragged, it's out ya come!"

Heman, Amos and I hoisted our fellows upright. Minutes more and every man had been herded outside. A biting wind carried right through our clothes. Azariah began at once to shiver.

Lined up a stone's throw away and facing us were ranks of soldiers - their coats too dark for Regulars. "Continentals, are they?" Amos asked.

"Prisoners," Heman replied. "Just like us."

But they were not like us. How straight flowed their lines, even by the light of lanterns. How shrunken and in disarray we seemed by comparison. The shouts of an officer jolted their ranks into motion. Straight towards us they marched. As they neared, I recognized the shocked, angry expressions of men newly captured. Those bloodied were freshly so, and more than one cried out in his private agonies.

"How well fed they seem..." murmured one of our number.

Truly flesh seemed to have melted from our bodies when these stout strangers approached to within an arm's length. "What regiment are you?" I asked a passing Corporal. "What befell your company?"

"Fort Washington," he spat back. "Them bastards took it from us. And Manhattan besides I should think." His words spread like a contagion throughout our huddled mass. Rank after rank of them carried on, straight into our refuge.

"We can't all of us fit inside there," someone muttered behind me. "Where are we ta sleep? What's ta become of us?" he wailed.

"Have no fear, rebel," scoffed Prod, and he a corporal. "We've a new home for the likes a you."

"A right floatin' palace it is," chortled one of his mates.

"Mind your duty you two," ordered the British sergeant. "If we lose even one of them that's fresh caught, I'll have the skin off your backs."

Our guards relished the work of forming us into a column. So plodding was our pace, however, that even the most cruel among them soon tired of driving us along the road heading north. On an impulse I glanced back. I regretted it at once. Though I could not discern the hole so near the corner of the rectangular black shape, I knew its location all too well. How many times, hundreds most like, had I dreamt of reaching this very spot; with none but my friends about me, and on the road to freedom.

"Keep moving!" the corporal shouted. The stock of his musket drove home his demand.

Northwards we went, till we passed through what had been our defensive line. Rather than continue to Fulton Ferry we veered right. Downhill we staggered. Wind and rain lashed at us but did not last. Not even my prediction of the weather had proven correct this night. At the coast the shore opened up in a sweeping curve, visible in the pale light of the moon. Wallabout Bay, I recalled from my study of Eli's map. Had he escaped that encirclement in August I wondered anew? And what of Daniel? Was he now home, and safe? Would the entire family be together this eve? And Jemima...

"A warship," someone muttered. "Will ya look at the size of it?"

We had reached a strip of sand. Not a quarter mile off the beach a dark, imposing shape rode at anchor. "A hulk," I whispered, remembering the mast-shorn vessels settling into the opposite side of this same East River.

"They cannot mean to take us aboard that," Azariah said. These were his first words since we'd been forced outside.

Within mere minutes a good half of us had been ordered into boats drawn up at the water's edge. Those able were forced to man an oar, and row. I hauled with neither skill nor relish, despite the prodding attention of the corporal seated behind me. Each creaking pull drew us closer.

"Man-a-war my eye," scoffed Amos on the bench beside me. "Sailed merchantmen as boy an' man, and that there's a transport as I live and breathe."

"It's breathe through yer back it'll be if ya don' pipe down!" the guard promised.

The helmsman must have yanked the boat's rudder hard over, for we circled 'round behind the wooden behemoth. Painted letters on the stern had long faded. "The *Whitby*," Amos whispered. I know of that name..."

"You there, tall fellow," the guard called. "Grab hold of that rope ladder. Hold it still whilst the others climb."

I did as he ordered. Ropes secured wooden slats along its entire length. The whole writhed like a serpent when each captive labored upwards. I held tight and surveyed the curving wall above. A double tier of small holes had been cut in the massive sides. Iron bars barricaded the squares, not two feet across. Every 10 feet or so another such dark opening loomed. As the last able man stepped clear, a sling was lowered. I hoisted up Azariah who had lain silent in the bottom of the boat. As I slipped the rope beneath his armpits, he stared at the distant shore. "It is up we must go now, Brother," I said.

"We will rot here. In this cage of theirs..."

A sharp haul on the sling stole Azariah from my grasp. He cried out upon banging the steep side. The rest of the ordeal he bore in silence. I scrambled up after him.

Chapter 68

We passed single file into a type of blockhouse constructed on the stern. Here our names were scribbled down. We were made to strip. Naked and shivering we stood whilst they searched our miserable rags.

"We've a cure for your stench," a private promised. He proceeded to douse me with a bucket of frigid seawater. His friend so relished my gasp that he scarce paid attention to my coat. Against my chest he tossed it a moment later, having failed to take note of the coins hidden there.

Hurriedly I dressed myself, and Azariah too, for he could not haul his breeches up over his soaked skin. At the ladder fixed to the wall of the upper deck, I guided him down to Heman. With one of us on either side we made our way. The line stopped at the main hatch, a large, raised square in the middle of the deck. My head rocked back at the indescribable stench that billowed up as though from hell itself.

Azariah twisted so in my arms that I nearly lost my hold. "No more of this, Brother! You'll do yourself a hurt."

"Down with ya, rebels! It's the ladder or the bayonet!"

"Go first, Heman! I'll hand Azariah down."

"That's a wild one ya have there," Prod noted. Was this Tory to pursue us even into the depths? Short and rotund he was, but with a sneer that seemed a permanent expression. His lip curled more deeply as he studied my reaction. "We'll soon learn him what's right. You as well if ya don' show respect."

Having heaved Azariah's lower body over the lip of the hatch, I now forced his head below. "He will be no trouble, corporal. It is his wounds make him..."

"To the devil with 'im and you besides. Now down ya go."

My companions had stayed close to the base of the ladder - with Azariah propped up by the other two. In the shaft of moonlight they huddled like apparitions. Told to clear away by those above, I led off into the blackness. A single collision with the low roof taught me to bend low. I professed apologies with every step, for torsos and limbs lay every which way at my feet. Like cordwood, men were entwined. Twice before I reached an open space, oaths and threats railed up from the depths. Once when entreaties failed, I offered to respond with blows. Nothing came of it.

Exhausted, we four sank down; I with my back to the sloped wall. A dim square higher up offered hope that dawn would reveal one of the openings. The earthier scent of beasts filled my nostrils. Cattle, I guessed, had been the *Whitby*'s prime cargo. Now men crammed its decks. And we smelled near as bad.

At some point I must have slept. I only recall waking, and with a start. The dream I did not remember, but it had drenched me in sweat. On an impulse I groped about, and found Azariah's back. Exhaling, I settled against the hull. Only then, intent on listening to every new sound, did I sense the movement. First a slow, ever so slight roll in one direction; then back again. Though deep waters had always filled me with unease, somehow this gentle rocking soothed me. Something at least, if only the sea, was alive in this place.

Ship's bells startled us awake. The unfastening and removal of the hatch drowned out the sound. A shaft of gray light dropped straight into the hold. Behind it, creeping along, came delicate fingers of air. Whatever freshness it promised died before reaching us, though the chill remained. Low, massive beams formed the ceiling of our prison. Groaning, writhing forms blanketed the floor. On the wall, an opening did exist but dawn had not yet found it.

On deck the full force of November's icy grip seized our sweat-drenched bodies. Our spasmodic jaws rendered speech nigh impossible. From the hatch upright forms surged onto the deck like creatures released from a nighttime crypt. Their upper bodies retained the hunched posture demanded by the unforgiving beams down below. Some hundreds there were.

Those who had belongings piled them to one side. Most wearing tattered naval uniforms laid ditty bags down. Rare it was to see a soldier who boasted a knapsack. Far too many lacked coats, while a few stumbled about half-naked and shoeless.

"Bless me," Amos said. "Look at the state of them." In truth, though we had compared but poorly to the captured garrison of Fort Washington, next to these gaunt figures we seemed fit as fiddles.

"You there," the British sergeant said, with his finger aimed at my chest. "Aye, you. You're to join the party that brings up the bodies." His was an order, not a request. I fell in with three others. Back down we went. For the next hour or so we dragged into the shaft of light men who had died overnight.

"Try ta avoid touching the flesh of them that's died a the pox," said the fellow paired with me. Gray hair he had, in a long plait that fell across broad shoulders.

Smallpox had ravaged those in Roxbury, but not till our company had returned to Connecticut. How fortunate we had thought ourselves then. "How will I know?" I asked.

"Trust me, lad. You'll spot he who's been taken by the pox soon as ya see it." He shuddered suddenly. "Jus' take me word fer it."

On deck at last I sank down, panting, beside my companions. "Nine," I said. "In a single night..."

Heman laid his hand on my back. "We know, my friend. They set Amos and me to wrapping them in strips of canvas; old sails by the look. He kept up a count as they lowered the bodies over the side."

"What? They simply tossed them in the sea?"

"Heaven forbid," Amos said. "They're rowing them back to the beach."

"So they are to be buried. We can be grateful for that, at least."

"Not to them right bastards," Amos replied. "Probably only planting 'em in sand so as they won't pop up against the side of their ship."

Normally our new companion's feistiness brought me a measure of joy. This conversation, however, I was beginning to find tiresome at best. "Amos! What is it you're doing with my brother's head?"

He rooted about in Azariah's matted hair and produced a small, gray, wriggling form. "Plucking vermin," he replied; popping it.

I turned away in disgust. Within minutes, though, I requested the same grooming, for I now knew the source of the itching that had plagued me since waking. Tucked close to the waist-high gunwale, and somewhat protected from the wind, we probed each other's scalps and clothing. Sometimes, especially in Azariah's case, one man worked on him, whilst in turn, his tiny tormentors were nabbed by another. For each we seized, however, many more scurried into whatever crease and fold that offered.

"Did you enjoy your biscuit an' beef?" Heman asked me one afternoon when the sun shined low and fierce across the deck, yet without heat.

"Biscuit an' gristle, more like," Amos answered.

"Then it must be a Tuesday," I said. "And in December, too. Soon a new year will commence."

Heman sucked on his pipe though he'd exhausted his supply of tobacco long before. He now raised it high as if to toast the coming season. Azariah ignored our chatter. As was often the case of late, he paid no one any mind.

"Can I check your bandage, Brother?" I asked him.

"As you wish."

Already I had near exhausted my modest stash of coin for clean wrappings, and the occasional scrap of real meat. My brother had never asked the source of these offerings. He'd certainly never thanked me. The British sergeant of the first watch had, in fact, proved far more gracious when accepting my pittance in return for medicine or food. Even Azariah's body resisted my ministrations, for his wound that once seemed so near to healing, had resorted to redness and oozing. "Brother," I said, pinning his breeches in place once more. "You really must eat up what they give us. I understand how meager it is, and how awful..." A tug at my sleeve brought me 'round.

Heman it was who had hold of me. "Elisha," he whispered. "Best leave him be."

"But have you seen how inflamed it is of late? It refuses to heal."

He leaned close. "Have you considered, my dear friend, that your brother may wish it so..."

I yanked my arm free. "Damn you for that, Heman Baker." Up I went. "Damn you all."

Disease had pursued us from the beginning. Ailments of various description claimed countless men, battered in limb and spirit. Some we carried aboard, no doubt. Other afflictions sprung from the foul kettles in which our putrid meats soaked, or crawled up from the rat-infested lower hold. All, in time, feasted upon our weakened flesh through open sores and bites. Half-starved we were. With winter's onset, and perpetually chilled to our bones, our remaining defenses crumpled.

So weak had we become, that the derrick used to bring water casks up from the boats was now employed in conveying corpse after corpse from below. How I loathed this task. A pair of lifeless feet, robbed of their shoes and as cold as dangling icicles, bumped hard against my temple in transit. I gave them a shove that sent them clear of the hatch. I cursed. Gathering my strength, I swung my leg up onto the deck. "That's the last of them, sergeant," I gasped.

"Very well." The sergeant made a check with a flick of the quill. "Sew this one up," he ordered Heman. "Corporal. Soon as he's finished have this body winched over the side. Do we have a name?"

I shook my head, leaving it to him to find one of the dead man's mates. My labors finished for the day, I took my place between Azariah and Heman. I still struggled to engage the one in talk, whilst the other I spoke to regularly - though without the warmth we had always enjoyed.

"That last had the pox," Heman said. I nodded. "That makes three in the one night," he added. This was not news to me for I had handed the larger share of them up from below. I had half a mind to tell him so. "Amos volunteered to help catch rats rather than be so near the dead." Yet another development that I did not wish to be reminded of. "Elisha. It's spreading."

"You think I don't know as much!" I practically shouted.

With his good arm he restrained me. "You might look to Azariah," he whispered. He then took his leave of me. I sat stiff against the gunwale, head turning neither left nor right. My breath came in shallow pants. In time my breathing calmed. Tears followed. How they burned.

There was no mistaking the pink rash. Advancing down from my sleeping brother's scalp it peeked out from his hairline. Surrounded by a sky and a sea fashioned of lead, his forehead fairly blazed.

Waking of a sudden he stared up at me. "A drink, Brother?" he begged. "I'm parched." I fetched the tin cup from its hook by the cask. With a rag I wiped the sweat from his brow, feverish despite the bite in the wind.

Each dawn I marked the progress of the dread disease. It proceeded stage by stage as was its wont. How well I knew its course. Flat, reddish lesions gained a foothold. Soon they ruled over those once-smooth cheeks. They advanced along my brother's neck to his shredded collar and beyond. Beneath the blanket and the remnants of his shirt the rash claimed all that remained of him. The body that had once served him so well, was now laid waste.

One evening, soon after they had sent us below, Amos announced his intention of leaving our mess. By the light of a distant lamp, tears glistened there in his eyes. Seeing them did nothing to lessen the pain of his desertion – at such a time. "If not for my wife," he said. "For the sake of my children..."

By way of reply I laid down his penknife. He shook his head. I left the farewells to Heman. He, at least, had stayed by our side. I concentrated instead on mopping Azariah's brow, only to find his eyes fixed upon me. "Forgive me, Brother," he said, in a voice I scarce recognized, "for having let you down."

"You've never," I replied. After a harried moment of confusion I asked, "Do you mean Roxbury? Fret not over that, Azariah. To kill another is a shocking thing. I know."

He grinned. The corner of his lips actually crinkled the way they always had. Oh, that there could have been more light. "No, not Roxbury, Brother," he said. "Though it is strange, is it not. That for all I loved to hunt, how I loathed killing. I am glad there'll be no more of it.

Not for me." He might speak of any topic whatsoever, even death, and I would welcome it. To have him back beside me. My little brother back again... "No, Elisha," he said, the voice weaker now. "I regret Gowanus Road. If I had but discovered a way out, you might have escaped this place."

"Fret not. There was none."

"Why even now, you might be with Jemima ... and she your wife ... my sister..."

His eyelids fluttered, then closed. I dabbed at his forehead and spoke to him. He needed no forgiveness. I told him so. Content I was to be at his side, I said. Yet no matter what I insisted, and pleaded too, he spoke no more. The fire in his body burned hot and hotter.

During the night Azariah arched up in a spasm of pain. I caught him before he pitched to the planking. I held him fast until at last his spent form sank back. His tortured limbs burned despite air that vaporized each breath. I had to break the thin crust of ice within the bucket with a closed hand. Gently as I could I laid the cloth upon his pustule-pocked skin.

"Who's there?" he asked in the darkness.

"It's me. Elisha."

"I'm cold, Brother. So cold."

I cradled his head to my chest. Side to side I rocked him. "I will never leave you, Brother."

"No," he whispered. "I know you never would."

It was Heman's arm upon mine that woke me. Dawn had come. Around Azariah my own arms still wrapped. How cool and still he lay within my embrace. At long last the invading heat had relinquished its hold. "Brother?" I asked.

"Let him be, my friend," Heman said. "He walks now with God."

Chapter 69

The others on our detail made no fuss when I insisted Azariah be hoisted up last. I clung to the hold's ladder so that I might prevent his body from banging as it rose. Panting, I guided him over the hatch and down onto the deck. There Heman knelt, canvas at the ready. I sagged beside him. He plied the needle as he had so many times before. Except in this case the gathering folds engulfed not a stranger, nor a comrade even, but my beloved Brother.

"The last stitch, my friend. Do you wish to draw it through?"

I shook my head no, but then stuck out my hand so suddenly that Heman nearly pierced it. "A moment..." My fingertips traced the pallid cheek. How cool felt his skin. How at peace his expression. "Azariah. Brother..."

"Clear away!" ordered the Tory corporal. "Off him now, or we'll have ya over the side with 'im." Prod circled the tip of his bayonet directly above Azariah's canvas clad feet.

"Stick him and I'll kill you," I vowed.

The corporal's eyes narrowed to slits. He positioned his feet for a thrust. I shifted mine to accept my weight.

"He died of the pox!" Heman warned. The guard hesitated. "Aye, infected from head to toe. If you sink your steel in his body you might as well cast it and your musket overboard. To touch it would be your death." The man's eyes widened now. They darted from us to his weapon, then to the prostrate form. Back shrank the blade.

"What's all this about?" the British sergeant demanded. "Speak up, Mister Loring!"

The corporal came to attention. "These prisoners, sir. They won't give up the corpse."

The sergeant glanced at the face in its shroud. "Your brother is it?" I nodded. "You did your best," he said. "No shame in that. His death was unavoidable. Once he caught the pox."

The humanity in his tone awakened the ache in my chest. "Let me accompany him, sergeant," I pleaded. "Allow me to join the burial detail." Instinctively my fingers clutched at the pocket of my coat. One coin remained and ready I was to tear the lining out to get at it.

His gaze followed my movement. His head shook side to side. "No," he firmly replied. "That I cannot do. Not for charity or any other cause. You no longer have the strength, and it is strong men needed for work with the shovels and picks."

Never had I felt my confinement, nor my condition more. Heman, having bitten off the thread, encircled me with his arm. "Sergeant!" I begged, falling forward on all fours. "Please. Would you see that he is buried above the high tide mark? And that his name be spoken at the last."

The man removed his cap. "That I can promise you. Now get up, man, for the sake of heaven!" I could have kissed his boot with gratitude. Instead I rose, slowly, painfully, and with Heman's help. "His name?" he asked.

"My brother's name is Azariah. Azariah Benton."

The sergeant gave a curt nod, then spun on his heel. "As the hoist is secure, Mister Loring," he said, "have the deceased lifted clear of the deck." With that he grabbed hold of the accommodation ladder and went over the side.

The guard gave us a last sneer before following. "You rebels may have the sergeant twisted 'round yer fingers but it's me who'll have the last laugh." He swung one leg over the rail. "It's piss on yer brother's grave I will."

Heman held me fast. The guard's brutish laugh echoed up along the hull.

I could make out the knot of soldiers on the distant beach, but relied upon Heman's sharp sight to tell me of the happenings. In silence I watched and waited, tears blurring my vision time and again. At last he turned, and pulled me down beside him.

"It unfolded as you had wished, my friend," he said. "The sergeant is proved a man of his word."

We all had spotted rotted corpses plucked forth by the tides and carried out to sea. To have Azariah safely beyond the reach of the waves somehow proved a great relief. With my hands I cradled my face. "And Prod?"

"He got nowhere near your brother's grave. It seems the sergeant put him in charge of those standing guard at the boat."

"Thanks be to God."

"Aye, our Father in heaven still looks down on us it seems. Perhaps some good tidings will come our way at long last." His hand had come to rest on my coat. There was no mistaking the bright rash. It shined on his outstretched wrist as might a beacon. Seeing it exposed, he drew back his arm.

"How long, Heman? How many days has it been?"

Ever so slowly he lifted his tattered sleeve. He stared at it. "The day before Azariah's delirium. Two days now."

I covered his inflamed flesh. There against the gunwale we sat, whilst the *Whitby* swung to and fro on her anchor chains.

A few days later the captors had us set up narrow cots close in to the port rail. Prostrate forms filled a score of them by week's end. January and a new year was to bear witness, it appeared, to ravages beyond comprehension. Holding each other for support, we made our way up one side of the deck, and down the other. No matter the wind or temperature we did so, prolonging every minute they let us stay above decks. Death lurked in the hold below, and only men destined to die lie on those cots.

"When I am close to dying," Heman said on one of our perambulations, on a day otherwise like any other, "I would have a favor from you. Suffocate me. In my sleep."

"What!" So quick had I stopped that we both nearly toppled over.

"I mean it, Elisha," he said. "I cannot bear to end as these men, gasping hour after hour like a fish tossed upon a dock. Mocked all the while by beasts like that Loring."

I started us walking once more. I could not bear to think of putting an end to him, my dearest friend in this world; now my only friend. Nor could I contemplate the pinkish glow I had spotted at dawn between two fingers of my left hand.

We had traipsed up and down until we could do so no more. Seated, as far from the cots as we could manage, we watched the milling mass of prisoners. Those recently captured stood as men among ghosts. It was more like the latter we now looked. How long had Heman and I left, I wondered? A few weeks, perhaps; maybe only days.

A sudden commotion twisted my head round. Down from the blockhouse came the sergeant, flanked by the corporal and trailed by a pair of privates. The British officer watched them as they departed below him. As the knot of men came forward, the sergeant glanced towards the bow where we hunkered. "Up, Heman!" I pulled at him though he grasped his tender arm.

"What is it, Elisha? You're hurting me."

"Hurry! Don't ask questions." As we approached, the soldiers were already threatening those lying flat out on the cots.

"They're not responding, sir," one of the privates explained.

"Then bloody well drag them off," demanded the sergeant. Never had he sounded so out of temper.

The corporal took a tentative step closer to his superior. "Why not exchange some of those below, sergeant? There's a trouble-maker or two I can point out. These here are half-dead and no trouble at all."

"You have tumbled the lieutenant's thinking, in your own peculiar way. You heard the order. Obey it. The flag of truce vessel is alongside and he wants these men on it."

Flag of truce? Amos had once spoken the term in regards to prisoner exchanges. I hauled Heman to the rail. Below us a smallish yet sleek warship rocked in the waves, not 100 yards off. Already one of her boats rode swiftly across towards us.

"What are you two men about?" I whirled to see the sergeant directly behind us. "Corporal Loring!" he commanded.

"Sir!"

"See to it that this pair are the first to be put aboard."

His harsh tone shocked me, yet something in his eye kindled hope. Even as the corporal leapt forward and grabbed hold of us, I stared again at the vessel dancing so near upon the sea. Ten guns to a side she boasted; all in a single row. A frigate, I thought – low and fast. The next moment the sling was fitted to me and over the side I went. Soon after, Heman was tumbled into the open boat beside me. Never would the corporal have taken such rough hold of us, no nor come within a rod I imagine, had he known what we carried.

We managed to prop ourselves up on one of the bench seats. Those dragged from their cots plopped one by one onto the boat's floor at our feet. Up and down the sling went until the man at the tiller cried out that any more might swamp him. The neck cloth he had knotted about his mouth and nose muffled his speech, but his alarm was clear enough. With their oars the sailors on the inner side immediately pushed off. The craft glided a few yards back. As we backed away from the *Whitby*, her sheer mass towered over us. A mighty mountain of rotting wood it was, wallowing on the sea. The oarsmen and their flashing blades now did their work. Farther and farther off we skimmed.

The British sergeant and his soldiers peered down. I had not even thought to thank him. His was a final kindness. Dozens upon dozens of haggard faces also lined the rail. How hungrily they stared down at us as we sped away. With a jolt, I recognized Amos among them. His hand rose slowly up. I hesitated a moment, then responded in kind. Light sparkling on the foamy chop lit the red lurking between my fingers. At the slight shift of Heman's head I dropped my hand. Swallowing, I whispered, "We are free of her, at last."

"Aye, my friend," he replied. "Free." In my heart I knew he had seen the tell-tale sign.

Chapter 70

The *Glasgow* had but the one deck. And scores of us had been jammed beneath it. Across this the sailors scampered back and forth, seemingly atop our heads. The decking, the beams, everything was of a diminished scale - yet possessing a grace completely absent on the *Whitby*. As the ship took life, she rose, then fell. Slowly at first, and then faster until wonderful, powerful notes sang along her curved sides. I who feared vast waters touched her planking. The vibrations of our passage dwelled there between the wood's fibers and liquid sea.

"Heman," I said, catching him as he bobbed, already half-asleep. "I never thanked you."

"For what?"

"When we prepared Azariah for the hereafter. If you had not interceded with the corporal, he would have stuck my brother's body, and run me through."

"Ah, that. Save your thanks, my friend. Consider what fate I may have saved us for."

"You have given me the hope of returning home. The chance to see my family once more."

Even in the half-light I recognized his familiar, freckled smile. "To see her, you mean."

"Jemima? Yes." Still smiling he laid his head against my shoulder. I smiled too; with the prospect of keeping a promise I had thought irrevocably broken. In this happy state of mind I dozed off.

Sometime later our sailing prison heeled. The movement was not great, and confined as we were I could not fathom our direction. What was most evident was the sudden presence of sharp lifts, and abrupt drops. Crammed into the narrow bow each impact rattled through my sopped breeches, jarring my spine. Mortal dread flooded up inside me. Might the very next fall end with a rending crash; the single, thin planking yielding to the pummeling wave; and we plummeting down to our doom. Groans all about signaled most had been awakened.

"We have left the bay," Heman said. "So claims the man beside me. Zadock is his name, and of the 17th as it happens. He says we journey north on the East River. Urged on by a following wind."

"I see. Yes of course." I turned away from the slop of the bilge water, for it was evidence of the sea working hard to claim us. I clung to the sun-kissed bottoms of the clouds, visible through the iron grate that covered the hatch. This coming night we would not be forced down into the pestilence of the hulk's bowels. Slowly my breathing calmed. The features of Eli's map took shape once more in my mind. The East River, of course. Its channel ran north till it reached, what, Long Island Sound? "Heman! Ask the fellow. Does not this way bring us to the shore of Connecticut?"

"Aye, it does, says he. Born he was in Lyme, and knows the passage well."

We careened along without means of marking the minutes or the miles. From above came the hum of wind in the rigging. Down below, men cried out or groaned in their privation and pain. Every so often Heman could be heard responding to his unseen companion, who insisted that we must have reached this point or that ferry landing in such and such a time. With each league Connecticut drew nearer, but would we stop along her shore? I dozed off again pondering this question.

During the night I awoke to the sound of unfamiliar voices. Their manner of speech told me they were likely a pair of junior officers. British midshipmen perhaps, come forward to use the head.

"When we are next in Halifax," said one, "I mean to sit for the lieutenant's examination."

"You must not mind this service overmuch, Henry," replied a reedy, eager voice. "They are only rebels, after all."

"Mind it? I detest it! Surely we neither of us joined His Majesty's navy to set ashore dying men, and why, so that they might spread pestilence. Ashamed, I am, to write Father as to my duties on this station."

"Come Henry, you fret overmuch. Besides, the lieutenant will note our absence."

The rushing wind and water soon smothered their conversation. In the pitch-black I slumped, rubbing the unseen patch that had encroached farther along my fingers.

A gray dawn revealed the looming mast amidships and the taut sail. Bells rang out then, and at intervals throughout the day. Clearly we were not to be allowed the freedom afforded by the deck of this warship – flag of truce or not. Towards evening a series of shouted commands launched pounding feet. The canvas sheet disappeared, though I could not make out the busy hands that gathered it in. The sea's song sank to a whisper. A long, rattling crash marked the running out of a chain. "Heman! Wake up. They drop the anchor."

"I am awake. But where are we? Even Zadock doesn't know."

The grate came away. Scarlet-coated marines ordered us to climb. Weak as we were, Heman and I did our best to help those less able to surmount the short flight. We half-dragged our companions to the low rail. Just below, boats bobbed on a shiny, black sea. With the butts of their muskets the soldiers separated us into two smaller groups. Thus were Heman and I divided.

Standing, sitting or sprawled flat out, we shivered uncontrollably on their deck. I could not stop my face, my arms, my legs from quivering; from the cold and exhaustion both. Our captors moved not a muscle. Fit and well-turned out in their coats of wool, they stood, still as statues and with glares quite as cold and hard. Lepers, we were, to them. When further orders came, these men would execute whatever was asked.

In the stern, the captain finished addressing his lieutenant. The latter saluted his superior with a touch of his cap. Descending from the quarterdeck, the lieutenant strode forward. His sharp gaze fixed on prostrate forms lying face up. Dead men, I realized only then. "Over the side with those two," the officer commanded. Up and over they went with shocking dispatch. Splashes followed. "Set the rest of the rebels ashore. Dry if possible."

"And if we are fired upon, sir?" The high voice identified the speaker as one of those from last night. He was indeed a midshipman.

"If the populace threatens you in any manner, Mister Hawkins, you are to dump your cargo in the surf."

"The surf it is," replied Mister Hawkins. In the dark I had disliked this man's manner of expression. Now I heartily detested his scrawny neck. Would that I possessed the strength to…

"You, there," the lieutenant said. I faced him. "You will lower this lot to the boat then descend. Mister Talbot. The order to dump cargo if threatened applies to you as well."

"Sir," replied the second of the midshipmen.

No more than two yards separated the ship's rail from the open boat, but the choppy seas and our wasted states rendered the span treacherous indeed. One fellow let loose my hand before he had a secure foothold, and dropped straight between the vessels. The hulls banged together. When they parted once more, the deep gave no sign it had swallowed the unfortunate whole. None chastised me for his loss. No one paused in their hurry.

Heman's boat pushed off mere moments before us. Mister Hawkins appeared to consider this putting of prisoners ashore a race, for he exhorted his men to bend their backs. With Mister Talbot, Henry as he had been addressed overnight, the pace was smart; his manner efficient. His crew pulled in unison and with their eyes fixed on him. He kept his gaze on the course he'd set, and I imagine, the boat ahead of us. Fog drifted across the surface, but not thick enough to conceal that we were steadily closing the gap. Even as the sound of the surf reached my numbed ears, we drew nearly even.

Hawkins fired a look back at us before shouting a series of commands. His oarsmen ceased rowing. Though well shy of the shore, the marine contingent forced their human cargo overboard. I sat upright as Heman staggered about in thigh-deep water. An oncoming wave swept past, swallowing him to chest height. Around him bobbed the heads of less fortunate men.

We surged by, leaving them rapidly in our wake. "Collins and Smyth!" Mister Talbot called as the beach rose up before us. "Ground the boat." A sailor hopped over each gunwale and held us fast. "Prisoners disembark."

I clambered over the side, pausing only to put fingers to my forehead, as I had seen his men salute him. He nodded and I turned to help those struggling to rise. The icy water gripped me, but only as high as my ankles. Farther out, where the rollers crested in frothy curls, Heman dragged a man towards shore. "Hang on!" I shouted. "I'll come for you."

As it turned out, by the time I had emptied Talbot's boat, Heman had collapsed on the stony slope. His good arm still clung to a waterlogged lump beside him. I stumbled over and dropped to all fours. Together we managed to roll over what in truth was Zadock, and he a lad the age of Azariah. Together we thumped his chest and hoisted him up and down until he coughed up some of the wave he'd swallowed.

"Who goes there?" demanded a voice.

I crouched facing the water and there I glanced first. The boats with their British crews had disappeared into the mist. Men thrashed and struggled out there still, but the hail had come from behind me. I twisted about just as two men emerged from a thicket of primrose. Both held muskets and these were leveled at us.

"I, we, are soldiers. Of the 17th Continental."

The lead man, a gray-haired gentleman by his look, pointed his barrel skywards. "Then you are Patriots, sir, and friends to us. Let us help you."

"Help them!" I cried. "Before they drown."

The pair set their weapons down and raced into the surf. They seemed oblivious to the cold and the power of the waves. I found I could not rise to offer aid of any sort. Within minutes they had hauled a score beyond the reach of the tide. Other civilians appeared and joined in the rescue effort. Some might have been lost, though of this who could be certain.

The gray-haired fellow approached. "We need to get you indoors. Here. Take my hand."

"You may not wish to offer it," I replied. "We are stricken. Some with the yellow fever."

He wavered in the light of dawn. "I have offered you my hand, sir. I'll not withdraw it now."

The next few days and nights passed in a blur. Those who had survived the journey and the immersion lay on comfortable bedding spaced about the floor. 'Milford, Connecticut', our rescuers proudly proclaimed, and this their town hall. The building's pew boxes had been stacked in the rear. When the 6th had passed through last spring, with Heman and I bent on joining the 17th, I had glimpsed the outside of this very structure. Never had I guessed that one day I would be...

"May God forever bless the kind people of this town," said Heman.

I rolled onto my side. "Amen." Though I faced my friend, my eyes came to rest on Captain Stow whom we had first met on the beach. There across the spacious room he bent low to wipe the brow of one of our comrades. Kind and courageous were these folk, for he and many others had taken us in - riddled with afflictions though we were, and cast unbidden at their doors.

Heman pressed a chunk of fresh bread against his cheek as though he might the better absorb its scent and warmth. I smiled. "Would you eat of it, Heman, or do you intend inhaling that loaf?" He laughed, but his laughter morphed into a cough that racked his chest. "Lie back," I counseled.

"Aye," he said, when finally able.

"It is good to have hot, wholesome food, is it not?"

"Ah, yes. And thawed out at last." Again he coughed.

Plainly I could see his lesions from where I lay. More of them now there were. A particularly angry one had erupted in the valley between his nostril and cheekbone. And I did not need to glance down to feel the heat of the rash, spread to the back of my hand. "Heman." He met my gaze. "You know we cannot stay."

"And why not?" he asked with rare fire in his eyes.

"Would you be content with a full, warm belly, if it means never returning home?" His sudden sadness filled me with regret. "Come, Heman, what of the girl by the lake. Will you not take to the road to set eyes on that lass?"

He looked away. "She'd not have me. Not now."

At this, I too, fell back. Even if we did not succumb to disease upon the road, what made me think Jemima would still have me? I stared up at the ceiling so that I would not catch sight of the most piteous cases about us. How we must look to those spared our afflictions. It required no effort to conjure up the horror visible in the eyes of the kindly townspeople who had left food and clothing at the doorway yonder.

"I do miss my parents something fierce," Heman whispered. "And how I long to see my new home once more."

"Yes, Heman," I said, drawn upwards by his hopes. "As do I."

He turned to me. The chunk of bread, still untouched, molded to his cheek. "Do you mean to set off, Elisha? On any accounts?"

"I do."

"Then I mean to accompany you."

"When your strength is restored. At week's end, perhaps."

"No. You are right, my friend. Time is not our ally. Tomorrow. Let us agree on tomorrow."

Chapter 71

The good Captain and his friend Doctor Carrington had employed numerous arguments to counter our intention of leaving. Still we persisted. Finally, in desperation and anger, the Captain cried, "For the sake of heaven it is the month of January!"

"And how many comrades did Heman and I lose overnight?" I asked him. "How many will you inter this day?"

"Very well, Sergeant Benton. I will have provisions packed for you both, though you scarcely have the strength to carry the half of what you'll require for such a journey." He stood. "And where will I find a greatcoat to fit? You with that frame of an ox and not an ounce of flesh to be found anywhere upon it." He went off shaking his head. As he had proven an intensely honest man, his current dismay deepened the fear in my guts.

"Perhaps we should sneak away whilst his back is turned?" Heman joked. He began to laugh but ended up hacking into his hand. I rubbed his back for want of being able to offer real comfort.

Captain Stow had taken us by cart as far as New Haven. Here he helped us down. "The Upper Post Road will take you clear to Hartford," he repeated.

"We are familiar with it," I replied.

Into my pocket he secreted something. I heard the clinking of coins. He covered the gift by snugging up the belt that he'd fashioned to keep my greatcoat from flapping about. "Keep this taut against the wind," he cautioned. His eyes paused at the rash on my hand. "You would be best to conceal your condition - from innkeepers and the like. But remember, Elisha, Heman. Touch no one. The risk to them is too great."

I slipped my hand inside the coat. Half a dozen precious, round objects nestled there. "Yet you, Captain; you never once hesitated to offer us succor."

"My affairs are in order. I have seen to that." His sudden smile shooed my fears away. Reaching up he patted my cheek. "Besides, you brave lads are like my own four sons. Should they ever be captured, or suffer some misfortune, I hope others will receive them with kindness. Trust that it has been my privilege to nurse you. I only wish that I could do more."

The road took us almost due north. A stiff and tenacious wind blew throughout the day from the northwest, smiting us upon the left side of our faces till our cheeks went numb despite the cloth wound 'round our heads. Many pauses had we made, and these to catch our breath or massage our aching limbs in the shelter of some outcrop or other. Barely a building or a fellow traveler did we come across. Finally, some miles from New Haven, we happened upon a cluster of homes.

"So this is the Northeast Parish?" Heman asked.

"So it appears. And that there must be the inn of which the Captain spoke." With Heman leaning heavily upon my arm, we stepped beneath the swinging sign. A gust of wind propelled us within.

"Close that blasted door!" the landlord demanded. "What have we here?" He cocked his head to one side and studied us from beneath his raised lantern. "Your mate is taken ill, friend. From whence do you hail?"

"Milford, sir. We seek a bed for the night."

"All that way and on foot you come?"

"We rode partway. To New Haven. From there we walked, aye."

He drew back. "In this weather? Well. If you've no money for the coach, you've likely none for a bed neither. An' I'm not one to be offering charity to strangers. Especially them as look sickly."

"Our journey, it weakened us. The Captain opposed our going. But as we insisted, he said we were to stay here in this very inn."

"Did he now? And this all-knowing officer; he has a name?"

"Captain Stephen Stow."

"You claim to know the Captain?"

"We broke bread with the good and kindly gentleman this very morning."

The lamp rose close once more. "Well, let me see now. I do have a room at the end of the hall. And I'd ask you to keep your friend inside of it; far from my other guests. They may not take to him as I have. I can have some bread and cheese brought upstairs. Hard cider, perhaps, to wash it down. If, that is, you keep him there till morning."

I shifted Heman's weight as my arm had begun to lose feeling. The prickly heat throbbed on the back of my hand. "We are much obliged, sir. And the cost?"

"Supper for two, and a room to be shared. Two shillings."

I proudly produced the coins that I had reassuringly rubbed this day, but not yet viewed. I set them on the bar so that I would not touch him.

On the way upstairs Heman whispered, "I thought us destined for the roadside."

"It was a near thing. If not for the Captain..."

"Elisha. Can we rest awhile?"

"Of course! The landing here; will this do?" Gradually his panting lessened.

"Captain Stow," he said at last. "Was it he gave you the silver?"

"Aye. A gift from him and the Doctor I would think. Perhaps their mutual friend Captain Miles as well."

"How, how can we ever repay such kindness?"

"Let us pray they find it in heaven, if not here on Earth."

"Are they in danger? The conditions in Milford. They were so unlike the prison ship..."

"We jeopardize everyone who so much as..." His expression stopped my mouth. "Enough of such talk," I said. "Let us get you to that bed. All will yet be well."

The Hartford Stage left early the next morning. We were not aboard. What monies we possessed must be husbanded so that we might once more sleep safe from the reach of the elements. At sunup this plan had proved convincing to Heman. Yet before the sun had reached the zenith of its low arc in the sky, my own faith in this scheme was fading.

For a third time I stopped our progress. The numbness that had taken hold in my toes now overspread both feet. Each footfall came to rest not upon my heels, but seemingly on blocks of ice strapped to them. And Heman, he had not uttered a word for near on an hour.

"Do you spy Durham?" he wondered. "Is that why we stop?" According to the marker at the roadside we had covered but five miles. Last spring we had logged five and 20 with nothing like this expenditure of body and spirit. "Elisha. Might we sit? Just for a time..."

"Wait. Stand. Something comes. Heavy by the sound of it." A rumbling grew in the still air. I glanced down, half expecting to see the ground shake. Around the last bend a team of draft horses appeared. "A dray," I said. "And heavily loaded at that." A man and a boy occupied the seat.

"They are enough alike to be father and son," Heman said, as if echoing my thoughts.

"The question is, will they take us aboard?" The man had been watching us carefully as they approached. Before they came abreast I called out. "Greetings, fellow travelers!"

At a single motion by the man, the boy hauled on the reins. "Shall I set the brake, Father?"

The man said neither aye nor nay. His large, calloused hand shifted his pipe to the opposite corner of his mouth. Through wisps of smoke he peered long and hard, as had the innkeeper.

"Might you be headed to Hartford, sir?" I asked.

"I trust you know this to be the Post Road and where it leads, for you and your companion stand upon it. As for me and my boy Seth here, we aim to follow it."

"To Hartford, then?"

"As that would be where these goods are bound."

"Then we share a common destination."

"Do we now?"

"We are wondering, my friend and I, whether you and your son might consider taking us aboard? As passengers of sorts."

"Thought you might work your way around to that. Just who are you men? What places you on the highway, without mounts, in such a month as this?"

"We, my friend and I, are soldiers."

"Soldiers is it?" The pipe shifted once more. "Soldiers without arms. No kit of any kind."

"We're not deserters if that is your meaning." The struggle to keep Heman standing served at least to keep my temper in check.

"Did I say you were? Besides, there are worse things than that even." He spat. "Perhaps you've heard the same tale as I. Back in Milford it was. I heard tell that the Regulars dumped prisoners on the beach. Diseased men from the prisons in New York. Dumped them in hopes of spreading the putrid fever and assorted miseries into the towns hereabouts."

One of Heman's legs gave out, nearly dragging us down. Grunting, I hoisted him upright. "Sir, I beg you. Hear me out. We, my friend and I, Heman Baker is his name. I am Elisha Benton. We were among those who marched in relief of Boston. Back in the spring of '75. We fought in Roxbury, and at Breed's Hill. And again last August on Long Island. There the British surrounded us. They shot Heman, and captured us both. We've not seen our families in near on a year. It's to them now we make our way."

"Father..." the boy said.

"Hush now." The pipe settled in the man's lap. "Your mate. What ails him?"

"He, he has the pox. And if we must walk the entire way to Hartford, I fear he'll not see his father again in this life."

"Father, please. Can we not help them?"

The man quieted the boy with a glance.

"I have a few shillings," I insisted. "Here in my coat. It is all we have. You are welcome to them."

"None of that now," the man said. He tapped out his pipe. "You will climb on at the back. The very back you understand. And I'll press you to touch nothing of my cargo." I could not staunch the tears that filled my eyes, and overran my cheeks. "You soldiers, you get aboard now. I've a schedule to keep."

Chapter 72

We parted from the man and his boy at Hartford's Meeting House Square. Flurries came and went but not so thick as to keep everyone indoors. Enough people thronged the market, huddled within their wraps, that the passage of a pair of ailing men went largely unnoticed. The boatman, however, rubbed his chin as if uncertain whether to allow us aboard his ferry. At the sight of my silver he relented. Again I made sure not to touch him during the exchange. Not until we reached the east side of the river did I recount our dwindling treasure.

"Have our friends provided us with enough?" Heman asked.

I turned the coins over once more but doing so did not increase the tally. "It will be a near thing."

"All will be well, my friend. You will see."

The ride on the dray had jostled our bones most certainly, but caused no more harm than that. Likewise the massive slags of ice on the Connecticut had alarmed us, but done no ill. Now, with each mile put between us and the river valley, the ground rose. We both sucked at the frigid air as though through a blanket. Step by plodding step we proceeded eastwards. The higher we climbed the more the snow squalls intensified. Homesteads became increasingly rare. At times our meager shadows crept along the road before us. At others, swirls of white erased them completely.

Long had my arm ached. Now my friend's sagging weight shot pulses of pain throughout my being. Like an anchor he dragged me down. Could he not try? For a wild moment I thought to cast him off. The notion shocked me.

"Why do we stop?" he muttered. "I, I can continue." His head did not rise from my shoulder as he spoke.

"I had hoped to reach Bolton. There is an inn..."

"Have we money enough, Elisha?"

"It matters not. Not now." I tried remembering how far back had been the last house. Too far, then, to retrace our steps. A burst of fading sunlight revealed a break in the forest, no more than a quarter mile distant. "That may be a field, just ahead," I murmured. "And where there's a field, there must be a farm."

The ground pitched more steeply than I had reckoned over that stretch. The opening was, in fact, a field, but merely the first of three. More than once Heman stumbled. To fall now meant death. I lacked the strength to lift him, and doubted he could do so on his own. Would I stay...?

"Elisha?"

"It is nothing. We must keep on. Shelter is near at hand."

A stiffening of the wind proved an unexpected blessing. It shoved at my back. It whipped one leg forward, then the next. The outline of a building rose up on our right hand side. I gave free rein to the urgings of the wind. Too much so, for our feet could not keep up. In a jumbled heap we fell between the farm's house and barn. Ice crystals jammed one ear as I twisted to locate the homestead. Heman's ragged breath echoed in the other. At a window a woman's face appeared. A moment more and the door was hauled open. A man emerged, the barrel of his musket pointing at our heads.

"State yer business!"

"Shelter! Please!"

The man took a step closer. He squinted against the white-flecked wind. "Fever!" he hollered over his shoulder. "Sure as I'm standin' here."

"We are soldiers! Connecticut soldiers. Exchanged, and trying to reach our homes." The woman called out something to her man. "Please!" I cried. "We beg shelter! For but one night."

The woman was shouting now, and crying too. Something about their son; their sons. He yelled back at her. From farther inside the home children began to cry.

Heman's breath came in gasps; divided by dreadful silences. I gathered myself. "Help us for the love of God! One night in your barn, for two Tolland men. For two sons of Tolland." The door closed. My head dropped back to its bed of snow. I could not take my eyes from the slats. Heavy, wet flakes whirled in eddies, and lent a coat of white to Heman's matted hair. "Please..."

Suddenly the man re-appeared. Musket gone, he made straight for us. He passed by without pausing, stomping a route 'round our fallen forms. At the barn he was, swinging open one of the double doors. "You're ta find yer own way inside fer I'll not come near! An' don' ya dare trifle with my beasts."

"Bless you," I said, though I doubt my words carried that far. I struggled to push Heman off me. When I'd managed to sit up, the man had gone. I took hold of Heman's collar. I dragged him for a bit. Clouds of my breath covered his head. We carried on like this - bouts of dragging and panting. I don't know how long it took. Near an inch of powder covered him by the time I backed into the entry. By then I had hold of my friend's bad arm. I dared not let it go. In near darkness I folded his feet inside. It took three tries to pry the open door from where it had wedged in the near frozen muck. It banged shut.

A pile of straw served as packing. I near buried the both of us in it. In time our bodies warmed the bristly bed. The animals quieted in their unseen stalls. In the dark, I listened to Heman's ragged breaths. Between each, I waited, waited for the next. I fell asleep waiting.

The lowing of the cows brought me round. Dawn had come. I lay quiet, listening. I did not hear Heman's breathing. I felt it. Faint wafts of warmed air came and went, causing the rash to flare on the back of my hand. I buried my face against his spine. Like a furnace he burned. I forced myself up. My breath burst, cloud-like, in the half-light.

There, moving amongst the animals' heaving flanks, was the farmer of yesterday. He toted buckets and his stool for milking. About his nose and mouth he'd wound a cloth tight. Not a word or a glance did he offer me. "Heman?" I tried once more but earned a groan and nothing more.

"Will ya be leavin' today?" called the farmer from the small door set in the rear wall.

"My friend. He lacks the strength."

"Ya promised. One night ya said."

"I am sorry. He's, I think he's, dying."

The man stood silent for a time. "Ya'll find water jes' outside the door there. That an' cheese. An' some bread. Baked fresh yesterday."

"We have money. A bit..."

"Ya've no need of it. The food. It's a gift from my missus. An' I'll charge no man to quench his thirst."

"Bless you. Most kind. Please, will you thank your wife for us? For my friend and me."

The man nodded. He re-claimed his full pails. "I'm grateful ta ya, fer beddin' down so far from my beasts. The cows, they're near all we've got now, what with our elder boys away. I'll come back by an' by, an' bring fresh straw. Put it 'round front fer ya."

The door closed before I could ask after his absent sons. "Heman? Wake! Wake up now." His groans grew louder till he woke sufficiently to choke them back. "Are you in great pain?" I asked.

"Like nails, driven into my back..."

I tried to massage his limbs but he stiffened in agony. "Here. Take something. They've brought us food, and drink." He attempted a bite. He could not swallow. A smile ghosted across his visage. Lost were his freckles in their bed of angry skin. His head hung heavy upon my hand. "You must try, Heman."

"I am not to see them, Elisha. Not Father, nor Mother, nor a one of my brothers."

"You're wrong. Remember how you spoke of..."

"Never again will I step upon the land. My own land..."

"Heman. Listen to me..."

"My friend. You must promise, to leave me, when the time comes."

"I shall not..."

"I promised her, you know. Your Jemima. She made both of us promise. In the town this was. Azariah and me. We were not to return without you." His chest lifted and fell with the effort, but he would not let me speak. "I, I will not," he gasped, "not be the cause of keeping you from her side. Leave me now. While you still can."

He fell into a type of sleep not long after. When he stirred I tried to get water down, but he merely coughed it up. I could do little more than dampen his feverish brow, and rock his head and shoulders to and fro. I too, drifted in and out. At times I thought I cradled Azariah. In lucid moments I recognized my friend.

A pounding awoke me, the slatted door fairly reverberating in my skull with the blows. "You there, inside the barn!"

"We're awake. What is it?"

"Yer home. Tolland was it?"

"Yes. Tolland."

"The town I recollect is but one day's ride - there and back. The missus asks if ya'd like word delivered. On yer whereabouts, a course."

How had I not thought to ask? "Yes! Oh, thanks be to God! Heman did you hear? Sir! We accept. Hello? Are you out there still?"

A noise from the rear drew my head around. The man moved rapidly to the lone horse and began saddling her. A mare she was. Though gray flecks coated her muzzle, her limbs appeared plenty sturdy for such a journey. "Sir! I am Elisha Benton. My friend is Heman Baker. If you but give our names to any in the town, they will get word to our fathers. Misters Daniel Benton and Heman Baker, the Elder. You've but to direct them to your home and they will come. I know they will."

"Benton. An' Baker. Aye."

"Heman! I insist you wake and eat at once. Word goes to our families. This very moment. Heman!" My hand knew the way of it before my head. And long after my head understood, my heart refused to accept that my friend was cold, and dead.

Chapter 73

The farmer had left a blanket and a rope; the first to wrap Heman's body, and the second so that it could later be dragged forth from the barn. A kindness was meant, of course, and the man had apologized that he could not do more - dared not. With that he had ridden off. And so the hours passed. Yet I lay, unmoving.

Occasionally one of the beasts shifted its weight within a stall. The hens set up a fuss at a later point over some imagined threat. Otherwise all within the barn made barely a sound. Even the breeze died away.

This fine spell, however brief, would surely improve the state of the road. Somewhere out there the farmer must be making good time. Even now he might be delivering word to a somber assemblage upon the town green. Even now the Baker clan might be burdened with the knowledge that their son had perished mere miles from home - lost to them forever, though so near their embrace.

"None can clasp you to them, Heman. Neither you nor me, for we are beyond the touch of our fellow man."

Slowly the line of shade had retreated, yielding up my friend to the light. The pus-swollen lesions that had crowded his face had caved in on themselves. Even the yellow hue of his skin had begun to fade. The voracious disease had met its match at last. In bringing death it died too. In the pale, lifeless form that remained, I glimpsed something of he whom I'd known so well. I breathed deeply. Slowly, methodically, ignoring the agonies of my burning limbs, I worked the woolen blanket up, over and about my friend. This done I secured the rope. Beside him I slumped, exhausted.

I awoke with a start. Of Jemima I had dreamt. I turned to Heman to tell him so. His shrouded form drove me back with a gasp.

A creak of hinges. Then, open wide the barn doors flung. Framed in the entry stood Daniel. Up went my arms as a strangled cry escaped me.

"Elisha! Brother!"

"No, Daniel! Back! Stay back!" His shocked eyes scanned the pair of us. "I beg you..." I pleaded. "Do not..."

His forward momentum had been checked, but there was no denying the resolve in his eyes - though they filled with tears. "You must let me come to you, Brother."

"You must not. The pox. You see what it's done to me. To Heman."

Daniel removed his hat. "I know of it. The farmer spared us nothing."

"He did right. You, everyone must know our fate. Tell me true, Brother. What is to become of me? Our father, will he allow me under his roof? As I now am..."

"It was he bade me ride April that I might retrieve you all the sooner. The farmer follows with our cart. And the Bakers, they are to journey to this place on the morrow." At these tidings I collapsed forward upon my hands. "Please, Elisha. Let me help you."

"You have, Brother. More than you can know..."

Though Daniel had backed the cart practically into the barn, I squandered a precious quarter hour of daylight scrabbling and clawing my way aboard. The farmer kept his distance, but my brother I was forced to warn off repeatedly. "I must do this myself. Don't you understand! You cannot touch me."

He withdrew but no farther than the mare. Despite his taut grip April kept turning her head rearward. Her whinnies set all the barn's inhabitants to lowing and neighing. "Sssh, girl," I said to her, but she would not heed me.

With a last surge I tumbled onto my back on the open bed. A blanket billowed high above and settled atop me. Armfuls of straw followed. A freshening breeze swept fragments of cloud across the sky. Daniel's voice, calm and strong, spoke words of comfort the while. Heartfelt thanks he lavished upon the farmer. My shallow, raspy breathing quieted at last. Motion, and the clattering of the wheels could not prevent my eyes from closing. "Farewell, my friend..."

Each time I came to, the light had diminished, turning the bare branches above yet darker. My teeth chattered though sweat drenched me. Every bump and hole traveled the cart's wood and iron frame, intent on smiting my aching limbs. Only by climbing did we keep the sun's company. Shafts of light illuminated the clouds from below. "God give you rest, Heman..." I prayed. "May you be seated with Azariah in heaven. And find Grandsire beside him."

In a waking moment I told Daniel of our brother, and how he now lay within a woodland so like those he loved to roam. He promised to tell Father and the rest. Then he related his escape, and that of precious few others including Eli. The tidings offered comfort especially since so many whom I loved had died. And in so short a span. Yet others lived - my family, and her. How would they receive me? Jemima - would she come...

"Elisha?" The cart had stopped. Daniel's face peered down at me from the seat.

"I'm awake. I am."

"You gave me a start, Brother. We are close now. I intend taking you to Grandsire's."

"If you think it best."

"Father's house, well, it is quite crowded. Mother Sarah lives with us now. She has since Grandsire's passing. His home is empty, and so, we..."

"I understand, Daniel, I do."

Even in the failing light, and in my current state, I sensed the turn onto the narrow lane. Not a tree nor rut had changed. I knew where stood the stone wall, raised along so much of its length by my own hand. Knew, too, where the opening commenced.

Mother's cry, it was, that pierced the dusk. Azariah's name she cried out; and mine. "Keep her off, Daniel!"

"Elisha! My son! My precious son. No, Daniel! Let go of me..."

Her sobs, Hannah's too, filled my heart and shredded it all at once. I fought my way onto an elbow. Daniel held Mother by the waist. At sight of me she nearly broke free. "Elisha!" Sister squirmed in Mother Sarah's grasp, her arms extended towards me.

To see them at long last. To see their dear faces, so close at hand and so little changed. I blinked fast - that I might keep them in my sight. Finally, somehow, Daniel shepherded the womenfolk inside. I fought the waves of pain, praying that they might come forth once more.

Daniel it was who re-emerged. Following him, with a lantern raised, came Father. How old he seemed, leaning there upon his cane. His hair had gone white, white as Grandsire's. From where I lay, his features even bore a resemblance to that beloved face, though they hardly ever had.

I focused on my right hand, somewhere there, trapped by the folds of the blanket. The harsh straw stabbed the sores as my fingers wriggled up from the depths. Father caught sight of my withered limb, quivering just above the cart's low side.

The white-haired head nodded, in time with his oft-repeated, "My Boy, My Boy..."

Daniel had at first pulled up before Grandsire's front door. He saw at once what I did not, that even should I simply tumble headfirst from the cart, never would I make it through the home's entry; to the bed that awaited me in the rear. With firm commands he positioned April alongside the house. "Wait but a moment," he said, and disappeared.

The familiar twelve-over-twelve-paned glass broke the line of clapboards in the wall beside me. This had been my very own room, in happier days, gone by. A lamp appeared within the kitchen bedroom. Daniel opened the window.

"The bed is just here, Elisha. Can you crawl through to it?"

I knew its location well enough, having slept many a night upon it. Now, however, the obstacles between where I lay and it seemed insurmountable. Even as I grasped the cart's side, and hauled myself to it, my grating breathing panicked me. How like Heman I sounded, when he neared his mortal end. What's more, the rash mocked me from the backs of both my hands.

"Brother," he said, so soft, and quiet. "Look to me." How steadfast were his eyes. I stared till I saw nothing but. With the deepest inhale I could manage, I heaved towards him.

Stabbing, hot pain contorted my limbs but I had made it. I dug my fingernails into both wall and bed-frame until the waves crested, then subsided. Heaving gasps echoed in the cramped space. Mine. Never again would I make such an attempt as that.

Sobs drew my head towards the room's entry. They were there. My kin. Daniel in front. Father, Mother, Hannah clinging to her, and Mother Sarah just behind. Eyes wide with shock, all of them and filling with tears, over what they had witnessed. Oh, that I could have spared them that. I scanned them frantically. "Jacob?" I whispered.

Daniel turned towards Father, who stepped up beside him. "Your youngest brother has gone off, my son, to join the fight."

"No! He must not!"

"He has, and it is right that he did so. An enemy who has done what these men have, they must be fought. I know that now."

"But Jacob," I said. "He is so young..."

"Your brother Daniel brought word of how the 17th fought on; you Elisha, and Azariah, when even men of parts had seen fit to run. Worry not about Jacob, my son. If he possesses but half the courage of his older brothers, I shall go to my grave a proud father." His one good hand lifted then, stretching out for me. Daniel it was who took hold of it, and led our father away.

They let me be for a time. This was good, for piteous enough I was without them seeing me weeping too. Purposeful sounds came from the kitchen. Iron met iron, and pewter found wood. Mother it was who looked in on me. She brought a stool upon which she set a pitcher and glass, followed by a bowl with a cloth draped over its side.

"Do no more than put them within my reach, Mother."

Though she bit her lip, she did smile for me. "You are come home to us. Yes, home at last."

"I am content, Mother, truly I am. If only Azariah had enjoyed so much."

"Oh, Elisha..." My upraised hand held her back. Crying again, she nodded. "And so must I be. Content."

"Mother," I said, when she had turned to leave. "I hope Father forgives me, as I forgave him long ago."

"Our boy. Our brave boy. You need no forgiveness. But I will tell your father. For it will bring him peace."

I slipped away from them for a time. When I awoke once more, soft voices carried from the parlor. Hers was not among them. Jemima had not come. Much as I reveled in my family's tender welcome, I could not bear that she had kept away. But blame her I must not. I had become the very horror I meant to spare her from. She must find another. Soon she would be free to do so.

"No," I argued in the near darkness, for the lamp had been turned down low. "I cannot bear it. Daniel," I called in a throaty whisper. I would have him ride to the town. Ride now despite the hour whilst there was still time. I tried to get hold of the glass that I might take a sip; make myself heard.

That's when the knock came. Footsteps followed, and then Daniel's voice. "Father. Jemima Barrows is come."

"Elisha. Is he truly here?" My name it was, and carried to my ears from her lips.

"Have you not heard that my son has the pox? To do more than lay eyes upon him is to court death."

"I died a hundred times waiting to learn his fate. The fear of dying will not keep me from him."

A silence was broken by Father's choked voice. "Then you are most welcome under this roof, Miss Barrows. Your presence will gladden him. But do prepare yourself. My son's appearance may startle you."

"Your son, yes, and my betrothed..."

No sooner had she said as much, that her face appeared in the doorway. In the shock of her first glance, I knew as never before how far death had advanced in me. In her next, gentleness and acceptance held sway, enveloping her, and sweeping forward. I saw, too, what she intended. "No. Jemima. NO!"

She came on regardless. Came on before any could stop her. The stool she set aside. My disfigured hand she clasped in her own. And beside my bed she knelt.

"Jemima..." I whispered. "You mustn't..."

"My God!" Daniel cried out in the entry. "Elisha, I am sorry!" Our family crowded hard behind him, imploring her to step away.

"I cannot stand by whilst he languishes alone," she told them. "Please do not ask it of me." To me she said, "I could not bear it..."

We Bentons gave in to her, then, to the love and resolve of Jemima Barrows. Together my family parted from us, and in peace. She dipped the cloth in the basin, and dabbed it along my forehead, bringing blessed cooling with her every touch.

"Oh Jem, my Jem," I whispered. "You must forgive my weakness, for I would have you stay."

"Sssh." Her delicate fingers smoothed the sweat-caked clumps of hair from my eyes. I saw her auburn tresses clear as she removed her hat, and cap too. Her lustrous hair spilled down, mingling with mine, as her head came to rest beside me. "We are together at last, Elisha - forever, side by side."

HISTORICAL NOTES

Few details are known about the lives of Elisha Benton and Jemima Barrows in the years 1774-1777. That any have survived nearly 250 years of American history are testament to their compelling nature. They sketch the outline of a tale of love and self-sacrifice that has few equals. Theirs is a story that deserves to be told.

So what, exactly, do we know? The record shows that Elisha Benton, first-born son of Daniel II, was born in Tolland, Connecticut in 1748 ***(see Drawing #1).*** By the fall of 1774 he had reached his 26th year. He was in love with a daughter of a townsman, though his prosperous and influential family opposed his choice of a prospective wife. In the spring of the following year an express rider carried news of the Lexington Alarm to eastern Connecticut. Private Benton marched off with the 5th Company 'in relief of Boston'. By 1776, as a sergeant of the 17th Continental, he fought and was captured by the British in the Battle of Long Island. Imprisoned, he contracted smallpox, a virulent and much feared disease. In January of 1777, with the winter raging, his captors released him onto the Connecticut shore in Milford with hundreds of similarly afflicted American soldiers. Despite his weakened state and the harsh conditions, he managed to complete the journey back to Tolland and his family's home. It was there that his betrothed, Jemima Barrows, and she only seventeen years old, risked her life to nurse him back to health. Though the Bentons had previously opposed the intended union, they did not dissuade the young woman from this courageous attempt to save their son. Tragically, Elisha died before the month's end in his 28th year. Jemima, too, contracted the dreaded disease, and did not survive February. The couples' infected bodies were buried mere yards from the Benton home which still stands. Their graves are some paces apart, for never were they wed. These things we know, but little else.

A good deal more is known about Daniel Benton I. Born in 1696, the second son of Samuel, he received from his father 40 acres of Tolland land in 1719 - a mere four years after the founding of the town. Though only 22 years of age upon the receipt of this gift, bestowed by the father '*...in consideration of love, good will, and affections which I have and do have unto my loving son Daniel...*' The grateful son immediately set about transforming the gift into productive farmland. By 1721 he had married Mary Skinner and taken up residence in what is still known today as the Daniel Benton Homestead on Metcalf Road in Tolland. Over the years their efforts enabled Daniel to acquire other parcels totaling hundreds of acres. His fellow accepted "inhabitants" of the town named him one of only five selectmen. Particular duties with which he and two others were entrusted included: surveying and selling new land divisions, collecting taxes, constructing new roads and creating a militia. There is little doubt that Daniel I became a prosperous and well-respected man, and patriarch to his family. When our story opens in 1774, however, he was nearing the end of his life. As did the man himself, the character of 'Elisha's Grandsire' passes in the summer of '76, in his 80th year.

He bestowed his name upon his first-born son. Born in 1723, Daniel II received both a house and five acres of land from his father when only 20 years old. Unlike his father, information is not readily available to attest to either his relative prosperity, or civic achievements. Nor do records indicate that he participated in the French and Indian War, despite mandatory militia participation requirements. His younger brother William did serve, rising to the rank of sergeant in this conflict, which cost him his life in 1760. Daniel II passed in 1777 at age 54, and only a year after his father died. It was the lack of evidence of Daniel II's contributions to the Bentons well-being or the town itself, coupled with his early passing, that led to the imagining of 'Father' as an ailing man, anxious about the family's lasting prosperity to the point of fear. His known opposition to Elisha's choice for his bride-to-be cements the imagined conflict between father and first-born son.

Jemima Barrows was not yet 16 in the fall of 1774. As many teenage girls wed in colonial America, it is believed that Benton opposition to the match concerned not her age but rather her low station in life. As the daughter of a landless cabinet-maker, neither she nor her family offered the dowry or political connections believed so necessary to a family's long-term welfare. To have the first-born son, especially, make such a disadvantageous match was not to be borne. The young people's actions proved the depth of their love: the dying Elisha survived a journey home that claimed many other men en route; the self-sacrifice of Jemima who tended him upon his arrival.

As Elisha served repeatedly and ultimately gave his life so that his country might exist free of tyranny, so too did Jemima freely offer hers. Their sacrifices are a metaphor for the efforts of countless men and women whose sacrifices in the years 1775-1783 gave birth to America.

The commitment of Tolland's people began well before the outbreak of hostilities with mother England. As the town meeting minutes reveal, as early as September 1774, authorization was given to a "*...Committee to receive and transmit to the towns of Boston and Charlestown, such charitable donations as shall be subscribed for the use of the poor and necessitous inhabitants of those towns.*'" They followed through on this commitment; driving 95 sheep along the approximately 90 miles of the Middle Post Road bringing desperately needed relief following General Thomas Gage's closing of the city's port. That the aid was gratefully received is evident in Henry Hill's letter from *Boston's Committee of Donations* received October of that year. Other notable members of this committee included Patriot leaders Samuel Adams and Dr. Joseph Warren. Once war broke out, this organization became the quartermaster organization serving the need for uniforms, provisions and ammunition of the entire Provincial Army.

Gentlemen.
This is to acknowledge the receipt of your kind and generous donation of ninety-five sheep by the hand of our worthy friend Mr. Hope Lathrop which shall be applied to the relief of our poor sufferers by means of the cruel and oppressive port bill, - according to the intentions of the generous donors. We are still struggling under the heavy load of tyranny. Our troubles are exceeding great, but the kindness and benevolence of our friends in Tolland, as well as other places, greatly refreshes and raises our spirts. You may depend upon it, that by divine

help and blessing, Boston will suffer everything with patience and firmness that a cruel and arbitrary administration can inflict upon us, even to the loss of fortune and life, rather than submit in any one instance to the power of tyranny. We trust we have a righteous cause, and that the Supreme Ruler of the Universe will in his own time and way, arise and scatter the dark clouds that at present hang over us. We submit to him and ask your prayer at the throne of grace for us. The sincere thanks of this committee in behalf of this greatly distressed and injured town are hereby presented to our worthy friends in Tolland, for their kind assistance in this our day of trial. We are with great esteem, gentlemen, your friends and fellow countrymen.

HENRY HILL, per order of the committee of Donations-October 24, 1774

As required of all men aged 16 to 60, Elisha was a member of the local militia. Though the town's population totaled only about 120 families and 1200 people at the time of the Revolution, it eventually boasted two companies of militia. Some men from smaller, neighboring towns such as Coventry, Stafford and Willington did muster with the Tolland militia. Even so, based on numbers alone (i.e. approximately 100 soldiers per train band or nearly 200 in total), every Tolland family was, in essence, represented by at least one soldier. When an express rider arrived on April 20, 1775 bearing tidings of the 'Lexington Alarm', it is amazing to consider that, in essence, the manhood of the town took up their arms and marched off to aid a neighboring colony - in a fight against their own monarch, and arguably the best army in the world at that time.

As further evidence that the burdens of service were shared, one only need consider the make-up of the Tolland 5th Company. (Note: to maintain the novel's emphasis on Elisha and his companions, only the

5th Company is described; characters names are chosen from those who actually served yet their actions and words are fictionalized. The intent is to shed light upon and to honor their possible contributions and sacrifice; in so doing it is hoped that no injustice has been done any individual via an incomplete or inaccurately chosen characterization). The ranks of the company(s) included men across all classes of colonial society. In 1775, not only did the affluent and influential participate, they were expected to lead. Prosperous farmers and community leaders are much in evidence on the list of those who responded to the "Lexisngton Alarm": Chapman, Hinckley, Loomis, Paulk, Stimson and West.

As William P. McDermott points out in *Tolland, A Connecticut Town 1715-1815*, the Chapmans, for example, were one of the most wealthy and powerful families. They owned numerous parcels as well as homes, but focused on utilizing slave labor and livestock that could produce income (e.g. oxen for rent to other farmers) rather than relying on farming to produce one's own food as was more typical. The family's prominence is represented by members such as Samuel Chapman, captain of the militia during the French and Indian War; and his son Colonel Chapman who served during the American Revolution; and another son, Deacon Elijah Chapman. It is the deacon's son Elijah who marched off to Boston, and who is portrayed as 'Eli' in the novel. The fictionalized bonds between this family and the Bentons are drawn upon the fact that Daniel Benton I witnessed Samuel Chapman's will.

In the case of the Bentons, brothers Elisha, Daniel III, Azariah and Jacob, only 15 at the outbreak of hostilities, all are proven to have served before the war ended. The Tolland militia, or the 5th Company of General Joseph Spencer's 2nd Regiment, was among the first to march 'in relief of Boston.' They took up siege positions in Roxbury ***(see Drawing #2)***. In the novel they entrench opposite the fortified gates of the city along the narrow causeway which then connected the port with the mainland. The three older brothers appear in the Connecticut archives as privates when the company encamped in May 1775. Captain Solomon Willes, their commander, had fought alongside the British during the French and Indian War. He also was a veteran of King George's expedition to Cuba that claimed numerous Tolland men - largely from disease.

When the Provincial forces learned the following month that British General Gage planned attacks upon the heights of Dorchester and Charlestown peninsula, they decided to preempt these assaults by fortifying Bunker Hill. A force drawn from the militias of Massachusetts, New Hampshire and Connecticut was hastily assembled the night of June 16, 1775. Captain Willes' 'duty book' notes that 16 men of the 5th Company participated in this historic battle. They joined the Connecticut force of some 200 men placed under the command of Captain Thomas Knowlton from neighboring Ashford. Like hundreds of their comrades, the Connecticut contingent, upon reaching Breed's Hill, which was lower and closer to the British forces than Bunker Hill, labored with picks, shovels and their bare hands. By dawn British naval observers spotted those workers and began cannonading them. Despite this and also lacking water or other provisions the men who had marched and dug all night continued adding to the redoubt's breastworks.

Meanwhile Gage's officers were assembling infantry in Boston. These were rowed over to Moulton's Point at the tip of Charlestown peninsula ***(see Drawing #3)***. When the assaults did come in the afternoon, they fell first upon the men of Connecticut; as well as upon the later-arriving regiment of New Hampshire troops. And so began the stubborn defense of the north slope of Breed's Hill. They successfully repulsed two attacks – despite these being supported by field artillery. The Regulars, strengthened by reinforcements, valiantly came on a third time. They charged on multiple fronts and as the defenders had exhausted their ammunition, overran the redoubt. The advantage now swung to the British, for not only were they well supplied with cartridges, their muskets were also fitted with bayonets. Lacking both, the Americans were slaughtered in the hand-to-hand fighting that ensued. It was in these close quarters that the influential and courageous president of the Massachusetts Provincial Congress, Dr. Joseph Warren, was slain.

The carnage might have been much worse if the Connecticut and New Hampshire troops still guarding the left flank had not put up a fighting retreat. Their continual fire enabled a good many of those fleeing the fortified hilltop to escape to Bunker Hill in the rear, and ultimately cross the causeway that led towards Cambridge. Captain Thomas Knowlton, who later formed the Rangers unit that constituted General George Washington's first intelligence gathering arm, was much credited for this action. While history records few names of the soldiers under him, including the 16 from the 5th Company, it is known that Elisha Benton was promoted corporal just two weeks later. Thus in the novel, the character of 'Elisha' is placed, with a degree of confidence, upon the slope of Breed's Hill on June 17, 1775.

Elisha and his comrades are shown returning home by the fall of 1775, when the plot shifts to affairs of the heart. In reality the enlistments of the 5th Company extended from May through December. Of note, the term of the militia enlistments (e.g. eight months in this case) proved a massive challenge for General George Washington who assumed command following the Battle of Bunker Hill. One can only imagine the challenges of commanding an army of wildly vacillating strength, which saw veterans replaced with raw recruits time and again.

As it happens, a stalemate developed outside of Boston following the fighting upon Breed's Hill. Having suffered 1000 casualties to achieve his nominal victory, General Gage, who English authorities soon saw fit to replace, was unable to launch offensive operations until reinforcements arrived from overseas. For his part, General Washington could not invade the city without the support of cannons. An attack was instead launched by Continental forces under Colonel Benedict Arnold upon Quebec. Captain Willes himself was believed to have joined this ill-fated expedition. Beset by supply and tactical difficulties and with the force reduced by the elements, the final attack on the northern city was launched in a blizzard. The campaign proved unsuccessful, but Captain Willes was promoted to Lt. Colonel soon after.

In Massachusetts, General Washington used the summer and fall to reorganize his new Continental Army. Apparently as a consequence of this activity and Willes' departure, Elisha joined the 8th regiment. This unit served alongside the 2nd in Roxbury, and was also under the overall command of General Joseph Spencer. Led by Colonel Jedediah Huntington, and with Elisha likely among their ranks, the 8th was tasked early in 1776 (then under General Samuel Parsons) with hauling the great guns captured from Fort Ticonderoga in New York to Dorchester Heights. The success of this effort led directly to the British evacuation of Boston - for the Americans could now bombard the city, while the occupiers' cannon could not elevate sufficiently to dislodge them. For the sake of continuity with the characters in the novel, Elisha and Captain Willes as well as their comrades continue their connection with the 5th Company of the 2nd Regiment through 1775. Thus the historical record tells us that the duration and nature of the service of Tolland's soldiers was even more extensive than appears within the pages of the fictional account.

One can only imagine the pent-up elation ready to burst free across New England upon learning that the Regulars had been driven from the colony of Massachusetts in March of 1776. Soon after entering the city, however, General Washington learned from patriotic Bostonians that General William Howe, the enemy's new Commander-in-Chief, intended to invade New York. Equally new were the regiments that Washington needed to organize to replace men whose enlistments had ended at year's end 1775, and to counter this anticipated thrust. Lt. Colonel Willes joined the 6th Connecticut State Levies under Colonel John Chester en route to New York ***(see Drawing #4)***. Colonel Huntington was charged with forming and leading the 17th Continental Regiment. Even at partial strength, he too hurried his command towards Manhattan. As archives confirm, among his soldiers were both Elisha and Azariah Benton. If Elisha was to ever begin a life with Jemima Barrows, those plans must once more be placed on hold. In the novel Elisha, Azariah and others from Tolland join the 6th's hurried departure.

On the home front many of the chores typically the province of men were now ably filled by women. Spring planting could not be delayed, whether a good portion of the male population was absent or not. Thus the women of Tolland stepped up in the spring of 1776, relying on skills acquired the previous spring following the militia's response to the Lexington Alarm.

The Continental Army arrived well ahead of the British. General Howe spent the spring and part of the summer re-outfitting his army in Halifax, which became Britain's northern military base. Once reinforcements arrived, Admiral of the Fleet Richard Howe, the General's brother, transported the army along the coast of New England and through The Narrows into New York harbor ***(see Drawing #5)***. Unlike in Boston where 'Rebels' had resisted them at every turn, on Staten Island the British troops found a warm welcome. So strong, in fact, was the Tory influence that the militia stationed on the island went over to the enemy en masse. In addition to arms and men, the 'Yorkers' provided the Howes intelligence on Continental troop deployments.

General Washington had a difficult challenge in attempting to defend numerous islands and land masses all of which were separated by great, tidal rivers like the Hudson and East. He divided his army in an attempt to defend Long Island, Manhattan and New Jersey. The lack of a navy made this a herculean task. Any movement of troops from one place to the other of necessity meant they had to be rowed practically under the wary eyes of an enemy which by August could rely upon the greatest naval force ever assembled - approximately 400 ships in total. The number and caliber of cannon jutting from the gun ports of any of Admiral Howe's first-rate men-of-war rivaled or even surpassed those of all of the Continentals' forts.

By the end of that month General Howe had made his decision. With the aid of his brother's ships he crossed The Narrows and began landing a force on Long Island that would swell to approximately 20,000 British and Hessian troops, supported by field artillery as well as naval guns covering his left flank. To oppose this landing, its extent unknown to him, General Washington reinforced his line of forts ringing the northwest tip of the island. Of approximately 6,000 soldiers positioned there, he ordered forward roughly half. These entrenched along a ridge line separating the two armies ***(see Drawing #6)***. In a critical tactical blunder, the Americans defended only three of the four passes.

General Howe initiated hostilities with a holding attack against the Americans right flank, up Gowanus Road that ran along the southwest coast. There, 7000 British infantry engaged 1,500 Americans under Lord Stirling. Colonel Huntington's 17th Regiment, which in previous days had already engaged Hessian troops at Flatbush, were ordered forward in the middle of the night to augment the thin line of Delaware and Maryland troops. Stirling sent these welcome reinforcements into the hills to prevent his left being flanked. This the Benton brothers and their comrades did, beating off numerous attacks by superior forces on this most isolated position throughout the long morning. Unbeknownst to them or Washington, however, was that Howe had spent the pre-dawn hours leading his main force around the Continental's left flank, and through the unguarded pass. Before noon he had encircled and routed the defenders of the remaining passes. Stirling and Huntington's regiments were thus completely surrounded. When the former turned to fight the enemy advancing on his rear, word never reached his flanking force. Thus Huntington's 300-man unit was subsequently cut-off. By the afternoon these few were the sole American forces still offering resistance upon the field. By the evening of August 27, 1776, the 17th ceased to exist – its officers or men killed or captured piecemeal by the combined British army of 20,000.

Of Stirling's stubborn and heroic stand against insurmountable odds much has been written. His efforts, and those of the Maryland, Delaware and Pennsylvania troops under him, enabled many other Continental army units to escape the encirclement and reach the line of American defenses. Among these were Elisha and Azariah's former captain, now Lt. Colonel Willes, who that day commanded Chester's Regiment a short distance northeast near Bedford Pass. Colonel Willes survived to become the Speaker of the House of the Connecticut Assembly. And history tells us that immediately after his defeat, General Washington then skillfully employed Colonel John Glover's men from the North Shore of Massachusetts in rowing the salvaged army back to Manhattan. What is largely unknown is the fate, and bravery, of the men of the 17th Continental Regiment of Connecticut troops. Colonel Huntington, suffering from malaria, was absent. Their senior officer that day, Lt. Colonel Joel Clark, died in captivity. Thus the most detailed chronicle of the resistance on what became known as Battle Hill was written by Colonel Samuel Atlee. Though junior to General Parsons and in command of the much smaller Pennsylvania detachment, Atlee's account describes the courageous decisions made as his alone; the defense conducted almost exclusively by his men. Only the barest mention is made of his superior officer and the 17th Regiment to which he had been attached.

In his 2009 book *Cut Off: Colonel Jedediah Huntington's 17th Continental (Conn) Regiment at the Battle of Long Island August 27, 1776,* Charles H. Lewis paints a vivid and well-researched depiction of this portion of the Battle of Long Island, and its aftermath, as well as the pivotal role of Huntington's Regiment in safeguarding Stirling's flank and thus assisting the safe retreat of Continental forces. To Mr. Lewis, I am indebted for the essence of the envisioned battle scene in the novel.

The portrayal of the capture leads to the imprisonment of Elisha and Azariah Benton on a prison ship on Wallabout Bay (*Cut Off* includes the brothers' names in an archived list of the Regiment's 'Casualties'). This shallow cove on the north coast of Long Island opposite Manhattan served as an anchorage for British ships previously used to transport soldiers and provisions including cattle from England. Having taken hundreds of prisoners and lacking secure facilities, the British converted the transports into floating prisons. What with overcrowding, lack of adequate food or medical care, neglect and in many cases abuse, these hulks became hotbeds of disease. Men perished nightly and were buried upon the beach each morning. The *Whitby* was one such vessel, and as it is known that men of the 17th were imprisoned upon it in 1776, so, in the novel, it was chosen to house 'Elisha', his brother 'Azariah' and many of their comrades *(**see Drawing #7**)*.

The Continental Army suffered more total casualties among these unfortunate captives than in battle during this long war (1775-1783). Among these was Azariah Benton, said to have died on the prison ships in December 1776. The barbaric treatment of American captives by their British and Tory guards was repeatedly protested at the time to little avail. Even entreaties by General Washington to General Howe met with no sustained improvement. Perhaps the worst abuser was a loyalist by the name of Joshua Loring. Having evacuated Boston with the

British in March 1776, we was given the role of commissary of prisoners. Some have even accused him and his British overlords of attempting to commit an act of biological warfare by allowing disease to run rampant among prisoners of war, who were then on numerous occasions deposited along the coastline to carry disease inland. Skeletons were found more than 100 years later during urban growth and renewal projects along Long Island's shore. As Edwin Burrows described the skulls found along the coast, *"...they were as thick as pumpkins in an autumn cornfield."*

By year's end 1776, Elisha Benton and hundreds of others were finally conveyed from their New York prisons aboard the British warship *Glasgow* - which coincidentally had been among those supporting the British assault on Breed's Hill. Confined below deck for 11days, 28 died during this voyage alone. The survivors were dumped on the Connecticut coast in the dead of a New England January. The people of Milford, Connecticut heroically sheltered and cared for these men. Despite their charity and sacrifice, 46 more former captives died and were buried in that town. Some of those brave souls tending to them also passed. Both former captives and caregivers are celebrated annually by the people of Milford.

Records prove that Elisha Benton was one of the few who retained the strength and will to attempt to reach home. Another was Heman Baker (Baker is the family name of another Tolland grantee). Tragically, he died along the route - succumbing only miles from Tolland. (Note: A plaque marks the spot on the grounds of Pratt and Whitney in East Hartford.) In the tale, these companions struggle homeward together. Elisha died within a few weeks of his return. As noted, in caring for him Jemima contracted the disease and passed soon after her betrothed. Their graves can be visited on the grounds of the Daniel Benton Homestead Museum **(see Photograph)**.

Against all odds, in unity and with resolve, the American people and their French allies eventually prevailed in this war of independence. Tolland's role in this birthing of America is quite amazing: her people provided sustenance to Boston's destitute in 1774; her sons contested Breed's Hill with the best Britain could throw at them in 1775; and in 1776 they held the field fled by so many others in Long Island. These outsized contributions for a small town in northeast Connecticut are somewhat astounding. That a fictional account serves to illuminate these historical realities is both ironic and bittersweet. Nevertheless, despite centuries of credit seldom extending to Tolland and her people; the story of Elisha Benton and Jemima Barrows presents clear evidence of the extent of the personal sacrifice and pain they and so many others endured in order that our country might live. It is my fervent hope that I have done justice to them and their contributions.

Two other Benton sons, Daniel and Jacob, fought in the Revolution and survived. It is said that as the eldest, Elisha laid the foundation that would enable the homestead, and thus the family, to expand. Upon these stones, Daniel and Jacob built an ell that sheltered Bentons for generations and which stands to this day. As evidence of the surviving brothers' sense of loss, and likely as a living tribute to the bravery of their departed siblings, each named his first-born son after those lost: Jacob chose Azariah and Daniel christened his boy Elisha.

DRAWINGS & MAPS

(Drawings & photograph by the Author)

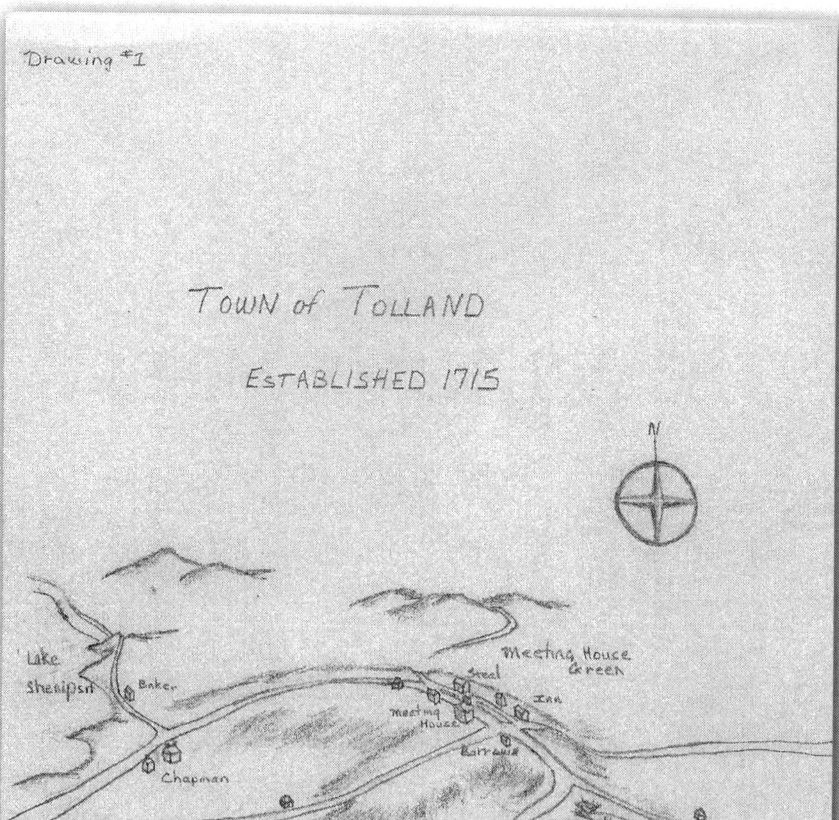

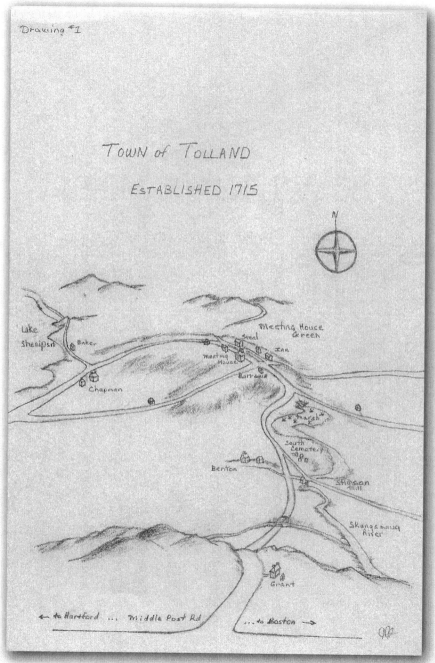

Map - Town of Tolland – Established 1715

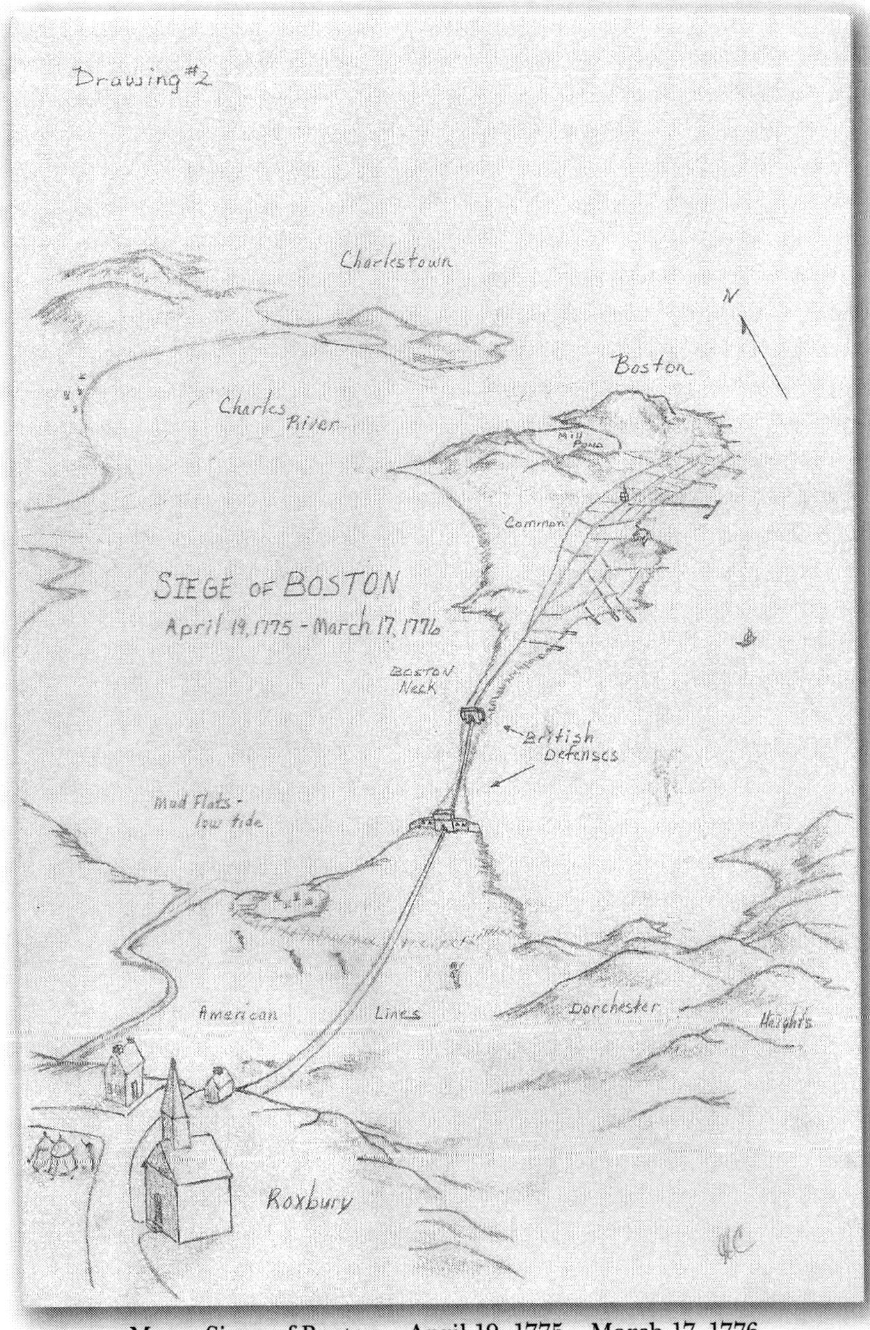

Map – Siege of Boston – April 19, 1775 – March 17, 1776

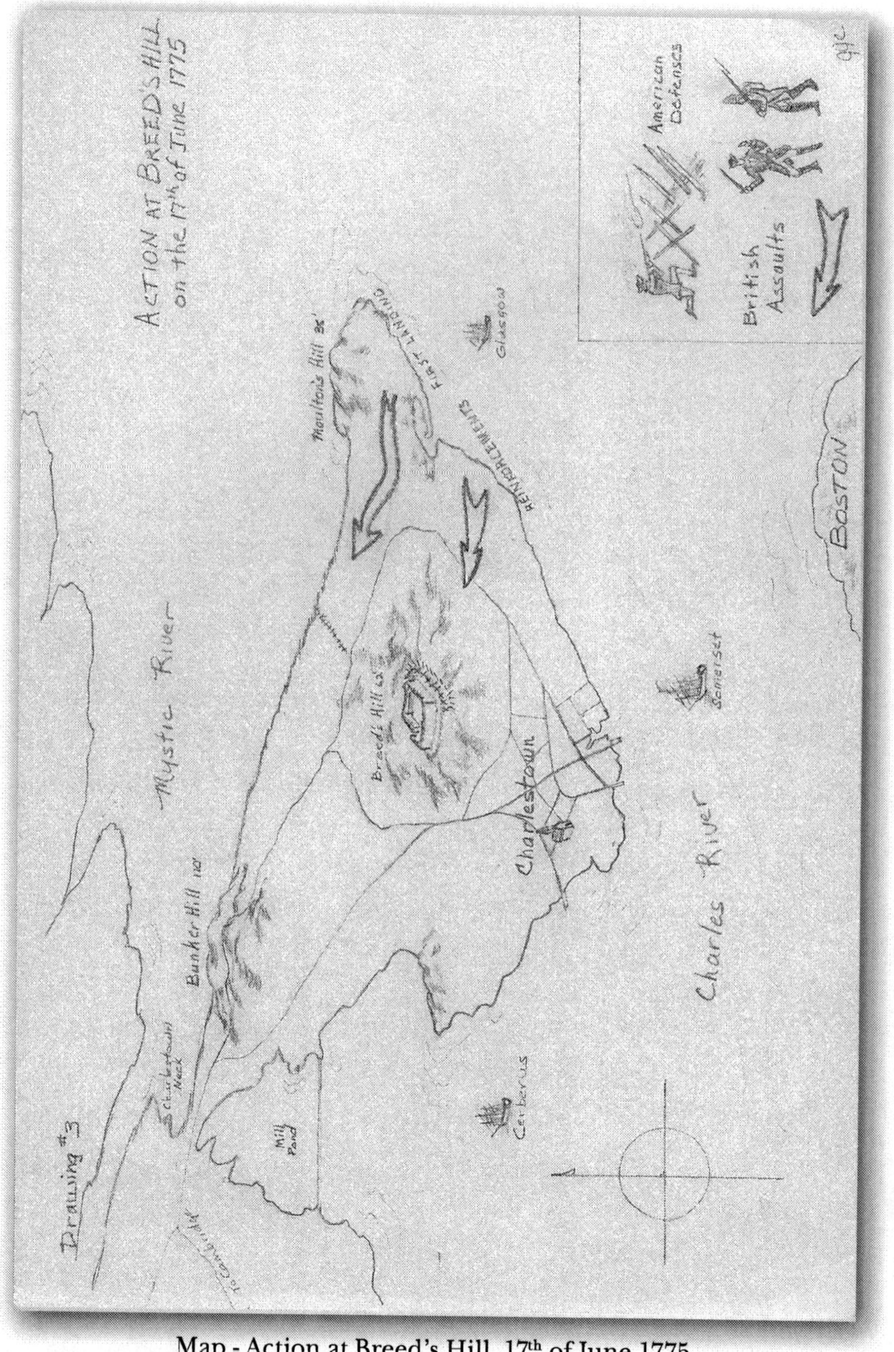

Map - Action at Breed's Hill, 17th of June 1775

The 6th Connecticut State Levies – March on New York Under the Grand Union Flag

Howe's Fleet Sails through The Narrows Into New York Harbor – July 1776

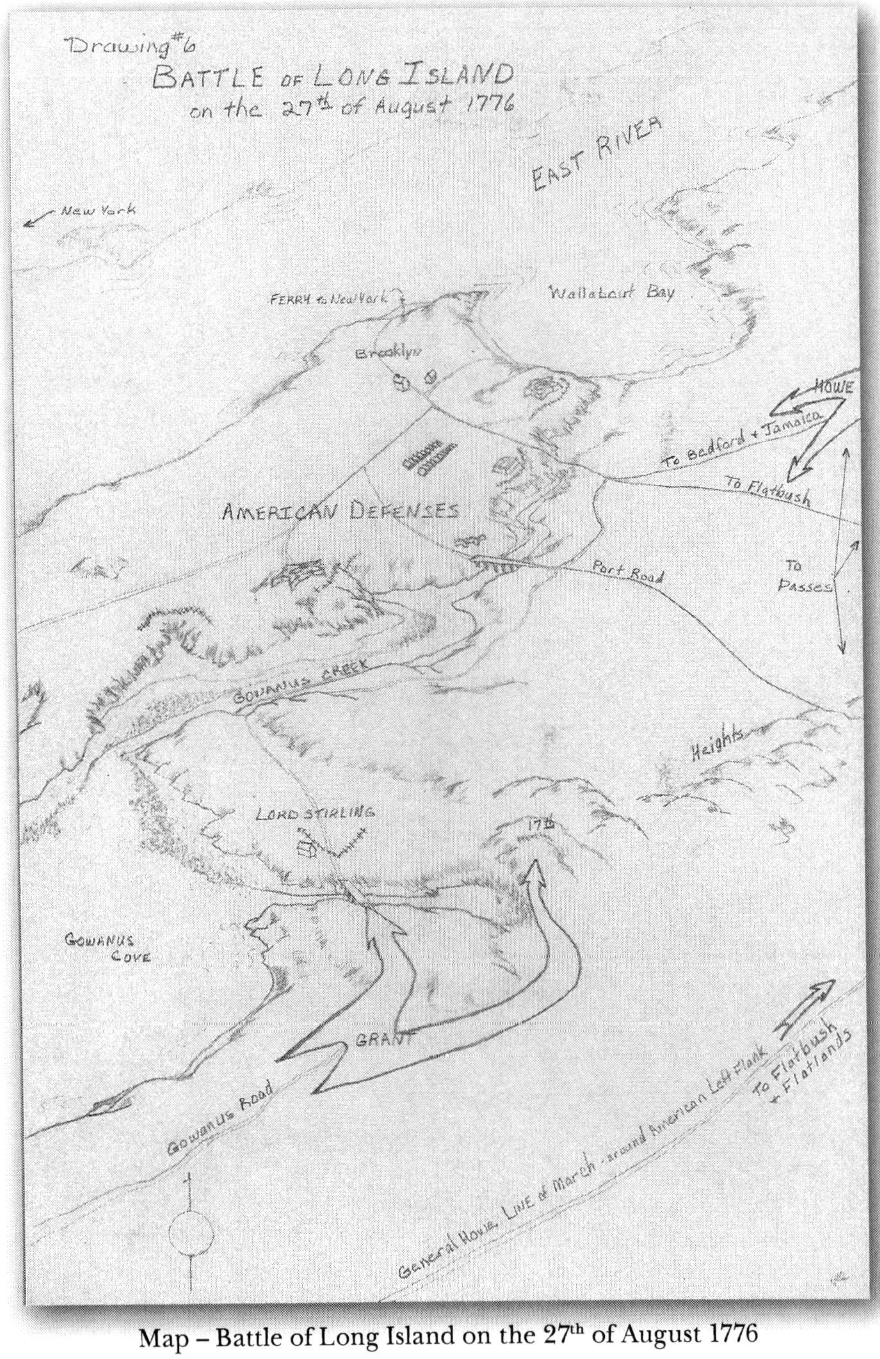

Map – Battle of Long Island on the 27th of August 1776

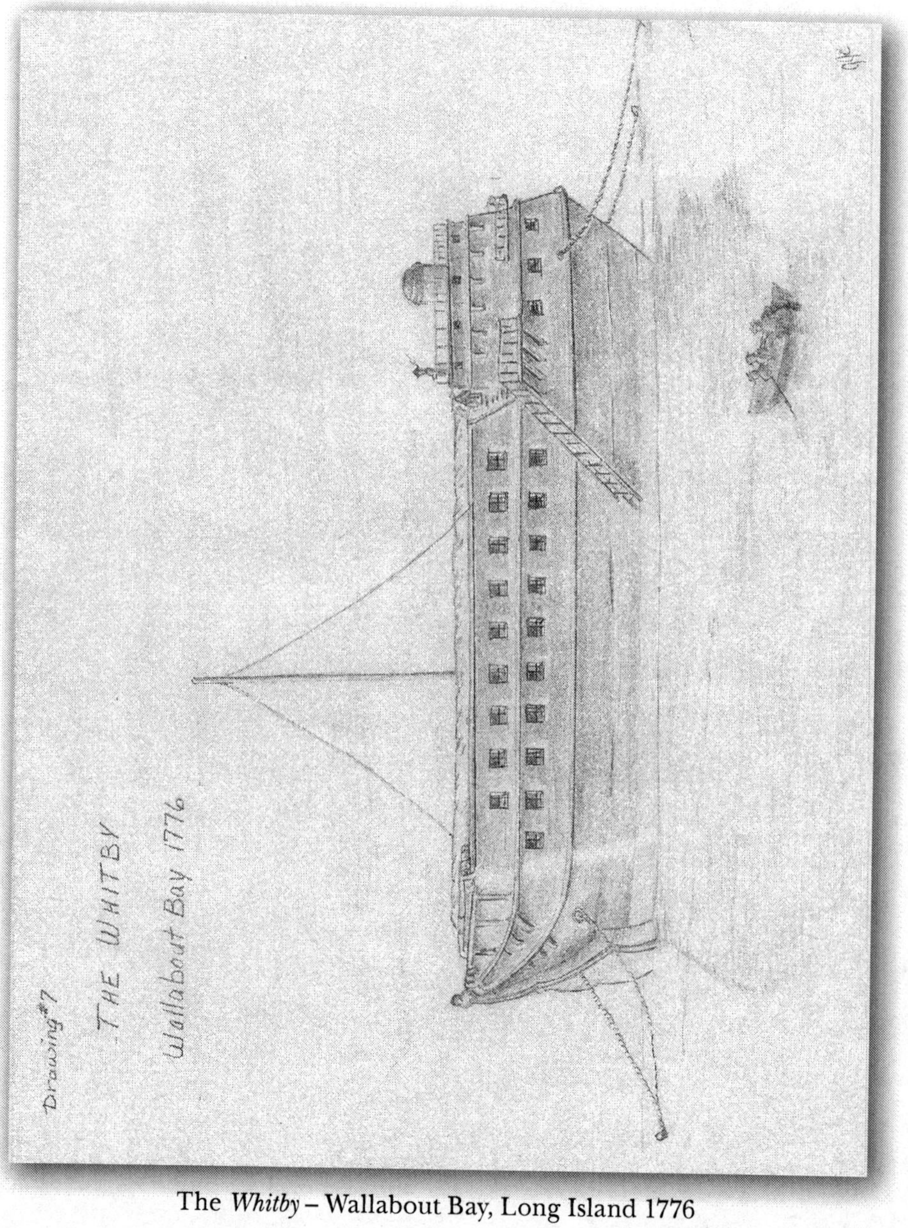

The *Whitby* – Wallabout Bay, Long Island 1776

The graves of Elisha Benton and Jemima Barrows may be visited at the Daniel Benton Homestead Museum on Medcalf Road in Tolland, Connecticut
(Photograph by author)

Of Gravesite of Elisha Benton and Jemima Barrows at The Daniel Benton Homestead, Tolland, CT

ACKNOWLEDGMENTS

I consulted many fine histories about the American Revolution. Two works were of particular value in crafting the narrative. William P. Mc Dermott's *Tolland, A Connecticut Town 1715-1815*, provided many useful insights into life in 18th century living. Charles H. Lewis' *Cut Off: Colonel Jedidiah Huntington's 17th Continental (Conn) Regiment at the Battle of Long Island, August 27, 1776,* corrects many inaccuracies in the historical record regarding the pivotal role of Colonel Huntington's 17th Regiment throughout the battle. His research enabled proper placement of our protagonist on the field. I am also grateful to both authors for their graciousness in responding to my inquiries. Bill shared insights which illuminated the world of self-publication, while Chuck cheerfully offered additional information concerning various forces and individual soldiers during the events of August 1776.

I was likewise fortunate that Joel Brown, author of the Libertyport mysteries, generously shared his knowledge of self-publishing. He also put me in touch with his editor. I am especially grateful to him and my friend Fay Salt for providing introductions to people who became instrumental in finalizing the novel.

The early drafts would likely have progressed no further were it not for the efforts of many dedicated readers, including Virginia Brousseau of the Tolland Library, Korina Moss, a fellow critique group member, and my friend Sherry Rains.

I am also grateful to the useful and motivational feedback of readers of the manuscript as it neared completion, especially my friends Bernice Thomas and Jonathan Salt. Thanks go, too, to Joe Thomas for his many suggestions as to how to guide the finished book into the hands of interested readers.

Two individuals who helped ensure the historical accuracy as concerns both Tolland and the Bentons of the 1700s are: Barbara Cook, Archivist and Town Historian; and Gail White-Usher, Director, Daniel Benton Homestead. Both enjoy long-term affiliations with the Tolland Historical Society.

The artwork gracing the cover evolved from a sketch to a credible composition with the input of Jerry Leone and Dave Brown. Rockport MA artist Christopher J. Coyne leveraged these initial efforts to create, in watercolors, the cover art which poignantly captures the essence of colonial New England.

I am indebted to my editor, Bill Brotherton, whose professional insights, encouragement, and perseverance led to the polishing of the final manuscript.

Lastly I wish to express my abiding gratitude and love for my daughters Rachel and Laura, and my wife Jeannette. The creation of a novel is a long and sometimes arduous journey. Throughout they showered me with encouragement, and never tired of reading yet another draft. Rachel and Laura, drawing upon their backgrounds in performing art, offered up wonderfully insightful suggestions regarding that which motivated the main characters in numerous scenes. Jeannette took each and every step with me, from the first chat about the bittersweet fate of Elisha Benton and Jemima Barrows, to the formatting of the final manuscript which we hope does justice to their story.

John J. Cuffe is a retired businessman whose short stories for young adults appeared in magazines when his daughters were growing up. A long-time resident of Tolland, CT, he and his wife now live on the North Shore of Boston.